The Handbook of Project Portfolio Management

T0313231

Managing large and complex organizations; balancing the needs of business-as-usual, new products and services and business change; assuring risk across everything the business does; these are all core requirements of modern business which are provided by the discipline of portfolio management.

The Handbook of Project Portfolio Management is the definitive publication that introduces and describes in detail project portfolio management in today's ever-changing world. The handbook contains the essential knowledge required for managing portfolios of business change with real-life examples that are being used by today's organizations in various industries and environments. The team of expert contributors includes many of the most experienced and highly regarded international writers and practitioners from the global portfolio management industry, selected to provide the reader with examples, knowledge and the skills required to manage portfolios in any organization.

Dennis Lock and Reinhard Wagner's definitive reference on project portfolio management explains: the context and role of the discipline; the practical processes, tools and techniques required for managing portfolios successfully; the capability required and how to develop it. The text also covers the recognized standards as well as emerging issues such as sustainability and environment. Collectively, this is a must-have guide from the leading commentators and practitioners on portfolio management from across the world.

Dennis Lock began his career as an electronics engineer in a research laboratory but subsequently served many successful years in project and administration management. Dennis has carried out consultancy assignments in Europe and the US, and was for eight years an external lecturer in project management to Master's degree students at two British universities. He is a best-selling author and has written or edited over 60 books, many published in multiple languages. He is a fellow of the APM, member of the Chartered Management Institute and is now a freelance writer.

Reinhard Wagner has gained more than 30 years of project-related leadership experience in sectors such as air defence, automotive engineering, machinery and not-for-profit organizations. As Certified Projects Director (IPMA Level A), he is experienced in managing projects, programmes and project portfolios in a complex and dynamic context. For more than 15 years, he has been actively involved in the development of project, programme and portfolio management standards. Reinhard is Past President and Chairman of the Council of the International Project Management Association (IPMA), Honorary Chairman of the German Project Management Association (GPM) and Managing Director of Tiba Managementberatung GmbH.

The Handbook of Project Portfolio Management

Edited by Dennis Lock and Reinhard Wagner

Routledge
Taylor & Francis Group

LONDON AND NEW YORK

First published in paperback 2024

First published 2019
by Routledge
4 Park Square, Milton Park, Abingdon, Oxon OX14 4RN

and by Routledge
605 Third Avenue, New York, NY 10158

Routledge is an imprint of the Taylor & Francis Group, an informa business

British Library Cataloguing-in-Publication Data
A catalogue record for this book is available from the British Library

Library of Congress Cataloging-in-Publication Data
A catalog record has been requested for this book

ISBN: 978-1-138-63501-2 (hbk)
ISBN: 978-1-03-283881-6 (pbk)
ISBN: 978-1-315-20659-2 (ebk)

DOI: 10.4324/9781315206592

Typeset in Sabon
by Swales & Willis Ltd, Exeter, Devon, UK

Contents

PART II
The practice of portfolio management   61

Figures

About the editors

Dennis Lock began his career as an electronics engineer in a research laboratory but subsequently served many successful years in project and administration management. His industrial experience is extraordinarily wide, ranging from guided weapons electronics to heavy special machine tool systems and mining engineering. Dennis has carried out consultancy assignments in Europe and the US, and was for eight years an external lecturer in project management to Masters degree students at two British universities. He is a best-selling author and has written or edited over 60 books, many published in multiple languages. He is a fellow of the APM, member of the Chartered Management Institute and is now a freelance writer.

Reinhard Wagner has gained more than 30 years of project-related leadership experience in sectors such as air defence, automotive engineering, machinery and not-for-profit organizations. As Certified Projects Director (IPMA Level A), he proved to be experienced in managing projects, programmes and project portfolios in a complex and dynamic context. For more than 15 years, he has been actively involved in the development of project, programme and portfolio management standards (for example as convenor for ISO 21500 *Guidance on Project Management* and ISO 21503 *Guidance on Programme Management*). Reinhard is Past President and Chairman of the Council of International Project Management Association (IPMA), Honorary Chairman of the German Project Management Association (GPM) and Managing Director of Tiba Managementberatung GmbH.

Notes on the contributors

Alicia Aitken has 20 years' experience working in the field of project, programme and portfolio management as a practitioner, researcher and author. As the CEO of Human Systems International, she led a global team that assessed, benchmarked and advised on the improvement of organizational delivery capability for organizations and government departments. Her cross-industry experience includes banking, finance, telecommunications, defence, aerospace, pharmaceutical, government, engineering and construction. Alicia held the first Chief Project Officer role for Telstra, Australia's largest telecommunications company and now works in investment management for an ANZ banking corporation. Alicia is also the current chairperson for the International Centre for Complex Project Management. She holds a PhD in project management and psychology.

Emma-Ruth Arnaz-Pemberton is a PMO, Project, Programme and Portfolio specialist with extensive experience in the change management industry and a particular focus on collaboration, PMO conception and strategy, method and capability development. As the Director of Consulting Services for Wellingtone Project Management, Emma-Ruth is responsible for all services within their PPM DNA concept, including the recently APM Accredited PMO Practitioner course, and the Wellingtone competency framework and Maturity Models. She is currently chair of the APM's PMO SIG, an APM Accredited Trainer and involved in various project management charitable organisations.

Steve Butler is a portfolio management practitioner with over 20 years of experience, having worked with organisations such as The Financial Conduct Authority, Allen & Overy, Credit Suisse, Barclays Wealth, HSBC, the FT, the NHS, Vodafone, Orange, Gazprom, Zurich Insurance and Old Mutual Wealth. Steve was on the core committee responsible for writing the PMI Standard for Portfolio Management, 4th edition (published October 2017) and the 3rd edition before that, and is co-authoring the companion practice guide due for publication during 2018. Steve is the current Chair of the UK Portfolio Management Forum. He was on the governance board that created the PMI's Portfolio Management Professional certification (PfMP), and sits on the global assessment panel for PfMP applicants. Steve holds a Masters Degree in Strategic Management and is in his final year of his PhD, researching for a dissertation entitled 'Complexity and its impact on portfolio delivery'.

Robert Buttrick is an international authority on business-led, programme and project management with a successful track record in a wide variety of large organizations, most recently at the UK's Cabinet Office and as BT's PPM Method Director. Before this he was with the PA Consulting Group, and specialized in business-led project management, advising across a range of sectors. His early career was as a civil engineer working in Africa, the Middle East and at the World Bank, in the USA. His published works include the best-selling book *The Project Workout* and he is an active contributor to project management handbooks, methods, professional journals and conferences. Robert received a Distinguished Service Certificate from British Standards Institution (BSI) for services to national and international project management standards; he is a Member of the Chartered Institute of Marketing, is a Chartered Engineer and an Honorary Fellow of the Association for Project Management. Robert currently works as an independent consultant and is a Visiting Teaching Fellow at the University of Warwick.

John Chapman is Programme Director for TouchstoneFMS, a business solutions company. He is the author of *Your Project Needs You, Kafka, Pulp Fiction, Beer and Projects, Project and Programme Accounting: A Practical Guide for Professional Service Organisations and IT*, and a member of the authoring group of the *Gower Handbook of Programme Management*, 1st edition. He regularly tweets at http://twitter.com/chapmanjs and is the author of a range of educational video podcasts which are published at https://www.youtube.com/user/theprogrammedirector. John is an experienced programme director, programme manager, project director and project manager, having led programmes of business change, implemented financial accounting and enterprise solutions, spend control systems, document management solutions and business intelligence solutions. He has international project implementation experience with a good understanding of the challenges of working with different cultures, and the logistics of international project delivery. As an active member of the Association for Project Management Specific Interest Group on Programme Management (www.apm.org.uk/progm), he leads the Communication Workstream.

Darren Dalcher is Professor of Project Management at the University of Hertfordshire. He is the Founder and Director of the National Centre for Project Management, an interdisciplinary centre of excellence operating in collaboration with industry, government, academia, third sector organizations and the learned societies. Following industrial and consultancy experience in managing technology projects, Professor Dalcher gained his PhD in Software Engineering from King's College London. He has written over 200 refereed papers and book chapters, and published over 30 books. His work has been translated into French, German, Spanish, Italian, Russian and Portuguese. He is Editor-in-Chief of Wiley's *Journal of Software: Evolution and Process* and editor of two established book series focused on managing projects and change initiatives, published by Routledge. He is an Honorary Fellow of the Association for Project Management, a Chartered Fellow of the British Computer Society, a Fellow of the Chartered Management Institute and the Royal Society of Arts, a Senior Member of the IEEE and a Senior Fellow of the Higher Education Academy.

Philipp Detemple started eight years ago at BNP Paribas Germany's Consorsbank with the mission to install a PMO. After this successful setup, he has now held for more than five years the position as Project Portfolio Manager in the Strategy and Transformation division. Here he has the central responsibility for project financing in the digital transformation programme of the bank. Starting nearly 20 years ago as a project manager for R&D in user-machine interfaces in the automotive industries, he also gained experience as a project management and PMO consultant in special purpose machinery manufacturing enterprises as well as in the surrounding event management for nation-wide marketing events and conventions. The educational basis of his diversified experiences is a Master's degree in Computational Linguistics and an MBA in International Marketing. He is certified in the *Management of Portfolios* framework of APMG.

Stuart Dixon has more than 25 years' experience in working in PMOs in a variety of sectors including retail, finance and travel, with more than 10 years involved with portfolio offices. He was one of the reviewers for the P3O standard and has contributed to the development of the APM *Body of Knowledge* and their competency assessment. He has previously been the chair of the APM specific interest group for PMOs and was one of the authors of the PMO competency framework. Stuart is a passionate supporter of PMOs and the difference they can make to the success of an organization.

Adrian Dooley is an honorary fellow of the Association for Project Management and the lead author of the *Praxis Framework*, the world's first free framework that encompasses the management of projects, programmes and portfolios. Originally a construction project manager, he became involved in the development of project planning software for PCs in the 1980s. In 1984 he set up a training and consultancy company, The Projects Group, and ran that until its sale in 2008. Adrian was a founding member of *Project Manager Today* magazine and Project Management Exhibitions Ltd. From 1996 to 2000, he served on the APM Council and during that time was the Head of Professional Development. A frequent author and commentator on project management, Adrian has been published in *Professional Engineer*, *Computer Weekly* and *The Daily Telegraph*, among others. With over 40 years' experience in the industry Adrian is well placed to discuss the evolution of project, programme and portfolio management and what can really make a difference.

Afshin Farahmandlou has gained more than 20 years of professional experience for well-known companies such as Ericsson, Lucent Technologies, Hughes, Atos and Siemens in different lines of business and positions, with more than 10 years at Siemens AG. He is currently responsible for the project portfolio management at one of the Siemens Divisions with the strongest project business portfolio. He developed a holistic approach for project portfolio risk management that is widely used at Siemens. He has strong expertise and understanding of project business, risk management and portfolio management, and gained long-standing experience as a project manager of complex large-scale projects at a global level in the automotive and IT sector. He is a certified Project Manager Professional PMP® according to PMI and PM@Siemens.

Jörg Floegel is a successful executive manager with more than 20 years of professional experience in professional services including programme and project management in the financial, retail and payments industries. As Director, Jörg is in charge of professional services businesses in an international and multicultural environment and leading NCR's Professional Services business for northern Europe. Jörg drives business development and emphasizes building partnerships. He has a thorough programme management background in all related disciplines such as programme planning, risk management, recovery management and project closeout.

Paul Gardiner is Professor of Project Management at SKEMA Business School, where he is the Director of the DBA and a GAC-accredited MSc programme. He gained experience in the manufacturing and oil and gas industries, before receiving his PhD from the University of Durham. He has held appointments at Heriot-Watt University, Edinburgh and the British University in Dubai. With a strong track record in programme design and development, he was lead academic in a European consortium winning 5 million euro to launch an Erasmus Mundus Master's. Other assignments have been held at Politecnico di Milano, Edinburgh Business School, the University of Edinburgh, Bristol Business School, Nottingham Trent University, ICN Business School, Nancy, University of Fribourg, Universitas Pelita Harapan (UPH), Jakarta, and the University of Manchester. He has held several external examinerships in the UK. His research interests are in project–organization interfaces, learning for business value and project management for competitive advantage. He has written over 70 scholarly articles and an international textbook. He is also a reviewer for several international journals.

Alistair Godbold is a programme director with the Nichols Group with over 30 years' experience. He has managed projects, programmes and portfolios ranging from high-integrity, safety-related systems, infrastructure, construction and business relocation, through organization-wide business change and IT projects in civil aviation, rail, nuclear, military and mining in the UK, Australia and Brazil. He has authored several chapters of project management books, publishes articles on project management and is regularly invited to speak at conferences. He is an Honorary Fellow of the Association for Project Management, a Fellow of the Institute of Engineering and Technology, a Fellow of the Royal Society of Arts Manufacturing and Commerce, a Registered Project Professional and a Chartered Engineer.

Manja Greimeier joined the automotive supplier Continental AG in 2017 as Vice-President for Sales and Customer Project Management in the business unit ADAS. Before that she worked for the automotive supplier Valeo in different positions in Finance, Project Management and General Management and gained more than 10 years' management experience. She developed a Leadership and Career Development Program for Project Managers based on the train-the-trainer principle, and launched organizational efficiency programs to cope with the increased complexity of large-scale projects. After completion of the General Management program at CEDEP in Fontainebleau, she gained experience in transforming organizations through change in leadership excellence and drive of cultural change. Her background is business administration, which she studied at the University of Mannheim in Germany.

Martin Haberstroh is Professor for Engineering Project Leadership and Quality Management in the Department of Electrical Engineering and Information Technology at the University of Applied Sciences Hochschule Konstanz (HTWG). Before joining the Hochschule Konstanz he had worked for around 10 years as project management consultant for strategic product projects in the Global Project Management Office Daimler Trucks at Daimler AG. Previously he was a consultant for automotive project management at Mercedes-Benz technology GmbH in Sindelfingen. Martin studied industrial engineering at the University of Karlsruhe (KIT) and earned his PhD in the field of project management at the University of Kiel. After many years of practical experience he is also an expert on New Product Development Processes—starting from the idea to successful manufacturing of complex products. His major tasks were the New Product Development Process of Daimler Trucks as well as consulting product projects during the project start. Before joining Hochschule Konstanz he was also a lecturer at several universities, teaching subjects such as innovation management, project management and new product development processes.

Michael Horlebein is Senior Vice President for ID Solutions in Veridos GmbH and is responsible for implementing identification and identity solutions for the international market. He joined Giesecke+Devrient GmbH in 2009 as Head of Project Business before moving to Veridos GmbH, a joint venture founded in January 2015 by Giesecke+Devrient GmbH and Bundesdruckerei GmbH. In addition, he heads the Corporate Project Management Office in the Giesecke+Devrient Group responsible for the definition of corporate project management standards, career model, training and leadership of the Giesecke+Devrient project management community. After studying electrical engineering at the Technical University in Munich Michael held a variety of national and international positions in Siemens AG and Nokia Siemens Network GmbH & Co. KG in both project management and sales. The author has been familiar with project business for more than 20 years.

Claus Hüsselmann is Professor for Industrial Management, leading the Laboratory for Business Process and Project Management within the department of Industrial Engineering at the TH Mittelhessen University of Applied Sciences (THM). His focus areas are multiproject management, embracing hybrid and lean project approaches. Before joining THM he gained experience for more than 20 years in the field of project and process management at IDS/Scheer/Software AG as a consultant, project manager, director project operations and risk control and, lastly, as management consulting partner. As a member of the Executive Board of the German Project Management Association (GPM), Claus accompanied the strategic transformation of the organization and is now working as co-director of the Multi-PM professional group. Claus earned his PhD in the field of Business Informatics after his academic studies of Applied Mathematics, Technical Physics and Data Processing.

Stephen Jenner is an author, practitioner and trainer in project, portfolio and benefits realization management. He is author of, and Chief Examiner for, APMG's 'Managing Benefits™' and co-author of the OGC (now Axelos) 'Management of Portfolios'. He is also the author of several other books in the fields of portfolio and benefits realisation management. Steve has extensive practical experience at senior management level as a member of the UK Senior Civil Service from 1999 to 2011. This included designing, implementing and operating the Criminal Justice System IT approach to Portfolio & Benefits Management that was recognized internationally in reports to the Organization for Economic Co-operation and Development (OECD) and European Commission, and which won the Civil Service Financial Management Award. He now develops and delivers Masters' level courses in project, supplier and investment management at a number of international business schools. Steve is a professionally qualified management accountant (FCMA), Fellow of the APM, with an MBA and Masters of Studies degree from Cambridge University.

Knut Kämpfert has more than 20 years' experience in project and portfolio management in the automotive industry. He founded and built up the corporate PMO at ZF Friedrichshafen AG. In this function he developed and implemented processes and tools for project and portfolio management. In addition, he coached and supported a lot of different types of projects in the organization. After several years in corporate function he moved to China to build up a TechCenter for Asia/Pacific. He is Global Program Manager for a customer group in a business unit. Knut was part of the ISO Technical Committee for ISO 21504 *Project, Programme and Portfolio management – Guidance on portfolio management.*

Soohong Kim is CEO of the Incheon Bridge Company Ltd and Director of the Institute for Korean Peninsula Project Research and Development at the Kyungnam University as a professor. He puts his utmost effort into developing project management in Korea as the Vice-Chairman of IPMA Korea. He is a regular member of NAEK (National Academy of Engineering of Korea), which is a special corporate body for the development of engineering and technology. Soohong serves as the Honorary Consul for the Republic of Uganda, representing the Ugandans in Korea and a central committee member of the Korean Red Cross as well. He has received many prestigious awards including the national highest Order of Industrial Service Merit-Gold Tower Medal awarded by the President of the Republic of Korea, and the best management awards from seven different institutions in Korea such as the grand prize awarded by the Deputy Prime Minister in charge of the Ministry of Strategy and Finance. He was selected as one of the 'Top 25 Newsmakers' in 2007 by Engineering News Record (ENR) as the first Korean honouree and recently awarded the Project Manager of the Year by the International Project Management Association (IPMA) as silver winner. He was the first Asian executive director in charge of the five project affiliate companies of AMEC Foster Wheeler and served as representative of AMEC Korea. He was educated at the University of California, Riverside, and has an honorary doctorate degree in business administration from the Kyungnam University, South Korea.

Donnie MacNicol is an experienced project and programme leader who is passionate about developing the leadership capabilities of individuals, teams and organizations to deliver success. He works with a broad range of organizations including nuclear, infrastructure, defence, technology, aerospace, parliament and government to improve delivery and leadership capability. Widely recognized as contributing to the 'people and organizational side' of project management thinking, he is much in demand as a lecturer, speaker and writer. Donnie is the Founder of The Delivery Club™ and member of the Acumen7 network of business leaders. He is a Visiting Teaching Fellow at Warwick Manufacturing Group (WMG) and was previously Chair of the PMI UK Chapter OPM Forum and APM's People Special Interest Group. He is the co-author of *Project Leadership*, 3rd edn (Gower, 2015), has had over 30 articles published and contributed to 5 books, including *Programme and Portfolio Management Demystified*. He has presented at over 150 events and conferences including for the MPA, IOD, APM, PMI, RICS and ICE, and a host of private and public-sector organizations.

Helene Metoui is a global PMO leader with extensive hands-on experience in delivery of various types of projects, programmes and portfolios, crossing countries, cultures and continents to achieve measurable results – amounting to a total revenue of more than a billion euros. His track record ranges from innovating sparkling business startups, applied artificial intelligence R&D programmes all the way up to complex large-scale software customization and global corporate IT and business governance transformation. She contributed to the success story of Fortune Global enterprises in several sectors such as Retail, Travel and Transportation as well as Financial Services at a Global Top Tier Technology Consulting giant. As a Europe Region PMO Leader for a Global FinTech partner, she was in charge of a technological portfolio that counted more than 500 projects and programmes delivered by more than 50 managers to more than 150 customers in more than 15 countries yearly – with the strongest performance around the globe. Currently, she leads a strategic Global PMO workstream determined to delight customers with a top-notch portfolio of cutting edge services, driving business reinvention through technology, infusing new energy and propelling growth worldwide.

Mey Mark Meyer is a managing consultant at Prometicon Solutions, a vendor-independent consultancy for digitalization in project management and project portfolio management software. He specializes in designing and implementing project management processes and the respective IT support, including the necessary organizational development. Mey Mark Meyer has advised several companies from different industries in successfully implementing IT support for project management and in choosing an appropriate software solution. He is the author of 'Project Management Software Systems', a market survey for PPM software. As a civil engineer, he started out managing construction projects before he joined the Institute for Project Management and Innovation at the University of Bremen as a Research Associate where he began to focus on the project management-orientated organization.

Elvira Molitor looks back on 20 years of experience in project and portfolio management in the agricultural industry. She has managed complex development projects both within and across company boundaries and, for the last seven years, she headed the Project, Program and Portfolio Management Office for Research & Development and then Production & Supply in Syngenta. In this role, Elvira owned the processes and tools, pioneered a new approach to portfolio structure, provided the single source of truth for all 3PM data and helped improve the organizational maturity in 3PM. Through founding the Project, Program, Portfolio Management

(3PM) Academy, establishing a trainee programme and a career path for project managers, she has also helped to build strong 3PMC capability in the organization. Elvira holds a PhD in Toxicology and a Master's degree in Project Management, and is MSP (*Managing Successful Programs*) as well as MoP (*Management of Portfolios*) certified. She is a member of PMI, GPM and the Swiss Corporate Networking group.

Michael Münzberg is a certified senior project manager GPM (IMPA Level B). After several years of experience in project management in the private sector, he joined the civil service at the German Federal Office of Administration in 2002. In 2016, as part of the IT consolidation federal government, he became deputy head of department at the ITZ Bund, where he is still responsible for all disciplines of project management and project governance. With his more than 15 years of experience in project management, he is actively involved on a voluntary basis in the GPM Deutsche Gesellschaft für Projektmanagement e.V. There he is co-founder and spokesman of the specialist group 'PM in public administration' and member of the committee for specialist work.

Christof Rink is a product portfolio manager and business model developer at Tiba Consulting. He joined Tiba in 2011 as consultant, trainer and project lead for PM implementation and integration, including analysis of various business models and product development assignments in the aerospace, automotive, healthcare, retail and renewable energy industries. Beginning early with business development as well as key account management, he created and successfully tested customer-centric services approaches focusing on business innovation. After studying aerospace engineering at the Technical University in Munich and the Universidad Politécnica in Madrid he did flight dynamics research at the German Aerospace Center before transferring to production process consulting at MTU Maintenance in Hanover. During this time, he achieved an MBA before joining Tiba.

Silke Schönert has been Professor for Business Information Systems and Project Management at the University of Applied Science in Cologne since 2013. Before she was Head of Strategic Planning and Controlling of the Program Management Department at BWI Informationstechnik GmbH – a joint venture of Siemens AG, the Federal Republic of Germany represented by the Federal Ministry of Defence and IBM Deutschland GmbH. With her experience in programme management, she and her co-authors wrote one of the first German books on management of programmes in 2012. She has 20 years' experience in several industries and academics, with a focus on project management and programme management for strategy and process optimization. She is a Certified Projects Director (IPMA Level A).

Alexander Schwarz is responsible for technical asset management in Leverkusen for Covestro Deutschland AG, former Bayer MaterialScience AG. After studies of Chemical Engineering in Germany and the USA he received his PhD at the University of Stuttgart. He started his industrial career at Bayer AG in 1999 with various positions in process design and analysis, engineering, plant management and project management, as well as heading the investment coordination and analysis team of a business unit. There, and in his following positions, he gained theoretical and practical experience in project portfolio management with a focus on investment projects and programmes for chemical plants and processes.

Martin Sedlmayer has gained deep experience in project, programme and portfolio management in various sectors, including process manufacturing, insurance, transportation and different services industries. He successfully realized complex change programmes, worked as project and programme manager, as line manager of projects organisations, as well as for a long period as an expert and consultant. He holds an MBA in International Management from six universities around the globe, a CMA/CFA diploma and has been certified Projects Director IPMA since 2002. He is a board member of the Swiss Project Management Association SPM and acts as an assessor Level A in various countries. In the role of project manager and lead editor Martin recently developed, for IPMA, the Individual Competence Baseline IPMA ICB® version 4. He actually serves IPMA as Vice-President, responsible for the delivery of products and services worldwide.

Jörg Seidl is managing director of Bonventis GmbH, a consulting company specialized in project and change management. After he studied business informatics at the Technical University of Darmstadt, Jörg joined Lufthansa German Airlines, where he was part of a major programme organization before he became responsible for a business intelligence department. After that he led the information centre of a leading German tour operator. Then Jörg changed tack to consulting business. In his new role he twice developed and led the consulting activities of midsized IT companies. As certified Senior Project Manager (IPMA Level B) he has gained nearly 30 years of experience in management of programmes and projects in finance industry. For more than 10 years he has been involved in several activities of the German Project Management Association (GPM). He is IPMA-Assessor for the 4-Level-Certification system, author of several project management publications and was involved in the development of project and portfolio management standards.

Tetsuro Seki is Professor at Bunkyo University, a former dean of the Graduate School of Information and Communications, a department head of the Information Society, and a member of the Board of Councillors of Bunkyo University Foundation. He received his Doctorate of Engineering in Applied Statistics, which was based on Quality Management and Reliability Engineering, and he worked at Teikyo University of Technology and Chiba Institute of Technology before joining Bunkyo University. He is currently majoring in Project Management for Large-scale Information Systems Development. He is a founder, the representative director and President of the Society of Project Management (SPM), the representative of the International Project Management Association (IPMA), Japan, and chair of the International Organization for Standardization (ISO) PC236/ TC258 Mirror Committee, Japan. He is also the chair as well as a member of the Expert Advisory Committees of the Ministry of Economy, Trade and Industry (METI) and Ministry of Land, Infrastructure and Transport (MLIT), JAPAN.

Akihiko Sekiguchi began his career as a systems engineer, working for Fujitsu Ltd, which is one of the biggest computer manufacturers in Japan. He has experienced a lot of system integration projects for customers of both private companies and local governments, and successfully completed many complex and large-scale projects as a project manager. He was also responsible for expanding offshore development for his company, making use of global companies in China, India, and so on, to contribute to improving project management in global projects. In recent years, one of his missions has been the standardization on projects, programme and portfolio management. He is a member of ISO/TC 258, which is a committee on the standardization of projects, programmes and portfolio management. He contributed to publishing ISO 21503 (*Guidance of programme management*) as a secretary of the working group. Akihiko is also chair of the Committee of Standardization in SPM (Society of Project Management) in Japan.

Fiona Spencer is the chief portfolio officer for the Home Office, one of the major departments of state within the UK, leading work on strategic investment and portfolio management and, as head of profession, building project delivery capability within the department. She is currently a member of the UK government projects council and is also involved in research on project initiation and transition under the government's Project X research programme. An early graduate of the Major Projects Leadership Academy, Fiona has over 20 years' experience in leading project delivery and change, and has led a range of major government projects in technology, shared service development and business transformation in the home affairs, criminal justice and mental health sectors.

Subas Subedi has more than 10 years' experience in developing and delivering social development projects. He is the winner of the Young Project Manager of the Year 2012 award from Young Crew, IPMA. He is an active member of the Project Management Association of Nepal (PMAN) and former President of the Young Crew Nepal. Currently, Subas is team leader of one of the impactful projects in skills and employment, and extending technical assistance to the government agency in Nepal. He has been associated with IPMA activities since 2009 and promotes the profession in Nepal where the contexts are not easy.

Alan Summerfield is a certified management consultant and experienced senior manager from the BBC with a long and proven track record working at a senior level. Alan has great experience in senior leadership roles across a number of disciplines, all high profile with substantial strategic, operational, change management and budgetary responsibilities. Alan now delivers coaching, mentoring, consultancy and training particularly focused on portfolio, programme and project leadership and risk management. He supports organizations in setting up governance arrangements for portfolios, new programmes and programmes in difficulty. He is an accredited trainer in MSP, MOP, M_o_R, Benefits Management and Change Management. He has led a number of major organizational change programmes within the BBC, building, developing, leading and motivating programme teams, chairing programme boards with senior membership from across a diverse organization, and has particular experience in involving and influencing executive stakeholders and customers at all levels. Alan is a member of the authoring review team for M_o_R, and the latest version of Prince2. He is a member of the Institute of Directors, the British Consulting Institute and the Institute of Consulting.

Thomas Walenta worked on projects from 1974 and chose project management as his distinctive profession in 1988. He is a coach and mentor for project management professionals and interim manager for organizations. In 2014 he retired from IBM after 31 years, where he gained experience with setting up complex programs,

PMOs and turning around troubled projects for IBM clients in diverse industries, geographies and technologies. In parallel to his work Thomas has been a Project Management Institute (PMI) volunteer since 1998, as Chapter President, global Board Director and being awarded as PMI Fellow in 2012. He has been a frequent speaker at global conferences since 2000 and a member of the GPM since 1995.

Michael Young is a serial entrepreneur with a passion for project management. With over 20 years' experience working in project, programme and portfolio management across many sectors, including government, defence, engineering IT and logistics. Michael's voluntary contribution to project management is remarkable, having developed numerous ISO standards, being of the authors of IPMA's ICB4, being a member of the IPMA research board, and through over 18 years' service in various roles with the Australian Institute of Project Management. His work has been featured in the *BRW magazine*, the *Australian Financial Review* and *Smart Company*. He has received over 25 awards, including Australian Business Awards for project management, innovation and sustainability. He also managed the Australian IT Project of the Year in 2006. As a prolific author and speaker, Michael actively advocates for an evolution of project management and the delivery of sustainable change.

Preface

Projects have been around almost since civilization began, but current management practices are a comparatively recent development, with their origins traceable back to the 1950s (mostly in the military and defence industries). Since then we have seen the extension of project management into multiproject and (more recently) programme management, where bundling interrelated projects together can achieve synergies and better alignment through joint management. Projects and programmes are temporary endeavours that strive to deliver products and services beneficially. That goal has to be achieved within set constraints, using resources as efficiently as possible.

With a few exceptions, the numbers and importance of projects and programmes before the year 2000 were relatively small compared with the 'business-as-usual' activities of organizations. As both the number and importance of projects and programmes grew significantly during the early 2000s, a fresh management approach was needed to align projects and programmes with the strategic ambitions of organizations, and to plan and control the utilization of finite (or even scarce) resources available to those organizations. Thus the idea of using the already existing concept of portfolio management in the area of projects and programmes was born.

The portfolio concept already existed in financial assets management, which seeks to align all investments to the strategic goals of the investor (balancing risks and opportunities as well as the available, typically scarce financial resources). International associations, researchers and literature picked up that idea and spread it through their publications.

Project and programme portfolio management (abbreviated to PPM and usually discussed simply as 'portfolio management') is a permanent function that supports the decision-makers in a defined part of the organization. Its main task is to ensure that the right projects are chosen and performed, so that defined strategic objectives are achieved for the organization's benefit. Thus selection and prioritization of project proposals and projects to achieve the strategic objectives are one of the key activities of portfolio management. In other words, portfolio management is the bridge between the strategic level and the project level of an organization. Strategic objectives are used to formulate the objectives of projects and programmes before executing them. In return, portfolio control collects information from all projects and programmes, and collates that information into high-level portfolio reports that keep senior executives informed and supports their decision-making.

Do we have enough resources to perform all the projects and programmes in our pipeline? How do we allocate resources in an optimum way in order to achieve the best results? These are two of the questions related to another important aspect of portfolio management. The more projects and programmes that are performed in an organization, the more important it is to have an overview of the resource requirements over time, so that the available resources can be scheduled and allocated efficiently to all portfolio elements, balancing the resources according to the strategic needs. One of the key risks of a project-orientated organization nowadays is a lack of resources for its projects and programmes.

Another significant risk in portfolio management is that resources could be reallocated from one project to another without knowing what the impact on the overall portfolio might be. This is just one of several reasons for having a portfolio management office or project management office (PMO), which includes responsibility for resource allocation. Another significant development in portfolio management has been the definition of its various processes (including the methods, tools and, most importantly, the human competences needed). These definitions are now available in international standards, and human competences are recognized by various qualifications and certifications from professional institutions.

This *Handbook* is the first of its kind on the subject of portfolio management. It provides an overview of what portfolio management is all about and allows deep insights into the application of portfolio management in various sectors and application areas. Almost 40 experts from a wide range of industries and professions describe the application of portfolio management in their areas of responsibility and thus provide deep insights into the profession.

Handbooks are not intended to be read from the first to the last page. Rather they offer a valuable source of reference from a range of expert writers. The first section of our *Handbook* provides insights into the foundations of portfolio management. It covers basic concepts, definitions and the purpose of portfolio management. It touches on the relevance of portfolio management and the value that it intends to deliver, and explains the different portfolio types, and the portfolio components and settings that could confront a portfolio manager.

Our second section includes 10 chapters which provide various insights into the practice of portfolio management, including (but not limited to) information and communications technology (ICT), research and development (R&D), change and business development, construction, banks, public administration and humanitarian aid. Through these chapters it will become obvious to readers that there is no 'one practice' of portfolio management. Instead it is rather a wide range of practices, which need to be tailored to the needs of a specific portfolio.

Through the third section it is made clear that effective portfolio management requires certain prerequisites to be in place. These include, for example, a governance system and a PMO, clearly defined roles and responsibilities, alignment with organizational structures, management systems and processes, competent people and effective software systems.

Our fourth section outlines the approaches for managing a portfolio. It covers a wide range of activities such as defining the portfolio, and identifying, selecting, prioritizing and planning the portfolio components. These chapters give advice on evaluating and reporting portfolio performance, balancing and optimizing the portfolio, as well as describing the portfolio-level benefits, risk, resources, change and people management.

The final section describes how the capabilities of an organization related to port-folio management can be developed. Here is included an interesting chapter with 10 questions and answers for the executives engaged in portfolios.

We gratefully acknowledge the contributions made by all our authors. These are people who are busy with their daily work, and yet they have made their time avail-able in the not inconsiderable task of sharing their expertise and experiences with us. You can read about them in our 'Notes of contributors' section, which precedes the main text. Holding the result of these joint efforts in hand makes us feel proud and confident that the practice of portfolio management will benefit considerably. We also owe special thanks to Jonathan Norman, who inspired us to move forward with this handbook, and to all the people at Routledge for helping us to make it happen.

Dennis Lock, Chesham, UK
Reinhard Wagner, Friedberg, Germany

Abbreviations and acronyms

Note: many abbreviations and acronyms have multiple meanings. Those given here are most relevant to this book.

AI	artificial intelligence
AIPM	Australian Institute of Project Management
APM	application portfolio management
APM	Association for Project Management
ARCA	amended and restated concession agreement
AXELOS	successor to OGC
BAU	business as usual
BCG	Boston Consulting Group
BI	business intelligence
BoK	body of knowledge
BM	business model
BSC	balanced scorecard
CA	concession agreement
CAPEX	capital expenditure
CBS	cost breakdown structure
CDC	change delivery committee
CEO	Chief Executive Officer
CFO	Chief Financial Officer
CIO	Chief Information Officer/Chief Investment Officer
CIP	continuous improvement process
CISR	Center for Information Research (MIT)
CoE	centre of excellence
COO	Chief Operating Officer
CPD	continuing professional development
CPPE	Certified Practising Portfolio Executive
CS	Construction Supervisor
CSR	corporate social responsibility
C-suite	collective noun for CEO, CFO, CIO and COO
DEDPI	detailed engineering and design plan for implementation
DFID	Department for International Development (UKAid)
DS	Design Supervisor

EA	enterprise architecture
EDP	electronic data processing
EI	emotional intelligence
EIA	environmental impact assessment
EPM	enterprise (and organizational) project management
EPMO	enterprise PMO
EPPM	enterprise project portfolio management
ERP	enterprise resource planning
ETM	Efficient Task Management
EY	Ernst & Young
Fintech	financial technology
FLSM	full span launching method (applies to steel girders in Chapter 14)
FM	financial management
GDP	gross domestic product
HMSO	Her Majesty's Stationery Office, now replaced by TSO
HRM	human resources management (once known as personnel management)
IC	investment committee
ICB	individual competence baseline
ICCPM	International Centre of Complex Project Management
ICO	integration and coordination office
ICO	interface control officer
ICT	information and comunications technology
IMF	International Monetary Fund
IoT	internet of things
IPM	infrastructure portfolio management
IPMA	International Project Management Association
ISO	International Organization for Standardization
IT	information technology
KCI	key competence indicator
KEC	Korea Expressway Corporation
KPI	key performance indicator
LFA	logical framework approach
LRFD	load and resistance factor design
LTA	lender's technical advisor
METI	Ministry of Economy, Trade and Industry (Japan)
MIT	Massachusetts Institute of Technology
MoP	Management of Portfolios (AXELOS, published by TSO)
MRG	minimum revenue guarantee
NGO	non-governmental organization
NPV	net present value
O&M	operation and maintenance
OBS	organization breakdown structure
OCB	Organizational Competence Baseline
OGC	Office of Government Commerce (succeeded by AXELOS)
OPM	operational project management
P3	portfolios, programmes and projects

P3M	portfolio, programme and project management
P3O	(AXELOS collective term for project management office, programme management office and portfolio management office)
PDG	portfolio direction group
PDP	product development process
PM	project management
PMI	Project Management Institute
PMO	project management office/programme management office/portfolio management office
PO3	AXELOS term combining all three PMOs listed above
POUNCE	projects overspent in uncontrolled environments
PPF	portfolio, programme and project management community
PPG	portfolio progress group
PPM	project portfolio management
PPO	project purchasing officer
PRINCE	**PR**ojects **IN** Controlled Environments (a management system for projects set up in the UK under the auspices of the Cabinet Office, now administered by AXELOS). Publications available from the TSO
PRINCE2	Successor to PRINCE
RAG	red, amber, green 'traffic light indicators', used in pictorial reports
ROI	return on investment
SAM	self-assessment method
SBU	small business unit
SDC	Swiss Agency for Development and Cooperation
SME	small or medium enterprise
SME	subject matter expert
SMO	strategy management office
SRO	senior responsible owner
SVP	senior vice-president
TBL	triple bottom line accounting
TQM	total quality management
TSO	The Stationery Office, based in Norwich
USAID	United States Agency for International Development
VP	value proposition
WBS	work breakdown structure

Part I

Foundations of portfolio management

Chapter 1

Basic concepts and definitions of portfolio management

Steve Butler

Project portfolio management is essentially managing information concerning the implementation of a strategy. At its heart it provides decision-makers with the insight, foresight and oversight to enable them to assess, select, prioritize, reprioritize, pause and even terminate initiatives.

Introduction

A number of activities are needed to make project portfolio management (PPM) successful. These activities involve creating the initial plan, maintaining that plan and delivering the portfolio. The process includes the following elements:

- managing risk;
- managing resources across the portfolio;
- balancing conflicting demands from competing portfolio components;
- monitoring progress;
- monitoring the budget;
- delivering the benefits of the portfolio components – the essence of PPM.

Corporations of all sizes often find it easier to formulate a strategy rather than implement it. The solution is to make effective use of PPM. Correct application of the appropriate knowledge, processes, skills, tools and techniques will have a significant and positive impact on implementing the strategy, as well as increasing programme and project success by selecting the right work.

This *Handbook* focuses on the discipline of PPM and is based on current best practice at the time of writing. 'Best practice' in this context means where there is general agreement that the application of these skills, tools and techniques can enhance the chances of success over a wide range of portfolios. It expands on existing standards and research (see, for example, Project Management Institute, 2017) as well as on considerable expertise and first-hand experience (such as that demonstrated by the contributors of the following chapters).

Definitions

Definition of a portfolio

A portfolio is the activity related to delivering the strategy of an organization. Indeed, the Project Management Institute (PMI) defines a portfolio as:

a collection of projects, programmes, subsidiary portfolios and operations managed as a group to achieve operational objectives

(PMI, 2017)

A portfolio will typically be the umbrella structure over a group of related and unrelated projects and other work. A portfolio might contain one or more programmes, but the reverse is far less likely to be true. A portfolio may also be defined to contain support, operations and non-labour expenses, although those types of work and expenses do not have to be included if there are good reasons for not doing so.

The portfolio allows us to optimize investment decisions by prioritizing and balancing all the work contained within it. For maximum effectiveness, a portfolio should encompass all the work that draws on common resources (such as that contained within an entire business unit or department). However, the work itself is not done at the portfolio level. Instead, the work is done through the projects, support teams and operational teams that work within the portfolio

Definition of portfolio management

Portfolio management (or project portfolio management to give it its complete name) is 'the centralized management of one or more portfolios to achieve strategic objectives. It includes a set of interrelated organizational processes by which an organization prioritizes, selects, and allocates its limited internal resources to best accomplish organizational vision, mission, and values' (PMI, 2017).

Although the focus of a project is to deliver capabilities, and that of a programme is to deliver benefits, the focus of portfolio management is to deliver value – in other words, portfolio management is concerned with delivering the right benefits. It provides an opportunity for governance boards to make decisions that control or influence the direction of a group of portfolio components as they work to achieve specific outcomes.

Another way of looking at it is that portfolio management ensures that all significant interrelationships between programmes and projects are identified and that resources (such as people and funding) are allocated in accordance with organizational priorities. Programme management's focus is on achieving the benefits expected from the portfolio components as determined by organizational strategy and objectives. Project management is largely concerned with achieving defined deliverables that support specific goals.

The interrelationship of projects, programmes and portfolios

A project will have a pre-agreed scope that is intended to deliver capabilities within constrained budgets and schedules. It will have a relatively discernible beginning, middle and end, with a clear path forwards. Projects are subject to strict change control for managing variances from their baselines (although the degree to which agility is applied will often impact this).

Programmes are often made up of related projects and other activities. They can have a wide scope and they focus on realizing organizational benefits from the capabilities enabled by projects. Programmes have a clear vision of an end state, but not necessarily a defined path on how to get there. Change should be expected (and is often encouraged) during the programme's lifecycle, so a flexible framework should

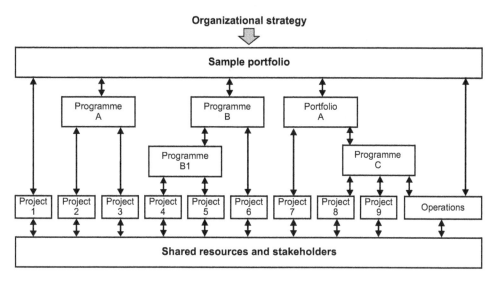

Figure 1.1 A portfolio composed of various components

be provided, while ensuring that any change is relevant and within the context of the big picture.

A portfolio is a collection of components that are grouped together to enable strategic objectives. Those components are projects, programmes and/or operational activity (operational activities are often referred to as 'business as usual'). All these components are not necessarily interrelated but they should be selected to provide the optimum mix of risk and investment for achieving the strategic objectives. Contribution to and alignment with the portfolio are often a main factor in project or programme selection criteria. Figure 1.1 shows how a portfolio might comprise a mix of projects, programmes and subportfolios.

Why portfolio management is important

Portfolio management is concerned with delivering value. While programme management delivers benefits, effective portfolio management will ensure that the *right* benefits are delivered. It therefore follows that disappointing and less than optimal performance and returns for the portfolio will result if management efforts are focused on executing individual portfolio components, but fail to give the same attention to the project portfolio itself.

Typically, a company wants to move towards its vision, and to do this it establishes goals. These goals will have objectives that are measures of goal achievement. Strategies are developed for how the goals will be achieved. These strategies direct the execution of work intended to achieve the goals, amounting to the organizational strategy that describes how the organization will be used for:

- capitalizing on opportunities;
- responding to changes in the market;
- minimizing the impact of threats;

- ensuring adherence to legislative or compliance requirements;
- activities for 'keeping the lights on';
- and so on (this is not an exhaustive list).

Other chapters throughout this *Handbook* assume that there is an organizational strategy in place, and that there are objectives containing mission and vision statements, as well as goals, objectives and strategies intended to achieve the vision. Linking portfolio management to strategy balances the use of resources to maximize the value delivered in executing project and operational activities.

After identifying what the organization wants to do (and why and when) it makes sense to ensure that it executes on those intentions. That is where portfolio management comes in, and that is why it is so important.

What successful portfolio management does

The previous section described the importance of portfolio management, but at a high level what does that involve? Before I describe in granular detail what is involved, it is helpful to take a more distant look. Essentially, portfolio management attempts to deliver the maximum value envisaged and intended by a strategic plan by the following means:

- *Making sure that projects and programmes remain aligned with business goals throughout their execution, and ensuring the right mix of projects at all times.* This involves ensuring continuous management oversight, regular communication and coordination, constant course correction to minimize project drift, and redirecting projects when business objectives change to maintain alignment. The concept of 'kill fast–kill early' applies (stopping a project as soon as it becomes apparent that it will not deliver the required returns).
- *Constantly ensuring that the risks posed by the projects and programmes in the portfolio are managed and balanced.* Just as an investor attempts to minimize risk and maximize returns by diversifying portfolio holdings, companies should assess and balance the risks of the projects in their portfolios. An aggressive project portfolio may have greater odds of hitting a 'big win', but that comes at the cost of a substantially higher risk of failure or loss. Conversely a conservative portfolio might minimize risk, but it would also limit the potential returns of the portfolio. Good project portfolio management diversifies the portfolio, balancing risks with potential returns.
- *Identifying performance problems and ensuring that they are corrected before they become major issues.* Although portfolio management cannot eliminate performance problems completely, it can help to deal with them early, before they become major issues. Recognizing, escalating and responding to issues quickly will keep projects on track and avoid compromising dependent or downstream projects.
- *Ensuring that projects receive the oversight and support needed to complete them successfully.* By elevating the prioritization and oversight responsibilities to the executive level, project portfolio management can ensure that projects receive the backing they need to succeed. Executives have the authority and business knowledge to ensure alignment between projects and business strategies, to: fine-tune

the timing and sequence of projects to exploit synergies, avoid reworking and eliminate redundancies; assign resources optimally; direct funds to the most valuable initiatives; and help to resolve critical performance issues.
- *Ensuring optimal resource allocation across those projects* – with limited resources there is a need to quantify and prioritize projects to help ensure that the right resources work on the right projects to produce the most value. High-level executive oversight should resolve resource conflicts between ongoing projects. It also incorporates formal sourcing strategies to determine the skill sets needed for each project and the best source of resources.

The portfolio structure

When portfolio management is introduced, the first step should be to identify the elements of the planned portfolio. The best way of doing this is to draw up an inventory of all the portfolio components in order to establish the key descriptors through which the components can be identified, assembled and compared. For example, the following list suggests possible descriptors that you could adopt and include:

- reference number;
- brief description of the component;
- class of component (for example, project or programme, business case, value proposition, subportfolio or other related work);
- strategic objectives supported;
- benefits – quantitative;
- benefits – qualitative;
- sponsor, client, customer;
- type of product, deliverable or enabler;
- estimated cost;
- risk category.

Based on these data, the potential components can be categorized using one or more of the descriptors such as class, objectives, type of benefits, client, cost or risk level, depending on whatever makes the most sense to the organization. In subsequent years, the principles will have been established so this step should prove to be easier. Nevertheless, the actual components in the various categories identified will change.

There may be more than one portfolio, each designed for a different division or a different focus. Selection of the respective components will depend on the individual portfolio plan's operational goals and objectives.

The next step is to design the portfolio, and there are two approaches to this process, as follows:

1. The top-down or strategic approach. The portfolio is designed to deliver the changes required to achieve the defined strategic objectives.
2. The bottom-up approach. This is appropriate where the strategy is more emergent and in more dynamic environments. Here change initiatives are proposed bottom-up, and are appraised and prioritized on a regular basis in the context of the current high-level strategic objectives

Skills needed by the portfolio manager

We have seen that portfolio management is critical to successful execution of a strategy. It therefore follows that the role of portfolio manager is equally critical. So what skills does a portfolio manager need to have and apply in order to achieve success?

Top of the list, and often not documented, is political awareness. The portfolio manager needs to be aware of the various political nuances in the area of the business where stakeholders exist (the stakeholder landscape) – and needs also to be aware of the interest in, power over and influence on the portfolio that each stakeholder has. The portfolio manager needs to be adept and confident in reporting the status of the portfolio to senior management – 'warts and all' – and in providing the appropriate recommendations for action.

Portfolio managers need to be experts at capturing the impact of their portfolios and the resulting values created relative to the strategic goals, and conveying to governing bodies how well the components of the portfolio are aligned to the strategy. They need to be able to negotiate for resources and work with functional leads to ensure optimum execution of the portfolio, including a constant and accurate awareness of the risk exposure of the portfolio. They need to be experts in understanding the implications of change management, experts in team management and leadership, experts in conflict resolution, able to understand financial reports and the implications thereof, and have an understanding of portfolio management tools and techniques. The list is seemingly endless!

Remember, project management is about doing projects right, portfolio management is about doing the right projects. So the skills needed to be a successful portfolio manager are considerable.

Reference

Project Management Institute (2017), *The Standard for Portfolio Management*, 4th edn, Newtown Square, PA: Project Management Institute.

Chapter 2

Delivering organizational strategy with portfolio management

Martin Sedlmayer

Every project, programme and portfolio should set out to satisfy established strategic objectives. So this chapter on delivering organizational strategy has particular relevance and importance in portfolio management.

Why strategy really matters

Industry 4.0 is the internet of things and services, digitalization of the value chain and disruptive technologies – the core strategic challenges of many businesses nowadays. Industry 4.0 will create a smart factory of things and services. Within modularly structured smart factories, cyber-physical systems will monitor physical processes, create a virtual copy of the physical world and make decentralized decisions. Over the internet of things, cyber-physical systems communicate and cooperate with each other and with humans in real time. Via the internet of services, both internal and cross-organizational services are offered and used by participants of the whole value chain (Hermann, Pentek and Otto, 2016).

But how will Industry 4.0 change the way in which we develop or implement a strategy? Does it influence strategic thinking? Although heavily discussed in research and practice nowadays, there seems to be the general understanding that strategy, strategic thinking and properly considered anticipation of the future remain important. Only long-term planning becomes less important. The general expectation is that an organization with a defined and declared strategy is (and will remain) more successful than an organization without. And because times are more changeable, more fragile and less certain than in the past, organizations are forced to think in shorter investment cycles and act accordingly. But an unpredictable future will not be made any more predictable only through more precise planning.

An organizational strategy, of course, is not a beautiful set of PowerPoint slides, but a plan of actions designed to achieve a major or overall aim. It is a blueprint that is developed, integrating all relevant stakeholders, a framework that provides guidance and makes sure that what you are doing is aligned with the overall objectives.

Without successful implementation as its core purpose, strategy will remain a dream and never become a reality. To implement the strategy in the most effective way, project portfolio management and the temporary organization's projects and programmes must offer solid processes, models, tools and competences.

Strategy scholars differ in principle about two main approaches to strategy development. The 'rationalist school' (Ansoff, 1965, Drucker, 1971, and others) derives strategy top-down from mission and vision, in a rather deterministic way. In contrast, the 'emergent school' (Mintzberg, 1978) focuses more on emerging ideas and how they shall be induced into the future strategy. These general approaches also determine the two principal approaches of how to set up project portfolio management:

1.   The emergent approach builds on a bottom-up process of innovation, asking primarily engineers and frontline staff to come up with innovative ideas. It runs a process on how to cope with these ideas and how to include them in the strategy.
2.   The rationalist approach drives a top-down planning process in which strategic initiatives are derived from the strategy, and implemented through projects and programmes.

Good governance practice nowadays explicitly requires a formal alignment of business, portfolio, programme and project plans, and transparent reporting of status and risks to the board of directors (Association for Project Management or APM, 2004). Consequently, the implementation of a corporate strategy is assertively a major task for today's chief executive officers (CEOs): 'The challenge for tomorrow's CEOs is not so much developing a sound strategy but rather getting it implemented consistently and in a timely manner' ([Heinrich von Pierer, former head of the Board of Directors of Siemens] Dammer, 2007).

The strategic alignment approaches

Recognition of the strategic importance of project management in the corporate world is rapidly increasing. One reason for this acceleration may be a strong belief by business leaders that aligning project management with business strategy can significantly enhance the achievement of organizational goals, strategies and performance. However, empirical literature that offers advice on how to achieve this alignment is scanty. Many companies are suffering from misaligned projects and a lack of a systematic approach to align project management with the business strategy. Although projects are the basic building blocks of organizational strategy in many companies, project management is not often recognized as a functional strategy and is rarely perceived as a business process, making the achievement of a project management/business strategy alignment even more difficult.

The emergent project portfolio approach

The 'emergent' project portfolio approach uses a well-defined process to identify, analyse, evaluate, and collectively manage current and proposed projects. This process shall ensure that all projects are in line with the organizational strategy. The objectives are to determine the optimal resource mix for delivery and to schedule activities to best achieve an organization's operational and financial targets, while honouring constraints imposed by customers, strategic objectives or external real-world factors.

To do so, project portfolio management usually aligns projects to the corporate strategy by applying a kind of gate approach: potential project ideas are compared against numerous key characteristics to reach a decision as to whether or not to launch the project. These key characteristics may include:

- Strategic fit;
- Coverage of customers' needs;
- Synergies with existing business;
- Profitability, net present value or a similar key performance indicator (KPI);
- Delivery time/time to market;
- Technical feasibility, chance of success;
- Risk exposure.

As a result of the evaluation, various reports can be generated, to support top management in their decision-making. Bubble diagrams are popular in this context, and there are several examples elsewhere in this Handbook (see, for example, Figure 26.2, Chapter 26).

As hardly any company has enough resources to deliver all ideas at the very same time, projects have to be put in an order of priority. Projects have to queue. This cyclic process generates a project pipeline, with the following principal stages:

1. Exploration/conceptual;
2. Scoping;
3. Initial feasibility studies;
4. Definition;
5. Execution.

The emergent approach focuses on balancing the portfolio, but a link to the strategy is most commonly superficial. Of course, strategic fit will be one of the key characteristics (hopefully the most important one), but strategic alignment remains 'artificial' and is not naturally linked to the strategy development process.

Although quite well implemented in major companies, this process has a couple of disadvantages, including:

- It does not provide any assurance that the strategy as a whole can be implemented with the sum of all activities planned, with all the projects in the project portfolio;
- Business ideas tend to be queued instead of being either delivered or eliminated.

Consequently, the lack of assurance about feasibility can lead to many strategies not being implemented. The consequential holding back of project ideas can generate quite a large backlog of projects, with increasing dissatisfaction among employees and top management. In addition, the window of opportunity to realize one or more ideas might be missed.

The rationalist project portfolio approach

In the 'rationalist' project portfolio approach, projects or (most probably) programmes (Lock and Wagner, 2016) become *the* vehicle of strategy implementation. Projects are directly derived from the strategy. The project lifecycle is naturally embedded in the strategy process as Gartner's analysts (Light and Hotle, 2006) suggest (Figure 2.1).

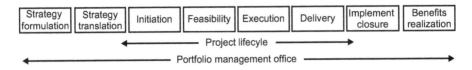

Figure 2.1 Projects embedded in the strategy process

Projects are no longer retrospectively or artificially aligned to the strategy. The integrated approach seeks to derive projects naturally and directly from the strategy (Sedlmayer, 2007). This requires working on the strategy in sufficient detail in order to be able to define the scope and the main deliverables of the underlying projects or programmes of projects with certainty.

Of course, a strategy may contain elements that can be implemented without special projects. These 'run the business' elements are allocated to the responsibility of line management. Nevertheless, most strategic statements indicate the need for changes, which implies the use of project methods and structures ('change the business').

The integrated process can be outlined as shown in Figure 2.2. The first part of the process is the strategy development. Whatever methods and tools a company may select, some elements of an environment analysis and some elements of a company analysis will be performed to formulate the strategy.

A point worth mentioning is that today CEOs believe it is not necessary to involve project managers in strategy development (Crawford, 2005), despite the fact that over 20 years ago Bourgeois and Brodwin (1984) proposed that project managers should be involved in strategy formulation. Project managers can hardly implement a project effectively without deep knowledge of the true factors that initiated the change for the project(s). The project management office needs to be linked into this process as early as possible, to enable a seamless handover to take place by clarifying the strategy and transferring the outcome into project realization. The specific knowledge has to be kept, especially the important aspect of 'knowing why' (Holland, 2002).

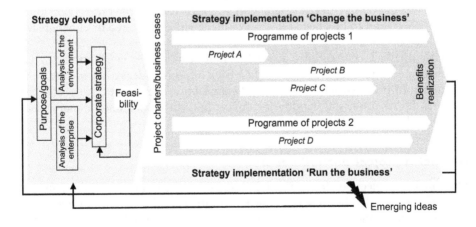

Figure 2.2 The integrated process

Most companies start the implementation of their strategy straight after the final steps of strategy definition without checking whether or not the strategy as a whole is feasible. They ignore the fact that the second-best strategy that can be executed is much better than an ideal strategy, which can demand capabilities that a company simply does not have (Aspesi and Vardhan, 1999).

Important questions should be answered in this feasibility check, before the final approval of any strategy. These questions include:

- Does the organization have enough skills to implement the strategy? Both numbers and competences? (IPMA, 2015)
- Is the organization – or part of it – able to bear the required change?
- Can the strategy as a whole be financed?
- Is there enough time to implement the strategy, fast enough compared with competition?
- What are the implications of the new strategy on current activities, both line activities and projects?
- Are there alternative ways of reaching similar or even the same objectives, but faster or with fewer resources?

Undoubtedly, the strategy has to be elaborated up to the point where it becomes clear how to implement it and whereby projects and programmes can directly be derived from it. This thinking through – making it concrete (Mankins and Steele, 2005) – has to be conducted with both the strategy team and the project management team.

One could argue that this check is not necessary if the analysis of the company has been done properly. However, the analysis phase does not usually include the strategy as a whole (the definition of a master plan of initiatives, the allocation of key resources, the funding, and the prediction of a date when all initiatives and projects could be completed are all missing). At this stage, the planning level remains quite broad. It is not necessary to have exact project plans in place, but a clear picture about the following needs to be elaborated:

- A rough picture about the solution, including its impact on current business;
- The way to get there (rough timeline, tranches, core milestones and so on);
- Key resources including management capabilities (for example, top management capacity, project managers) to steer the implementation process; and
- Financial implication (financing and cost).

Without the feasibility check, it is not possible for the management to predict the likelihood of the strategy to be implemented at the given time. It could be argued that this is the most important step in defining a sound, reliable strategy.

The optimum approach

Obviously, the rationalist approach is more effective (Srivannaboon, 2006) simply because the projects are directly derived from the strategy. But to apply this process, the management needs to have a clear picture of the path to follow, a clear and well-elaborated strategy and, most important, the will and power to execute.

The emergent approach is more suitable for organizations that are looking for creativity and innovative ideas. They constantly scan the markets for opportunities. The strategy development process and the strategy implementation include more stakeholders, especially more front-line staff. It is more of a bottom-up approach for managers in favour of making constant decisions.

However, as in strategy development there is no universal or 'one-size-fits-all' solution for the optimum approach to implementing the strategy. That is why organizations most probably apply both approaches and deliberately let them interfere in the project portfolio. But nowadays a super-session of strategic programmes over the 'normal' project portfolio can be observed in many organizations. From the overall capacity of an organization, the 'absolute must' projects are given first priority and implemented. After this slice (which should really be small) all strategic programmes are resourced. Any other ideas, projects and activities can be supplied from the remaining resources. This approach finally guarantees the right of way to the strategic programmes and timely implementation of these important initiatives.

Measuring strategic alignment

Although a sound portfolio process already leads to a sound strategic alignment, it is not sufficient for success. Strategic alignment means that all elements of a business are arranged in the way that best supports fulfilment of its long-term purpose. This includes not only the 'run the business' parts, but especially the development parts, projects and programmes.

Strategic control systems

Strategic control systems (Bungay and Goold, 1991) are used by organizations to control the execution of strategic plans. These are a specialized form of management control, and they differ in respect of the need to handle uncertainty and ambiguity. Strategic control is focused on the achievement of future goals and benefits, rather than the evaluation of past performance.

Strategic control processes are cybernetic in nature (Beer, 1972). They use one or more 'closed-loop' feedback controls to detect and highlight deviations from expected results, so that management can intervene and apply corrections. It is important that this process is forward looking when used to control strategy, so that measures can be implemented that are future directed and anticipatory.

A related concern for strategic control processes is the amount of time and effort required for the process to work. If either of these is too big the process will be ineffective, or it will simply be ignored by the organization. To work properly, a strategic control system needs a small set of standard elements, the absence of any one of which makes strategic control impossible to achieve (Muralidharan, 2004). These essential elements are:

- Articulation of the strategic outcomes being sought;
- Description of the strategic activities to be carried out (attached to specific managed resources) in pursuit of the required outcomes;
- Definition of a method to track progress made against these two elements (usually via the monitoring of a small number of performance measures and associated target values);

- Identification of an effective intervention mechanism that would allow observers to change, correct or adjust the organization's activities.

These elements imply active involvement of senior managers in the determination of the strategic activities pursued by the component parts of an organization and (more importantly) by following up the implementation of the measures defined to ensure delivery.

Usually, such a strategic control system contains KPIs to set targets and to monitor their degree of fulfilment. Also important in such a system is the anchoring of these targets within the permanent organization. These targets can be achieved only if line managers follow the same set of strategic targets as the project managers. For more on KPIs, see Chapter 23.

Balanced scorecard

A balanced scorecard (Kaplan and Norton, 1992) monitors the performance of all or parts of an organization towards strategic or operational objectives. It uses financial and non-financial performance measures to focus on areas where the organization is failing to do what is required or expected (Figure 2.3).

The balanced scorecard (BSC) is a strategy performance management tool that can be used to keep track of the execution of activities and monitor the consequences arising from these actions. It is widely accepted as a useful tool for monitoring the alignment of projects to the organization's strategy. At its core, the balanced scorecard is simply a table with a few numbers recording features associated with an organization,

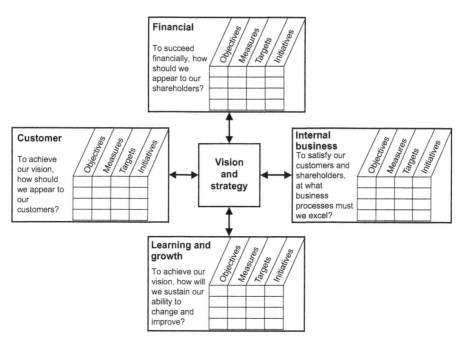

Figure 2.3 The classic balanced scorecard framework

Adapted from Kaplan and Norton (2003)

matched to target values. The table is reviewed periodically, and by comparing actual performance achieved against the target managers can spot issues more easily. They can then choose to intervene and correct these issues before they become problems.

However, for maximum effectiveness a balanced scorecard has to include the right measures and targets, which can be a difficult thing to achieve. The balanced scorecard is useful only when the measures and targets chosen are appropriate. The early balanced scorecard designs featured a small number of performance measures. Kaplan and Norton (2003) proposed four perspectives:

- Financial;
- Customer;
- Processes;
- Learning and growth.

Modern approaches describe the balanced scorecard in terms of a (individual) set of high-level objectives to be achieved. Measures are then chosen for each objective as part of a second design step. A strategy map illustrates how the various objectives are related. Objectives and linkages help providing a stronger basis for choosing measures.

Business case

The business case is an important element of the strategy implementation process, but is it often weak or even missing in many organizations. For each of the different initiatives, it is essential to have a clear view of how much it will cost, which and how much benefit (monetary and non-monetary) it will generate, and how these benefits shall be realized. The results of each project have to increase the value of the organization and/or its customers. The benefits may come from increasing revenues (new or improved products or services), by decreasing operational expenses or business risks, or by decreasing or improving return on a particular investment. Even further, in all business cases the important question of alternative ways for reaching the same targets has to be addressed. Is the proposed way for implementation the most effective and efficient one? Are there alternatives for reaching the same objectives with lower cost, or in a shorter timescale or with fewer risks? A sound business case should include at least the following items:

- Description of the current situation, environment, market demand and core requirements;
- Aim, target, objectives, strategic direction;
- Key deliverables;
- Influence on the company's business units and the IT department;
- A rough plan, including key decision points;
- Prerequisites, outside influence, dependencies, constraints and conditions;
- Key roles (including sponsor, project manager, architect and so on) and sourcing (for example, IT partners, outsourcing);
- Key opportunities and risk analysis;
- Details of the required funding (for the whole lifecycle, not just the investment phase) and the expected benefits.

Benefits realization

It is imperative to realize the predicted benefits during and – at the latest – after project completion. The predicted values have to be realized to ensure a sustainable business (Söderholm, Gemünden and Winch, 2008).

Progress of the benefits realization and prediction has to be measured during and after the execution of the project. Only when sponsors are required to demonstrate how the benefits have been realized will it be possible for an organization to increase the level of maturity concerning strategy implementation and benefits generation (Sedlmayer, 2009). The most effective way to do so is to include all benefits predicted in the business case in mid-term financial planning (revenues, costs, profits) of the line managers, simultaneously with the acceptance of the particular business case.

Of course during and after the project the sponsor is given the possibility to correct these (predicted) benefits. These changes of the expected benefits will lead to better decisions and more realistic expectations. In addition, this would enable the management to decide on how to proceed with these strategic undertakings (by adjusting their content, timescale, resource allocation or even early project termination).

Conclusion

Industry 4.0, digitalization of the value chain and disruptive technology are some of the factors that will provide organizations with big challenges. A sound strategy, although with a shorter time horizon, remains important for future success. But a strategy is not enough: the organization needs to be aligned and the strategic initiatives have to be implemented. Projects need to deliver the expected benefits. To delivering an organizational strategy, the portfolio management system requires some key elements, as follows:

- The strategy needs to be sound and concrete enough for all (top) managers to have the same understanding of the organization's aims;
- Every strategy needs a feasibility check before it can go into realization. Otherwise there will be no understanding possible as to whether or not the strategy can realistically be implemented in the timeframe required and within the costs that the organization can afford;
- Competent, accountable and available sponsors funding and steering the strategic initiatives need to care about the strategy implementation;
- A strategy control system with a small number of KPIs enables the management to review progress regularly and initiate timely corrective actions if required;
- A project portfolio management system that is interlinked with the strategy process should ensure that the executing project manager has the correct knowhow and, especially, the 'know why';
- Stricter prioritization by top management (Sedlmayer, 2007) and the use of programmes to focus on strategic initiatives that supplant nice-to-have projects.
- A sound business case for every undertaking, including integration of the predicted benefits into the standard planning processes of the organization.

References and further reading

Ansoff, I.H. (1965), *Corporate Strategy*, New York: McGraw-Hill.

Aspesi, C. and Vardhan, D. (1999), 'Brilliant strategy, but can you execute?', *McKinsey Quarterly*, 89–99.

Association for Project Management (2004), Directing Change: A Guide to the Governance of Project Management, High Wycombe: APM.

Beer, S. (1972), Brain of the Firm: Managerial Cybernetics of Organization, London: Allen Lane.

Bourgeois, L.J., III and Brodwin, D.R. (1984). 'Strategic implementation: Five approaches to an elusive phenomenon', *Strategic Management Journal*, 241–264.

Bungay, S. and Goold, M. (1991), 'Creating strategic control systems', *Long Range Planning*, 32–39.

Crawford, L.H. (2005), 'Senior management perceptions of project management competence', *International Journal of Project Management*, 7–16.

Dammer, H. (2007), *Ergebnisbericht Multiprojektmanagement-Studie 2004–2006*, Berlin: Technische Universität Berlin.

Drucker, P.F. (1971). *Drucker on Management*, London: Management Publications Ltd.

Hermann, M., Pentek, T. and Otto, B. (2016), *Design Principles for Industry 4.0 Scenarios*, 49th Hawaii International Conference on System Sciences (HICSS) (S. 3928–3937). Hawaii: System Sciences (HICSS).

Holland, D. (2002). *Projektmanagement für die Chefetage*, Weinheim: Wiley.

International Project Management Association (2015), *IPMA International Competence Baseline Version 4.0*, Nijkerk, Netherlands: IPMA.

Kaplan, R.S. and Norton, D.P. (1992), 'The balanced scorecard: Measures that drive performance', *Harvard Business Review*, 71–79.

Light, M. and Hotle, M. (2006), *The Emergent PMO: Projects, Programs and Portfolios*, Geneva: Gartners Project Portfolio Summit Europe (S. 1–20).

Lock, D. and Wagner, R. (2016), *Gower Handbook of Programme Management*, Abingdon: Routledge.

Mankins, M.C. and Steele, R. (2005), 'Turning great strategy into great performance', *Harvard Business Review*, July/August.

Mintzberg, H. (1978), 'Patterns of strategy formation', *Management Science*, 934–948.

Muralidharan, R. (2004), 'A framework for designing strategy content controls', *International Journal of Productivity and Performance Management*, 590–601.

Sedlmayer, M.R. (2007), *The Architecture for Effective Strategy Implementation*, Berne: University of Applied Sciences.

Sedlmayer, M.R. (2009), 'Leadership assessment for sponsors and project managers', a case study, in: Knöpfel, H., Schäuble, M., Scheifele, D., Witschi, U. and Baumann, D. (eds), *Behavioural and Contextual Competences for Project Management Success*, Nijkerk: International Project Management Association, pp. 136–144.

Sedlmayer, M.R. (2016), 'Mastering integration in programme management,' in: Lock, D. and Wagner, R. (eds), *Gower Handbook of Programme Management*, Abingdon: Routledge.

Söderholm, A., Gemünden, H.G. and Winch, G.M. (2008), 'Projects and programmes: Strategies for creating value in the face of uncertainty', *International Journal of Project Management*, 1–3.

Srivannaboon, S. (2006), 'Linking project management with business strategy', *Project Management Journal*, 88–96.

Chapter 3

The value of portfolio management

Michael Young

The project portfolio has been defined as 'a collection of projects or programs and other work that are grouped together to facilitate effective management of that work to meet strategic business needs' (Project Management Institute or PMI, 2008). Portfolio management (PPM) involves identifying, prioritizing, authorizing, managing and controlling the component projects and programmes, and the associated risks, resources and priorities (ibid.) in order to deliver value to the organization.

Introduction

The concept of project portfolio management has emerged from two complimentary, yet independent, drivers, these being the need to make rational investment decisions that result in the delivery of organizational benefits (Markovitz, 1952) and the need to optimize the use of resources to ensure that the delivery of such benefits occurs in an effective and efficient manner (Dye and Pennypacker, 2000).

In 1952, Markowitz first introduced the concept of the portfolio to the financial sector. He proposed the *Modern Portfolio Theory* and suggested that rational investors use diversification to optimize their portfolios: the portfolio in this case being a collection of financial assets and investments. His theory also suggested that investors can reduce their exposure to individual asset risk by holding a diversified portfolio of assets with the portfolio allowing a higher return with reduced risk, compared with the inherent risk and return ratios of the individual investments that comprise the portfolio. Although applicable to a project portfolio, the diversification advice offered by Markowitz does not necessarily take into account resource constraints and the interactions between various portfolios across the organization.

McFarlan (1981) introduced the use of the portfolio management approach to the field of information technology (IT), suggesting that projects, rather than assets or investments, are the components of the portfolio and that the collective management of these unrelated projects could occur in a manner that optimizes the organization's desired business outcome while minimizing the organization's overall level of risk. The desired business outcomes to which McFarlan refers are not static, but instead change over time as a result of shifts in the various legislative, political, economic, social and technological drivers. Although individual projects represent specific risks to the organization, they also provide particular opportunities. Achieving an optimum balance between risk and reward across the diversified set of projects was seen as the key to success in the business environment (Hubbard, 2007).

Although portfolio-level project management approaches were inspired by value optimization methods from the financial world (Cooper, Edgett and Kleinschmidt, 2000), the PPM methods and philosophies in use bear little resemblance to financial portfolio management methods. Various PPM approaches and techniques were drawn from the new product development and commercial research and development (R&D) sectors (McDonough and Spital, 2003), and similar approaches have been developed in the IT, construction and pharmaceutical sectors, leading to the recognition of common PPM approaches for use in any type of project portfolio (Cooper et al., 2000; International Project Management Association or IPMA, 2008; PMI, 2008).

PPM is focused on creating, continually reviewing and updating the selection of projects and programmes under management within the organization at any time. The process is continuous, akin to the line management of an operational area of the business. Numerous books, papers and texts have been published on the topic. Many authors suggest that PPM is all about delivering the 'right projects' and that (through the process of selection, prioritization and regular rebalancing) the project portfolio delivers value to the organization. Levine (2005) goes as far as to claim that PPM is the most exciting development in project management since the critical path method, largely focusing on the benefits that the practice brings to an organization.

We have also seen the emergence of enterprise and organizational project management (EPM) approaches, which aim to provide a consistent delivery approach for all projects being undertaken by an organization, implemented through the enterprise project management office (EPMO) or other similar structures. More recently, PPM software has been developed to help organizations to improve management of their collection of projects and to provide a 'single source of truth' on the status of all elements of their portfolio.

PPM research has gained significant momentum in recent years with the emergence, formulation and popularity of the concept being heavily influenced by industry. However, it is clear that industry has not yet fully mastered PPM concepts in practice. In a study conducted in 2003, Jeffery and Wilson (2004) found that, of 130 CIOs of Fortune 500 companies surveyed, 89 per cent were very aware of PPM but only 17 per cent were realizing its full value. A challenge for organizations is managing this potentially diverse range of projects (Prifling, 2010) while ensuring that the right projects are selected (Elonen and Artto, 2005).

In this chapter, I explore the value of PPM and whether or not current practices help to deliver value to organizations. I examine the subject of PPM software and how such platforms help or hinder the delivery of value. I also explore the related practices of EPM to determine how they complement PPM and collectively add value to an organization.

Before examining the value of PPM it is important to understand the concept of value. So I start my examination of this topic by discussing the notion of value and how it is measured and defined.

Value

Value is a highly subjective term. It is conceptual and intangible in nature and is a fascinating subject with which philosophers have wrestled for centuries. It is recognized that the notion of value is fundamentally a matter of perception. Thus value will be perceived to be different from person to person, organization to organization and time to time. So measuring or attempting to demonstrate value can often be fraught with danger and often lead to arguments and disagreements. The word value is used in so many different ways and in such very different contexts that there is no universally agreed definition.

Value is often equated to money and intangible measures are assigned money amounts so that the actual costs and benefits of a particular activity or decision can be determined. This happens particularly in business cases where a project needs to be justified through the analysis of both costs and benefits. Value is also used as an abbreviation for 'value for money', which is another subjective term that is equally difficult to define or quantify. With such a wide range of perceptions and understandings it is worth pondering why anything does have value at all.

Value is also a relative term, so it exists only in the context of comparing a number of discrete options. It is these three factors that are drawn together and used in the comparison of options.

Consider for a moment going to a café and looking at the menu for coffee. Not only are there different types of coffee, but often there are different sizes available at different price points. Often the comparison is made between the price of each size and the relative perceived value obtained by purchasing a particular size. You might be able to get double the size for only a small increase in price, and therefore the larger cup size may have their highest perceived value.

The Australian Standard for Value Management (Standards Australia 2007) identifies three core elements that can be used to determine the value of a project or solution. The first of these three factors is 'useful purpose'. If an entity is perceived to have no 'useful purpose' it is likely to have no value at all (to the person perceiving it). The second of these factors is 'benefits', or 'beneficial outcomes', that is to say, the set of benefits or beneficial outcomes that will flow from fulfilling the useful purpose. The third factor is the set of 'important characteristics' relating to the entity. Barton (2012) provides an excellent example of the three aspects of value, as follows:

> The way in which these three factors work together to determine value may be seen by considering an example such as the Singapore MRT. From the point of view of the passenger, the useful purpose of the train is that it takes one from point A to point B. If the train does not do this, then to the customer, it has no value at all. But assuming that it does take the customer from point A to point B, the question of value does not end there. One benefit of fulfilling the useful purpose might be that the train enables the customer to get to work: so this is also a factor in why the train has value. Something that is most important to the customer is the frequency, regularity and reliability of the service. A more reliable service is likely to have more value in the eyes of the customer. We could add other points, too, such as personal safety and comfort. Indeed, if we were to bring together a group of MRT passengers and discuss these factors with them, we would probably produce quite a long list of elements but we would be able to place them all beneath the headings of: useful purpose, benefits and important characteristics.
>
> If, for a moment, we were to change perspective and consider the value of the train from the point of view of the train driver, an entirely different set of value factors would emerge. For example, the 'useful purpose' of the train would have

nothing at all to do with taking someone from point A to point B. Rather, the useful purpose of the train would be to provide employment. A benefit of this is that it enables the train driver to 'put food on the table'. An example of something that is most important might be health and safety at work. So even though we are considering the same train, the value factors from the point of view of passengers and train drivers are substantially different.

We could keep the exercise going and consider the value of the train from the point of view, say, of the Ministry of Finance or a major shopping centre. Again, each would have their own perspectives. So it is with any entity. There will always be multiple perceptions of useful purposes, benefits and important characteristics.

The goal of PPM

The academic literature identifies a number of goals that PPM is intended to achieve. Cooper (2011) suggests that these goals are:

- Value maximization for the organization;
- Achieving portfolio balance by having an appropriate selection of projects which will deliver both short-term and long-term value; and
- Ensuring a strategically aligned portfolio that accommodates the requirement for non-economic factors to influence project selection.

These goals are also seen in industry, where 'best practice' suggests that high performing organizations employ high-level decision-making teams to align projects with strategy, achieve a balance in the project portfolio and maximize the value of the portfolio (Killen, Hunt and Kleinschmidt, 2008). I now explore the key goals identified in the literature in turn.

Maximizing the value of a portfolio

A commonly cited goal of PPM is to maximize the value of the portfolio against one or more business objectives (Cai et al., 2000, McDonough and Spital 2003). The objectives might be profitability, strategy or risk, for example (Iamratanakul et al., 2009). According to Iamratanakul et al. the constraints could be financial budget, staff limitations, supporting constraints of activities and other considerations. In this case, portfolio selection methods are suitable for the selection of projects with multiple constraints (Ghasemzadeh and Archer, 2000).

Achieving the 'balanced' portfolio

Portfolio balancing considers the constant utilization of resources along the project execution and the constant generation of cash flow (Archer and Ghasemzadeh, 1999; Cooper, Edgett and Kleinschmidt, 2001; Killen et al., 2008) as well as the balancing of corporate resources against projects' operational risks (Laslo, 2010). The notion of 'balance' is a modern interpretation of the Modern Portfolio Theory of Markovitz (1952), in which he balanced risk and reward. It is often noted that strategic values generated by projects should be balanced according to the importance and range of strategies. Portfolio balancing may also cover financial, commercial and technical issues.

Strategically aligned portfolio

A common theme that has emerged from the literature is the need to build and maintain a link between corporate strategy and the project portfolio. This alignment is intended to ensure that the organization can achieve the goals specified in their business plans (through project selection) and to prioritize resource allocation. The literature also highlights the importance of aligning resources through prioritizing their allocation to strategic business objectives (Cooper et al., 2001; Levin, 2005; Iamratankul et al., 2009). The level of agreement within an organization regarding the relative importance of cost, quality, delivery and flexibility to organization's operational goals, as well as the relationship between competitive priorities and policies, has been discussed as strategically aligned (Iamratanakul et al. 2009).

Other academic goals

There are other goals, to which only a few papers refer. These include selecting the right number of projects (Cooper and Edgett, 2001), providing a centralized source of information (Cao, Ding and Tian, 2006) and ensuring portfolio sufficiency versus overall product innovation goals, although it is unclear as to how this could be applied (Cooper, 2005). A number of spurious goals have also been found in PPM literature. These include arguments suggesting that PPM:

- is a software process (Wideman, 2004);
- reduces costs and eliminates waste (Rongzeng, Wei and Chunhua, 2005);
- reduces IT expenditure by as much as 40 per cent (Verhoef, 2002; Kersten and Verhoef, 2003);
- provides organizational agility (Laslo, 2010).

When the arguments for these claims arguments were explored in more detail, it was discovered that there was no empirical supporting evidence.

Literature from vendors of PPM software

Another aspect to consider is the promotional literature for PPM software offered by vendors. This purports to offer a practical method by which an organization can achieve its PPM goals. PPM software has been developed to assist organizations to select and prioritize projects by considering strategy of organization, and manage projects with the scarce resources available to gain maximum benefits. Vendors are attempting to provide a variety of products to their customers to help them manage multiple concurrent projects across the organization, with the promise that the organization will achieve maximum benefits.

Sarbazhosseini and Young (2012) undertook a comparative analysis between the academic literature and PPM software vendor literature to determine whether there is any alignment between both sources. This analysis revealed a gap between the academic literature and the vendor offerings; in particular, software vendors do not appear to deliver solutions that allow organizations to select the right number of projects, or to ensure portfolio sufficiency versus overall product innovation goals. Instead, software vendors have been focused on goals that are not specified in the academic literature, including the following:

- Improve customer satisfaction;
- Increase competitive advantage;
- Effectively and efficiently manage projects;
- Easy to use and maintain;
- Appropriate tool for managers; and
- Take timely correct actions.

These goals appear to be marketing-based concepts to promote the use of PPM software. It is unclear how PPM software would achieve these particular goals or, in particular, how PPM software would help an organization achieve competitive advantage.

The value of PPM

Value maximization has been stated as one of PPM's key goals. The starting point for value measurement is often through the organization's objective of long-term profit, return on investment, likelihood of success, or some other strategic goal (Cooper, Edgett and Kleinschmidt, 1997).

A 2014 study by Martinsuo and Killen highlighted that strategic value has primarily been tackled in the form of long-term business success measures. This paper reviewed the extant literature and identified a number of value dimensions of PPM, which included the following:

- Delivering benefits to the organization including improved efficiency, profits, organizational learning and waste reduction;
- Delivering benefits to stakeholders, including social and environmental impacts, user satisfaction and learning, and community benefits;
- Delivering strategic value and influence in the society, health, safety, security and environmental responsibility, economic profitability and stakeholder admiration;
- Improving managers' perceptions of the organizational impacts of development projects in terms of financial, market and technology value;
- Creating competitive potential and future business opportunities; and
- Strategic renewal.

These authors observed that many of the existing measures focus clearly on commercial value. However they also indicate that there is a growing recognition of need for non-commercial and future-oriented metrics that may be more difficult to measure.

> We have shown that firms' strategies increasingly feature long-term and stakeholder-oriented interests of sustainability, societal influence, and knowledge diffusion and

state them as part of single project goals; therefore, it is also necessary to include these strategic value measurements as part of project portfolio management.

(Martinsuo and Killen, 2014)

Research (Martinsuo, 2013) has shown that the practice of PPM is much more interactive, political and path dependent than suggested in the academic literature. Observations from the practice of implementing PPM approaches in organizations have identified a number of key benefits, including the following:

- *Improved resource allocation.* Often many projects of low value are selected and an attempt is made to resource projects where the demand for resources exceeds the available resource supply. Engwall and Jerbrandt (2002) talk about the 'resource allocation syndrome', which occurs where resources are shared across all projects so that all projects suffer some element of resource shortage. Through the organization-wide prioritization of work, high priority projects are fully resourced and are subjected to fewer resource constraints. Resource allocation in project management has always been a key issue for success in organizations managing several projects and it is clearly a critical aspect for consideration when striving for the best possible balanced portfolio.
- *Understanding future resource needs.* Through resource forecasting and examining the resource view of the portfolio, managers across the organization can identify future resource requirements in the short, medium and longer terms with greater clarity. They can develop appropriate workforce plans, recruitment strategies and staff development plans so that the appropriate resources are available when needed. This can reduce costs and eliminate the need to hire temporary contract labour (that might not be available, or may be costly at the time of need).
- *Improved scrutiny of work.* Through a formal prioritization and approval process a committee is often involved in making decisions that determine whether or not projects shall be funded. Outside this process, managers make funding decisions for their own work and they are not open to challenge and review. However, the committee process is open to more scrutiny because managers know that, when work is approved in one area, it removes funding for potential work in other areas. Although some 'horse trading' might still happen, the committee dynamic usually leads to approval of projects that have absolutely the highest priority and the highest value.
- *Improved transparency of project approval.* Use of a formalized project selection and approval process shows how projects are approved and get funded. By communicating this process throughout the organization, all aspects of the business can propose projects and new initiatives. This can build engagement and also help managers across the organization to understand the business priorities and apply strategic goals.
- *Reduced ambiguity in project authorization.* The PPM planning process provides criteria for evaluating work more consistently. This makes it easier to compare work on an 'apples-to-apples' basis and do a better job in ensuring that the authorized work is valuable, aligned and balanced.

- *Ensuring informed decisions and governance.* The portfolio prioritization and selection process brings together key project stakeholders, data points and processes in a single, unified view of project, programme and portfolio status. This provides greater visibility and often leads to improved governance and decision-making, particularly in relation to ensuring that approved projects consistently deliver the planned benefits.
- *Increased focus on possible project cancellation decisions.* The balancing and prioritization processes of PPM are akin to those in an assets or investment portfolio. When an organization examines its investment portfolio, there may be a need to divest assets or, in the case of a project portfolio, put projects on hold or cancel them entirely. This overview provides managers with a process for identifying potential problems earlier in the project lifecycle, and gives the visibility for taking corrective action before those problems impact financial results.
- *Improved alignment of projects.* In addition to making sure that only high priority work is approved, PPM also results in the work being aligned to the organization's goals or strategic objectives. When projects are prioritized and presented to the investment board or portfolio committee for approval, only those projects that contribute (or directly deliver) according to the strategic plan are usually funded. The scrutiny of the committee process challenges any 'pet projects'. Such projects are really often low priority and would not meet or align with the organization's goals or strategic objectives.
- *Shift in focus from cost to investment thinking.* The prioritization and review process inherent in the project prioritization and selection process often draws out the value of the project relative to the cost. If the proposed project does not represent sufficient value relative to its cost, the proposed project is either rejected outright or added to a backlog of potential future work. Through these discussions that take place during the review process, a shared understanding is developed across the management team as to what is and what is not important to the organization. This often leads to a subtle shift in focus from cost to investment.
- *Increased collaboration, communication and engagement.* In many organizations, senior managers make business decisions but take only their own department into account. In many organizations today, functional departments do not communicate well with their peer departments or even within their own groups. PPM requires a continuous dialogue across the organization. As a result, there are often many more opportunities for discussing the value of the portfolio and its constituent projects.
- *Improved organizational flexibility and agility.* PPM's regular prioritization and balancing process provides organizations with flexibility to alter plans, priorities and resource allocation across key initiatives. The world in which organizations operate is often rapidly changing, and agility is needed to adapt and change priorities continuously. Regularly reprioritizing projects in the portfolio gives managers greater flexibility concerning how, where and when they allocate resources according to need. Also, resource changes can be made quickly in response to a crisis.
- *Improved deployment of practices.* PPM requires a base level of data to be delivered in a consistent manner to enable comparison across all projects in the

portfolio. This can often drive the need for a maturing of project management practices and, through a continuous improvement process, the adoption of best practice can be championed.

These benefits have been observed across many consultancy assignments in large organizations where PPM has been implemented (either at the whole enterprise level or within a specific business unit). Although this is not an empirical study of the benefits of PPM practices, many organizations have continued to use and refine the processes implemented over an extended period (often because of the improved levels of visibility, clarity and consistency in project delivery that are achieved).

Measuring portfolio value

One shortcoming in the PPM domain is the lack of valid studies that quantify the value delivered through effective PPM. Most value measurement is restricted to financial measures such as NPV (net present value) or ROI (return on investment) for each specific project rather than a collective or holistic measure of the entire portfolio. Of note, Sanchez and Robert (2010) assert that all performance of project portfolios cannot be assessed in terms of immediate financial measures because many of the expected benefits are intangible and evolve over time.

Qualitative or non-financial measures (McDonough and Spital, 2003) are limited and often include considerations such as brand awareness and reputation, consumer satisfaction, environmental and social responsibility, and development risk.

The literature identifies several comprehensive value measurement systems that span non-commercial value in combination with financial considerations. These value measurement systems are sometimes drawn upon for PPM approaches. Three of the common value frameworks are outlined briefly below.

Logical framework approach

The logical framework approach (LFA) is used in international development projects and includes a wide range of measures (such as environmental, economic, social measures) from local and global perspectives (Cooper, Edgett and Kleinschmidt, 1999; Cooper and Edgett, 2001; Gareis, 2002).

A study of the ways by which sustainability is incorporated in the investment analysis of projects shows that, in addition to economic aspects, the social as well as environmental aspects must be considered. The study found that the LFA is able to represent these aspects holistically (Cao et al., 2006).

Triple bottom-line accounting

Triple bottom-line accounting (TBL) is an accounting framework that incorporates three dimensions of performance: social, environmental and financial (Cooper, 2005). TBL accounting is increasingly popular with non-profit organizations and government agencies (Wideman, 2004). Several approaches have been developed to include TBL considerations in project planning and decision-making using comprehensive TBL project evaluation criteria (Kersten and Verhoef, 2003; Rongzeng et al., 2005).

Balanced score card

The balanced scorecard is a strategic planning and management system used to align organizational activities to the vision and strategy of the organization. For more about this system, please refer to Chapter 2 and Figure 2.3.

Conclusion

This chapter examined the value of PPM and has explored aspects including the goals of PPM, the notion of value and how PPM delivers value to organizations. I have shown that what is considered to be of value to one person at one time may be different at some other time. Likewise, the value perceived by one person in an organization at a particular level may not be viewed in the same way by another person operating at a different level. Thus, it is important to understand to whom the value is created. It is important to consider:

- The value that PPM creates for organizations as a whole;
- The value delivered to a particular project;
- The associated value created for project sponsors; and finally
- The value created for project managers.

References and further reading

Archer, N.P. and Ghasemzadeh, F. (1999), 'An integrated framework for project portfolio selection', *International Journal of Project Management*, 17(4).

Barton, R.T. (2012), *Value for Money in a Whole of Government Context*. Singapore: Value for Money in Product Development.

Cai, X., Teo, K., Yang, X. and Zhou, X.Y. (2000), 'Portfolio optimisation under a minimax rule', *Management Science*, 46(7), 609–618.

Cao, R., Ding, W. and Tian, C. (2006), 'Using resource and portfolio management solutions to align IT investment with business', *International Journal of Electronic Business*, 4(3), 239–246.

Cooper, R. (2005), Product leadership: pathways to profitable innovation. Retrieved from egully. com: egully.com

Cooper, R. (2011), *Winning at New Products: Creating Value Through Innovation*, 4th edn. New York: Wiley.

Cooper, R. and Edgett, S. (2001), 'Portfolio management for new products: picking the winners', Product Development Institute Conference 2001, Ancaster, Ontario.

Cooper, R.G., Edgett, S.J. and Kleinschmidt, E.J. (1997), 'Portfolio management management in new product development: lessons from the leaders', *Research Technology Management*, 40, 5, 6.

Cooper, R., Edgett, S. and Kleinschmidt, E. (1998), *Portfolio Management for New Products*. New York: Perseus Books.

Cooper, R., Edgett, S. and Kleinschmidt, E. (1999), 'New product portfolio management: Practices and performance', *Journal of Product Innovation Management*, 16, 333-351.

Cooper, R., Edgett, S. and Kleinschmidt, E. (2000), 'New problems, new solutions: making portfolio management more effective', *Research Technology Management*, 43(2), 18–33.

Cooper, R., Edgett, S. and Kleinschmidt, E. (2001), *Portfolio Management for New Products*. New York: Basic Books.

Dye, LD. and Pennypacker, J.S. (2000), 'Project portfolio management and managing multiple projects: two sides of the same coin?', *Proceedings of the Project Management Institute Annual Seminars and Symposium*, Houston, TX: Project Management Institute.

Elonen, S. and Artto, K. (2005), 'Problems in managing internal development projects in multi-project environments', *International Journal of Project Management*, 21, 395–402.

Engwall, M. and Jerbrandt, A. (2002), 'The resource allocation syndrome: the prime challenge of multi-project management', *International Journal of Project Management*, 21(6), 403–409.

Gareis, R. (2002), 'Professional project portfolio management', *IPMA World Congress 2002*. Berlin: International Project Management Association.

Ghasemzadeh, F. and Archer, N.P. (2000), 'Project portfolio selection through decision support', *Decision Support Systems*, 29(1), 73–88.

Hubbard, D. (2007), *How to Measure Anything: Finding the Value of Intangibles in Business*. Hoboken NJ: Wiley.

Iamratanakul, S., Shankar, R. and Dimmett, N. (2009). *Improving Project Portfolio Management with Strategic Alignment*. Portland, OR: Management of Engineering and Technology (PICMET).

International Project Management Association (2008), *IPMA Competence Baseline*, Version 3.0, Newtown Square, PA: IPMA.

Jeffery, M. and Wilson, D.C. (2004), 'Best practices in portfolio management', *Sloan Management Review*, 45(3), 41–49.

Kersten, B. and Verhoef, C. (2003), 'IT portfolio management: a banker's perspective on IT', *Cutter IT Journal*, 16(4), 27–33.

Killen, C.P., Hunt, R.A. and Kleinschmidt, E.J. (2008), 'Project portfolio management for product innovation', *International Journal of Quality and Reliability*, 25(1), 24–38.

Laslo, Z. (2010), 'Project portfolio management: an integrated method for resource planning and scheduling to minimize planning/scheduling-dependent expenses', *International Journal of Project Management*, 28(6), 609–618.

Levine, H.A. (2005). *Project Portfolio Management: A Practical Guide to Selecting Projects, Managing Portfolios and Maximising Benefits*. San Francisco, CA: Jossey-Bass.

McDonough, E.F. and Spital, F.C. (2003), 'Managing project portfolios', *Research Technology Management*, 46, 40–46.

McFarlan, F.W. (1981), 'Portfolio approach to information systems', *Harvard Business Review*, 59(5), 142–150.

Markovitz, H. (1952), 'Portfolio selection', *Journal of Finance*, 7(1), 77–91.

Martinsuo, M. (2013), 'Fragility in project-based organizing, and the ways towards robustness', *International Journal of Managing Projects in Business*, 6(1).

Martinsuo, M. and Killen, C.P. (2014), 'Value management in project portfolios: identifying and assessing strategic value', *Project Management Journal*, 45(5), 56–70.

Project Management Institute (2008), *A Guide to the Project Management Body of Knowledge*, 4th edn. Newtown Square, PA: PMI.

Prifling, M. (2010), 'IT project portfolio management – a matter of organisational culture?', *14th Pacific Asia Conference on Information systems*, Taipei, pp. 761–772.

Rongzeng, C., Wei, D. and Chunhua, T. (2005), 'Using resource and portfolio management solutions to align IT investment with business', *ICEBE 2005*, IEEE.

Sanchez, H. and Robert, B. (2010), 'Measuring portfolio strategic performance using key performance indicators', *Project Management Journal*, 64–73.

Sanchez, H., Robert, B. and Pellerin, R. (2008), 'A project portfolio risk-opportunity identification framework', *Project Management Journal*, 97–109.

Sarbazhosseini, H. and Young, M. (2012), 'Mind the gap: exploring the world of PPM software and theory', *Proceedings of the Australian Institute of Project Management National Conference*, Melbourne.

Standards Australia (2007), *AS/NZS 4183–2007: Australian Standard for Value Management*. Sydney: Standards Australia

Verhoef, C. (2002), 'Quantitative IT portfolio management', *Science of Computer Programming*, 45(1), 1–96.

Wideman, R.M. (2004), *A Management Framework for Project, Program and Portfolio Management*. Victoria: Trafford Publishing.

Chapter 4

The relevance of portfolios and portfolio management in today's organizations

Thomas Walenta

Every business has to assess its potential projects and programmes and decide which will actually be included in its active portfolio. That involves making decisions based on the purpose of the organization, the availability of resources and the relative merits of the individual portfolio components.

Three core characteristics of portfolio management

The three core characteristics of portfolio management can be summarized by the following:

- Purpose;
- Work;
- Resources.

To introduce this subject, consider the case of medical emergencies that occur after a serious epidemic, a major accident or some other catastrophe. Hospital staff are often confronted with many sick or injured people. They cannot all be treated immediately, so the medical team employ a kind of portfolio management system, which in this case is called 'triage'.

This case example is set in a busy hospital, faced with a mix of patients with various medical conditions and different degrees of risk to their healthy survival. With limited resources, hospital staff have to make critical decisions on which of those patients should be given priority for treatment. Hospitals manage this difficulty using a system known as 'triage' (see https://en.wikipedia.org/wiki/Triage).

To illustrate how this works, consider the accident and emergency department of a hospital that is suddenly faced with the arrival of people who are injured during a major incident. The triage system helps by selecting those individuals for the next immediate treatment who are in most urgent need and have the best chance of survival. The term 'triage' is derived from the French word *trier* which means sorting. So, triage means that doctors assess the status of all the injured people, and sort them into one of the following three categories:

1. Heavily injured people who have little chance of survival. They will be given treatment to ease their pain.

2. Heavily injured people who need to be treated urgently if they are to have a chance to of survival. These people are given priority for treatment and are treated immediately, or as soon as possible.

3. People with injuries that are not immediately life threatening. These patients can be made to wait for treatment. One method used is to ask all who are able to leave the immediate scene and collect at a gathering point, from where they can be called for treatment later, when medical staff and facilities become available.

The three core characteristics of a triage are as follows. First, there is an overarching *purpose* and goal to save as many lives as possible, while doing no harm to anybody. Second, a mechanism exists to elect, sort and prioritize the *work* presenting itself (the patients), including predefined criteria about how to categorize and select the work. The third core characteristic of the triage concerns the capacity of medical *resources*. This third characteristic should be understood well, because it is dependent on the number of available doctors and nurses, emergency rooms, medicines, and so on, for dealing with the work on hand.

The same three core characteristics apply to any organization in fulfilling its purpose. In organizations these characteristics can be explained as follows:

1. *Purpose*. Achieving a known purpose or goals of the organization. The purpose could be implicit or explicit. It might be developed further into a vision, a strategy to achieve that vision and strategic goals that detail that strategy. For a fairly recent discussion, see 'hierarchy of purpose' as described by Antonio Nieto Rodriguez in *Harvard Business Review* (2016 – see https://hbr.org/2016/12/how-to-prioritize-your-companys-projects).

2. *Work*. Categorize, prioritize and select the work that should be executed (which is always represented by changes, initiatives, projects and programmes). Sometimes work also includes operations, and business-as-usual or other related work.

3. *Resources*. The available resources should be assigned to work so that the purpose is achieved in an optimal way. This sometimes explicitly means financially optimal (which might not be sufficient even for for-profit organizations, but is a nice simplification that can be tracked by accountants). Resources include funds but also staff with certain capabilities, contractors, partners, materials, management oversight and so on.

Even an organization that does not call this process portfolio management will practise some way for selecting work and assigning resources. Management itself can be seen as providing resources to work to achieve organizational goals. For example, Mary Parker Follet (1868–1933) defined management as 'the art of getting things done through people'. In that context, management is involved by the following:

- Setting the organizational goals through strategy development;
- Implementing the strategy by defining the work (operations, projects);
- Assigning resources (staff, contractors, locations, material, funds, and so on) which are already available or must be developed or acquired.

Management itself can then be defined as balancing these three characteristics, just as project management is balancing the 'magic triangle' of scope, cost and schedule.

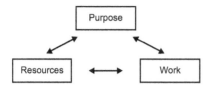

Figure 4.1 The magic triangle of portfolio management

© 2017 Thomas Walenta.

Portfolio management provides good practices and techniques that can help management to achieve that balance (Figure 4.1).

Representation of the three core characteristics in portfolio management standards

There are a handful of standards and guides available for portfolio management. Unfortunately it seems that these are not yet in line with each other, which means that there is no generally accepted understanding. Organizations have either to choose one standard over the other or to develop their own.

ISO 21504, the standard providing guidance on portfolio management, defines a project and programme portfolio as a 'collection of portfolio components grouped together to facilitate their management to meet, in whole or in part, an organization's strategic objectives'. So, we see that the *purpose* is represented by the strategic objectives. The portfolio components (which represent the *work* at hand) are described as 'projects, programmes, portfolios or other related work', while the *resources* are represented in the definition indirectly by 'to facilitate . . . management' of work and later in the standard by 'optimizing organizational capability and capacity' (ISO, 2015).

Project portfolio management (PMI) defines a portfolio across its foundational standards as 'projects, programs, sub-portfolios, and operations managed as a group to achieve strategic objectives'. This definition also refers to *work*, specifically including operations. The reference to 'strategic objectives' can imply that there is a *purpose* and a strategy leading to these. *Resources* are not explicitly covered in the definition, although the PMI Project Portfolio Management Standard does refer to the organizational resources needed to be assigned to work (see also Figure 1.3 on page 8 of PMI's PMBoK Guide).

UK's application portfolio management (APM) defines portfolio management as: 'the selection, prioritization and control of an organization's projects and programmes in line with its strategic objectives and capacity to deliver. The goal is to balance change initiatives and business-as-usual while optimising return on investment.'

The *work* is represented by projects and programmes, the *purpose* by the strategic objectives and the *resources* by the 'capacity to deliver'.

The International Project Management Association's (IPMA's) ICB4 provides the definition that: 'A portfolio is a set of projects and/or programmes, which are not necessarily related, brought together to provide optimum use of the organization's resources and to achieve the organization's strategic goals while minimising portfolio risk. Important issues on a portfolio level are reported to the senior management of the organization by the portfolio manager, together with options to resolve the issues.'

Wikipedia defines 'Project Portfolio Management (PPM) as the centralized management of the processes, methods, and technologies used by project managers and project management offices (PMOs) to analyse and collectively manage current or proposed projects based on numerous key characteristics. The objectives of PPM are to determine the optimal resource mix for delivery and to schedule activities to best achieve an organization's operational and financial goals, while honouring constraints imposed by customers, strategic objectives or external real-world factors'. The *work* is defined here as merely the projects. The *purpose* is represented quite narrowly by the organization's financial and operational goals and might not cover strategic goals. Finding the optimal *resources* mix is mentioned as one of the two objectives of PPM. Furthermore, Wikipedia mentions pipeline and resource management as two of five key capabilities of portfolio management, the other three being risk, financial management and change control.

In summary, all these standards describe the *purpose* as strategic objectives or goals, in the case of Wikipedia narrowed down to financial and operational goals. The *work* is defined as projects, in the case of the Project Management Institute (PMI) extended to operations. *Resources* are defined variously and not in depth, as 'optimal resource mix', 'capacity to deliver' or 'optimum use of resources'. PMI and the International Organization for Standardization (ISO) do not give further guidance on how to manage resources. Figure 4.2 shows these results. Portfolio management standards are described in greater detail in Chapter 7.

What happens when one of the three core characteristics is missing, ill-defined or not implemented

Lack of purpose

Lack of purpose leads to bad decision-making and inappropriate resource capabilities. Imagine a doctor arriving at an emergency site with multiple casualties. Suppose that doctor has no guiding purpose (a purpose based on the oath of Hippocrates and a criterion laid down in the applicable triage procedures). The doctor might just jump at the first person encountered and treat a broken leg while another person is bleeding to death. Triage requires and enables the doctor to make an overall assessment and prioritize the treatments before starting the work of treating patients.

Lack of purpose will create a tendency to launch any idea without looking at the strategic fit and the capacity/capabilities to deliver. Organizations in this situation will tend to have a huge portfolio of projects. A clear purpose and derived criteria help to make the tough decisions: killing or not launching projects. Research shows that this is a characteristic of high-performing organizations (see, for example, Muller et al. 2008).

If there is no agreed purpose of the organization, or no strategy or no set goals, it will be impossible to identify rational selection criteria with which to categorize the work at hand. Then work cannot be adequately prioritized.

If there is no process or procedure defined for making decisions based on data (evidence and facts), decisions will be delayed and eventually made based on individual perspectives (mostly 'gut feeling', experience). These will probably be suboptimal decisions. This might be appropriate for day-to-day situations, but at the organizational

Standard	Purpose	Work	Resources
ISO 21504	The organization's strategic objectives	Projects, programmes, portfolios or other related work	Facilitate resource management
PMI	Strategic objectives	Projects, programmes, sub-portfolios or other related work	Not explicitly mentioned
APM (UK)	Strategic objectives	Projects/programmes	Capacity to deliver
IPMA ICB4	The organization's strategic goals	Projects/programmes	Optimum use of resources
Wikipedia	Financial and operational goals	Projects	Optimal resource mix
Triage	Do no harm. Save as many lives as possible	Treat patients to survive	Doctors, nurses, medical equipment, medicines

Figure 4.2 How project portfolio standards reflect the magic triangle.

level decisions have deeper and farther-reaching consequences, because they apply to a larger set of resources and impact the organization in the long term.

Furthermore, it will be difficult or impossible for the organization to develop capabilities and resources if there is no agreed purpose. Each piece of work (project or programme) will require specific capabilities and, with no organizational purpose, would have to acquire these capabilities individually. If, for example, an organization decides to move into a new business area, it will consider the necessary capabilities and can acquire or build the needed resources. In the case of triage, a doctor coming to an emergency will have an emergency kit, including a triage kit needed to do the selection process, so the required resources are acquired based on that purpose.

In some cases, a purpose, strategy and set of goals might exist on paper, but are not fully driving day-to-day operations and decisions. Management might make decisions that, instead of being based organizational requirements, are based on individual targets. Then it could happen that 'pet projects' are selected (or business cases are constructed) to satisfy formally stated but not accepted selection criteria. Check the 'hiding hand principle' on Wikipedia to see how this type of decision-making was promoted for decades, even though it contributed to the planning fallacy and failing projects rather than proving beneficial. Even if portfolio management processes are in place, management may deviate from them and hence devaluate them. In these cases, portfolio management is not working for the benefit of the organization.

Bad work prioritization

Badly prioritized work leads to waste, staff overload and portfolio failure. In the case of a medical emergency, if a doctor starts a treatment for saving a patient's life, this treatment must not be interrupted. The treatment has to be continued to the point where the patient's immediate condition is no longer life threatening. Ideally the emergency room should have only one patient at a time.

If there is no rationalized selection made from all the possible work, and there is more work than can be accomplished, multitasking prevails, causing lack of focus. Work is done that does not satisfy organization targets in the best way. Work is being re-prioritized frequently. Work is begun but not finished, often leading to staff overload and poor results. If selection and prioritization processes are defined on paper but not followed, acceptance of the process is hampered and the results might be like having no process at all.

The selection and prioritization process is important for initially finding the work to be prioritized for the next period of business activity. This work includes not only projects and programmes, but also operational work. It is important to understand that input to the process is not confined to new work; unfinished work in progress must be reconsidered. This is even more relevant if the frequency of portfolio selection is increased (for example) from an annual planning cycle to quarterly prioritization sessions – or even down to two-weekly backlog assessments in agile scenarios.

Besides prioritizing and selecting, work in progress has to be monitored and its categorization and justification should be reassessed periodically. Following this, work in progress might be stopped or changed and the portfolio can reduce the new work pipeline. Organizations using 80 per cent or more of their resources for ongoing work (projects or operations) will only have 20 per cent of their capacity available for tackling new work requests. This is not enough for an environment that becomes increasingly competitive and sees disruptive changes with increasing frequency.

A good practice for handling existing work is to disregard sunk costs as a primary reason for continuing. At times it becomes necessary to 'pull the plug' and overcome the inherent inertia of stakeholders involved in that work in progress.

One example of the importance of a selection process is how outsourcing providers choose which opportunities to pursue or disregard. When pursuing an outsourcing opportunity, a provider makes a significant investment in time (it can typically take 6–18 months) and cost (a team can consist of 6–20 people). A prudent and professional provider will set a threshold for the number of opportunities they can pursue at any time and may reject requests for proposals if they happen to arrive when the portfolio is already full.

Insufficient or badly managed resources

For a medical emergency, there is a wealth of knowledge and training available for first aid and basic life support (in some countries, drivers are required to obtain certificates as first responders). Medical doctors may be trained to serve in emergency situations as a speciality. This shows that communities and governments provide resources to have the capabilities and capacity to be deployed to patients in life-threatening conditions.

If there is no or limited understanding about the *resources* available for the portfolio work, how they are utilized and which capabilities they represent, it will be hard to select the best resource mix to fulfil the organization's purpose or goals. An example of this is seen when an organizational change is implemented in changing processes and tools without considering the culture and capability of staff, which must change in parallel but normally takes much longer. A part of such a change must be to define resource parameters, which can include factors such as:

- which roles and responsibilities are needed;
- which skills and capabilities are needed;
- the numbers of each skill or resource;
- the timing of when those people will be needed, taking into account variations over time;
- how the resources and skills are to be acquired, built or trained.

Human resource departments play a key role in these activities. Resource management is not given the cover it deserves in the literature, but Lock (2013) deals with resource planning and allocation at the project and multiproject levels.

If an organization choses to limit the scope of a portfolio (for example, to strategic projects and programmes), but fails to assign a specific pool of resource to that scope, resources can be split between the portfolio and other work. This other work might be operations (such as ongoing production) or maintenance (keeping the operational infrastructure running). Some companies chose to divide their resource pools (for example, into production and research and development [R&D]) and in some cases, use outsourcing to accomplish this (such as for IT maintenance and IT projects).

Another concept for tackling the resource issue would be to regard all the work of an organization as a portfolio, following the PMI's approach, and to subdivide this portfolio into sub-portfolios with separate resource pools and different responsibilities and targets/purpose. For example, each business division (such as R&D, or sales and services) might want or need to take control of their own purpose, portfolio and resources, all these being hopefully aligned to the overall organization setting. The hierarchy of portfolios would follow similar standards and procedures, and would be mapped to the organization's structure and governance. In this case, it is mandatory to ensure cross-portfolio alignment.

Some organizations follow the approach of defining a *resource-based strategy* (Wernerfelt, 1984), trying to understand their unique resources and capabilities and deducing from that:

- Their potential strategic competitive advantage;
- In which area they could best deploy the resources;
- On which kind of work.

Portfolio management then allows them to select the work activities for the market that makes best use of the capabilities and resources available.

Other organizations set their purpose and strategy based on other, external criteria rather than internal resource capabilities, such as perceived market need, a customer requirement, an opportunity (for example, IBM entering the cloud and artificial intelligence [AI] business). They then acquire resources and build capabilities pertinent to these strategic needs. In these cases, purpose and strategy drive the work selection. Resource capabilities are built as needed. This approach is described as the *industrial organization model.*

Many organizations look at their strategic projects and portfolios only with portfolio management processes, while having a resource base that spans all the work of the organization. This makes resource optimization more difficult, because the resource-dependent work comes not only from the portfolio but also from other sources, such as operations. That risks resource overloads. Decisions about priorities are then made at an operational – not the strategic – level. A possible measure to avoid this problem is R&D departments that are solely concerned with the portfolio of research projects and programmes.

In IT departments, a plan-build-run operating model and organization is often used (see www.mckinsey.com/business-functions/digital-mckinsey/our-insights/using-a-plan-build-run-organizational-model-to-drive-it-infrastructure-objectives). This can result in different resource pools for each of the plan, build and run areas. In this case, project portfolio management would deal with the 'build' area. Another popular idea for focusing resources on the core purpose of the organization is to outsource IT operations and maintenance and focus the organization's internal resources on the IT projects or build area.

Further considerations on the practical use of PPM in organizations

As we have seen, all three characteristics (purpose, work and resources) are necessary and interlinked to establish successful PPM for an organization. In the following I present three considerations that can help an organization in how it implements professional PPM.

Portfolio categorization considerations

It is argued in the literature (in ISO 21504, for example) that the target of portfolio management is to meet strategic objectives. Besides this strategic view, however, in practice criteria such as law and regulations, availability of resources, risk attitudes and appetite, and individual management priorities (including 'pet projects') play a role in portfolio selection.

In many cases, a portfolio consists of interdependent components. These components can include, for example, the following:

- Establishing a technical pre-requisite;
- Acquiring resources;
- Analysing a new field of activity (new market, new product, new target group, new technology).

All these might be required before realizing the benefits needed to fulfil the strategic objectives. It might be appropriate to cluster prerequisites, with components targeted directly at objectives into a programme, and then prioritize that programme. Or the dependency is managed at the portfolio level, if a certain prerequisite affects the organization and most of the strategic objectives.

Scenario considerations

When choosing the best scenario (mix of work), it might well be that the components with the highest priority are not considered (Figure 4.3). Consider this in the following three steps.

1. The first step is to analyse and categorize each component by itself.
2. The second step is to find interdependencies between components. For example, 'If we include project B, we should do project A as a prerequisite, even if A by itself does not have a ranking to include it into the selected portfolio'.
3. A third step is then to look at overall portfolio requirements such as 'We want to assign at least 20 per cent to a certain area or goal'.

Then we can build different portfolio scenarios that reflect the individual rankings, the dependencies and the overall portfolio requirements. These scenarios should be analysed, categorized and prioritized based on scenario-specific criteria. It may well be that the most important project is not part of the scenario finally chosen. The resulting scenario will probably have a reverse impact on the strategy and goals. The portfolio selection process provides insight into the effects of strategic goals and may therefore alter them.

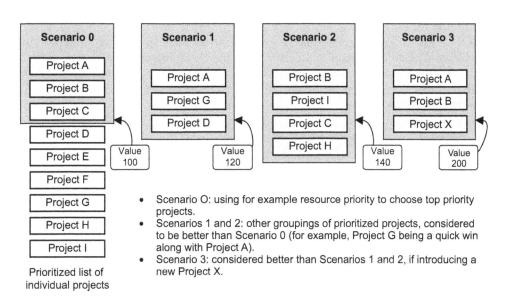

Figure 4.3 Portfolio scenario selection differs from simple project prioritization and requires a valuation of scenarios in addition to projects

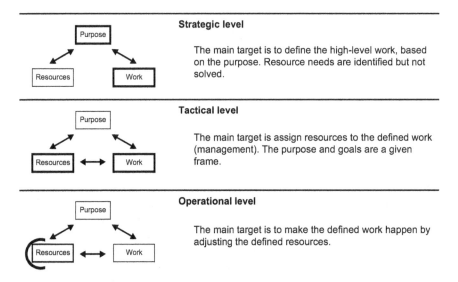

Figure 4.4 Three different levels for decision-making

Project portfolio management has a different focus on strategic, tactical and operational levels

Decision-making is required at different levels by different management groups (for example, strategic at an organization or division level), tactical at a team, programme or project level and operationally at the day-to-day level). There is merit in defining the purpose for each of these levels.

At the strategic level, the work needed to achieve the strategic goals and the purpose is at the core of decision-making. Resources are merely considered at a level of needed capabilities. As resources may not be available and their specific capabilities not yet understood, they will be built or acquired when the tactical level needs to deploy them to work.

At the tactical level, based on the strategic project portfolio decisions made, management decides how to implement the prioritized work using the available resources. Here decisions are often concerned with optimizing resource allocation. The strategic goals and purpose are regarded as firm.

At the operational level, the main purpose is efficiency, avoiding waste, overcoming roadblocks and using available resources in the optimal way. Scrum teams do that well, because they are fixed teams, understand their sprint targets for the next 2–4 weeks, have daily stand-ups to ensure progress and identify roadblocks, and provide good visibility for the contribution of each team member.

Looking at these levels simplifies decision-making and focuses each management level on the relevant parameters for project portfolio management (Figure 4.4).

Conclusion

Every organization is doing portfolio management, if they have a purpose and work at hand, and use resources. They can do this consciously, and more efficiently and effectively, if they describe, measure and improve what they are doing.

The organization should make sure that its purpose is described clearly, and understood and shared by everyone in the organization. This might involve establishing values and setting a culture, providing a meaningful vision and formulating a strategy. The purpose informs which selection criteria are defined to evaluate possible work (project, programmes, operations) and which resources are needed and should be built or acquired.

The work to be prioritized can be all the work of an organization or a sub-portfolio (for example, only the strategic initiatives). This process should not only look at the pipeline of new work but also periodically reassess the ongoing work.

Resources that are available may drive the purpose and strategy of an organization. New external triggers or strategy decisions might result in the need to build and acquire new capabilities, and capacities to be assigned to selected work, projects and programmes. This acquisition itself might justify a programme. On a tactical level, projects and programmes need to be equipped with resources.

Every organization is doing portfolio management – whether or not they give it that name – if they have a purpose and work at hand, and apply resources. They can do it consciously (more efficiently and effectively) if they describe, measure and improve what they are doing. Or, by doing it unconsciously, by gut feeling, they might end up treating the wrong patient while others die.

Acknowledgements

I would like to thank the following individuals for their support and feedback on this chapter:

- Antonio Nieto-Rodriguez;
- Henning Zeumer;
- Kerstin Tammling;
- Manuela Heinisch.

References and further reading

International Organization for Standardization (2015), ISO 21504, *Project, Programme and Portfolio Management – Guidance on portfolio management*, Geneva: ISO.

Lock, D. (2013), *Project Management*, 10th edn, Farnham: Gower.

Muller, R., Martinsuo, M. and Blomquist, T. (2008), 'Project portfolio control and portfolio management performance in different context', *Project Management Journal*, 9 September.

Wernerfelt, B. (1984), 'The resource-based view of the firm', *Strategic Management Journal*, 5(2): 171–180.

Chapter 5

Portfolio components

How everything fits together

Paul Gardiner

This chapter explains the elements of a typical portfolio, and how they fit together in the portfolio's composition.

The basic ingredients

The first important ingredient to consider when studying the composition of a portfolio is its raison d'etre. Without a clear and valid justification, a portfolio can end up becoming a drain on organizational resources rather than a means to business efficiency. Fortunately, most organizations today have a reasonable understanding of why managing their projects in a portfolio is a really good idea. We can describe the purpose of a portfolio as facilitating the management of a multiproject environment to create synergies for the projects inside the portfolio, and the integration of the outputs of those projects to achieve systemic business benefits, and gaining efficiencies not achievable by managing the projects individually. So having a portfolio can lead to better organization and control of an enterprise's resources. This is achieved by ensuring that these resources are working on a mix of projects that collectively represent a set of projects for competitive business value and customer satisfaction (at the current time and in the given context).

The obvious 'ingredients' of a portfolio include its projects and programmes, and the virtual 'container' in which these assets reside. But it is also necessary to consider the structural mechanism that provides the means and method of control for accepting, retaining and rejecting the projects and programmes in the portfolio. Furthermore, there are also less obvious but important ingredients in the complete list of components that make up a successful portfolio. I consider these shortly.

For now, let's explore this idea further by considering an analogy. Imagine the exploded product breakdown structure of a powered model aircraft kit. To create a fully functioning model aircraft capable of flying, we need to have not only all the parts in the exploded model view, but also the instruction manual to explain how they fit together, and some assembly tools as well. We also need the correct glue, paint and brushes. We will need wires and a motor to make it functional, a source of power and a control device. And before we attempt to fly it, there must the right outdoor environment – not too much wind, a suitable take-off and landing area, plus enough time to learn how to fly it and improve our technique. The parts in the exploded view are the obvious components, but when we consider the whole system there are many more components that we must take into account for a successful flight.

The same is true for a portfolio. There are the obvious components. Then there are the additional components which can make the difference between having and not having a successful portfolio.

A portfolio as a container

Portfolios are dynamic structures, but they also tend to be relatively permanent structures within an organization (unlike the projects and programmes that they contain (which of course are temporal organization structures). Figure 5.1 shows a typical diagrammatic representation of a portfolio and its basic components.

Projects, programmes and business as usual

A portfolio is a dynamic entity, not a static one. The concept of project portfolio management is simple – create a place (the portfolio) where all project investments in an organizational unit are visible. Then manage the flow of projects in and out of the portfolio to support the organization's strategy. Figure 5.1 shows how a portfolio might look with some projects bundled into programmes and others existing as stand-alone projects. Programmes are themselves collections of projects that are somehow related, usually by objectives, project type or dependency.

As already mentioned, the products of a portfolio are temporal, which in practice means that the duration of programmes and projects inside the portfolio are bounded by start and end points in time. However, the dynamic nature of business environments and their contexts mean that the precise start and end points of projects and programmes can be difficult to pin down. Programmes, in particular, can be trouble-some to predict in terms of a calendar date for their final closure. Indeed, some programmes exhibit characteristics similar to portfolios, with new projects being added over time. Programmes are also more closely related to the organization's strategy than the individual projects in a portfolio.

To fulfil its purpose, the portfolio must contribute to the strategic objectives of its host organization by systematically optimizing the project-based work. For simplicity,

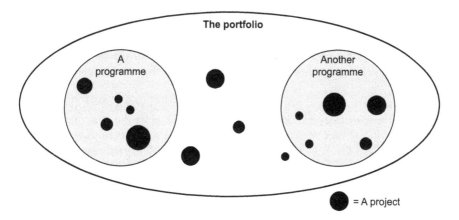

Figure 5.1 Bubble diagram representing a portfolio

it can be convenient to consider the work done in an organization as consisting of two types: project work and business as usual or BAU. In this way, projects are considered as the work done inside the portfolio and BAU is the work done outside the portfolio. Project and programme management, as a discipline or profession, can then focus on one type of work while operations management can focus on generating efficiencies for the BAU work.

Unfortunately, this rationalization is overly simplistic. It fails to consider that over the last 15–20 years there has been a steady shift in organizations steering them towards a way of organizing and working called 'managing by projects' (Crawford et al., 1999; Geraldi and Teerigankas, 2011). This has paved the way for organizations to take advantage of the benefits of project working by repackaging the BAU tasks as relatively discrete projects. On the other hand, some projects seem to exhibit substantial amounts of standardization and repetitive tasks, similar to BAU activity. This apparent ambiguity between what is, and what is not project work has resulted in a concept described by van der Hoorn and Whitty (2016) as degrees of 'projectyness'. In other words, very little work is purely BAU or purely project: rather organizations must learn to manage a range of activities that span a spectrum of projectyness. This ambiguity can lead to difficulties in organizations when it comes to deciding which activities should be added to a project portfolio or continue to be managed as BAU (Ndoye, 2017).

Despite the simplicity of the basic concept of a portfolio, there remain differences of opinion as to what constitutes portfolio management. Although project work and BAU are often regarded as being mutually exclusive approaches, the Association for Project Management (APM) recommends that they be 'thought of as points on a gradual scale of managing effort to deliver objectives' (APM, 2012).

Hierarchy and relationships

Another dimension of portfolios that must be considered is that of hierarchy and relationships. Typically, an organization will have several portfolios. Each portfolio sits within its own parent organization, which could be a department, a business unit, a geographical region, a corporate business structure, or some other organizational form or entity at national or international level. At the highest level, an organization might have an enterprise project management office within which there is a super portfolio (an enterprise-wide portfolio) that tries to bring a holistic and systemic world view across all the organization's portfolios. An added complexity would be when there are strong interdependencies between portfolios in different parts of the organization, so that they share some project resources on projects, in a way that resembles an internal joint venture.

The projects in a portfolio will typically have a close relationship with the organization strategy; indeed, strategy execution is often thought of as the enactment of the projects in the portfolio (MacLennan, 2010). However, the projects and programmes in a portfolio do not exist (and are not managed) in isolation. Their success depends on a number of factors, including the organization strategy itself, the level of interdependency between the portfolio products, the structural aspects of the organization and the IT/digital capability of the organization. In a high-performing organization, there is a dynamic and agile balance between all these elements which contributes to the competitiveness of the organization. These synergies at the strategic level contribute to achieving effective portfolio management in an integrated strategy–project system.

Another important component to consider is how many active projects there are in the organization that are not accounted for in a portfolio. At one level, a portfolio is a tool that can help an organization to be efficient at the business unit level – but only if all the projects are visible, accountable and represented in the portfolio. In many organizations, some projects have resources working on them without transparent portfolio accountability. These could be small pilot projects, pet projects of senior executives or personal projects of knowledge workers. A key question for organizations is not just which projects are in the portfolio but which projects are active and not included in the portfolio. These projects are typically not covered by portfolio governance or clear reporting lines. Collectively they dilute business efficiency. The resources that work on them are unavailable for other projects, even though they appear to be available in the formal portfolio management system.

Dynamism, variety and change

The effectiveness and success of a portfolio are in part shaped by the products it contains. For example, if individual projects in the portfolio perform well, then that augers well for the overall portfolio efficiency (Martinsuo, 2007). For the state of Delaware, in the USA, managing the construction programme of roads and bridges involves hundreds of projects with thousands of resources to be managed all across the state. 'Throw in a mixture of large-scale multi-year projects with multiple smaller projects and poor project scheduling, and you can end up literally stopping an entire city in its tracks.' This portfolio has extremely high project variety, which increases the portfolio management challenge. In this case, advanced project scheduling and resourcing can help to obtain the visibility they need through the centralization of project information to achieve project success, while keeping the general public satisfied. (Source: Bob Perrine, www.pmwarstories.com/pmwarstories/2009/06/pm-war-stories-28-.html.)

Then again, a project portfolio is similar to a financial portfolio – not least because projects can be rightly viewed as investments. Some organizations (for example, the General Accounting Office in the USA) refer to project portfolio management as investment management. Executive leadership teams can select the right project investments from the mix of opportunities in the pipeline, including research initiatives, new improvement projects and new business endeavours to provide compounded benefits through the synergy between projects and programmes.

Just as a financial portfolio changes over time with the short-term and long-term goals of the investor, portfolio management keeps projects aligned with the company's short-term, mid-term and long-term goals by making changes in individual projects, as well as adjusting the mix of the portfolio. The ability to maintain a dynamic equilibrium between the changing strategy and the projects that execute strategy and contribute to emergent strategy is an area in which organizations can find competitive advantage through the use of a portfolio. In a volatile market or economy, organizations that have developed and nurtured competences in organizational agility will tend to fare better than their counterparts over the long term.

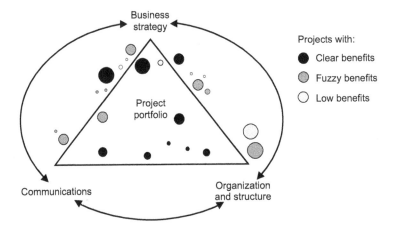

Figure 5.2 Example of a project portfolio

The portfolio skin

A portfolio is an open system rather like a biological system. In a biological system the regulation of nutrients is achieved by a semipermeable membrane, which selectively allows certain molecules to enter or leave the system. In the same way, every portfolio has a virtual skin that somehow regulates which projects and programmes are given the go ahead to start and then, once started, to continue or be stopped. The characteristics of the portfolio skin (that is, what the controls are regarding as adding new projects, keeping existing projects or removing projects) are explained below. The skin is the selective barrier that determines which projects and programmes get into the portfolio, which ones remain and which ones are ejected.

The portfolio shown in Figure 5.2 has nine projects inside it. The size of each circle indicates the size of the project relative to the other projects in the portfolio. Seven are projects with clear benefits, one has fuzzy benefit expectations and the other has low expected benefits. It might be expected that an optimized portfolio would contain only projects with clear benefits. Obviously this is not the case in this portfolio. Consider for yourself possible answers to these three thoughtful pondering questions:

1. Why might a portfolio contain projects with fuzzy or low benefits as well as those with clear benefits?
2. What actions might the manager of this portfolio consider taking at the next portfolio review meeting?
3. What options can you recommend concerning the fuzzy benefits projects inside and outside the portfolio?

Optimization and decision-making

To achieve its purpose a portfolio will have some intangible components – for example, a decision-making process and a governance structure that determine how the portfolio operates, and how it relates to the rest of the organization, top executives, project managers and other employees.

Optimization of the portfolio requires an evaluation of different sets of projects and of the synergies achieved by these alternative combinations of projects. Having an optimization engine is a critical success factor of a portfolio – otherwise the question can be asked: 'Why have a portfolio in the first place?' A multiproject environment can be just a collection of projects managed individually. A portfolio should be different. Portfolio optimization seeks to achieve synergy across the portfolio and to maximize benefits for the organization. There is no single approach to portfolio optimization that works in every organization, industry or culture (Bridges, 1999). There are many different relationships between projects in a portfolio and they simply cannot be modelled in a single model to reflect the actual decision-making process (Aalto, 2001). Nevertheless, most authors agree there are three key tasks in portfolio optimization:

1. Prioritization and selection of projects in the portfolio;
2. Resource allocation of projects in the portfolio;
3. Evaluation and optimization of the portfolio based on the portfolio's value, balance and strategic fit.

The role and purpose of a portfolio optimization tool is described by Poskela et al. (2001) as follows:

- To establish a set of projects that reflects the organization's strategy;
- To balance overall risk, focusing on go/no-go risk and portfolio risk;
- To optimize resource allocation across all projects;
- To implement the organization strategy.

Aalto (2001) draws attention to four portfolio management frameworks in particular. These are the following:

- The integrated framework by Archer and Ghasemzadeh (1999) – a prioritization model based on prioritizing individual projects and selecting those that score the highest;
- The action-orientated strategy table model of Spradlin and Kutoloski (1999) – consideration of alternative portfolios rather than individually prioritized projects in rank order;
- The strategic buckets model of Cooper et al. (1997) – the purpose of strategy is to allocate funds to different types of projects, each type representing a discrete part of the strategy;
- The narrative and discussion approach by Martinsuo and Lehtonen (2013) – recognition of the complexity of portfolio management: portfolios can be where narrative and discussion take place and decisions are made through iterative reflection and negotiating rather than through an objective algorithm. Decisions typically decisions involve objectivity, narrative and heuristics.

Each framework adopts a different approach to portfolio management and optimization, although the underlying goals remain the same.

In reality the portfolio mix is managed by the portfolio director, who uses strategic plans, portfolio frameworks, programme and project data, expert judgement, software tools and input from key stakeholders to evaluate, shape and reshape the portfolio periodically. Data on projected project benefits are updated and fed into the portfolio model. If a project begins to stray from strategic goals, or its potential return on investment (ROI) reduces owing to unforeseen events or market changes, then it may be downgraded and ultimately ejected from the portfolio, releasing resources to work elsewhere.

Projects and stakeholders are continuously competing for time to meet their own agendas. Getting portfolio decisions right is subject to many challenges, influences and potential biases. For example, there can be a tendency to prefer new projects to ongoing projects: 'Senior project managers have expressed concerns comparing the ROI calculation of new projects versus those later into their lifecycle. In fact, new projects at the beginning of their lifecycles often are forecast to more than 75 per cent ROI, in contrast to the more mature projects estimated at a 10–15 per cent ROI. It's no wonder that organizations and project managers want to move on from older, mature projects and pursue new ideas.' (Source: Hugh Woodward, 31 July 2010, www.pmwarstories. com/pmwarstories/pm-manufacturing.)

A means of learning and the portfolio scorecard

Another component of the portfolio is the way in which it learns and adapts. All portfolios are dynamic systems which change with the projects and programmes that compose them and which coexist within the parent structures that sustain them. As dynamic systems, and as vehicles of change for the parent organization, portfolios have an added critical component which is called *learning capability* (Gardiner et al., 2018). In an ideal world all the projects in a portfolio would be well matched for optimum performance, but in today's dynamic and uncertain marketplace this can be unobtainable. So portfolios must include components in their structures that enable them to be agile – to respond quickly to changes in strategy, the market or the economy.

The ability to learn, change and operate new practices, giving the organization new capabilities, has seen a surge of interest in mature successful organizations such as Ford, Thales, Walmart and NASA. The need to learn from experience is well expressed by Cooke-Davies (2002) in his research on success factors for consistently successful projects, which identifies the following three factors related to project portfolios:

1. Portfolio and programme management practices that allow the enterprise to resource fully a suite of projects that are thoughtfully and dynamically matched to the corporate strategy and business objectives;
2. A suite of project, programme and portfolio metrics that provides direct 'line of sight' feedback on current project performance, and anticipated future success, so that project, portfolio and corporate decisions can be aligned;
3. An effective means of 'learning from experience' on projects, which combines explicit knowledge with tacit knowledge in a way that encourages people to learn and to embed that learning into continuous improvement of project management processes and practices.

Conclusion

The final component of a portfolio that I want to mention in this chapter reflects the requirement that a portfolio must be accountable to the organization it serves and ultimately be fit for purpose. The use of quantitative measures of benefit, such as risk-adjusted value (a tool adapted from financial portfolio management theory) is not widespread, except in certain sectors such as new product development. However, estimating the expected benefit of a project is a fundamental requirement and critical to effective portfolio optimization. A portfolio is a tool for creating dynamic alignment and balance between the projects and programmes it contains and the strategy of the organization. To achieve this, a portfolio is usually associated with a scorecard set of measures that look at the efficiency of the portfolio and the effectiveness of the individual projects and programmes it contains. Without such a scorecard, it is impossible to manage the portfolio effectively because there will be no guiding reference or standard to against which to make decisions.

References and further reading

Aalto, T. (2001), 'Strategies and methods for project portfolio management', *Project Portfolio Management: Strategic Management through Projects*. Helsinki: Project Management Association, Finland.

Archer, N. P. and Ghasemzadeh, F. (1999), 'An integrated framework for project portfolio selection', *International Journal of Project Management*, 17(4), 207–216.

Association for Project Management (2012), *APM Body of Knowledge*. High Wycombe: APM.

Bridges, D.N. (1999), 'Project portfolio management: ideas and practices', *Project Portfolio Management – Selecting and prioritizing projects for competitive advantage*. West Chester, PA: Center for Business Practices, pp. 45–54.

Cooke-Davies, T. (2002), 'The "real" success factors on projects', *International Journal of Project Management*, 20(3), 185–190.

Cooper, R.G., Edgett, S.J. and Kleinschmidt, E.J. (1997), 'Portfolio management in new product development: Lessons from the leaders – II', *Research–Technology Management*, 40(6), 43–52.

Crawford, L., Simpson, S. and Koll, W. (1999). 'Managing by projects: A public sector approach', *Proceedings for NORDNET*, 99, 608–626.

Gardiner, P.D, Eltigani, A. Williams, T. et al. (2018), *Learning Mechanisms in Strategy–Project Systems*. Newtown Square, PA: Project Management Institute, in press.

Geraldi, J. and Teerigankas, S. (2011), 'From project management to managing by projects: Learning from the management of M&As', in: *(Proceedings) X IRNOP*. Montreal: International Research Network on Organizing by Projects.

MacLennan, A. (2010), *Strategy Execution: Translating strategy into action in complex organizations*. Abingdon: Routledge.

Martinsuo, M. (2013), 'Project portfolio management in practice and in context', *International Journal of Project Management*, 31(6), 794–803.

Martinsuo, M. and Lehtonen, P. (2007), 'Role of single-project management in achieving portfolio management efficiency', *International Journal of Project Management*, 25(1), 56–65.

Ndoye, M. (2017), 'Project management as the catalyst of change: the future of technical data services in the commercial aeronautics industry', MSc dissertation, Lille, SKEMA Business School.

Poskela, J., Korpi-Filppula, M., Mattila, V. and Salkari, I. (2001), 'Project portfolio manage-
    ment practices of a global telecommunications operator', in: *Project Portfolio Management:
    Strategic Management through Projects*. Helsinki: Project Management Association Finland.
Spradlin, C.T. and Kutoloski, D.M. (1999), 'Action-oriented portfolio management', *Research–
    Technology Management*, 42(2), 26–32.
van der Hoorn, B. and Whitty, S.J. (2016), 'Projectyness: a spectrum of greater or lesser capa-
    bility', *International Journal of Project Management*, 34(6), 970–982.

Chapter 6

Different types of project portfolios and settings

Darren Dalcher

Project portfolios offer an established way of organizing and prioritizing projects, programmes and investment opportunities for both private and public sector organizations. Yet, project portfolios differ greatly in the assumptions they embody and the way they are set up and utilized. This chapter explores the diversity of different types and settings of project portfolios.

Portfolios, definitions and strategies

Although the term 'portfolio management' can mean different things to different people, the basic idea of organizing investment (or projects) into a planned structure that allows the full range of investments (or projects) to be scrutinized is relatively straightforward. The 6th edition of the *APM Body of Knowledge* defines portfolio management as 'the selection, prioritisation and control of an organisation's projects and programmes in line with its strategic objectives and capacity to deliver' (Association for Project Management [APM], 2012, p. 16). The aim of such an arrangement is to enable an organization to make the most of its existing resources, select the most appropriate investment or projects, and maximize throughput and value to the organization.

The management of portfolios enables organizations to focus on investments and the potential value that they deliver, especially in terms of proposed change initiatives, product ranges and/or agreed activities. This is often achieved by balancing project and change initiatives and business as usual, while optimizing value, or return on investment. Portfolio management offers a range of benefits (Jenner and Kilford, 2011), because it:

- Helps achieve the best return from the total investment in change programmes and projects;
- Ensures successful delivery;
- Realizes the full benefits in terms of efficiency savings and contribution to strategic objectives across all sectors; and
- Provides the tools for and techniques to identify and prioritize overall investment.

However, it is important to note that portfolios are initiated for a variety of reasons. Pellegrinelli (1997) makes a reference to a portfolio programme configuration, which enables the grouping of relatively autonomous projects with a common theme. The existence of a theme enables the performance of the individual projects to be improved through the coordination of common resources or of a common technology. Artto (2001, p. 8) likewise emphasizes the need to share similar strategic objectives and shared resources among projects in a portfolio that are subject to similar sponsorship and management arrangements.

Other early work in this area (Combe and Githens, 1999) recognized a wider variety of rationales for adopting a portfolio approach and therefore proposed the three general types of: value-creating, operational or compliance portfolios. These types are further elaborated as follows:

- *Value-creating portfolios*, which encompass enterprise projects concerned with improving the organization's bottom line, which are viewed to be of strategic importance;
- *Operational portfolios*, which comprise functional projects that make the organization more efficient or improve organizational performance;
- *Compliance portfolios*: comprising essential projects that are required to meet legal, environmental, health and safety, or other regulatory compliance purposes. Note: similar setups may be required to respond to compelling market forces or dominant new technologies.

It is worth pointing out that the typology put forward by Combe and Githens appears to reflect the general distinction across vision-led programmes, emergent programmes and compliance programmes identified in *Managing Successful Programmes* (Office of Government Commerce [OGC], 2011). Generally, vision-led programmes (OGC, 2011) are derived in a top-down fashion (Rayner and Reiss, 2013) from a clearly defined strategy (Thiry, 2015), representing a deliberate attempt to shape the required activities to align with organizational strategy and match the strategic objectives. In contrast, emergent programmes (OGC, 2011) roll together existing activities, which emerge in an ad-hoc (Thiry, 2015), yet bottom-up, fashion (Rayner and Reiss, 2013), and are better managed in a coordinated fashion (Thiry, 2015), as also identified by Pellegrinelli (1997). Compliance activities can fit into either the strategic, vision-led, or the emergent ad-hoc type of activities, depending on the perceived level of urgency and strategic value (see also Thiry, 2015, p. 51).

Portfolio: why and where?

Portfolio management systems allow organizations to make the most of their investments and projects, especially in comparison with the expected returns. Given that the demand for project work is greater than the capability to deliver such projects, portfolio management plays a crucial role in determining which aspects of the work are feasible and achievable and identifying their wider contributions to the organization.

Cooper et al. (2001) summarized a set of detailed interviews conducted in 35 leading organizations. Their study identified the three main goals of portfolio management as follows:

1.   Maximizing the value of the portfolio against an objective, such as profitability;
2.   (Finding) balance in the portfolio. Portfolios can be balanced in many dimensions, with the most popular being risk versus reward, ease versus attractiveness and breakdown by project type, market and product line;
3.   (Providing the) link to strategy – looking for strategic fit and resource allocation

The three main goals observed in the research, also agree with Bridges' (1999) proposed paradigm of focusing on fit (identification of opportunities and assessment), utility (analysis of the usefulness and value) and balance (development and selection of balance) as the three core concerns of portfolio management.

Small enterprises may typically employ a single, company-wide project portfolio management system (Rayner and Reiss, 2013) to deal with the full range of concerns. However, the majority of larger organizations are likely to define more than one portfolio to account for the product line, geographical, political or technological divisions of the organization, sector, industry, market or multi-party collaboration.

In the context of the UK Government a portfolio is often used as an umbrella term encompassing the total collection of projects, programmes and initiatives currently being undertaken, thereby providing a perspective on the total investment. Indeed, the OGC's Management of Portfolios (Jenner and Kilford, 2011) defines a portfolio as 'the totality of the organization's investment in the changes required to achieve its strategic objectives'. The methodology developed by the OGC (ibid.) consists of two management cycles – one dedicated to portfolio definition and the other to portfolio delivery, five principles and twelve portfolio management practices.

In more general terms, portfolio management is used as the continual process of creating, delivering and evaluating the set of initiatives, activities and projects at the enterprise level, as they go through the repeated cycles of fit, utility and balance considerations. The approach allows the enterprise to manage the full portfolio and the results, in tandem with the evolution of the business strategy, in an effort to optimize and maximize the value of business investments while exploring new and emerging business opportunities.

One portfolio or more?

While portfolios have traditionally been viewed in terms of a central enterprise resource, they can also be adopted within functional areas, domains or departments. Indeed, the 6th edition of the *APM Body of Knowledge* clarifies that 'Portfolios can be managed at an organisational or functional level and address three questions:

*   Are these the projects and programmes needed to deliver the strategic objectives, subject to risk, resource constraints and affordability?
*   Is the organization delivering them effectively and efficiently?
*   Are the full potential benefits from the organization's investment being realized?' (APM, 2012, p. 16).

There is no 'one-size-fits-all' ideal arrangement for allocating projects or devising portfolios. Martinsuo (2013) notes the contextual nature of portfolio decisions and setups.

Portfolios are initiated for a variety of reasons. Rather than simply having one major project portfolio within each organization, many businesses would have multiple portfolios. Moore (2009) maintains that projects targeted at innovation and those concerned with improvement should be managed separately. The reason is because the metrics for success and the expectations for success are quite different. Moreover, the timing for returns on innovation will differ significantly. An extremely innovative project may yield nothing in the first five years, before experiencing dramatic growth thereafter, whereas a maintenance project will yield a steady single digit return. Managing innovative and process improvement projects in a similar manner, or even in the same category of portfolio, 'is likely to lead to mismanagement of either the innovative or the incremental projects, and most likely it is the innovative that will be curtailed. In the worst case, grouping together different types of projects could even caused both to be mismanaged' (Moore, 2009, p. 27). Different management styles are needed for different project portfolio types: for a conventional project portfolio the power of management rests primarily in the veto, innovation projects, in contrast, will need to bring ideas together and let them coalesce into workable solutions.

Although it may seem efficient to run a single project portfolio, and although it may make optimization simpler, in practice it is important to ensure that innovation is managed appropriately and allowed to develop over time. From a purely pragmatic perspective, there may be a single portfolio utilized to monitor where resources are allocated, but the different treatment of innovation and improvement projects would justify the division by type of activity, with different work flow and selection criteria applied in different parts of the organization.

Pennypacker and Retna (2009) acknowledge that most companies do not attempt to run all their projects at the enterprise level, and therefore make a case for tiered portfolios, where stand-alone portfolios may exist at a business unit or organizational level, as well as at the wider enterprise level.

Different sectors create their own functional portfolios. IT is particularly recognizable as having distinct structures and portfolios, often accompanied by their own approaches, methodologies, theories and a more comprehensive approach to encourage strategic alignment, portfolio flexibility, project pipeline, architecture, asset and resource management, and portfolio prioritization (see, for example, Bonham, 2005; Jagroep et al. 2014; Krebs, 2009; Rothman, 2016).

Many organizations have dedicated research and development (R&D) or innovation portfolios that focus on new product development, new discoveries or even underground oil exploration projects. New products are vital to the success of pharmaceutical, aerospace and heavy engineering constructors, and therefore merit their own dedicated portfolios.

Organizations are faced with different settings and hence need to match the complexity of their decisions with adequately sourced management and decision-making structures. Exxon Mobil Chemical uses six categories of projects to identify the right balance for investment, across:

1. Cost reductions and process improvements;
2. Product improvements, product modification and customer satisfaction;
3. New products;
4. New platform projects and fundamental/breakthrough research projects;

5. Plant support;
6. Technical support for customers.

Senior management reviews the spending split between the different categories, before considering the target breakdown of the ideal split against the current reality and making judgements based on future priorities and intentions.

Successful operation requires a balance between the different types of activities required for sustainable and effective performance. Christensen et al. (2012) assert that executives and investors might finance three different types of innovations with their capital, and manage each as a portfolio. The economy, they argue, requires all three types to occur regularly. The current economy has been overly focused on efficiency innovations, missing opportunities for new markets and empowering innovations, which all need to be managed in distinct portfolios. The three portfolio types are defined as follows:

Empowering innovations portfolios: transform expensive products into affordable ones that many more people can buy. These are innovations that create new jobs – because they require more and more people who can build, distribute, sell and service these products. Empowering investments also use capital to expand capacity and to finance receivables and inventory. Such innovation requires many millions of new jobs – that go unfilled because people do not yet have the skills to fulfil them.

Sustaining innovations portfolios: replace old products with newer models. They keep the economy vibrant, and in dollars they account for most innovation. But they have a neutral effect on economic activity and on capital.

Efficiency innovations portfolios: reduce the cost of making and distributing existing products and services. These are a natural part of the economic cycle, but they are the innovations that streamline process and actually reduce the net number of available jobs. They also preserve many of the remaining jobs (because without these entire companies and industries would disappear in competition against companies from abroad that have already innovated to become more efficient).

Ultimately, it appears that there are at several different ways of setting up portfolio management boundaries, including the following:

1. The boundaries of specific organizational units, functions or small business units (SBUs);
2. The enterprise level;
3. A specific project or innovation type.

However, additional arrangements may be needed to deal with specific types of initiatives concerned with satisfying the particular strategy required for the wider organization.

The case for strategic initiatives

Robert Kaplan and David Norton followed their pioneering work on balanced scorecards, strategy maps and strategy-focused organizations by zooming in on the need to link strategy to operations in order to develop and maintain a competitive advantage. Their book, *The Execution Premium*, focuses on the implementation of formal systems for the successful implementation of strategy. They describe the need to translate a strategy into strategic themes, objectives, measures and targets that represent *what* the organization wants to accomplish. However, execution requires bridging the execution gap, and therefore strategic initiatives are utilized to represent the *how*.

> Strategic initiatives are the collections of finite durations discretionary projects and programs, outside the organization's day-to-day operational activities, that are designed to help the organization achieve its targeted performance.
>
> (Kaplan and Norton, 2008, p. 103)

Although the need for an explicit link between long-term strategy and immediate actions may appear obvious, they point out that their own survey reveals that 50 per cent of organizations fail to link strategy to short-term plans and budgets (ibid., p. 4). 'A senior executive summarized many executives' frustration with the lack of alignment between strategy and action plans when he said, "half my initiatives achieve strategic goals. I just don't know which half"' (ibid., p. 103).

Reading between the lines: so why do strategic initiatives fail?

Kaplan and Norton (2008) propose an initiative management process model encompassing three distinct core activities required to align action with priorities:

1. *Choose strategic initiatives*: identify what action programmes are needed for executing the strategy;
2. *Fund the strategy*: identify a source of funding that is separated from the operational budget;
3. *Establish accountability*: determine who will lead the execution.

However, in reading the discourse related to the specific steps, it would appear that the true insights into the nature of the execution gap reside in the limitations and barriers associated with each of the steps.

Strategic plans require coordinated action that often extends beyond organizational boundaries, functions and business units. Kaplan and Norton reflect that in their original conception of scorecards, they encouraged companies to select initiatives independently for each strategic objective. However, they subsequently concede that selecting initiatives independently ignores the integrated and cumulative impact of multiple related strategic initiatives (ibid., p. 104). Those following only the earlier writing of these authors may thus miss the opportunity for integrating and choosing rather than optimize around individual activities and initiatives.

The new advice is that initiatives should not be selected in isolation because the achievement of a strategic objective 'generally requires multiple and complementary initiatives from various parts of the organization. . . . We continue to recommend that each nonfinancial objective has at least one initiative to drive its achievement but also that the initiatives be bundled for each strategic theme and considered as an integrated portfolio' (ibid., pp. 104–105).

In other words, in order to achieve the associated performance objectives of a strategic theme, it will often be required that the entire collection of initiatives, or the full portfolio of actions, is implemented. Successful execution with regard to organizational strategy thus requires a synergistic perspective rather than localized optimization at an initiative or unit level.

There are a number of additional barriers to the successful execution of strategic initiatives that require a unified enterprise response: They include the following:

- *Integrated justification*: strategic initiatives may be justified on a stand-alone basis in different parts of the organization, leading to strategic drift over the duration of the initiative;
- *Integrated funding*: cross-business portfolio funding is not common. However, the risk is that only parts of the initiative will be supported in different areas, leading to patchy or partial execution. Budgets typically focus on local accountability and responsibility centres or functional departments. However, strategic initiatives require uniform funding to secure delivery across the different business units and areas;
- *Integrated resources*: a similar logic applies to the availability of people and project resources. To avoid local interpretation and prioritization, strategic initiatives need to be resourced and justified centrally;
- *Integrated governance*: responsibility and accountability for the wider initiative need to rest with executive team members who can manage across teams, units and silos.

Strategic initiatives will often have a compelling business case that specifies the proposed benefits and the expected value proposition, and these can be used as the basis for leading and delivering successful initiatives.

Potential principles for collecting projects and programmes into a portfolio

I have already identified multiple reasons for assembling projects and programmes into distinct portfolios. These include the following:

- Strategic ambition;
- Maximizing value;
- Balancing different needs (or types of innovation);
- Managing common resources;
- Common technology;
- Shared sponsorship and management arrangements;
- Allocating budget;
- Justifying investments;
- Achieving enterprise visibility;
- Prioritizing initiatives;
- Reducing/enhancing risk profile;
- Enhancing a particular product line;
- Matching to a particular risk/investment appetite;

- Increasing the flow of value through a pipeline;
- Creating a particular funnel for a product or type of project;
- Responding to opportunities;
- Diversification;
- Delivery of benefits;
- Justifying compliance work.

Portfolios often endeavour to achieve multiple objectives by offering a link between the execution of initiatives and the wider enterprise strategy, and hence may pack together multiple aspects and rationales.

Agile portfolio management endeavours to distil the key principles of portfolio management by focusing on the rapid creation of value. However, it is important to align value realization with the relevant strategy and rationale. By identifying the general rationale and balance needed in a portfolio, it is possible to refine the key principles driving the leading choices and decisions, and begin to determine the dimensions and rules of success in setting up the portfolio.

Rethinking portfolio success

The track record of project portfolios is sometimes difficult to decipher. Jonas (2010) notes that it remains difficult to determine the overall success or failure of a portfolio, especially as it needs to be realised at different points during the lifespan of a portfolio. Marnewick (2015) summarizes the main portfolio success criteria according to Beringer et al. (2013) and Meskendahl (2010), as:

1. Maximizing the portfolio's financial value;
2. Linking the portfolio to the organizational strategy;
3. Balancing the projects within the portfolio while taking into account the organization's capacities; and
4. The average single project success of the portfolio.

Given the diversity observed in the types of portfolio setups, and the key criteria applied to each, plus the subtleties of determining success and failure, at multiple levels and perspectives (Dalcher, 2014), it should be clear that the key criteria applied should be context specific. Indeed, Martinsuo (2013, p. 798) asserts that 'recent studies show evidence that the success of portfolio management in highly dependent on the context'.

Indeed, it is clear that we must measure success in different ways. Success is a complex and multi-layered concept (Dalcher, 2014), especially in the context of portfolios. The multiple bases and rationales highlighted above identify a starting point in the conversation about success in portfolio settings. Generally accepted criteria in the extant literature appear to offer little value or guidance. Moreover, given the different needs and requirements of specific setups, such as strategic initiatives, this implies that specific criteria need to be applied and tailored to each context individually. The balance between the different components and interests should also be taken into account. Completion of a small part of a portfolio can be significantly less critical than the successful completion of a strategic initiative. Indeed, in a strategic context, specific actions and their completion may seem irrelevant against strategic imperatives.

Overall, therefore, the specific scenario for success needs to be tailored to the specific initiatives and activities that are invoked. Their relative importance to the overall sustained performance of the enterprise should play the key part in planning for (and measuring the achievement of) long-term intended performance, measured in terms of the fit, utility and balance of the achieved portfolio.

References and further reading

Association for Project Management (2012), *APM Body of Knowledge*, 6th edn. Princes Risborough: APM.

Artto, K.A. (2001), Management of project-oriented organization – a conceptual analysis, in: Artto, K.A., Martinsuo, M. and Aalto, T. (eds), *Project Portfolio Management: Strategic management through projects*. Helsinki, Finland: Project Management Association.

Beringer, C., Jonas, D. and Kock, A. (2013), 'Behavior of internal stakeholders in project portfolio management and its impact on success', *International Journal of Project Management*, 31(6), 830–846.

Bonham, S.S. (2005), IT Project Portfolio Management. Boston, MA: Artech House.

Bridges, D.N. (1999), 'Project portfolio management: ideas and practices. Project portfolio management – selecting and prioritizing projects for competitive advantage', in: Dye, L.D. and Pennypacker, J.S. (eds), *Project Portfolio Management: Selecting and prioritizing projects for competitive advantage*. West Chester, PA: Center for Business Practices, pp. 45–54.

Christensen, C.M., Allworth, J. and Dillon, K. (2012), *How Will You Measure Your Life?* New York: Harper Business.

Combe, M.W. and Githens, G.D. (1999), 'Managing popcorn priorities: how portfolios and programs align projects with strategies', Proceedings of the PMI 1999 Seminars and Symposium. Philadelphia, PA: Project Management Institute.

Cooper, R.G., Edgett, S.J. and Kleinschmidt, E.J. (1997), 'Portfolio management in new product development: Lessons from the leaders – II', *Research–Technology Management*, 40(6), 43–52.

Cooper, R.G., Edgett, S.J. and Kleinschmidt, E.J. (2001), *Portfolio Management for New Products*, 2nd edn. New York: Basic Books.

Dalcher, D. (2014), 'Rethinking success in software projects: looking beyond the failure factors' in: Ruhe, G. and Wohlin, C. (eds), *Software Project Management in a Changing World*. Berlin Heidelberg: Springer, pp. 27–49.

Dye, L.D. and Pennypacker, J.S., eds (1999), Project Portfolio Management: Selecting and prioritizing projects for competitive advantage. West Chester, PA: Center for Business Practices, pp. 45–54.

Jagroep, E., van de Weerd, I., Brinkkemper, S. and Dobbe, T. (2014), Framework for implementing product portfolio management in software business, in: Ruhe, G. and Wohlin, C. (eds), *Software Project Management in a Changing World*. Berlin Heidelberg: Springer, pp. 193–221.

Jenner, S. and Kilford, C. (2011). *Management of Portfolios*. Norwich: The Stationery Office.

Jonas, D. (2010), 'Empowering project portfolio managers. How management involvement impacts project portfolio performance', *International Journal of Project Management*, 28(8), 818–831.

Kaplan, R.S. and Norton, D.P. (2008), The Execution Premium: Linking Strategy to Operations for Competitive Advantage, Boston, MA: Harvard Business Press.

Krebs, J. (2009), *Agile Portfolio Management*. Redmond, WA: Microsoft Press.

Marnewick, C. (2015), 'Portfolio management success', in: Levin, G. and Wyzalek, J.P. (eds), *Portfolio Management: A Strategic Approach*. London: CRC Press.

Martinsuo, M. (2013), 'Project portfolio management in practice and in context', *International Journal of Project Management*, 31(6), 794–803.

Meskendahl, S. (2010), 'The influence of business strategy on project portfolio management and its success – a conceptual framework'. *International Journal of Project Management*, 28(8), 807–817.

Moore, S. (2009), Strategic Project Portfolio Management: Enabling a Productive Organization, vol.16. New York: John Wiley & Sons.

Office of Government Commerce (2011), *Managing Successful Programmes*. Norwich: The Stationery Office.

Pellegrinelli, S. (1997), 'Programme management: organizing project-based change'. *International Journal of Project Management*, 15(3), 141–149.

Pennypacker, J. and Retna, S. (2009). Project Portfolio Management: A view from the management trenches. Hoboken, NJ: John Wiley & Sons.

Rayner, P. and Reiss, G. (2013), Portfolio and Programme Management Demystified: Managing Multiple Projects Successfully, Abingdon: Routledge.

Rothman, J. (2016). Manage Your Project Portfolio: Increase Your Capacity and Finish More Projects. Raleigh, NC: Pragmatic Bookshelf.

Thiry, M. (2015), *Program Management*, 2nd edn, Aldershot: Gower.

Part II

The practice of portfolio management

Chapter 7

Best practice standards for portfolio management

Reinhard Wagner

Many standards exist for project and programme management. These include national and international, generic and sector-specific, process-orientated and competence-based standards. It is sometimes confusing to understand the commonalities and differences of those standards and apply them adequately in a specific context. Portfolio management is quite a new approach, which has gained more recognition since the early 2000s. Thus, there are only a few best practice standards available for portfolio management. These are explained in this chapter, together with their key concepts, contents and how various target audiences could use them. For simplicity, I focus on international standards.

Portfolios and portfolio management in the finance sector

The terms 'portfolio' and 'portfolio' management can be traced back to the late 1930s. After the Great Depression in the USA, people were reconsidering their investments in stocks, bonds and other forms of financial assets. Focusing on one or only few assets turned out to be too risky and therefore the concept of diversification became popular. John Burr Williams raised this idea in 1938 in his book *The Theory of Investment Value* (Williams 1938). Later Harry Markowitz described the concept and modern portfolio theory and won the Nobel Memorial Prize in Economic Sciences (Markowitz 1952). A key aspect of portfolio selection was that an ideal portfolio is one in which no added diversification can lower the portfolio's risk for a given return expectation, or alternatively, no additional expected return can be gained without increasing the risk of the portfolio. In the 1980s and 1990s the portfolio theory was also used for investments in tangible assets such as infrastructure, production equipment and computer systems. Finally, the concept was utilized in the field of management in order to manage projects from a strategic point of view.

Competence standards for portfolio management

Portfolio management is all about people. People manage portfolios and thus human competence is at the core of competence-orientated standards. All people involved in portfolios and their management can learn about the competence requirements by reading the competence standards. Training and many other ways of competence development can provide relevant best practices and enable the participants in gaining experiences (for example, through learning by doing). Certification bodies could use competence-orientated standards for portfolio management as a baseline for assessing and certifying personnel. Competence-orientated standards are typically not intended to be used as process models or methodology. They do not describe detailed input/output relations and activities for all process steps of portfolio management.

Currently there is only one international competence standard for portfolio management available, which is the International Project Management Association (IPMA) Individual Competence Baseline (IPMA 2016a).

The IPMA Individual Competence Baseline

The IPMA is the world's oldest international project management association, founded in 1965 in Europe. The IPMA approach was mainly:

- to enhance the competences of individuals involved in projects, programmes and portfolios through a standard;
- to offer education and training plus certification schemes through its national certification bodies in more than 70 countries worldwide.

The first version of the IPMA ICB was published in 1999. It was based on the approaches of four European project management associations (France, Germany, Switzerland and the UK). Portfolio management was not mentioned directly. However, some of the 28 competence elements described in this standard dealt implicitly with the management of multiple projects. Versions 2 and 3 of the IPMA ICB explicitly addressed the topic of portfolio management for projects and programmes. A range of competences, split into 'technical competences', 'behavioural competences' and 'contextual competences', were described. Two of the 'contextual competences' addressed the topic of portfolio management. One of these was titled 'portfolio orientation' and the other was 'project, programme and portfolio implementation'.

The IPMA certification scheme contains specific requirements related to particular categories of people to which the same standards and rules apply. For people managing a portfolio the IPMA ICB describes competences on the highest of four levels. Training providers could help to attain these competences, for example to obtain a certificate as Certified Project Director (IPMA Level A), which means that a person can direct an important portfolio (or programme), with corresponding resources, methodologies and tools. IPMA's certification bodies use IPMA ICB as the baseline for assessments.

IPMA published the fourth edition of its IPMA ICB in 2016 (IPMA 2016a). This goes a step further and separates the three domains of project, programme and portfolio management. For each of these three domains, a set of competence elements is described with key competence indicators (KCIs). These KCIs provide definitive indicators of successful project, programme and portfolio management for one, two or all three domains. Based on IPMA ICB Version 4.0, the certification bodies will offer certification in the domain of portfolio management on two levels: 'Certified Portfolio Manager' and 'Certified Portfolio Director'.

Practice standards for portfolio management

Management standards typically build on what is called 'good practice'. They try to capture this practice and extract key concepts, principles, processes, methodologies and tools for any type of organization, and for any type of portfolio, irrespective of project types or assets managed. There are three internationally acknowledged standards available for programme management, ISO 21504 *Project, Programme and Portfolio Management – Guidance on portfolio management* (International Organization for Standardization or ISO 2015), the *Standard for Portfolio Management* of the Project Management Institute (PMI 2013a) and the Office of Government Commerce's (OGC's) best management practice standard *Management of Portfolios* (now published by AXELOS 2013).

ISO 21504 Guidance on Portfolio Management

In 2007, the ISO chartered a project to develop an international project management standard, the ISO 21500 *Guidance on Project Management.* This is a process-orientated standard for the management of a single project. In the conceptual part of this standard, portfolios and portfolio management are defined as follows:

> A project portfolio is generally a collection of projects and programmes and other work that are grouped together to facilitate the effective management of that work to meet strategic goals. Project portfolio management is generally the centralized management of one or more project portfolios, which includes identifying, prioritizing, authorizing, directing and controlling projects, programmes and other work to achieve specific strategic goals.
>
> (ISO 2012, pp. 5–6)

Before finishing ISO 21500, a new technical committee was established, the ISO/TC 258 Project, Programme and Portfolio Management. That committee developed a standard for portfolio management, which was published as ISO 21504 *Project, Programme and Portfolio Management – Guidance on portfolio management* (ISO 2015).

The ISO portfolio management standard differs from ISO 21500, and does not follow a process-orientated approach. It defines terms, principles and prerequisites of portfolio management, as well as concepts for managing portfolios. A portfolio is defined as:

> A collection of portfolio components grouped together to facilitate their management to meet, in whole or in part, an organization's strategic objectives.'
>
> (ISO 2015)

Portfolio components could be projects, programmes and other related work. The main purpose of setting up portfolio management is the need for a consistent approach to manage strategically aligned projects, programmes, portfolios and other related work, within an organizational environment of varying complexity and uncertainty. It may:

- enable investment in portfolio components to be aligned with the organization's strategy;
- optimize the organizational capability and capacity;

- maximize benefits from investment;
- identify and manage stakeholders' expectations; and finally
- provide visibility of portfolio component activity and status.

Portfolio management 'aligns the portfolio components with an organization's strategic objectives, stakeholder priorities and values, such as sustainable practices and ethical principles. It may also be described as a continuous decision-making process, whereby an organization's list of portfolio components is subject to periodic review for alignment with the organization's strategy. In this approach, new opportunities or threats are evaluated, selected, prioritized and authorized. Portfolio components may be modified, accelerated, postponed or terminated' (ISO 2015, p. 2). The main practices mentioned are:

- defining the portfolio;
- identifying, assessing and selecting potential portfolio components;
- defining the portfolio plan;
- validating portfolio alignment to strategic objectives;
- evaluating and reporting portfolio performance; and
- balancing and optimizing the portfolio.

The other sections of this standard cover aspects such as governance, roles and responsibilities, and the context of the organization. The ISO portfolio management standard is a guidance standard, which means that its intent is neither to be certified against nor to replace other (national or sector-specific) standards.

Standards in the UK

There is a long tradition of project, programme and portfolio management in the UK. The Association for Project Management (APM, some universities and industry experts made specific expertise available, such as the APM Body of Knowledge (BoK) which is currently in its sixth edition. This publication defines portfolio management as follows:

> Portfolio management is the selection, prioritization and control of an organization's projects and programmes in line with its strategic objectives and capacity to deliver.
>
> (APM 2012, p. 14)

The stated goal is 'to balance change initiatives and business-as-usual while optimizing return on investment. Projects and programmes aim at making change happen'. This demonstrates a different focus in the UK from the rest of the world.

This is also the case with the UK best management practice standard *Management of Portfolios* (MoP). In 2011 the OGC published the first and only edition of MoP (OGC 2011). The OGC function later moved into the Cabinet Office as part of HM Government, which then merged the function with a private organization into a joint venture, called 'AXELOS'. AXELOS now owns all UK best management practice standards. MoP claims to provide practitioners with 'universally applicable principles and practices that will enable individuals and organizations (large or small) to successfully introduce or re-energize portfolio management approaches'. It defines a portfolio as:

> totality of an organization's investment (or a segment thereof) in the changes required to achieve its strategic objectives.

Portfolio management is defined as:

> a coordinated collection of strategic processes and decisions that together enable the most effective balance of organizational change and business as usual.
> (OGC 2011, p. 11)

It is claimed that MoP does not represent a new discipline. Portfolio management seeks to build on, and better coordinate, existing processes such as strategic planning, investment appraisal, and project and programme management. It is not concerned with the detailed management of the component projects and programmes; rather, it approaches the management of change projects and programmes from a strategic viewpoint. Some of the benefits of applying portfolio management are undertaking the 'right' projects and programmes, utilizing resources more efficiently, realizing greater benefits, enhancing transparency, accountability and governance, as well as improving stakeholder engagement, including but not limited to the senior executives of an organization. MoP describes five portfolio management principles, as follows:

1. Senior management commitment;
2. Governance alignment;
3. Strategy alignment;
4. Portfolio office; and
5. Energized change culture.

These principles provide the context within which the portfolio definition and portfolio delivery based on constituent practices operate. The portfolio management activities focus on either 'defining the portfolio' or 'delivering the portfolio'. The first set of activities ('cycle') mentioned covers practices such as 'understand', 'categorize', 'prioritize', 'balance' and 'plan'. The second set for delivery outlines the practices 'management control', 'benefits management', 'financial management', 'risk management', 'stakeholder engagement', 'organizational governance' and 'resource management'.

> The effective operation of these practices will be facilitated by tailored application of the techniques described in this guide. Success also depends on organizational energy – that is, the extent to which an organization, division or team has mobilized its emotional, cognitive and behavioural potential to pursue its goals.
> (OGC 2011, p. 13)

In separate appendices MoP provides a portfolio management health check, role descriptions, templates for programmes and projects, an example for benefits management and a glossary.

'The Standard for Portfolio Management' of the PMI

Founded in 1969, the PMI has developed into a US-based, internationally spreading, not-for-profit, professional membership association for the project, programme and portfolio management profession. In the 1980s the PMI developed a white paper on a project management methodology, which was published in 1996 as the first version of the *Guide to the Project Management Body of Knowledge* (PMBOK Guide). It identifies that subset of the PMBOK Guide that is generally recognized as good practice for project management. The PMBOK Guide is process based, which means that it describes work as being accomplished by processes. The processes are described in terms of inputs, tools and techniques, as well as outputs.

In 2006, the PMI published its first edition of *The Standard for Portfolio Management*. Since then, this standard has undergone significant updates and at the time of writing is available as the third edition (PMI 2013a). However, since 2016 a project for updating the standard is under way. The release of the fourth edition is expected to happen during 2018. The third edition of this standard states that it 'identifies portfolio management processes generally recognized as good practices' [PMI 2013a, p. 1] 'Generally recognized' means that the knowledge and practices are applicable to most portfolios, most of the time. This standard defines a portfolio as 'a component collection of programs, projects, or operations managed as a group to achieve strategic objectives' [PMI 2013a, p. 3]. Portfolio Management is defined as:

> The coordinated management of one or more portfolios to achieve organizational strategies and objectives. It includes interrelated organizational processes by which an organization evaluates, selects, prioritizes, and allocates its limited resources to best accomplish organizational strategies consistent with its vision, mission, and values.
>
> (PMI 2013a, p. 5)

Through its standards suite for project, programme, portfolio and organizational project management, PMI shows the interrelationships of projects, programmes and portfolios, and ways of managing them in an integrative way. All standards deal with the business value delivered, the various roles involved and competences required. PMI offers – like all professional associations – training and certification schemes for people involved in portfolio management.

PMI's *Standard for Portfolio Management* is a process-orientated standard. It defines five knowledge areas and three process groups with sixteen processes. Thus, this standard follows the process-orientated approach of the PMBOK Guide. The knowledge areas are specific for portfolio management and are called 'portfolio strategic management', 'portfolio governance management', 'portfolio performance management', 'portfolio communication management' and 'portfolio risk management'.

The three process groups are called 'defining', 'aligning' and 'authorization and controlling'. They have clear dependencies and are typically performed in the same sequence for every portfolio. All processes are outlined with their inputs, tools and techniques, as well as the outputs. Some of the key deliverables across the portfolio management processes are provided in PMI's standard, such as the 'portfolio strategic plan', 'portfolio charter', 'portfolio management plan', 'portfolio roadmap' and the 'portfolio'.

The *Standard for Portfolio Management* sets portfolio management in context with other activities in an organization, such as recurring and project activities, the development and implementation of an organization's strategy as well as the management of available resources. It (shortly) defines the roles of portfolio managers and the PMO with regard to portfolio management and other associated roles.

Other related standards for portfolio management

There are other standards with relevance to portfolio management, including national standards (for example, the AIPM Competence Standard for Portfolio Managers), regional standards (such as PM² Standards of the European Commission), sector-specific standards (for example, portfolio management standards for IT) and standards for assessment and certification of maturity in portfolio management (such as IPMA Delta). There are also many books and articles about portfolios and portfolio management, which could be seen as best practice standards. I now focus on standards with a specific approach to portfolio management.

The AXELOS Standard on Portfolio, Programme and Project Offices

Besides the aforementioned MSP Standard, AXELOS offers a best management practice standard called *Portfolio, Programme and Project Offices (P3O®)*. This was first published in 2008 and the current edition is dated 2013. P3O provides guidance with regard to portfolio, programme and project offices, aiming primarily at senior managers and managers responsible for the implementation of a P3O. It defines P3O as follows:

> The decision-enabling and support business model for all business change within an organization. This will include single or multiple physical or virtual structures, i.e. offices (permanent and/or temporary), providing a mix of central and localized functions and services, and integration with governance arrangements and the wider business such as other corporate support functions.
>
> (AXELOS 2013, p.7)

The standard explains why an organization should have P3Os, and how to design, implement or re-energize and operate the office(s). Several appendices of this standard include:

- roles and responsibilities;
- a business case example for the development or enhancement of P3Os;
- examples of tools and techniques through links to a knowledge centre; and
- case studies on model tailoring.

The IPMA Organizational Competence Baseline

In 2013, the IPMA released its first version of a new standard, the IPMA OCB, which was updated in early 2016. It introduces the innovative concept of an organizational competence in managing projects as a holistic approach for organizations to strengthen their management of projects, programmes and portfolios. The IPMA OCB describes the concept of organizational competence in managing projects, programmes and portfolio-related work, and how this should be used to deliver the organization's vision, mission and strategic objectives in a sustainable manner. It also demonstrates how the governance and management of projects, programmes and portfolios (PP&P) should be continuously analysed, assessed, improved and further developed.

The main target audience for this standard is senior executives. They can use the standard to understand the role of PP&P for executing and controlling mission, vision and strategy. It can help them to understand their own role in the concept of organizational competence in managing projects, to analyse the status of their organization's competence in managing projects, to identify areas for improvement, and to direct stakeholders, resources and activities for the development of the organization's capabilities in managing projects. IPMA OCB defines organizational competence in managing projects as:

> Ability of organizations to integrate people, resources, processes, structures and cultures in projects, programmes and portfolios within a supporting governance and management system. Organizational competence in managing projects is specifically aligned with the mission, vision and strategy of the organization and is intended to achieve results as well as to ensure continuous organizational development.
>
> (IPMA 2016b, p. 19)

One chapter elaborates on ways to implement or improve the competence of an organization and explains the tools to be used. IPMA's certification bodies use IPMA OCB as the baseline for assessing and certifying the competence of organizations: the approach is called 'IPMA Delta'.

ISO 21505: Project, Programme and Portfolio Management – Guidance on Governance

Another standard that was developed within the context of ISO/TC258 is a governance standard, ISO 21505 (ISO 2017). The primary target audience for this standard comprises governing bodies and executive managers who influence, impact or make decisions about the governance of projects, programmes and portfolios. The definition for governance is:

> Principles, policies and framework by which an organization is directed and controlled.
>
> (ISO 2017, p.2)

Governance should be aligned with the overall organizational governance and (if existing) the governance of all projects and programmes. The governance of portfolios as described in ISO 21505 comprises the principles, governing body responsibilities, guidelines and framework by which an organization directs and controls its portfolios. Examples mentioned in ISO 21505 for governing bodies are an investment committee and a portfolio board consisting of a body of executive or senior managers.

The PMI Organizational Project Management Maturity Model

PMI is also interested in elaborating on frameworks beyond the management of a single project or programme. A standard called *Organizational Project Management Maturity Model* (OPM3 – PMI 2013b) was developed, providing guidelines for improving organizational project, programme and portfolio management. The first edition was released in 2003, the second in 2008 and the current standard in 2013. The PMI is presently working on the next edition which will most likely be published in late 2018. In general, this standard is a knowledge foundation that can be used by many interested parties for learning and improving organizations. It can also be used as a check for assessing organizations.

OPM3 is based on the strategy execution framework 'Organizational Project Management (OPM)', utilizing portfolio, programme and project management as well as organizational-enabling practice. OPM is integrating knowledge, processes and people, and supporting tools to achieve business value.

The maturity of an organization is 'the level of an organization´s ability to deliver the desired strategic outcomes in a predictable, controllable, and reliable manner' (PMI 2013b, p. 240). OPM3 is described as:

> A framework that defines knowledge, assessment, and improvement processes, based on best practices and capabilities, to help organizations measure and mature their portfolio, program, and project management practices.

The improvement process is designed to start with acquiring knowledge about organizational project management. Then (after an assessment to evaluate the current state) managing improvement to gain the capabilities that have been identified as being needed. Finally the impacts of these changes are measured. OPM3 delivers a 'self-assessment method (SAM)' and an encyclopaedic list of best practices for comparison.

Conclusion

The international journey of developing standards in the field of projects and programmes started in the 1950s in the USA, especially in the aerospace and defence sector. Portfolio management standards were created about 50 years later.

National and international standards bodies as well as professional associations started to develop their own standards. Depending on their focus, these are competence-based, process-based or practice-based portfolio management standards. It is up to the user to decide which approach suits best. Other portfolio-related standards touch on organizational settings, roles and responsibilities, including the governance of portfolios and the maturity of its application.

Before reading the standards, the problem should be analysed and defined. Objectives and constraints should be clarified with all stakeholders and an implementation project started. All the above-mentioned standards disclose their target readership, the content and the main area for application. This will give guidance for choosing from the available standards.

International standards are typically very generic, because they are intended to fit all portfolios and all organizations. It means, that a user needs to understand the standard as guidance for developing their own, situation-specific solution. Implementing or improving portfolio management is a project on its own. Managing such a project also encompasses change activities (for example, stakeholder engagement, communication and conflict resolution). The long-term goal is to improve the performance of portfolio management and deliver value to the organization.

Other chapters in this handbook elaborate on several if not all aspects mentioned in this chapter. They may also refer to one or the other standards of portfolio management, showing the significance of the standards in daily application. As standards are not mandatory, there are many derivatives and interpretations at hand, which also help to move the profession forward by exchanging experiences and learning from the application.

References and further reading

Association for Project Management (APM) (2012), *APM Body of Knowledge*, 6th edn, Princes Risborough: APM

AXELOS (2013), *Portfolio, Programme and Project Offices*, 2013 edn, Norwich: The Stationery Office (TSO).

International Organization for Standardization (2015), ISO 21504 *Project, Programme and Portfolio Management – Guidance on portfolio management*, Geneva: ISO.

International Organization for Standardization (2017), ISO 21505 *Project, Programme and Portfolio Management – Guidance on Governance*, Geneva: ISO.

International Project Management Association (IPMA) (2006), *IPMA Competence Baseline for Project Management*, Version 3.0, Amsterdam: IPMA.

International Project Management Association (2016a), *IPMA Individual Competence Baseline*, Version 4.0, Amsterdam: IPMA.

International Project Management Association (2016b), *IPMA Organisational Competence Baseline*, Version 1.1, Amsterdam: IPMA.

International Organization for Standardization (ISO) (2012), ISO 21500 *Guidance on Project Management*, Geneva: ISO.

Markovitz, H. (1952), 'Portfolio selection', *Journal of Finance*, 7(1).

OGC (2011), *Management of Portfolios*, 2011 edn, Norwich, The Stationery Office. (Also available from AXELOS.)

Project Management Institute (PMI) (2013a), *The Standard for Portfolio Management*, 3rd edn, Newtown Square, PA: PMI.

Project Management Institute (2013b), *Organizational Project Management Maturity Model (OPM3)*, 3rd edn, Newtown Square, PA: PMI.

Williams, J.B. (1938), *The Theory of Investment Management*, Cambridge, MA: Harvard University Press.

Chapter 8

Portfolio management for IT

Tetsuro Seki and Akihiko Sekiguchi

The information technology (IT) portfolio derives from the financial portfolio. It realizes a well-balanced distribution of organizational IT investigation and total optimization of organizational IT assets. This chapter gives an overview of the application of IT portfolio management.

Role and nature of IT portfolio management

Portfolio management is the top level of project, programme, and portfolio (PPP) management. The strategic goal of organizational management is expressed quantitatively as the expected benefit from the management of portfolios. In IT portfolio management, high-level decisions are related to IT investment in the workflow required by the organization's strategy, as follows:

- Drafting and revising policies for IT investment;
- Drafting and revising processes aimed at gaining benefits;
- Creating, operating and discontinuing programmes, projects, and operations;
- Operating, remodelling and disposing of existing IT assets.

These decisions are made using the maximization of benefits as an evaluation index. IT portfolio management therefore refers to the processes by which an organization creates single or multiple programmes, projects and operations in line with its management strategy to achieve concrete benefits. That is a top-down approach for optimizing IT investment.

By contrast, IT *project* portfolio management demotes the operational evaluation of a programme or project to determine the redistribution of management resources. That is a bottom-up approach for optimizing IT investment.

It is the role of programme, project and operation management to ensure that individual programmes or projects operate properly. The role of IT portfolio management categorizes all IT investments according to compliance (return) and feasibility (risk) criteria related to the organizational management strategy. It then allocates resources either by category or for overall optimization.

Depending on the subject, IT portfolio management can be classified as follows:

- *Application portfolio management* (APM) evaluates the organizational assets of software applications and software-based services using such quantitative indices as age, importance, number of users, maintenance cost and interrelationship with other applications. It then revises the entire organizational portfolio (including software applications and software-based services) according to business benefits, such as the expected rate of return;

- *Infrastructure portfolio management* (IPM) is a management approach in which the philosophy of APM is applied instead to the organization's common IT infrastructure.

However, the definition and scope of these terms, and the scope of IT portfolio management, IT investment portfolio management and IT project portfolio management, are not immutable. The limits (or boundaries) to such management are ambiguous, depending on the literature or the individual organizations providing these services. Moreover, the concepts of IT portfolio management overlap with those of enterprise architecture (EA), enterprise IT governance and others.

History of IT portfolio management development

The philosophy of early IT portfolio management involved a theory that described four stages in the growth of electric data processing (EDP) (Gibson and Nolan, 1974). Meanwhile, the Massachusetts Institute of Technology (MIT) Center for Information Systems Research's (CISR) *IT Portfolio Framework* (2003) clearly presented the assumption behind IT investment portfolio management, which became the basis of many subsequent templates for IT investment portfolio management.

Benefits of implementing IT portfolio management

To motivate an organization to implement IT portfolio management, it is important to clarify the benefits that can be obtained. However, there has been little theoretical or empirical consideration of this aspect. Jeffery and Leliveld (2004) provided the following reasons for the need to introduce IT portfolio management:

- In 2002, IT investment in the USA reached US$78 billion, of which 68 per cent was evaluated as failing in terms not meeting delivery date and budget. In the previous two years, US$100–150 billion of IT investment was lost because of such failures, and the strategic goals could not be achieved initially;
- It is difficult to select projects that match organizational strategy from numerous simultaneous projects spanning functions, business units and locations;
- It is essential to be able to respond to management queries, such as how to derive business benefits from IT investment.

As a result, IT portfolio management is applied to measuring and increasing the benefits, and reducing the risks, of existing and planned individual IT investments and aggregated IT investment revenues.

Recently, the expansion of IT investment to include such technology as Fintech (financial technology), AI (artificial intelligence) and IoT (internet of things), plus the emphasis on improving the IT environment in terms of the organizational strategy, all support the need for introducing an IT portfolio. According to a study by Accenture

(2016), the total investment in Fintech was approximately US$1.8 billion for 2010, whereas the investment in 2015 reached approximately US$22.3 billion. In addition, the introduction of investment trusts boosted investment in AI, with the total investment in the 2016 fiscal year reaching a record high of US$5 billion. Consequently, as the amount and strategic importance of IT investment increase, so does the necessity for IT portfolio management to allocate resources appropriately and secure the success of projects.

IT portfolio frameworks

MIT CISR's model

The model from MIT CISR is often considered as a template for evaluating the importance of potential IT projects. Based on the approximate strength of the risk impact for each, this model categorizes IT projects into the following four different asset classes for the IT investment portfolio:

1. Strategic, with the strongest impact on the project's success;
2. Infrastructure;
3. Informational; and
4. Transactional.

According to MIT's summary of several sources, 18 per cent of IT investment is categorized in the first of these classes, with a 50 per cent failure rate against the potentially large benefit. Therefore, the projects (the opportunities and potential components required by the organizational strategy) can be categorized into four classes to ensure that the IT project portfolio is implemented appropriately.

At this stage, a grid model is employed to evaluate the importance of individual IT projects. The MIT CISR's model uses axes of 'value of business' and 'risk' to assess importance. This process is similar to financial portfolio management.

METI's model

Japan's Ministry of Economy, Trade and Industry (METI) issued the *IT Portfolio Model Utilization Guide Using Performance Evaluation Reference Model (PRM)* in 2003 to evaluate the government's IT investment and procurement. This model, based on the CISR's IT portfolio framework, aims to optimize the IT investment strategy for administrative systems. The Performance Reference Model (PRM) is one of the reference models for EA, along with the Business Reference Model (BRM), Technical Reference Model (TRM) and Data Reference Model (DRM), used to improve and optimize business and information systems from the perspective of an entire organization. PRM provides key performance indicators (KPIs) and outlines for each target business classification of the IT investment, which enables a comprehensive evaluation of the compliance and feasibility axes in relation to the management strategy for IT investment.

METI's model employs three different asset classes for IT investment portfolios, as follows:

1. Achievement of strategic objectives;
2. Business efficiency improvement; and
3. Infrastructure development.

These categories express the aims and criteria of the evaluation for IT project portfolio management, which uses a similar grid model to MIT CISR: 'strategic suitability' and 'feasibility'.

Strategic suitability consists of three items: effectiveness (10), inevitability (10) and area of influence (10). Feasibility consists of four items: internal risk (3), human and organizational risk (7), technology risk (5) and project risk (5). The numbers shown in brackets indicate the full scores, or the weight, for each item. The total score for each of 'strategic suitability' and 'feasibility' is therefore 30 and 20, respectively. These scores are then plotted for each IT project on a two-dimensional scatter diagram, as shown in Figure 8.1.

In this example, five potential IT projects for investigation are plotted on the scatter diagram. Clearly, the first quadrant is a top priority sector: Project A, an 'honours student', is urgent and low risk, and will move to the next stage. For the potential projects in the first quadrant, sometimes the existence of problems over budget and/or resources would force a choice between project B and C. In this case, the three different asset classes, representing organizational objectives in the IT investment portfolio, indicate priority to projects B and C. So the priority between the axes that indicate strategic suitability and feasibility decides an order for these two candidates. The same problem often occurs between projects D and E. In this case, the same treatment for projects B and C will apply to this selection problem.

As shown in the above-described process, the score for each potential project is determined by the function of the IT project portfolio (strategy and feasibility).

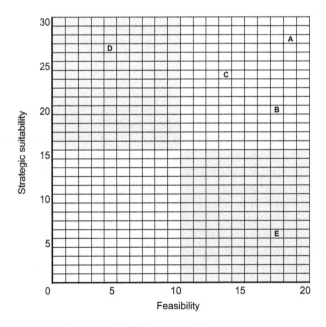

Figure 8.1 Example of METI's grid model

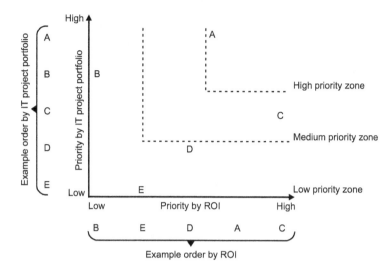

Figure 8.2 Example of prioritization by IT project portfolio and return of investment

Furthermore, METI's model requires examination based on further compilation of this result and the value of the return on investment (ROI) assessment, before finally deciding on IT investment. Figure 8.2 illustrates this final process of prioritization. A score is determined by the X axis (priority by IT project portfolio) and Y axis (prioritization according to ROI) in the final prioritization of projects as shown in Figure 8.2. This is achieved after the step in Figure 8.1 where the projects in the portfolio were prioritized according to strategy and feasibility.

Despite the fact that all examinations up to this stage might be completed, sometimes the process for prioritization cannot be achieved completely, because this model does not provide a straight answer to the problem. In such cases, an additional discussion based on the organizational objectives for IT investment is required.

This model is optimized for government procurement. Generally, the urgency for stakeholders is an absolute and necessary condition for a public IT project, whereas the budget, in-house capability and capacity are often treated as a precondition or a sufficient condition. On the other hand, for IT projects in the private sector, securing the budget, in-house capability and capacity (including technical skills) comprise important problems that should be considered in IT portfolio management. Based on this comparison of requirements in the government and private sectors, optimization and adjustments will be required to establish an optimum IT portfolio management for each application. This role would be played by the IT investment portfolios.

The appropriate selection of asset class is a goal of IT investment portfolios. It becomes the basis for choosing items to be questioned in the process of scoring to create a portfolio. Thus it is important to generate flexible and wide-ranging categories of asset classes. Satisfactory prospects and ease of operation are also essential factors. An example of IT portfolio management services by a private company is provided in the next section.

Please note that, at the time of writing, there is no English-language version of METI's IT portfolio model, and we have translated the terms and definitions used here into English from Japanese.

Vendor's role in IT portfolio management services

We mentioned in the previous section that the IT investment market is big. Thus, to satisfy this market, many companies worldwide provide consultation services on prioritizing IT investment projects and optimizing application assets. In fact, the market size of outsourced application services in Japan was 555.7 billion yen in the 2015 fiscal year (approaching the equivalent of £4 billion). IT portfolio management services accounted for 61.2 billion yen of that annual expenditure. IT solution vendors (hereafter called IT vendors) undertaking business applications development and related operational maintenance for companies in Japan were typical. Although the concepts of IT portfolio management are now well known, their application requires advanced skills in organizational strategy, IT investment consistency evaluation and IT asset analysis, as well as an extensive knowledge of future technological trends. All this requires the specific expertise offered by major IT vendors.

Clearly IT projects include the investment in hardware and infrastructure development. However, the IT vendors focus on applications development (including maintenance). They provide portfolio management services that consist of related projects. One aim of the IT vendors is to expand their applications services, because it is difficult to attract new clients for whom a competitor is already undertaking applications development and operational maintenance (owing to the lack of contact points and details of information system renewal). In addition, this type of service offers the opportunity to expand clients' businesses that struggle with IT investment optimization. By implementing this service for clients, the subsequent understanding of their information systems strategy and status of application assets leads to business expansion. Furthermore, IT vendors do not include infrastructure projects in their portfolio management services because customers tend to refuse budgetary advice (for which they engage other companies) and having fewer projects also reduces the workload.

From the aforementioned market size of outsourced applications services in Japan, it is evident that IT portfolio management services account for only an 11 per cent share. This is often because they are conducted as a spot service, large discounts are applied when used, and so on. However, such IT vendors undoubtedly contribute significantly to the transfer of IT portfolio management skills to user companies.

Example of an IT portfolio management service in practice

In this section we present an example of the IT portfolio management services provided by an IT vendor. This vendor offers the three types of services that we have shown in Figure 8.3. All three types of service depend on the progress of project, programme and portfolio (PPP) management and the IT service development process.

Stage 1: IT portfolio management service for planning

The outcome of IT investment is usually not to achieve a corporate strategic goal, unless projects are related to renovating infrastructure and ensuring higher information security (which are sometimes in response to an urgent corporate issue). Generally, management portfolios collect and select from many potential opportunities and components – programmes, projects, other portfolios and related work items.

Planning	Implementation for IT investment projects identified during mid-to-long-term business planning: adjusts the balance of investment between new projects and determines the prospects for IT resources over the mid-to-long term.
Reviewing and optimizing	Implementation for all IT investment projects during the drafting of the annual budget: examines and optimizes investment and allocation of resources in the current business environment.
Monitoring and reviewing	Periodic implementation for individual units of projects or during project audits: reviews the balance between projects to achieve optimization.

Figure 8.3 Three types of portfolio management service

Selection criteria for the evaluation of potential projects in terms of their strategic suitability are therefore very important for the portfolio manager in making agile and accurate decisions, and executing corporate management. These criteria should be based on reports covering topics such as the following:

- Organizational strategy;
- Organizational capability and capacity;
- Business benefit of the investment; and
- Stakeholder interests.

This service offers a solution to the problem of selection, as shown in the bubble diagram in Figure 8.4. The vertical and horizontal axes represent the 'business effect' and 'business risk', respectively, with the highest risk and lowest business effect set at the origin of the graph. As a result, the top right quadrant plots the set of projects for 'optimum

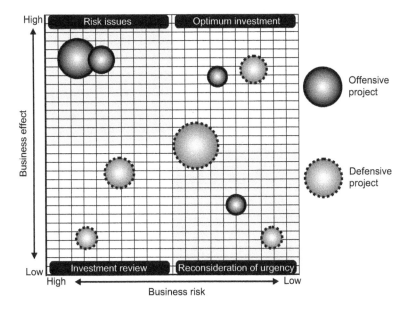

Figure 8.4 Example of an IT project portfolio in practice

investment' and, moving counterclockwise, other quadrants depict areas of 'risk issues,' 'investment review' and 'reconsideration of urgency' for each potential project.

Different-sized circles depict the amount of investment, whereas the different line patterns (solid and broken) illustrate the different investment views of corporate management and/or project type: offensive and defensive. Such categorization is equivalent to a procedure used within the IT investment portfolio (prioritization of IT investment depends on the assessment of each IT project). For example, a project that must be implemented by a deadline determined by legal reforms usually has a slight business effect; however, as no delays are permitted, business risks are increased. An analysis of this type of project would position it in the third quadrant as a defensive project (broken line circle). Although its implementation is essential, it still requires a review of the investment's validity.

The unique idea of this example is in moving the categories of project nature from strategic objectives for corporate IT investment to offensive project and defensive projects. The validity of this idea is supported by a market survey conducted by a user-side industrial association. The result of that survey categorized the IT investment items into offensive projects and defensive projects. For example, IT investment for improving channel management, global competition efforts, corporate innovation and customer experience focus are categorized as offensive projects. Improvements of in-house processes, communication management systems and information security, and supporting the agile corporate management are categorized as defensive projects. This provides part of the criteria for IT investment portfolios, with some flexibility in implementation for its users.

IT portfolio management service for reviewing and optimizing

This service is implemented when budgets are set for a new financial year. It follows a similar procedure to that for planning. The service includes all IT projects requiring a budget, whether new or ongoing, to achieve a complete analysis under the latest business environment, and to optimize budget and resource allocation. This service performs a similar function to the stage-gate control system (the process that results in go, hold or no-go decisions), which is systematically applied in the periodic examination of each project during its progress.

IT portfolio management service for monitoring and reviewing

This service analyses the status of ongoing individual projects when required. This might be periodically (such as quarterly) or at specific stages (a project audit, for example). Thus, all projects are analysed not simultaneously but according to the schedule of each business sector. Generally, the main purpose of a project audit is to assess the progress of an individual project towards achieving its objectives, which is the role of project management, not usually portfolio management.

However, it is useful to review the balance between this and other projects because conducting a portfolio analysis in parallel with the project audit will reveal up-to-date priorities for resource allocation. The practice of portfolio management consequently supports the activities of programme management, as well as greatly assisting decision-making at the portfolio management level.

Notes on terms and definitions

ISO 21504:2015 discusses IT portfolio management within the framework of PPP management. It defines the term 'portfolio component' as a 'project, program, portfolio, or other related work'. The boundary between portfolio and programme, and the concept of a programme in IT portfolio management, is not currently clear in IT investment and development management. Accordingly, a connotation of 'IT project portfolio management', a term often used in IT portfolio management, limits the meaning of 'portfolio component'. For most IT investment, especially in large-scale developments, portfolio management should be implemented to build a log of programme components. Apparently, 'programme portfolio management' is not a popular term in IT portfolio management; therefore we shall continue to use the term 'IT project management' until another expression becomes acceptable, such as 'IT programme management' or 'IT programme/project management', to avoid confusion caused by the different uses of terms in well-cited sources. [Editor's note: this argument is further complicated by the alternative spellings of program (US) and programme (UK).]

References and further reading

Accenture (2016), *Fintech's Golden Age*, available at: https://www.accenture.com/t20160724T
  221504Z__w__/us-en/_acnmedia/PDF-26/Accenture-FinTech-New-York-Competition-to-
  Collaboration.
Gibson, C.F. and Nolan, R.L. (1974), 'Managing the four stages of EDP growth', *Harvard Business Review*, 52(1), 76–88.
Jeffery, M. and Leliveld, I. (2004), 'Best practices in IT portfolio management', *MIT Sloan Management Review*, 45(3), 41–49.
International Organization for Standardization (ISO) (2015), ISO 21504 *Project, Programme and Portfolio Management – Guidance on portfolio management*, Geneva: ISO.
Office of Management and Budget (2017), 'Capital programming guide – supplement to office of management and budget circular A-11: planning, budgeting, and acquisition of capital assets', available on line at: https://www.whitehouse.gov/sites/whitehouse.gov/files/omb/ assets/a11 _current_year/a11_2017/capital_programming_guide.pdf.
United States General Accounting Office (2004), 'Information technology investment: a framework for assessing and improving process maturity', available at: www.gao.gov/new.items/ d04394g.pdf
Weill, P. and Broadbent, M. (1998), *Leveraging the New Infrastructure: How Market Leaders Capitalize on Information Technology*, Cambridge, MA: Harvard Business School Press.

Chapter 9

Portfolio management for research

Steve Butler

The significance of research and development (R&D) for the future competitiveness of a firm is well accepted, and this has placed an increasing interest in the process of generating innovations and creating new knowledge. Indeed, the very term R&D comprises not only activities in research, but also the development of new products – in other words, research provides the fundamental knowledge, whereas development tries to turn such knowledge into new and innovative products.

Introduction

In the 1950s and 1960s, R&D efforts adopted the basic procedures of project management. In the 1970s and 1980s efforts were becoming more effectively aligned with company's business objectives and strategies – that is, they became market-driven. In addition, from the 1990s a multitude of technological consortia, consisting of users (both competitors and allies) and suppliers, have increased demand-driven innovation, employing the maturing concepts of portfolio management to reduce investment risk. Most recently concept R&D has the following characteristics:

- The core of R&D activity is based on innovation;
- The innovation process is managed (for example, by project management techniques);
- Multiple projects, tied to a long-term strategy and combined into portfolios, are undertaken simultaneously to reduce associated risks (portfolio management);
- Partnerships of government, academia, industry and individual firms are becoming more common, and are often primary grant vehicles.

And so with the intensification of global competition, today's innovation strength is more than ever determined by a company's ability to differentiate from the competition by delivering value at pace, using available and often emerging technology. R&D is one of the means by which the stock of new knowledge can be increased in an organized way and, as with other portfolio components, the way to control and take full advantage of this activity is with effective portfolio management. However, R&D environments can present unique problems, and these are discussed and explained in this chapter.

The challenge of R&D

Innovation and R&D managers are constantly challenged to ensure that R&D budgets are allocated to the optimum set of R&D projects to reach their innovation targets in both the shorter and the longer term. This presents many challenges – not least of which is that, in R&D environments, traditional factors such as business opportunity and the feasibility of a project do not necessarily predict project success. In the case of R&D environments, some of the factors influencing the feasibility of a project are a competitive answer to a threat or opportunity, the amount of advantage over the competition and the sustainability of the innovation.

There are of course other factors. Typically, research outputs trigger new knowledge about materials, processes and ways of recombining these to produce new goods and services. Sometimes such benefits cannot be fully internalized within a business, industry or even a country. Indeed, R&D varies from other forms of investments in numerous respects, and one of the main distinguishing factors is that payoffs from R&D may not be restricted to the original investors, but can also accrue to other firms, competitors, suppliers, customers and society at large. This can make them extremely difficult to monitor and manage using the portfolio management processes outlined in this book.

Here are some examples of other challenges:

- Projects are effectively tools for delivering a business's strategy. Innovation projects in particular can question the existing business strategy and trigger change – sometimes fundamental change.
- Most project management frameworks assume that projects compete for the same limited resources and that all relevant resources are known and controlled. However, an increasing number of companies collaborate with external partners in research.
- Most frameworks assume that companies are completely aware of all internal and external factors affecting project portfolios. This is often not the case with innovation activities.
- It is often claimed that planning is typically effective only if projects are operating in a stable environment and no unforeseen deviations occur. In reality, portfolios are affected by multiple factors, which change or require adaptation of plans in order to achieve the goals and objectives. At times, the goals and objectives might change during the portfolio life cycle, consequently affecting all the initial planning and effort already undertaken. Accordingly, there is an element of dynamism and uncertainty in projects that directly affects the project portfolio and/or its environment – and this is particularly the case in R&D environments.

Another major challenge in an R&D environment is that of finance and budgets. Given that innovation projects typically span several years, determining the overall budget for the current year must be done in the context of the overall costs as programmes mature, which can be difficult.

Consistency in research is essential. It may be that little is accomplished in a year or two. Starting a new programme is easy; the challenge is to have enough planning and tenacity to ensure execution. It is insufficient to look at the initial costs; however, you must traditionally look at the expected cost over the life of a programme and reconcile this with the institution's financial strategy. This is further complicated by the unavoidable lag between the investment in innovation and the resulting cash flows from the new product or process. For example, in the pharmaceutical industry it can take up to 20 years to translate an inventive thought into significant financial return.

Bringing a new material to market usually means long specification cycles with a series of key customers downstream. The materials industry does not sell a new product until the customer sells a product, and in many cases raw materials are four to five steps or more removed from the ultimate end user. Each step in the supply chain has its own new product introduction procedures, and the timeline for these can range from a year for electronics products to more than a decade for aerospace products. Additional delays can occur if the design of the end product (such as an automobile or wind turbine blade) changes in a way that requires a redesign of the material properties.

Another factor that complicates budget decisions further is the fact that economic cycles are now 6–8 years in length at most, whereas the product development cycles for most materials range from 5 years to 20 years. There is increasing pressure on public companies to achieve quarterly results, but successful innovation requires a long-term vision. True leadership is required to sustain that vision and ensure successful innovation.

Portfolio management applied to R&D environments

One of the R&D management approaches that has gained prominence and acceptance in recent years encompasses the various product/project portfolio management techniques. The practice of portfolio management using the methods described in this handbook usually enables businesses to do the following:

- Maximize return on R&D investment;
- Maintain competitiveness;
- Properly and efficiently allocate scarce resources;
- Create a link between strategy and project selection;
- Achieve focus;
- Achieve balance between short- and long-term projects and high- and low-risk ones;
- Communicate priorities within an organization;
- Improve the objectivity of project selection.

The concept of business portfolios and strategic options was originally developed in finance and business. It is now a common practice. Recently, portfolio planning is also becoming standard practice in corporate R&D activities. The purpose of both business and R&D portfolio planning is typically to reach the optimum point between risk and reward, stability and growth. The definition of optimum, however, varies widely depending on the circumstances, and in particular on interdependency of risk, uncertainty, technological maturity, technological impact, competitiveness and other factors.

Multiple approaches to R&D portfolio management have been developed over the past few years. These include techniques such as financial methods, business strategy methods, bubble diagrams, scoring models and checklists. From the existing approaches, a combination of strategic and financial methods is most commonly used.

Portfolio management is a dynamic decision process through which a list of active projects is constantly updated and revised. In that process new projects are evaluated, selected and prioritized, existing projects may be accelerated, terminated or de-prioritized, and resources are allocated and re-allocated to the active projects. The portfolio decision process is characterized by uncertain and changing information, dynamic opportunities, multiple goals and strategic considerations, and interdependence among projects.

R&D projects are considered analogous to risky assets with some expected returns. The risk and return inherent in R&D projects makes the role of R&D portfolio manager more challenging in terms of prioritizing projects to optimize the return of the research portfolio, considering all the risks involved in those projects. The similarity between the portfolio of R&D projects and the portfolio of financial securities, in terms of balancing the risk and return, creates an opportunity to apply the rich resources available in financial portfolio theory.

Portfolio management provides a broad context for understanding the interactions of systematic risk and reward. It has profoundly shaped the way in which institutional portfolios are managed, and has motivated the use of passive investment management techniques.

Risk in R&D

Good R&D management requires that the innovation pipeline produces a constant and predictable profit flow, so that the company will continue to excel, particularly during turbulent economic times. Managing the balance between long- and short-term projects in the pipeline is fundamental to mitigating the risk associated with R&D. When done correctly, the result is an optimal mix of long- and short-term programmes that should provide the maximum return.

When the goal is innovation, invention and execution are exceptionally time sensitive. Success requires delivering game-changing, disruptive technologies, products and processes to customers in such a way as to improve their quality of life measurably. Customers will then spend their money on your products or processes, and the result is growth for the company. All risks associated with R&D management come about from trying to achieve that goal.

Industrial R&D management has the following three key elements:

1. Determining how much money you will spend, understanding that an appropriate R&D budget that effectively manages risk will be aligned with the goals of the supporting organization.
2. Determining which projects your team will take on. This requires prioritization using a robust method and a focus on the most current technologies while managing fads.
3. Managing these projects so that they result in execution. This includes the allocation of funds and resources, definition of metrics and the management of people.

Prioritization, risk management, resource allocation and people management are fundamental to any research effort. R&D leaders who understand how to accomplish this will promote innovation, whether they are in industry, universities or government laboratories.

Risks in R&D can come from several sources, which could be technical, financial, market related and administrative. The level of these risk components typically varies from project to project. Although in finance risk quantification is based on performance of stocks or other financial instruments, in R&D risk assessment is much more difficult to quantify.

The need for management tools

Management tools are playing an increasing important role in the current practice of research and development. Today's project management tools were initially introduced in the 1950s and 1960s to increase the effectiveness of R&D efforts. Effective use of such tools usually has a strong impact on meeting project schedule and budget objectives. Their impact on the project success in terms of meeting either functional or technical specifications is much less predictable, however.

The growing need for alignment of R&D with business objectives, market-driven strategies and investment risk reduction are the drivers for employing portfolio management techniques. Most recently, the need for tools to manage the knowledge creation and innovation on demand has come to the fore. The recent proliferation of multidisciplinary and team-based efforts, which involve big and diverse groups of people working with big budgets, calls for increased efficiency of R&D activities. However, care should be taken to ensure balance between innovation and return, and this is most easily done using a conceptual framework governing the R&D environment.

The advantage of a conceptual framework

R&D has increasingly contributed to business strategy, project portfolio management, innovation and dynamic capabilities, ensuring sustainable competitive advantage. Through new business models, companies create and deliver value for customers, and then convert payments received to profits. The approaches that help organizations efficiently manage their research and development investment project portfolio in uncertain business environments require some context for what is considered to be 'efficient'. This requires examining the results of the portfolio management or the portfolio performance in terms of value maximization, business strategy alignment and portfolio balance.

As already stated, evaluating the performance of a portfolio in an R&D environment can be problematic. Long-term R&D outcomes need to be included in the performance evaluation of the portfolio on a continuing basis through continuous management and monitoring. Various frameworks and methods are adopted, but they mainly focus on evaluating short-term R&D outputs despite the fact that there is a time lag between R&D inputs and outputs. Long-term R&D outcomes can easily be neglected, and a conceptual framework can be the answer.

A conceptual framework is a technique that:

1. Structures experiences; and
2. Provides coherent ways of discerning about relationships.

Both of these are necessary in the creation of new knowledge. Conceptual frameworks are potentially valuable for problem-solving in companies and environments that are multifaceted and complex. They are also necessary in the formation of a world view.

Everyone has a different world view. We all have different constructs of reality, our perceptions, connotations, associations, sensations and languages. Our interpretation of our world view is based on our unique perceptual combination of internal communication (attitude, personality and so forth). Also, the sharing of explicit and tacit knowledge is an important part of the creative process and the generation of creative and innovative ideas, thereby jumping from one conceptual space to the other and thus expanding our world view. Owing to rapid changes in R&D projects in the industrial markets (emerging technologies, changing customer needs, emerging and shrinking markets, and accelerating competition), deploying and understanding dynamic capabilities are key portfolio managerial concerns.

An example of a conceptual framework might consist of the following six dynamic capabilities:

- *Sensing*: processes to sense, filter, shape and interpret events and uncertainty;
- *Seizing*: opportunities seized, selection rules, business model used and decision-making protocols;
- *Transforming and reconfiguring*: characterization of changes to project portfolios; preserving competiveness by combining, enhancing, protecting and, where needed, reconfiguring the business's tangible and intangible assets;
- *Absorbing*: external knowledge is taken in;
- *Innovative*: the business's innovativeness to products is linked to market opportunities;
- *Adaptive*: resources and capabilities are aligned.

The more efficient an organization is in its project portfolio management of R&D projects, the more efficient will its ability be to generate beneficial returns and minimize risk. A conceptual framework is also characterized by the following factors:

- *The business environment*: the market, the economy, technology, political influence, industry type, the rivalry, legal aspects and how dynamic the environment is;
- *The business strategy*: it is assumed that the strategy for organization, project portfolio and project is already decided;
- *Governance*: which refers to decision structures at corporate, portfolio and project level. Governance and structure cover how projects are structured, including functional organization and alliances with external firms, especially where collaboration is at play;
- *Project portfolio management*: looks at the characteristics of the portfolio, including the history and dependencies between projects as well as reviews. It also refers to the process of selecting and evaluating possible new projects, introducing those that are suitable into the portfolio and removing others;
- *Efficiency and business return on investment*: estimating the degree to which the portfolio fulfils its objectives; strategic alignment/fit, balance across projects, and value maximization and the return on investment.

Monitoring the performance of an R&D portfolio

The concept of R&D performance includes not only research outputs, but also direct and indirect social and economic effects, such as converting these outputs into businesses, inputting them to other research projects and tasks, and technology transfer. This definition also includes records, information on outcomes, information on technologies and statistics on R&D performance. Meanwhile, performance monitoring itself includes the activities designed to conduct a long-term evaluation of outputs, and their technological, economic and social utility – thus, to study, arrange, convert into statistics and analyse the value of R&D in an effort to manage R&D performance. So, two aspects have to be considered in this concept of performance monitoring and evaluation. Likewise, the concept involves monitoring and management as to how and who should investigate, monitor and analyse the utility produced by research (another important consideration).

Nowadays, successful R&D depends not only on the development of technologically superior products, but also on the improvement of management processes and procedures that might turn into the true new core dynamic capabilities of R&D-intensive companies. It is therefore essential to foster the capability of learning from every single R&D project. One way of encouraging such learning in R&D is to conduct post-project reviews of aborted R&D projects. If that knowledge is lost, future projects can suffer from repetition of past mistakes (lessons learned). It is also argued that post-project reviews can have a positive impact on the learning capacity of R&D units, as such reviews have the potential to contribute to the development and continuous improvement of R&D management processes

R&D evaluation metrics

A proper system of metrics is crucial to ensuring that an R&D strategy is producing the desired results. Ultimately, the only real measure of innovation is company earnings. However, there are two challenges to relying solely on earnings. First, many things affect earnings, such as price, volume and cost of the existing product. Second, the time lag between investment and earning can be as long as a decade and that can be problematic. For what is essentially a creative process, developing a useful set of metrics is particularly important when measuring innovation, partly because the goal is to bring focus and discipline. R&D leaders have to remember that existing metrics developed for R&D and new product development do not necessarily offer a complete view of a company's overall innovation capability or health. Some companies that excelled based on historical R&D metrics no longer exist.

University researchers have also embraced the market driven approach to R&D. In 1986, it was estimated that 3.3 per cent of all academic scientists consulted for industry or owned their own business; this has increased by a factor of more than 10 since then (depending on the specialism). These academic entrepreneurs have an increasingly important role in the technology transfer between universities and industry.

In the current state of the industry, it is not obvious that standard metrics actually measure the qualities associated with R&D success. For instance, the quantity of R&D spending as a percentage of sales is a measure only of how much money is being spent. Although this does take into account whether or not the R&D budget is in line with the company's profits, it does not consider whether or not R&D efforts are being translated into sales. The ratio of new product sales to R&D is a better measure of research productivity and provides a way to assess research effectiveness. Therefore, depending on the environment, it is clear that great care must be taken to ensure that the success and sustainability of innovation are measured with appropriate metrics.

People in R&D

People are the most essential element of the innovation process. No innovation process can overcome a lack of talent. Creative, organized and intelligent people are often successful in spite of the bureaucracy that the innovation process has the potential to create. Thus, any discussion of innovation execution must begin and end with people.

In many ways, an R&D team is analogous to a sports team. Invariably the team with the best talent (and the best coach) wins more often than the teams with marginal players. Every leader's first and foremost responsibility is to recruit and develop world-class people. R&D leadership is no exception, whether it be industrial or academic. Few would debate that it is not the quality of the facilities but the quality of the faculty that defines world-class research. Most faculties would agree that the quality of their graduate students and postdoctoral fellows has a profound effect on the amount and quality of research that they can produce. Effective execution demands regular and detailed assessment of the personnel in an organization. People must be measured against goals; those who excel must be appropriately rewarded, whereas those who miss the mark need appropriate, constructive coaching. These organizational realities apply equally to industrial and academic institutions.

Chapter 10

Portfolio management for product development

Manja Greimeier

This chapter describes the challenges for the portfolio management of product development in the automotive industry.

Introduction

Portfolio management in the automotive industry is changing dramatically. There are four disruptive technology-driven trends:

1. Diverse mobility;
2. Autonomous driving;
3. Electrification;
4. Connectivity.

The tremendous increase in the complexity of product development linked to these trends makes it even more important to have the competence to make the right choices as a company. Questions to be asked include the following:

- Which new projects should we invest in to attract new customers?
- Which existing projects have to be staffed and invested in today to deliver what has already been ordered?
- Which projects need to be phased out of the portfolio to free up resources?
- Which projects need to be restarted to ensure that the product remains profitable?
- What is a good mix of new, existing and phased-out projects to ensure continuous profitable growth?
- How can my organization stay aligned and focused in a complex stakeholder network to give confidence to my employees, customers and partners, and not end up in firefighting mode, overload and with the company drifting into a different direction?

Existing projects that get out of control often have a lack of clarity on project targets, scope, roles and responsibilities from the very beginning. Critical issues endanger project delivery and can even delay production start-up date. Too many resources from the limited pool are taken from other projects in the portfolio. We face very limited choices for new projects when launching innovations and we need to grow and stay competitive. Existing projects and projects being phased out are negatively impacted.

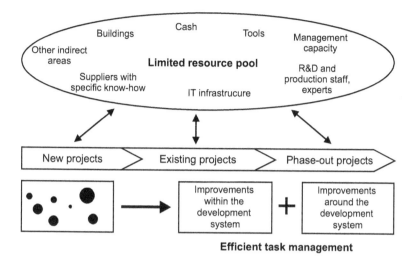

Figure 10.1 Overview of portfolio management in product development

So how do we stay in balance and manage our project portfolio in product development in a complex and changing world? Figure 10.1 illustrates this portfolio environment. Efficient Task Management (ETM) is a possible methodology that is described later in this chapter.

Aligning new projects with company strategy

What does our future portfolio look like? We must plan, make choices and adapt. All projects access the same limited resource pool and are therefore in competition with each other. In the automotive sector product development projects can be clustered into the following categories:

- Research;
- Pre-development;
- Serial development;
- Product application projects;
- Projects restarted to improve product quality or margin.

All projects and corresponding products are summarized in a product road map. The road map is presented to the customers to align with the product strategies and discuss future market trends and end-customer needs. Each year the product roadmap is planned and adjusted for a midterm horizon of 3–5 years. Based on this product roadmap, new projects are forecast for the year and resource needs are planned and budgeted for.

Usually customer vehicle planning is the starting point for the sales planning to identify which vehicles might use the new products, analyse the competitor's situation and identify the target price to calculate future projected sales. Based on the sales planning and a target margin for the financial year, the affordable resources can be derived to calculate the budget. This calculated budget is the basis for the project portfolio planning and its iterative adjustments for the financial year. However, this has to be adapted, based on market evolution during the year. The calculated budget can be regarded as the limited resource pool.

The decision about whether or not a new project should be started not only depends on resource limitations but is also based on a risks and opportunities rating for the project. There are various things and risk areas to consider, such as finance, resources and competence, milestones and the supplier portfolio, make or buy strategy and the technical feasibility of being able to manufacture the product. These risk areas are rated (for example, from 1 to 3) and are summed up to an overall risk rating number for the new project. In the same way the opportunities such as future growth potential, innovation to gain competitive advantage or fit into company strategy are each rated accordingly, and summed up to an overall opportunity rating number. A decision matrix supports the decision for a company proceeding with the new project, or indicates whether further evaluation is needed. It can also happen that a project with low risk and low opportunity is linked to another customer project portfolio, so the new project will be started owing to customer requirements. Figure 10.2 shows the format of risk and opportunities decision matrix.

The overall portfolio balance is important, which is why it is helpful to visualize how many planned projects are already (for example) high risk – which would clearly influence the decision to start another new high-risk project. Awareness of the organization is important to influence the project portfolio actively, adjust the planning, mitigate risks, and ensure that sufficient resources are taken on board and that competence gaps are understood to avoid bad surprises during the year.

The decision matrix is also helpful as a communication tool for visualizing and informing all involved departments of the current and future project portfolio. During the decision-making process for a new project the functions of sales, research and development (R&D), project management and general management should be involved. Indicators can be defined upfront to assess the financial health of the new project and incorporate the financial view. Regular project portfolio reviews are essential for adapting to changes and supporting the project teams to achieve the company goals.

The project type plays an important role for any new project decision. Existing serial development projects and products already launched determine the financial basis for affording new projects. Therefore, it is essential that the planned budget and

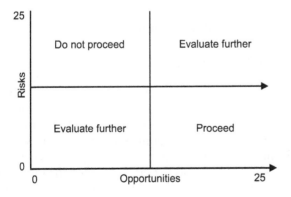

Figure 10.2 A risks and opportunities decision matrix

product margin stay in line with the target and provide the planned project profitability. All new projects compete with a limited resource pool and budget, which means that the following limitations must be taken into account:

- Number of employees available;
- Available competence within the company;
- Investment;
- Tools; and
- An organization that can support the project portfolio successfully.

So if, for example, the existing projects use all the resources and a new project would require more, this would impact on the possibility of financing and any new project.

Managing projects in the current portfolio

All existing projects of the project portfolio need to be managed and the status has to be monitored regularly. There is often more focus on serial development and application projects than on research and pre-development projects, because the milestones cannot be compromised and each deviation can have a potential negative impact for the customer. All projects compete with the same pool of resources and therefore all project types need basic processes, project governance and reporting.

For any new project decision, the risk rating assesses the criticality of the project, for which we use the RAG indicator system (red, amber or green). This rating allows us to prioritize projects and decide actions. It often provides more transparency within the wider organization.

Each project manager should be empowered to alert the organization urgently, if there is a critical milestone that cannot be met or a resource shortage that prevents one or more critical work packages being completed. A flat hierarchical organization helps access and communication across the management team. Empowered project teams solve problems more quickly and move on. Apart from a direct communication in case of issues, each project runs through a project steering committee which meets on a regular basis and uses a comprehensive project reporting method to review critical issues, discuss customer feedback and take decisions.

All project functions such as sales, purchasing, industrial engineering, R&D, quality and finance should be involved. The report for the project should at least provide an overview of the next milestones, actual costs, delivery performance and quality status, as well as listing any critical issues and providing recommendations for decisions and anything else needed to support the project team. This project report is aligned with the portfolio reporting of the company and also used the RAG indicator method to show the red, amber or green status within the project landscape.

The project portfolio review is also carried out on a regular basis. Its purpose is to ensure that the project portfolio is in line with the strategy of the company and the company targets. The project director presents these portfolio reports to the general management team, based on portfolio key performance indicators (KPIs) such as each project's profit over lifetime, risk rating and strategic importance. Decisions to start and end new projects, arbitrate resources and review the quoted status of each new potential project are normally part of the agenda.

There are many challenges to keeping the project portfolio under control. The first main difficulty is being able to measure the current status of the project clearly and correctly, especially for large-scale projects. The scale can be classified by the number of stakeholders, local or global scope, and product and process complexity, as well as the innovation level of the product. Product lifecycles have shortened drastically which provides additional challenges for keeping all levels and locations informed, aligned and decisive when changes occur. Having the right speed to react to disturbances and changes becomes a competitive advantage.

If projects are not managed properly, too many projects will become red. This would overwhelm the organization on all levels. Then managing the project portfolio and carrying out the company strategy become more difficult. The trust in the customer–supplier relationship will be called into question and might impact future business opportunities (new projects).

Phasing out projects

This section describes the phasing out of projects (transferring them from their launch phase to the maintenance phase) and explains how to release projects from the portfolio and ensure that the products remain profitable over their lifecycles. The mantra here is 'Keep on track, be realistic and prepared for continuous change'.

Several different challenges have to be considered when phasing out a project. It is necessary to ensure the following:

- The product remains profitable over its lifetime and opportunities are seen and implemented to improve the product margin;
- Serial product components are monitored and potential discontinued components get replaced;
- Change requests from customers are implemented properly;
- The production volume is monitored and all suppliers can support volume changes sufficiently to ensure delivery and robust quality of the product over its lifetime.

The list of possible changes is long and all these typical scenarios have to be managed. Some organizations hand over serial development projects to a project maintenance team or to the functional organization of the production plants. This depends on the innovation level and complexity of the product and its production processes, and is also linked to customer needs. In both cases a handover session must be organized to transfer the project documentation and history, lessons learned, open issues and a productivity action list for improving the product margin.

The customer is involved in the hand-over process because the stakeholders on the customer side can also change. Depending on the organization and the nature of the product, there is normally a period of three to six months after the start of production before the handover starts. This ensures that the project team can monitor the quality and reliability of the product until a representative high volume of production is reached.

Continued accountability of the project team during the start-up phase has big advantages because it keeps the competence and routine of the team in place to resolve any disturbance during the launch phase very quickly. After that the project team can be released from the project. Besides formally handing over all project documentation, it is also important to appreciate that the project team members will be impacted by ending the project. Often a big challenge comes to an end with high workload, work under pressure and focus on the final goal to launch the product for the customer. This event has to be acknowledged by the management team to show their appreciation and celebrate the successful launch with the team. A special focus on re-integrating the project team members into new projects should be planned in advance and managed proactively. Also, individual career aspirations have to be supported.

The organization is often much more focused on managing existing projects and winning new business than planning a proper project phase out of the project from the portfolio. This can mean that opportunities such as improving the margin of the product are missed, and that the danger of losing skilled and experienced employees when the project ends is not managed. Another aspect to consider is that very short-term projects are liable to be restarted to manage change requests from the customer or to carry out internal changes: these restarts could be delayed because resources are not available owing to lack of planning, visibility and priority.

The project portfolio review has to provide clear transparency on the planned phased-out of projects, so that the organization is able to learn lessons from completed projects. Inefficiencies should be identified, addressed and improved for new projects, and a continuous monitoring of customer and employee satisfaction after project end has to be put in place.

Managing the project portfolio by efficient task management

The keywords in this section are *clarity, transparency* and *consequence*. The objectives are to reduce the number of escalated issues and ensure that problems are resolved on the right level in large-scale complex projects. So, how do we keep the project portfolio under control?

Projects can get out of control if their scope, targets and work packages are not clearly defined and there is misalignment with the customer. It is more and more difficult to have this essential clarity in projects, because of the following:

- There is a change from a local to global scope;
- Products and processes are more complex for suppliers and their customers;
- There is stronger competition in global markets;
- Roles and responsibilities within growing organizations can become unclear for the project teams and the functional departments, and thus more issues are escalated and passed on to higher levels.

All this results in red projects and an organization in firefighting mode. Some of these difficulties and concerns are shown from different points of view in Figure 10.3.

Sufficient project execution with on-time transparency and increased problem-solving abilities will allow a higher adaptability to these new challenges. The risk is that, if companies are not able to execute projects efficiently and satisfy their customers, too many projects might have to be managed with high priority within the project portfolio, the organization becomes overloaded and new business opportunities are missed.

These projects are highly urgent and important, and burden all levels of the organization and slow down the resolution of issues. Projects can no longer be sequenced

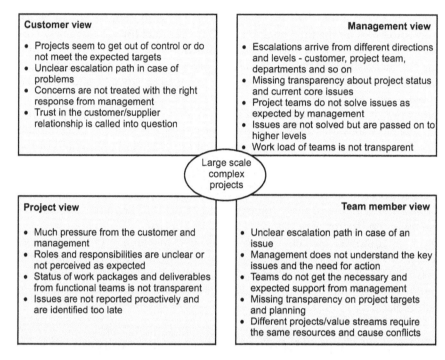

Customer view

- Projects seem to get out of control or do not meet the expected targets
- Unclear escalation path in case of problems
- Concerns are not treated with the right response from management
- Trust in the customer/supplier relationship is called into question

Management view

- Escalations arrive from different directions and levels - customer, project team, departments and so on
- Missing transparency about project status and current core issues
- Project teams do not solve issues as expected by management
- Issues are not solved but are passed on to higher levels
- Work load of teams is not transparent

Large scale complex projects

Project view

- Much pressure from the customer and management
- Roles and responsibilities are unclear or not perceived as expected
- Status of work packages and deliverables from functional teams is not transparent
- Issues are not reported proactively and are identified too late

Team member view

- Unclear escalation path in case of an issue
- Management does not understand the key issues and the need for action
- Teams do not get the necessary and expected support from management
- Missing transparency on project targets and planning
- Different projects/value streams require the same resources and cause conflicts

Figure 10.3 Difficulties and concerns from different points of view

and the organization is getting out of control. How can we achieve project execution for single large-scale complex projects and allow sufficient portfolio management at the same time?

ETM is a methodology that follows a simple base principle to ensure a short cycle for issue management and problem-solving (Staufen, 2017). Three essential features are as follows:

1. Clarity on targets, scope and timing within the project at any level;
2. Transparency on project status and current issues in relation to targets, scope and so forth;
3. Consequence – solve issues, make decisions and act in order to achieve targets.

The basis of ETM is regular communication in the organization and proper visualization at all levels. Communication follows a clearly defined cascade within the project organization and is aligned to the communication cascade of the functional organization (Figure 10.4).

ETM requires not only sufficient communication and visualization but also sufficient leadership skills. For example, the software project manager manages a team of software engineers and reports to the system engineering leader. The software project manager needs to learn the methodology of how to visualize targets, scope and timing, ensure regular communication, and lead the software team to solve issues autonomously.

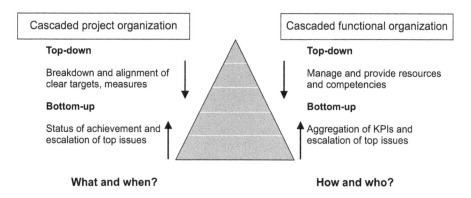

Figure 10.4 Structured regular communication cascade aligns project and functional teams

This is supported by an information board using either a paper-based version on a white board or a virtual digital whiteboard in a later step.

The software team meets at a defined time slot during the day and briefly discusses top issues, checks if planned tasks can be carried out or if there are any deviations from the plan. The team also reviews whether or not all team members are fully occupied or if anyone has free capacity to support others. If there is, for example, a capacity or competence issue, the software team is asked to solve the issue within the team first. Only critical issues that cannot be resolved get escalated.

Any action will clearly depend on the nature of the problem. For example, if the software project manager needs more resources, this issue will be escalated to the system engineering leader. The system engineering leader will support the software project manager to align with the hardware team and set the right priorities so as not to endanger the next delivery. Alignment within the functional and project organization ensures early warning for potential delays of critical issues. Rigorous follow-up on a daily basis at all levels supports a flow of information as well as ensuring an execution sequence that reduces escalations and focuses only on urgent and important matters. Empowerment of the sub-teams and their leaders is essential.

So how is efficient task management implemented in an organization? First the organization for the single project has to be clearly defined and visualized within the team:

- Who is responsible for what?
- Who is my next internal customer to deliver to?
- How do we align the project planning over all work packages?

So ETM requires an improvement within the development system, which means the following:

- Targets, tasks and status have to be visualized for the different subproject teams;
- Project and functional cascades need to be clear;
- Project planning needs to be aligned;
- Regular communication needs to be put in place, based on the defined cascades.

ETM also requires analysis and leadership improvement in the organization for each project team leader and functional leader. The ETM process (clarity, transparency and consequence) needs to be reflected and adapted after each meeting. Employees need full empowerment from the management teams and to foster continuous improvement with the new methodology. Structured problem-solving techniques are essential for resolving issues and team moderation. In the start phase of implementation, ETM coaching is necessary and helpful, especially to improve the leadership skills alongside learning the methodology based on the information board.

As soon as the single project is transparent and the status can be visualized clearly, consolidation over the complete project portfolio must be organized. When the functional departments and project teams are all trained and coached for ETM, the next step is to use a consolidated view over all projects. This allows real arbitration between projects and simplifies decision-making because all people at all levels are constantly aligned.

ETM enables the flow of information and decision-making process to have the complete organization aligned and focused on the same issues and sharing the same priorities and goals. Having fewer escalations leads to the higher satisfaction of project teams and reduces pressure on the functional departments and management.

Applying the ETM methodology requires extreme discipline, daily meetings and improved leadership behaviour on all levels. The project portfolio can be actively managed as soon as large-scale complex projects are executed efficiently so that the company strategy can be implemented.

References and further reading

Cooper, R.G., Edgett, S.J. and Kleinschmidt, E.J. (2001), *Portfolio Management for New Products*, 2nd edn, New York: Basic Books.

Staufen AG (2017), Virtuelles Shopfloor Management: Proaktive Projektsteuerung durch getaktetes Aufgabenmanagement im Entwicklungs- und Anlaufprozess, *12. Fachkonferenz Ramp-up – Anlaufmanagement in der Fahrzeug-Produktion, Neckarsulm*, 3/4 May 2017. ETM named 'getaktetes Aufgabenmanagement'.

Chapter 11

Portfolio management for strategic change

Fiona Spencer

This chapter describes the role of portfolio management in delivering strategic change, and identifies five key factors playing a key role in doing so, drawing on experience of driving and supporting transformation within a major UK government department, the Home Office.

The role of portfolio management in delivering strategic change

In today's world, change is an inherent part of organizational life – and, if anything, becoming more so: more critical to organizational strategy, more ambitious, more complex and more agile. The challenge for many organizations is, however, how to achieve *strategic* change – change guided by an overarching strategic purpose, designed to change the way in which the organization operates for the longer term – rather than just a succession of seemingly disconnected tactical initiatives. Increasingly, the importance of portfolio management in helping organizations to deliver strategic change is being recognized, particularly where this involves significant scale and complexity over time. Portfolio management supports an adaptive, dynamic approach to change, enabling the organization to manage evolving requirements while maintaining the focus on broader strategic goals for transforming the organization.

In a world where change is often seen as the only constant, all organizations face the challenge of how to adapt to keep pace and stay relevant. Success – sometimes just survival – depends on how effectively organizations adapt. The challenge for many is, however, how to deliver not just a succession of tactical changes, but also *strategic* change: change guided by an overarching strategic purpose, designed to change the way in which the organization operates over the longer term.

Through various theories of strategic change management, one thing is clear: strategic change does not just happen. It has to be managed purposefully. Project-based approaches have long been recognized as a way of managing strategic change. 'Change, and the need to manage change through projects, is now an endemic part of business life; it is the new normal' (Turner, 2014, p. 1).

Mostly, however, strategic change in organizations (particularly at the enterprise level) cannot usually be achieved through a single project or programme. Strategic change is likely to be complex, involving multiple projects of different kinds over successive periods. Sometimes these are sufficiently closely coupled to be manageable as a single transformation programme. Often, however, they are not – which is where portfolio management comes into its own.

Portfolio management provides a framework for managing multiple change initiatives over time. It enables the organization to select and prioritize, direct and manage a large number of programmes and projects in a coordinated way, designed and targeted to meet broader strategic goals for transforming the organization.

Unlike programmes and projects (which are structured to deliver specific outputs) portfolios are open systems that can readily adapt and evolve. As such, portfolio management can support an adaptive, dynamic approach to change management over time – while none the less staying focused on overall strategic goals. It is, therefore, particularly useful as an approach to managing adaptive transformational change, usually characterized by multiple, complex, disaggregated change initiatives, which also evolve over time (Heifetz et al., 2009).

All portfolio management is designed to facilitate the achievement of strategic objectives (Jenner, 2011). However, the significance of its role in driving and supporting strategic change within an organization, and the key considerations in doing so successfully, are less well understood. The next section therefore looks at some of these factors in more detail, drawing on recent experience within a UK government department, the Home Office.

How portfolio management is helping to deliver strategic change within the Home Office

The Home Office has an ambitious strategic agenda over recent parliaments, designed to support continued delivery of the department's mission (to keep the country secure and its citizens safe) and its strategic objectives (to prevent terrorism, cut crime, control migration, protect vulnerable people, manage crises effectively and promote growth).

The department needs to make sure that the services it delivers to and for the public are able to keep pace in a changing world – a world in which expectations continue to grow while the pressure on budgets becomes ever greater. Even without the need to become more efficient, new threats and opportunities, including those presented by exiting the European Union (EU), make it necessary to change ways of working and modernize technology and service delivery.

The Home Office has a phased plan for transformation, designed to achieve excellence through transforming systems and services across its areas of responsibility, and then maintaining this through continuous adaptation and improvement.

This is not a simple task. Different agencies within the overall umbrella of the organization operate in very different contexts, and face different threats and opportunities. There are multiple different pressures for change – and not all of these changes can be afforded, or at least not at once. Initiatives impact on different parts of the organization at different times. Moreover, the nature of government, and the political process, mean that demands are not always readily predictable and can change at short notice (with the calling of an election, for example, or the outcome of a referendum).

How, then, can organizations like government departments drive strategic change in an inherently complex and changeable environment? There is no magic formula. However, experience in recent years suggests that taking a portfolio-based approach to strategic change can help significantly, and that there are some key factors (considered below), which are particularly important in doing so successfully.

Five fundamental factors for delivering strategic change through portfolio management

Factor 1: strategic vision and agreed long-term goals

All portfolios need a purpose. For a portfolio to drive strategic change, however, it needs a clear *strategic vision* for how the organization plans to change and what outcomes are needed by when. There needs to be an agreed view of strategic priorities and of the overall design for change, set out, for example, in a target-operating model, blueprint or as an agreed set of design principles. These provide the overarching framework within which the portfolio will operate.

The Home Office's plans for transformation, agreed in the UK government's spending review in 2015, were designed to protect and modernize core strategic capabilities while driving down costs, in line with reducing government expenditure. The overall vision for the future organization and strategic goals for transformation were focused around four key themes:

1. Demand;
2. Digital;
3. Data; and
4. People.

These four themes were developed into strategic design principles for the future organization, as follows:

- Early intervention;
- Use of digital technology;
- Data-based decision-making;
- Developing people;
- Collaborative working; and
- Continuing adaptation on the basis of evaluation.

From these strategic goals and design principles, an overall strategy for investment was agreed, with three priorities: to protect and modernize critical national infrastructure; to drive for savings; and to help keep the country safe in a changing world.

The initial intent was simply to ensure a coherent investment strategy to underpin the Home Office's bids for funding during the 2015 spending review, and then for subsequent reshaping of the portfolio following the outcome. In practice, however, having a clearly articulated investment strategy, with a clear line of sight through to business design principles and strategic objectives, has proved equally valuable in guiding the continuing evolution of the portfolio.

Despite the natural inclination of many portfolio managers, this does not have to be a detailed view. Most organizations find it difficult to envisage future strategic outcomes several years hence, other than at very high level, and the portfolio director may as well recognize that from the outset. In fact, however, experience suggests that keeping it high level may be better, particularly where outcomes are far off and subject to change. The more detail there is, the greater the risk of the portfolio becoming fixed and drawn down into the tactical, losing the guiding focus on strategic outcomes that need to drive it instead. The detail may change: what matters is the overall strategy.

However, ensuring strategic alignment also needs to be a continuing task. In any complex portfolio, new developments arise and changes happen. An overarching vision and principles are not enough: checks, balances and levers are needed. Building these into governance, for example in testing strategic alignment at project or programme initiation, at strategic outline business case approval and other key investment gateways, is important. So too, we found, is a strong business design authority charged with ensuring alignment to the overall design for strategic change – and with the authority to intervene where plans threaten to diverge.

In summary, a sustained focus on strategic outcomes and high-level business design is critical for any portfolio intended to deliver strategic change. This is, moreover, not just about ensuring that the portfolio is designed to deliver the changes needed – but also that it does so on a continuing basis. Managing a strategic portfolio is an active business.

Factor 2: structuring the portfolio for strategic change

No portfolio is the same, and rightly so. To be an effective agent for the delivery of strategic change, the portfolio needs to be designed and structured to drive the kind of changes needed. There needs to be a clear understanding of what the portfolio is for and of its relationship, both with the programmes and projects within it, and with the wider operating environment.

Even more importantly, the portfolio, its structure and management, should be shaped by the needs of the organization, in terms of not just *what* it is designed to deliver, but also *how* it is designed to do so (the organization's ambition and risk appetite, the scope and timescale over which change needs to be delivered, the balance between control and flexibility, the organization of the delivery landscape and the organization's culture, or cultures). In short, the portfolio needs to be shaped to reflect the organization's overall strategy for change in order to deliver it.

What does this mean in practical terms? As an example, the Home Office as an organization has responsibilities across three major areas of business, or systems: its border, immigration and citizenship functions; law enforcement (including overall responsibility for policing and fire services, which operate at arms' length); and national security. Each of these areas operates very differently. Although core design principles are common across them, the nature of the changes involved and the way these are delivered differ significantly. Moreover, a core aim of transformation was to strengthen local ownership of individual systems while also building shared capabilities and mutual collaboration across them. The portfolio was therefore structured to recognize and provide space for these differences, with each system owning its own portfolio, but designated strategic capabilities protected on a cross-cutting basis as corporate priorities.

The portfolio (and the programmes and projects within it) were also structured as far as possible along modular lines: a deliberate decision to move away from old-style 'waterfall' programmes towards agile delivery where possible, given the rapid pace of change in the operating environment and the predominant focus on digital and data in the portfolio. This modularity provided flexibility to respond to changes in strategic priorities, enabling different elements of delivery to be reprioritized and rescheduled in response to external changes and major events (such as the decision to leave the EU) while managing impact on other parts of the portfolio.

Alongside modularity, proportionality is also a key principle. Many strategic change portfolios will include a mix of larger and smaller programmes and projects, and the Home Office portfolio is no exception. Visibility and control of the overall portfolio are key, but the disciplines and controls required around a major infrastructure programme are very different from those required for small agile projects, or an operational business transformation programme built on continuous improvement principles.

Our response was to design an approach based on tiered controls, aligned with the different strategic priority levels of the portfolio described earlier. Budgets and accountability for delivery were also aligned, assigned through portfolio directors at system level and senior responsible owners (SROs) for individual programmes and projects. The aim was to push ownership and accountability for delivery out from the centre to other parts of the portfolio – in line with wider transformation strategy – while maintaining an overall view and control of programmes delivering critical strategic capabilities. It also helped ensure that small and medium projects can compete fairly for resources and do not just 'get lost in the noise' (Turner, 2014, p. 73).

In summary, the way in which the portfolio is structured matters, and can be a core part of driving the strategic changes envisaged. Portfolio management, of course, lends itself particularly well to this, enabling different areas of activity and different levels of priority to be protected and managed proportionately, with an overall view of the critical dependencies between different elements. This is key in managing complex transformation, where there may be multiple different contributors at different levels involved in delivering strategic organizational change.

Factor 3: the ability to prioritize – and reprioritize

In most organizations, strategic change does not happen overnight. It usually needs sustained effort over a period of time, often over years, to deliver long-term outcomes, particularly in large and complex organizations. Yet this is inherently problematic. The operating environment for most organizations is increasingly volatile: rapid evolution of technology, changing customer expectations, social and political change mean that any strategic change takes place within an environment that is also changing, sometimes very rapidly and in unexpected ways. This is certainly true in the business of government. A new government may change priorities. Shifts in the economy can mean changes in departmental budgets or impact on markets in particular ways. External events, domestic and international, may significantly change requirements. But this is equally true for most organizations.

How, then, can we deliver long-term strategic outcomes amidst this volatility? Are the original outcomes still even relevant? These are inherent challenges for any organization that seeks to deliver strategic change over time. This is, again, where portfolio management can help. A strategic vision and an agreed portfolio plan are clearly an important starting point. But no plan of operations survives first 'contact with the enemy' – particularly when the plan is for complex transformational change.

Portfolios are open systems: projects are delivered and leave the portfolio, new ones are added (Hitchens, 2007). Even within a relatively stable portfolio, things change: projects slip or need to be accelerated or change course for particular reasons. Increasing use of agile approaches in project delivery accelerates this: although overall goals and outcomes for a programme may be known, the route for getting to them will develop along the way, in the light of learning from each phase of delivery; and developments will often not be linear but concurrent. Adaptive transformational change approaches, similarly, are designed to adjust and flex in response to differences in pace, sequence and timing in different change initiatives, and to help manage the relationships between them (Ruddle, 2008, p. 329).

The business of portfolio management is, therefore, not about managing a static portfolio. It is inherently about balancing changes and managing volatility, continually adjusting to keep the overall portfolio within agreed parameters and on track to deliver intended strategic outcomes. One of the most important tools for the portfolio manager is, therefore, the ability to rebalance the portfolio on a regular basis, and this requires the ability to prioritize.

Inherent in the Home Office approach to portfolio management, therefore, is the principle of regular review against strategic priorities, with regular reprioritization to reflect changes – whether in the external environment (the decision to leave the EU, for example, changing the priority of particular projects) or internal changes (such as changes in funding, timing or delivery requirements). The predominance of digital and data programmes delivered through agile methodologies has made this even more important.

To manage all this, we put in place a quarterly medium-term planning process, involving portfolio, finance, strategy and transformation functions, and designed to enable a rolling review of the portfolio against strategic priorities and overall outcomes, as part of wider organizational planning. Where necessary, changes to funding, scope or delivery plans are recommended by the departmental portfolio and investment committee to the executive board and ministers, to address particular changes in requirements or to rebalance spend to optimize investment against strategic goals.

The risk here is, of course, that, in responding to changes in the environment, the portfolio becomes increasingly tactical, dependencies become misaligned and the drive towards strategic outcomes is lost. As mitigation for this risk, designated strategic programmes have been given greater protection for funding, more visibility and stronger governance around the programme and key dependencies, to ensure continuing progress. At the same time, authority over smaller tactical projects is delegated to individual business areas to manage as local transformation portfolios, with the ability to adjust and retarget spend in line with evolving requirements and priorities at local level. Oversight is maintained through the quarterly planning process, with any rebalancing made between portfolios where necessary to support overall strategic priorities.

In summary, slavish adherence to the original portfolio plan is unlikely to deliver strategic change in the most effective way. At worst, although it may deliver the changes the organization wanted at the outset, it may completely fail to deliver the changes it needs by the time they are delivered. One of the key benefits of portfolio management in delivering strategic chance is the ability to adapt and evolve where necessary, and to do so in a differentiated way. However, this needs active management to ensure that portfolio delivery plans stay aligned with the evolving strategic needs of the organization, and to avoid the risk of delivering against yesterday's targets in tomorrow's world.

Factor 4: keeping the focus on outcomes

Ultimately, the delivery of strategic change needs to be translated into deliverables and benefits. There needs to be a clear line of sight between the overall strategic outcomes envisaged by the organization and how these are delivered through programmes and projects in the portfolio. In practice, however, there is often a gap between individual deliverables and wider transformational benefits, which can prove very hard to bridge.

Much depends on how the organization's vision for strategic change is articulated in the first place. Is there enough clarity on how the organization will be different and how success will be measured? Is it clear what the key assumptions and dependencies are? An agreed view of strategic deliverables and outcomes, and how programmes and projects deliver them, is important; so too is keeping a rolling view of progress, as both are prone to evolve.

Strategic change and benefits are, however, often not the same thing. We can readily track progress on individual milestones, outputs or even programme outcomes (such as new digital services or automated gates at the border). We also know how these contribute, through strategic benefits mapping, to wider outcomes. But it is much harder to quantify how much these changes contribute to overall strategic goals, for example in terms of keeping the country safe in a changing world: the many factors involved in socio-economic outcomes make this impossible to quantify in any ways that would be meaningful.

This does not mean that the programmes delivering these changes are not being delivered, or are not worth doing – far from it. It also does not mean that it is not worth trying to track specific benefits, and seeking to establish their relationship with broader indicators. However, it may be necessary to accept that there will be a gap – and that delivery of strategic change may have to be measured through high-level indicators (for example, on wider economic impact) which can be validated only in very broad terms.

In summary, therefore, it is important to be clear on what the portfolio is designed to achieve in terms of deliverables and benefits, and to track progress against them. However, there may still be a gap, and assessing delivery of overall strategic outcomes may ultimately be a matter of judgement rather than measurement.

Factor 5: telling the story of change

Nevertheless, there will always be pressure to bridge the gap between what the portfolio delivers and delivery of strategic change itself in the organization – even if it cannot be factually evidenced in terms of quantifiable benefits. From the outset, the portfolio needs to be seen as an integral part of the change journey, and the portfolio manager has a key role to play in telling that story.

There is extensive academic literature on the importance of sense-making and sense-giving (or, more simply, story-telling) in strategic change (Gioia and Chittipeddi, 1991; Alderman et al., 2005; Boal and Schultz, 2007), first, as part of creating the imperative for change and why the organization needs to be different, and then on a continuing basis in maintaining a sense of progression through a series of disruptive and destabilizing changes for the organization. This is particularly critical in complex, adaptive change in building a sense of connection between multiple, apparently disconnected changes that may feel chaotic and threatening for those caught up in it (or, conversely, random and distant for those at the edges).

This is also why formal structures, processes and tools are not enough in portfolio management designed to deliver strategic organizational change. As Boal and Schultz note: 'routines and rules capture only a limited part of explicit knowledge. They do not capture the past and the historical journey of the organization. They don't capture tacit knowledge or the emotional component of knowledge' (Boal and Schultz, 2007, p. 420). Strategic change is designed to bring about fundamental change in the organization's life story: portfolio management must also help the organization make sense of that change.

The importance of this became clear as the Home Office strategic change portfolio developed. In a complex and evolving environment (with a range of different partners and different kinds of deliverables), and with outcomes sometimes very hard to articulate in hard, quantifiable terms, being able to provide an overall view of change and its evolvement over time was central to building engagement and maintaining alignment.

Setting the vision for change is primarily a strategic leadership responsibility. The particular role of the portfolio manager lies in understanding how (and ensuring that) the different elements of change fit together and how these contribute to broader strategic change over time. So it is also a fundamental responsibility for the portfolio manager to help tell the story of change, through the portfolio and what it will deliver, both for those delivering the changes and in helping the wider organization engage in and make sense of them.

For some stakeholders the story may be understood as progress against portfolio delivery plans and performance data. For others, different ways of telling the story will be needed – whether these are a one-minute elevator pitch, the 'change story' slide pack, pictorials, infographics and posters, case studies or personal tales. And the story of change, and the ways in which it is communicated, needs to be refreshed and updated continually as the picture evolves.

The complexity of the portfolio often makes this a challenge, and thus all the more important. Helping the organization to make sense of complex, apparently disconnected and potentially threatening changes, and creating a sense of structure and progression towards longer-term goals must be a core priority for portfolio management.

Conclusion

Portfolio management has a key role to play in managing complex adaptive change – something that increasingly characterizes the nature of organizational transformation and strategic change in today's environments. As such, it has a key role in helping organizations manage through the instability and disruption of complex change.

To do so, however, portfolio management must be recognized as more than a set of structures, tools and processes. The portfolio needs to be driven by a strategic purpose, a vision for the future organization, to reflect the shape of the organization and the changes it seeks to make, to recognize the continuing need for reprioritization and evolution, to recognize its role in helping the organization understand these changes as part of its life story, and to drive and support the organization's continuing strategic change journey. In doing so, however, the portfolio becomes a powerful agent for change in its own right.

References and further reading

Alderman, N., Ivory, C., McLoughlin, I. and Vaughan, R. (2005), 'Sense-making as a process within complex service-led projects', *International Journal of Project Management*, 23, 380–385.

Boal, K.B. and Schultz, P.L. (2007), 'Storytelling, time and evolution: the role of strategic leadership in complex adaptive systems', *The Leadership Quarterly*, 18, 411–428.

Brion, S., Chauvet, V., Chollet, B. and Mothe, C. (2012), 'Project leaders as boundary spanners: relational antecedents and performance outcomes', *International Journal of Project Management*, 30(2), 708–722.

Cooke-Davies, T, Cicmil, S., Crawford, L. and Richardson, K. (2007), 'We're not in Kansas any more, Toto: mapping the strange landscape of complexity theory and its relationship to project management', *Project Management Journal*, 38, 50–61.

Gioia, D.A. and Chittipeddi, K. (1991), 'Sensemaking and sensegiving in strategic change initiation', *Strategic Management Journal*, 12, 433–448.

Heifetz, R.A., Linsky, M. and Grashow, A. (2009), *The Practice of Adaptive Leadership: Tools and tactics for changing your organization and the world*, Harvard, MA: Harvard Business Press.

Hitchens, D. (2007), *Systems Engineering: A 21st century systems methodology*, Hoboken, NJ: John Wiley & Sons.

Jenner, S. (2011), *Management of Portfolios*, London: AXELOS.

Ruddle, K. (2008), 'In pursuit of agility: reflections on one practitioner's journey undertaking, researching and teaching the leadership of change', in: Dopson, S., Earl, M. and Snow, P. (eds), *Mapping the Management Journey*, Oxford: Oxford University Press, 16, pp. 319–34.

Turner, J.R. (2014), *The Handbook of Project-based Management: Leading strategic change in organizations*, 4th edn, New York: McGraw-Hill Education.

UK Comptroller & Auditor General, National Audit Office (2015), *Lessons for Major Service Transformation*, Norwich: The Stationery Office.

Chapter 12

Portfolio management for business development

Christof Rink

Particularly in the service industry and its consulting business we can see a dynamic market development. On the one hand, digitization seems to have no limit at all, leading to a very high degree of disruption for all businesses and a high number of new players. On the other hand, there is a clear trend towards implementation and expert consulting that results in a big increase in the number of different service options for the customers. All this brings tough competition and a constant need for organizations to reinvent their business models. Thus we see various innovative and agile approaches and a clear trend towards business globalization. This chapter shows a way to manage the high number of business models in different stages of the portfolio.

The purpose of business development portfolios

The service industry is a 'people business' in which long-term investments tend to be poor. The resulting conflict between limited resources and high expectations for growth and profitability requires the ability to make fast decisions with a clear strategy. Portfolios support making strategies and their following processes transparent by using clear and well-chosen key performance indicators (KPIs). This means that decisions made on the basis of these KPIs might not limit the need for fast, flexible and creative developments.

Creativity needs having the right people at the right time, which can make time objectives almost impossible to realize. Involving all relevant players (such as creators, partners and clients) is more important for realizing a business model successfully than meeting the annual objectives of the investor.

Process overview of business development

Business development (with a clear focus on developing new business models) is a creative process that always starts with customer needs. Those needs have to be translated into business opportunities. Ways of matching these needs and opportunities need methods like the business model generation described by Osterwalder and Pigneur (2010) and the value proposition design described by the same authors (involving design thinking and classical business methods like market analysis, business planning and control – see Osterwalder and Pigneur, 2014.

To combine these approaches for business development to extend an existing business, it is essential to differentiate between the core business and the totally new

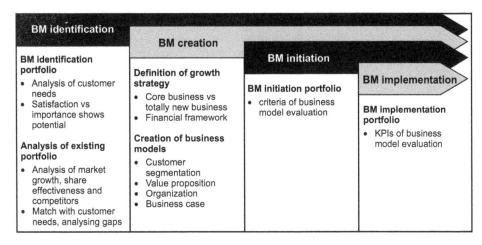

BM = business model

Figure 12.1 Process overview

business. It is also necessary to differentiate depending on the phase or maturity of the relevant business model. Hence, the process of business development could be seen in the four iterative stages depicted in Figure 12.1. These stages are as follows:

1. Business model identification;
2. Creation;
3. Initiation; and
4. Implementation.

Business model identification

The first stage of business development is a truly analytical process. It should compare both sides of a value proposition (the customer's needs versus the existing portfolio of the business and its competitors). The business model identification portfolio compares satisfaction with the importance of customer needs, and should result in a clear business potential.

However, analysis of the existing portfolio needs some more steps. On the one hand, it is necessary to collect facts and figures such as market growth, market share, market attractiveness and competitors' strengths. On the other hand, the competitors' strengths should be matched with the analysed customer needs to identify gaps for even more unique business potential.

Customer analysis using the business model identification portfolio

Using the customer segment of the value proposition CANVAS (Osterwalder and Pigneur, 2014), we must differentiate between the work to be done for our potential

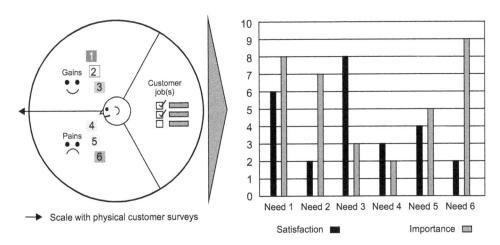

Scale with physical customer surveys

Figure 12.2 Analysis of customer needs.

customer and that done for customer's gains and pains to get a proper understanding of the customer's needs. The more emotional aspects we are able to identify here, the more important needs we can identify. Thus we use two aspects of categorization for the customer's needs in physical customer surveys, which are (a) importance and (b) satisfaction for all the gains and pains. These can be charted on a scale from 1 to 10, as shown in Figure 12.2.

So, having the systemized evaluation of the customer needs, the next step is to identify business potentials. Thanks to the ETC Institute (a market research organization based in Olathe, Kansas) we have a direct transfer from customers' satisfaction and importance to the whole range from over- to under-served markets. These markets can be categorized as follows:

- Ripe for disruption (reduce value);
- Potential for disruption;
- Appropriately served (sustain value);
- Solid, high and extreme opportunity (create value).

Placing our evaluation in the matrix allows us to see directly from which gain or pain we have the potential for opportunity or disruption (Figure 12.3).

Competitor analysis of the product portfolio and potentials

Collecting the right figures for competitor analysis is usually a rather difficult and time-consuming task (which can make the business model of strategy consultants quite interesting). But with a clear focus on the perspective of business model creation and the will to collect the figures on a sustainable basis, it will be completely worthwhile in the long term. To achieve this, we have to challenge our existing product portfolio in three dimensions, which are:

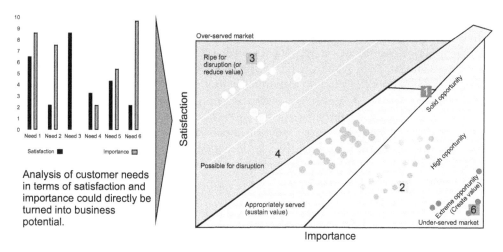

Figure 12.3 Creating the business model identification portfolio

1. Market;
2. Investment;
3. Emotional facts.

As best-practice examples, I recommend the classic Boston Consulting Group (BCG) matrix (BCG, 1968), competitor potentials in the business model identification portfolio (from the ETC Institute) and the core of the value proposition CANVAS (Osterwalder and Pigneur, 2014). The outcomes would be as follows:

- Comparison of the market growth with its share in the BCG matrix (BCG, 1968);
- An analysis of the competitors' fit with the identified customer needs;
- Aspects for growth strategy needs from the business model identification portfolio.

This results in the value proposition CANVAS comparing gain creators with pain relievers with costumer needs and identifying the level of the served needs of the real customer value.

Case example

To make all this theory more tangible, I introduce a case here from the business for which I work (Tiba Consulting). I do not introduce the whole business model of Tiba Consulting (Ger. Tiba Managementberatung GmbH) but describe the existing business model of Tiba's management consulting training and operations (with the core competences of project, change and process management for all industries), where the aim is to be able to serve any customers' project management needs. We call our method the PM4.0 approach.

Starting with the business model identification we found out that (especially for project management directors of bigger companies or the heads of project management offices [PMOs]), neither the classic 'waterfall' nor the agile project management approach met the full importance of customers' needs. (Those needs are: less trouble, with more efficiency, transparency, visibility, flexibility, vitality and innovation.) When it came to satisfaction, the existing hybrid approaches, such as GPM (2016), Project Management Institute (PMI, 2017) or AXELOS (2015) provided only limited satisfaction owing to their inflexibility (especially in fully dynamic environments).

Also analysing a bit deeper into our existing portfolio, we could see that our classic project management approaches in the market are seen more as a 'cash cow', and the agile-plus hybrid approaches were still more in the question mark area for us. Checking our competitors and possible customer values, we realized that fuller flexibility with existing approaches to our customers could lead to a specific growth for this customer segment.

Business model creation

As the next stage of our business development process we were able to start with the creation of our business model. As an important aside, I want to clarify that, in my opinion, the creation of a business model never ends until it is dead. If we accept this as a firm rule, it is clear why we have four iterative phases in our process. However, in the creation of various business models the definition of a growth strategy is essential.

Another consideration is (as you probably all know) that growth by itself does not automatically mean more revenue. A proper profit–growth strategy (especially in disruptive markets) is very often a key requirement for staying in the competition. Therefore, the outcomes of this stage are a comparison between the core and totally new business, using a financial framework in the growth strategy and when creating business models having the following:

- A crystal-clear customer segmentation;
- Value proposition;
- Appropriate organizational framework; and
- A fully calculated business case.

To find the right model for a growth strategy we have the same case of difficulty and effort I discussed earlier for the market analysis of the existing product portfolio (BCG, 1968). This is why I suggest the Ansoff Matrix here (Ansoff, 1988) (which compares existing and new markets with existing and new products). What needs to be derived out of this matrix should also be customer's needs. By combining this with the level of innovation (IDEO, 2008), and evaluating the desirability, viability and feasibility of a single business idea, you come straight to the creation of the necessary business model. Of course, this is again a rather iterative and creative environment and therefore sometimes it makes more sense to start with a prototype than with the full business model. Figure 12.4 shows the drivers for business model creation.

When describing the various business models by considering the creative, collaborative and iterative environment, the business model CANVAS (Osterwalder and Pigneur, 2010) represents the state-of-the-art methodology and makes good sense. To make this easier to describe, I have randomly summarized the nine necessary fields into four. These lead to four necessary factors to consider:

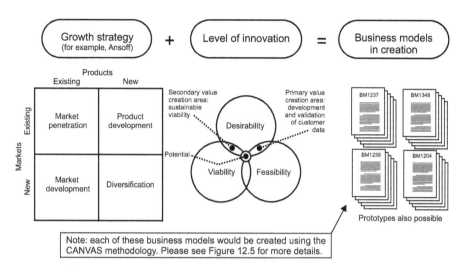

Figure 12.4 Drivers of business models creation

1. Customer segmentation (ideally coming from the business model identification);
2. Value proposition (again coming from the business model);
3. The organizational framework;
4. The business case.

I know that this will not work for all cases and it might be necessary to consider all nine fields. This is an iterative process, carried out step by step, which should be free from time constraints. The fields (components) of the business case using this methodology are illustrated in Figure 12.5. The process will depend on whether the business case is for an incremental optimization of a product or for a revolutionary new development.

In the case of our PM4.0 approach it was clear that we were talking here about a recombination of existing products and services and new business aspects into a unique approach. What made it especially easy for us was that the business case uses the flexibility of resources inside the existing organization – using these resources for the new approach as well as for agile approaches. This was possible because agile consultants, trainers and coaches typically have experience in both approaches. By being adaptive to different situations we could focus on our customers better. So we established our new centre-of-competence 'PM4.0'. This development continues in our organization and we are able to derive our products easily from the existing business and focus the right values by empowering our customers in this approach, as well as applying appropriate training and tool development (which is still continuing).

Business model initiation portfolio

The third stage of business development again needs a clear portfolio, owing to the need for a definite go or no-go decision. From my perspective as the author of this

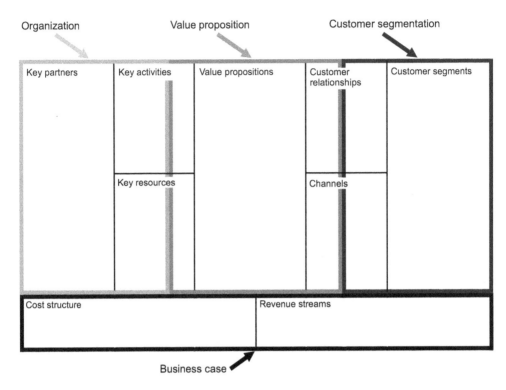

Organization   Value proposition   Customer segmentation

Figure 12.5 Business case modelling using the CANVAS methodology

chapter I took the decision to go for the description of each business model using the CANVAS system (Osterwalder and Pigneur, 2014).

Based on this decision, I clearly recommend using the following seven criteria of business model evaluation provided in Strategyzer (2016), weighted using a scale from 0 to 10:

1. *Switching costs*: 'Nothing holds my customers back from leaving me' versus 'My customers are locked in for several years';
2. *Recurring revenues*: '100 per cent of my sales are transactional' versus '100 per cent of my sales lead to automatically recurring revenues';
3. *Earning vs. spending*: 'I incur 100 per cent of my costs of goods and services before earning revenues' versus 'I earn 100 per cent of my revenues before incurring the costs of goods and services sold';
4. *Game-changing of cost structure*: 'My cost structure is at least 30 per cent higher than my competitors' versus 'My cost structure is at least 30 per cent lower than my competitors';
5. *Others who do the work*: 'I incur costs for all the value created in my business model' versus 'All the value created in my business model is created free of costs by external parties';

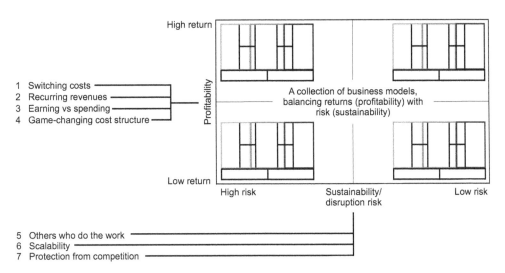

High return

1 Switching costs
2 Recurring revenues
3 Earning vs spending
4 Game-changing cost structure

Profitability

A collection of business models,
balancing returns (profitability) with
risk (sustainability)

Low return

High risk

Sustainability/
disruption risk

Low risk

5 Others who do the work
6 Scalability
7 Protection from competition

Figure 12.6 Criteria for a business model initiation portfolio

6. *Scalability*: 'Growing my business model requires substantial resources and effort' versus 'My business model has virtually no limit to growth';
7. *Protection from competition*: 'My business model has no defences and I'm vulnerable to competition' versus 'My business model provides substantial defences that would be difficult to breach'.

While I was writing this chapter, Osterwalder and Pigneur (founders of the business model and value proposition CANVAS) published a new proposal (Osterwalder and Pigneur, 2017). This gave new insight into how a business model portfolio could be visualized. It unifies criteria 1–4 in one group called 'profitability' and criteria 5–7 in a different group called 'sustainability/disruption risk' (Figure 12.6). The simplicity of this model convinced me to choose it and add the following three states:

1. 'Initiated', which means moving a project from the business model initiation portfolio to implementation after decision;
2. 'On hold', which means that more information should be gathered, perhaps (for example) by producing more prototypes;
3. 'Declined', which results in archiving the project and releasing its team for other duties.

In the third part of Osterwalder and Pigneur (2017), the authors developed 'the business portfolio map'. In this they added an 'explore' portfolio in front of the initiation step to track business model creations focusing on 'design' versus 'test'. For me this is a very valuable addition, suitable for very lean and focused businesses. However, although big organizations often intend to act like this, it is from my experience a big transition for them. So, the faster this can be used inside a business group the better, but you will need to decide when the business group is ready for it.

All this leads me directly back to our case and I must say that the evaluation was not enormous but, owing to the little business case and the strategic potential for further businesses, we decided to launch based on the following results:

1. *Switching costs*: low to middle, customers should more be empowered here but we could generate some partnership based on trust for that;
2. *Recurring revenues*: limited, again owing to the empowerment focus;
3. *Earning versus spending*: very good, based on a different price market for agile services and the low investment;
4. *Game-changing of cost structure*: middle, because of slightly different pricing but with more transparency given by focusing on empowerment;
5. *Others who do the work*: very good, owing to the empowerment of our customers;
6. *Scalability*: middle to high, by empowering the customers but by using human resources for consulting, coaching and training;
7. *Protection from competition*: middle, owing to a high first-mover advantage and a unique hard-to-copy wide network.

Business model implementation portfolio

After initiating a business model, it should logically be further tracked with all running business models, while understanding its implementation maturity. This also means evaluating running businesses which maybe would have not been evaluated in the past, or which would have been evaluated differently. To make the whole business development process as simple as possible we use a set of key performance indicators (KPIs) that are directly linked to the criteria of the business model initiation portfolio. As an example, I list below our designated KPIs. However, note that these have to be selected for each business group individually, trying to match the axes of 'profitability' and 'sustainability/disruption risk' (Osterwalder and Pigneur, 2017) (Figure 12.7).

1. *Switching costs*: customer return on investment (ROI) versus budget in euros;
2. *Recurring revenues*: average income per customer in euros;
3. *Earning versus spending*: profit per customer in euros;

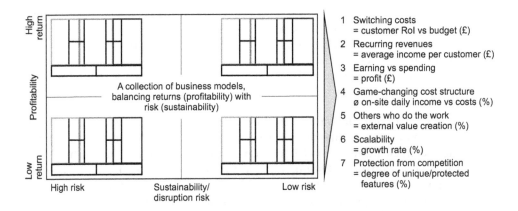

Figure 12.7 Example for a business model initiation portfolio in business development

4. *Game-changing of cost structure*: average on-site daily income versus costs expressed as a percentage;
5. *Others who do the work*: external value creation as a percentage;
6. *Scalability*: growth rate as a percentage;
7. *Protection from competition*: degree of unique/protected features.

Coming back finally to our PM4.0 case I have to say that progress is in its early stages and I cannot publish any results or figures. But we are running very well against our plan, with really happy customers as we build more and more internal resources to feed the request.

Summary: consideration of customers leads to success

The key to realizing a successful business development in its ongoing creative, collaborative and iterative process is to transfer the customer needs into the realization of business potentials. Applying the state-of-the-art business model method and value proposition CANVAS described by Osterwalder and Pigneur is essential.

Tracking the business models (BMs) in portfolios we must consider, in BM identification, high-quality analysis results for the BM creation. In the BM creation, this focus on a high-quality, customer-centric concept as a result should be continued. Finally, a clear profitability and sustainability focus are tracked in the BM initiation and implementation portfolio.

Our case showed you an example reinventing our own business with very low disruption. Using the appropriate models to create fast ideas for BM creation and implementation, we see, as the first results, a growing amount of orders and of human resources.

My final statement on business development portfolios will probably not surprise you. The more you consider your customers in your portfolio, the more you know them and the more successful your whole business group will become.

References and further reading

Ansoff, H.I. (1988), *Corporate Strategy (Business Library)*, 2nd edn, London: Penguin Books Ltd.

AXELOS (2015), *Prince2 Agile*, Norwich: The Stationery Office.

Boston Consulting Group (1968), *Perspectives on Experience*, Boston, MA: BCG.

GPM Deutsche Gesellschaft für Projektmanagement e.V (2016), *IPMA 4-L-C Zusatzzertifikat hybrid+ (GPM)*, available at: https://www.gpm-ipma.de/qualifizierung_zertifizierung/ipma_4_l_c_zusatzzertifikat_hybrid_gpm.html.

IDEO (2008), *A Toolkit for Human-Centered Design*, Palo Alto, CA: IDEO LLC.

Osterwalder, A. and Pigneur, Y. (2010), *Business Model Generation: A Handbook for Visionaries, Game Changers, and Challengers*, Hoboken, NJ: Wiley.

Osterwalder, A. and Pigneur, Y. (2014), *Value Proposition Design: How to Create Products and Services Customers Want*, Hoboken, NJ: Wiley.

Osterwalder, A. and Pigneur, Y. (2017), *Business Model Portfolio, Part 1: Manage The Existing Business, Part 2: Manage New Business Initiatives, Part 3: The Business Portfolio Map*, available at: http://blog.strategyzer.com/posts/2017/8/23/business-model-portfolio-part-1-manage-the-existing-business, http://blog.strategyzer.com/posts/2017/8/28/business-model-portfolio-part-2-manage-new-business-initiatives, http://blog.strategyzer.com/posts/2017/9/4/business-model-portfolio-part-3-the-business-portfolio-map

Project Management Institute or PMI (2017), *PMI Agile Certified Practitioner (PMI-ACP)*®, available at: https://www.pmi.org/certifications/types/agile-acp

Strategyzer, A.G. (2016), *Seven Questions to Assess Your Business Model Design*, available at: http://blog.strategyzer.com/posts/2016/4/26/access-30-free-strategyzer-tools-in-our-resource-library?rq=7 per cent20questions per cent20to per cent20assess.

Tiba Managementberatung GmbH (2017), *Projektmanagement 4.0 – Gemeinsam Projekte erfolgreich machen*, https://www.tiba.de/index.php?cid=2229.

Chapter 13

Portfolio management in a bank

Philipp Detemple

When I was asked to write this chapter I wondered about what the differences would be in project portfolio management (PPM) between different kinds of industries. The basic principles for PPM are always about choosing projects within the limitation of human and financial resources to achieve the organization's predefined goals, whether these are strategic or something else. So, the special points in industrial areas are more likely to be found in specific circumstances in which the portfolio is maintained, rather than in the methods used. Therefore, this chapter focuses more on the environment influencing a bank's project portfolio management than on PPM methods, because these methods are much closer to standards than one might assume.

Project portfolio management environment in the banking industry

When considering the principles of PPM we say that its purpose is to steer a couple or a big bunch of projects in order to reach the best contribution to an enterprise's strategy within the limits of time and budget. This is the same in banking industry.

The highest priority in your strategy is to survive. This is often unwritten because it is a key objective of every business. But with PPM in banking this survival objective has to be written down, because banks are faced with a continuously increasing number of challenges that may cause their business to stop. Contrary to other industries, these challenges have no economic reason but come from regulatory requirements, which, if not fulfilled, could prohibit parts of the business from continuing. They could cause extremely high penalties or could even mean losing the banking licence. Thus the top priority projects in a bank's portfolio are always regulatory projects.

The level of this regulation is increasing and is accompanied by an increase in administrative costs. This means that back offices have to be optimized for more efficient processes and automation, because present-day processes are too complex and will have to be leaner in the future. So, via the cost factor, efficiency partly builds a bridge to those parts of your strategy that lie more within your own choice than regulatory requirements – real business or growth projects.

On the market side, banks also have challenges to overcome. A very important issue in the current market is the very long duration of low interest rates, which have had a tremendous impact on all banks because interest rates are one key component of their income. So, new products have to be developed that are not that dependent on interest rates. Also, gaining new customers is key. But the environment for these tasks is also challenging because the typical banking market is entered by new competitors.

The impact of these (often contradictory) challenges – regulation and market – are described in more detail in the following sections.

Regulatory requirements

The bankruptcy or fatal loss of value of huge banks in 2008 started a worldwide crisis in the banking industry. Thousands of people lost their jobs and customers lost millions in savings. Analysis of the reasons for the crashes made government authorities aware that banks and their products had almost had a free run for decades. For a long time some banks cared only for increasing their earnings on an inter-institutional level instead of at the advisory level for private customers. As a result of these findings, the authorities started to compensate for their former blindness by producing tons of laws to implement more regulation in the financial industries. Most of these laws were absolutely necessary to minimize the risks for customers and to avoid further critical situations in the financial world.

First initiatives dealt with customer care by inventing better documentation of the advisory process with each customer. Here, a bank has to collect confirmations signed by the customer, stating that each person has understood what she or he was going to do with her or his money. Also process steps (such as the right to cancel the contract within a certain period) have to be made clear and the customers have to confirm this was explained to them.

Next initiatives required the separation of advisors paid out of commissions from their colleagues who were independently paid directly by the customer for their advice. In other words, a bank offering both kinds of services had to change the organization of its teams, which brought technical and real impacts.

In addition to the customer care regularities, information about the customers' own activities came more into the focus of authorities in order to identify illegal activities. For the sake of public safety, banks were obliged to gather detailed information about customers and prospects who wanted to become customers. This 'Know your customer' information is used to prevent money laundering and money transfers from people who might foster terrorism, criminal organizations or politically exposed persons. In the context of possible criminal activities, money transfers have to be checked according to several criteria and suspicious findings must be reported to the authorities.

However, it is not only public safety that is in the regulatory focus. Tax authorities also have an increasing appetite for data that will enable them to chase tax evasion. In the globalized economics of today, this causes requirements to report on a frequent basis, not only to local authorities within the operating country of a bank, but also to state unions like the EU or to countries like the USA.

As the banking industry is a key player in the economics at territorial and global levels, the activities of the bank itself are also now followed more closely. From the detection of simple frauds in favour of a single person, up to market abuse by the bank and its customers, systems and processes had to be invented for identifying such actions. And in any case of suspicious, action authorities have to be informed within a very short time to enable them to trace and stop it.

Customer care, the prevention and tracing of global crime, tax evasion, fraud and market abuse are just examples, shown to give you an idea of how heavily a bank's project portfolio is constrained by the environment of our economic world (Bock 2014). The influence of regulatory requirements is extremely high and is therefore often called the 'priority 0' part of a bank's project portfolio. The next section shows you which things need to be done from an economic perspective.

Market situation

The banking crisis that emerged in 2008 was critical for the world's economy. The critical loss of money and the following drop in economic activities led to one measure that is still the tool of choice (in Europe) to stabilize economics: the reduction of the cardinal rate of interest. For the banks this measure has several critical aspects.

The most important critical aspect is a reduction of income, because interest rates are, so far, a key income of a bank. But this money has to be spent to fulfil the regulatory requirements as well as being needed and used to develop new products and refine existing processes.

Indirect impacts include the significant increase in loans taken out by customers, which cause future risk for the bank. The very low interest rates have made loans attractive to customers, and have led to a significant increase in loans made by banks to their customers. The low interest rates enable thousands of customers to take out loans for real estate or luxury things (such as very well-equipped cars), which are in many cases calculated to the edge (sub-prime loans). These long running loans may become critical when the cardinal rate increases. Here, then, is another big danger of losing money if customers are no longer able to pay back. The first notifications of this risk from too many and too expensive loans taken out by US customers for buying cars were posted in newspapers at the end of August 2016 (Buchter 2016).

The loans situation bears some risk that cannot be ignored, but it is not a key problem of today. Today's problem is that the low income earned from interest rates can be balanced only by developing other products and getting as many new customers as possible to bring additional money into the system. Gathering customers is a hard challenge in every industry. In the banking industry the first point is to gain customers' trust. The next step is to differentiate from competitors. As the variety of products in banking is limited, the key for differentiation is the number of services offered and how those services are performed. One of the most important things in the strategic area of portfolios is therefore the customer experience. This means lean processes and a high quality in advisory and other services. All this is additionally within new sales channels, because shops will be replaced by a variety of different sales channels in the future.

Following a study with German banks (Lünendonk 2012), 58 per cent of bank managers support the hypothesis that the biggest part of customer interaction will be online until 2020. They also state that mobile applications will play a significant role in this. To cope with this, banks have to invest in mobile development as well as in automation of their back-office processes to have competitive, fast backup behind mobile applications. However, many customers (often elderly people) find the highest value in their relationship with their bank, being able to enter a bank branch and speak to real people, instead of using impersonal technical appliances that they hardly understand. As elderly people are a rapidly growing group of society, banks will also have to cope with this most costly sales channel – at least for a decade or two – until today's middle-aged people who are familiar with modern techniques become elderly themselves.

The quickly developing new technologies not only have the effect of creating a continuously needed improvement. Another effect is that they bring new competitors into the market, which nobody thought about a few years ago. Key banking domains (such as transfer of payments) are being entered by other companies (Apple and Amazon are examples). For a bank this means a loss of visibility by the customer, because the customer's visible front end is Apple Pay or Amazon Payments, which are more convenient because there is no media break inside the shopping process.

It is not only the big players that reduce a bank's visibility. An increasing number of startup enterprises, developing highly customer-orientated tools for banking business, are also entering the market. In previous years banks were frightened of this evolution because these small enterprises were able to bring good ideas into the market in a very short time. More recently this fear has widely disappeared and banks look for cooperation with these companies in order to participate in both the speed and the startup from the experience.

The core problem with these two groups of new competitors is not to be seen within the task they are taking over. In particular, payments are more expensive than what the users can be charged. Also some other services (especially those offered by FinTech) are limited by regulatory requirements that a small company can never fulfil without also losing their highest value, which is their speed. The real problem for the bank is the loss of visibility that comes when services, used by millions of people, are provided with other front ends.

The real challenge of all this is that it has all happened in a very short time. Regulation increase has now lasted for close to 10 years and the end is still not in sight, because currently many of the regulatory laws are already being updated. So, this will not be finished any time soon and the market evolution also gives us no room for a rest – otherwise new competitors will take over.

The impact on PPM

As we have seen so far in this chapter, the current circumstances under which a bank's project portfolio is to be managed are really complex. Regulatory requirements, project budgets melting under high cost pressure and new players in the market have to be aligned with each other in the project portfolio. And here is the problem faced by portfolio management in every industry: limited resources. For a long time this limit was more on the labour resources (staffing bottlenecks) if a project portfolio was to be performed. Now, budget restrictions have become a more serious factor within financial industries – a fact that many years differentiated financial industries from other industries.

So, now bank portfolios have to be built containing as many regulatory projects as necessary and as many business growth projects as possible. In the middle of this, in an ideal world integrated into the projects from both lines, work efficiency and lean process design are clearly essential as the cost perspective becomes more and more important.

The remainder of this chapter describes in a nutshell how the usual portfolio management methods are used to deal with all the points mentioned so far.

How to handle the complex banking requirements in PPM

Having giving you an overview of the difficult problems between surviving from a legal point of view and using limited resources for further growth I now describe how PPM is performed in the financial industry. The main points here are prioritization and always keeping a good overview on what is going on. So, I deal with the decision boards as well as with the aspects to be considered while making decisions.

Building the portfolio

When a portfolio is to be designed, the first questions are:

1. What goals are to be achieved?
2. What will be the duration of the portfolio under investigation?

Most portfolio goals are based on the strategic goals of an enterprise. Three important examples are:

- Growth of the enterprise;
- Making the company fit for the future to stay competitive;
- Doing things needed to survive.

In banking, you are always faced with all the three of these goals, as explained previously.

Depending on the goals, the duration of the portfolio must be decided. Knowing the run time is important, in order to become clear about the limitation factors of the portfolio. From the run time, you can derive the financial budget and the amount of human resources (person days) that can be used to perform the portfolio. In most cases the horizon is the calendar year, because financial cycles for tax and balance of accounts are bound to this.

As a next step, it is necessary to get an insight into the project ideas handed in to portfolio management. Without such information the portfolio management is not able to decide how an idea will fit the portfolio goals. Therefore, a process is needed to obtain the outcome of a minimum set of information about any idea (for example, the intended goal of the idea, an estimate of the effort needed to perform the project and a rough picture of skills needed). This step can be seen as the 'demand phase' of a project.

For the demand phase, it should be defined in the building process that people are allowed to contribute their demands to portfolio management. It is useful to define that demands from employees have to pass an approval by their line manager, to avoid the organization being flooded with demands. In our bank only demands that have been approved by a divisional head of business or IT are accepted.

The way in which project proposals are collected should also be well defined in the portfolio process. This must prevent portfolio management from receiving too many project ideas that are badly defined, perhaps only with a headline. Whichever medium you choose for these project demands, be it a form on paper or the interface of a PPM system (as in our case), it is strongly recommended to have a predefined structure to make sure that the needed basic information will be collected.

When the demands are collected, they have to be prioritized to decide which ones will enter the portfolio for the next period and which are to be postponed or even completely to be skipped. Prioritization follows the principle of identifying first those things that are mandatory. In the banking environment, this clearly includes the legal requirements that have a deadline within the period for which the portfolio is to be built. Following this, other mandatory topics can enter the portfolio, such as big IT changes to keep systems up to date in technical standards or changes for security reasons (particularly those changes that are too costly and would require so much effort that they cannot be done as usual maintenance).

After these two most important points, the next is to check the maturity and the progress of projects already running. Portfolio management has here to align with the top management if the strategy is to be maintained. Should projects that are running be kept and finished, or are new projects seen as being more important from a strategic point of view? This prioritization could mean that projects already running should be put on hold or even aborted. Stability and rigour should lead the decisions here and it is sometimes the role of PPM to counsel the top management with regard to this.

Dealing with the already running projects in the phase of portfolio building is a crucial point, because their impact on the planning of the next period is considerable from several aspects. The first and most visible impact is the use of resources already committed by the teams of these projects. Newly upcoming things, especially from the first prioritization category (the mandatory topics), could have a strong need for the same resources. At the next level budget aspects are taken into account, because the running projects have granted budgets that will consume parts of the budget given for the next portfolio period.

Looking at these two aspects could lead to a wrong decision, such as that stopping a project with not much progress made to date would be good to assure the portfolio and fulfil objectives for the next year. Here another strategic point comes into consideration: growth projects usually have financial goals to which they are committed at their start. It is necessary to check very carefully if the returns of these projects can be postponed or even skipped, because this could harm the cost/income ratio for a long time. But, also, projects with no big returns are the subject of deeper investigation because these can be enabler projects for further economic or efficiency goals.

In the build phase of the portfolio, PPM's duty is to make proposals on the portfolio for the next period following the steps mentioned before. The decisions are then taken by a portfolio committee. As described in PPM standards, this committee is, depending on the size of the organization, the senior or C-level management of the enterprise or a round of people empowered by the management. In real life, the committee should be a subset of the executive committee because this guarantees direct alignment with the top management and it will not bring up discussion afterwards about the empowerment. This last requirement is necessary because portfolio building will not always fulfil every wish from all parts of an organization, which then causes complaints about the decisions.

Maintaining the portfolio

Although a portfolio is in its lifecycle (meaning the period for which it was built) the duties of PPM look different from those during the build phase. PPM should now at first have processes to maintain an overview of the running topics. These processes usually mean maintaining contact with project managers and project owners on a regular and frequent basis. The first measure of choice is a report on project status in a predefined structure, which project managers have to prepare on a regular basis. Another good way of retaining insights is attending steering committees of the most important projects. This can also prevent deviations between the reported information collected and what is communicated to the stakeholders. A situation that sometimes happens is that the written reported information is collected at a different date from the committee meeting date, so that reported information becomes out of date.

The focus on the projects in the reports is on information that has impact for the portfolio. As PPM has to watch the consumption of the overall allowed budget, financial information out of each project is a crucial point. At the start and in the middle of each portfolio period, it is necessary to track whether projects are within their budgets and not going into overdraft. In the last quarter of the period, it is necessary to check with project managers, through deep investigation, whether or not the allocated budgets will really be spent. This is important for the financial long-range plans of the company, as well as to get an idea about budget needs within the following period. The possible impact on the following period's budget has to be checked because, most times, unused budget is not just surplus but comes from delayed project work that must be performed in the following period.

The point just mentioned leads directly to another important aspect of information in the running portfolio, which is the progress of the projects. On the one hand, quick progress could free up resources earlier for other projects. On the other hand, delays in projects (which are unfortunately much more likely) affect the timeline of the whole running portfolio and are therefore a risk for the existing period and the subsequent portfolio. This makes progress and its strong link to resource allocation very important.

It is very helpful to have a PMO supporting the collection of reports as well as some other operational duties. Here, it can also be assured that ideas and demands coming up within the current period are collected and checked for their priority. This could apply especially for demands with regard to new legal requirements, which cannot wait for the next portfolio period. The PMO can report on new demands to PPM. This assures that PPM gets the input without delay and can react in time to satisfy the new demand (in this case dealing with the short time before a new law is due to become live). Then the running portfolio has to be revised and re-prioritized in order to integrate the new topic urgently.

Maintaining a portfolio requires two kinds of committee for decisions to be taken. On a very frequent level, an operational portfolio committee has to be installed. Attendees of the committee are, besides PPM, product owners or those responsible for business lines (depending on the structure of the enterprise). The purpose of these meetings is to align the status of projects and possible inter-project dependencies. The committee then decides on resource and budget reallocation to overcome issues (for example, caused by project delays).

The second committee required is a strategic one, with the same participants as the committee that took the decisions in the portfolio-building phase. This committee need not meet frequently depending on the stability of a company's project portfolio. The purpose of this committee's meetings is to keep top management (those who determine the strategy) informed about the progress of the most important projects and the portfolio performance in the sense of budget and resource consumption. Decisions in this committee are to be taken if the portfolio has to be revised or re-prioritized or in case of remarkable deviations from overall budget.

Conclusion

For many years now, the banking industry has been under a great deal of pressure from different directions. On the one hand, they have to fulfil increasing regulatory requirements, causing cost increases; on the other, revenues are decreasing, meaning that banks have to find ways to assure further growth. An additional phenomenon is a massive change in the banks' markets, driven by the quick evolution of internet technique and mobile appliances. In the middle of this, PPM has a central role to enable the bank to perform the right initiatives to cope with the problem.

In this environment, a crucial point in PPM is the prioritization of projects. Attention to priority is crucial at portfolio building and also while performing a portfolio. Budget and resource conflicts can be solved only with a clear priority of the topics. The decisions needed are taken in two committees. An operational committee is responsible, together with PPM, for the performance of the running portfolio. A strategic committee, usually a subset of the executive committee, is responsible for decisions about priorities and as trouble shooters in case of excessive budget deviations.

References and further reading

Bock, M. 2014, *Kostensteuerung aus Bankperspektive – CRD IV/CRR Erste Erfahrungen und zukünftige Handlungsfelder*, https://www.wiwi.uni-muenster.de/fcm/downloads/praxis/schmalenbach/tagung_2014-03-14/20140314_Schmalenbach_AK_BOCK_DRUCK.pdf (accessed 14 August 2017).

Buchter, H. 2016, *Angst vor der US Autoblase*, http://www.zeit.de/wirtschaft/2016-08/autokredite-usa-finanzkrise-ausfallquote-kreditqualitaet (accessed 15 August 2017).

Lünendonk 2012, Trendstudie 'Zukunft der Banken 2020', available at: https://www.de.cgi.com/sites/default/files/files_de/white-papers/LUE_Bankenstudie_f221012.pdf (accessed 14 August 2017).

www.ey.com/Publication/vwLUAssets/EY_Bankenbarometer_Januar_2014/$FILE/EY-Bankenbarometer-Januar-2014.pdf.

Chapter 14

The Incheon Bridge Project

Soohong Kim

This chapter describes a successful project to build a very large bridge in Korea. The project is described by a central figure in the project, Dr Soohong Kim. Although technically this was one big project, it was split into a portfolio of three projects to achieve the best possible degree of control.

Introduction and project description

The Incheon Bridge is the Korea's foremost bridge connecting the Incheon International Airport and Songdo International Business District. Its total length is 21.38 km. This bridge is widely recognized as one of the world's leading civil engineering marvels for its grand scale, aesthetics and traffic management system (which integrated the newest cutting-edge technology).

At the time when the Incheon Bridge Project was being designed in 1998, Korea was experiencing economic hardship in the wake of the International Monetary Fund (IMF) financial crisis. Under Korea's conservative business circumstances, there had been no open-door policy exercised for foreigners to get into the market. In particular, the concept of project management was not appropriately recognized. In spite of these difficult conditions, AMEC (currently known as AMEC Foster Wheeler), the UK's leading global engineering company, decided to enter the Korean market through investment in this project. At that time I was the Representative Director of AMEC Korea, and strategically placed to be the centre of this project.

The main project became a portfolio of three independent projects or phases:

1. Financing;
2. Construction;
3. Operation and maintenance (O&M).

Each phase was developed and carried out with individually defined objectives and processes, and accomplished through the process of analysing stakeholders and putting management into practice to satisfy their demands and expectations.

As the most exemplary case of a project jointly pursued by the private and public sectors, the Incheon Bridge is appreciated as the first successful project in Korea led by a foreign partner.

This created fertile ground for foreign investment policies and free economic zones, as well as establishing a framework for new private sector finance business, raising the nation's global competitiveness. The Incheon Bridge Project, as the symbolic infrastructure of Korea, has achieved the world's best benchmarking case at each phase. It stands as the most successful public–private partnership project of Korea and has received over 120 awards from leading domestic and foreign institutions in finance, technology and operation, including the International Project Management Association's (IPMA's) Project Excellence Award (Premium Gold Winner).

The Incheon Bridge Project was designed under the premise that nature, the nation and the people are the clients of the project, and this has served as the strategic direction of the project to realize sustainability. This project is now in operation. It was the first public–private partnership project in Korea where the goals of the nation and the people have driven the entire journey from planning, financing, construction through to operation and maintenance.

The project was first proposed in 2000, before the concept of a portfolio was introduced into IPMA's Individual Competence Baseline 3.0 (ICB 3.0) (IPMA, 2015). There are three phases in the project and each phase has been planned and executed as an independent project. The Incheon Bridge Project contains the components defined in ISO 21504 (International Organization for Standardization [ISO] 2015) and incorporates sustainability as a concept to expand the existing project scope. As mentioned above the Incheon Bridge Project received the IPMA's Project Excellence Award and is now used as a global benchmark for projects. Figure 14.1 summarizes the whole project. I now describe each of the three phases in more detail.

The financing phase

Completion of financing is a concept that is possible only after meeting the expectations of all stakeholders through completion of the concession agreement (CA) and the amended and restated concession agreement (ARCA). Thus this established the objectives covering all the expectations, and the investment agreement for the cost of the project was signed and concluded. The core objectives were to gain approval to

Name	The Incheon Bridge Project
Project cost	Total project cost US$ 2.382 billion, comprising US$ 1.52 billion for the private section and US$ 862 million for the connecting roads
Facility scale	Total length 21.4 Km, comprising 12.3Km private section and 9.1Km of connecting roads Bridge: cable-stayed bridge, viaduct, approach bridge, hybrid through arch bridge, butterfly-shaped cable-stayed bridge and an extradosed bridge Six entering facilities as follows: airport new town JCT, Youngjong IC, Yeonsu JCT, Songdo IC, Oakyrun IC and Kakeik JCT Toll Plaza 1
Construction period	July 2005 to October 2009 (52 months)
Connected areas	Songdo International Business District - Youngjongdo

Figure 14.1 Summary of the Incheon Bridge Project

bid for construction expenses in a privately funded project for the first time in Korea and to secure minimum revenue guarantee (MRG) to preserve the principal sum during the operation. In addition, investors were guaranteed a range of profitable returns through a satisfactory rate of return, and the stability of shareholders and lenders was achieved by establishing stable management operation for 30 years, eliminating the risk of management costs during the operating period.

The risk of change in the demand forecast was managed through guaranteeing prevention of the competition route. An international design standard that could utilize an advanced technique to integrate aesthetics and the environment within space and time was implemented for the first time in Korea. Furthermore, it became the first case for project management to be recognized by establishing prior agreement of the design plan and the project management plan with the government (the detailed engineering and design plan for implementation [DEDPI]) milestone. By coming to a consensus between the government and the public's demand on main span expansion, aesthetics and environmentally friendly operation, the negotiation yielded an agreement that was a win–win for the public and the private sector.

By obtaining a government guarantee for the construction and timely completion of connecting roads between the Incheon Bridge and other expressways, a key element of traffic volume and conduct that met all stakeholders' expectations of the stakeholders was established during the ARCA. These were the terms of the agreement before obtaining the investment amount (which was the equivalent of US$1.3 billion). Thus, conclusion of the agreement meant the simultaneous completion of the financing.

The construction phase

In the construction phase, the fast-track method was used. Five core management elements were identified by the project management (PM) plan during the proposal stage, which facilitated the objective of timely completion. Process management was carried out through detailed and quantified milestones, especially during the construction phase.

For quarterly payments, AMEC's project manager was notified of the interim payment application information provided by the contractor. Reviews were conducted by the construction supervisor (CS), design supervisor (DS) and lender's technical advisor (LTA). The project manager then delivered the progress inspection record to the project owner, establishing a method for managing the contractor within the procedure. The remarkable point is that the construction supervisor was directly contracted and managed by Korea Expressway Corporation (KEC), an authorized agency of the government. Ultimately, this indicated that the responsibility for quality control was within the domain of the government of the system. Through this system, the concerns of the shareholders and lenders with regard to the quality assurance of implementing foreign project management for the first time was alleviated.

The operation and maintenance phase

Incheon Bridge Company, the concessionaire of the project, has managed its operation within the confirmed yearly budget, committed to achieving the following three future business objectives:

1. Realizing perfect maintenance management;
2. Supplementary projects to increase traffic volume;
3. A model social enterprise that practises love.

Once these annual objectives had been set, they separated into team objectives. Team objectives were achieved under the direction of the team leaders, who checked the objectives' completion against budget each quarter. Thus the Incheon Bridge Project is one that achieves its objectives through governing the management board and the lenders with yearly efficiency management.

Stakeholders and their expectations

This project was conducted as a public–private partnership project. The phase-specific expectations of all stakeholders were analysed from the beginning. These expectations are summarized and listed in Figure 14.2. By the time construction had been completed, the toll charges had already been set at 75 per cent compared with other private investment projects. This was based on the concept that the project's highest client is the nation, including its people and nature. Ways to reduce the toll further have been looked at continuously, contributing to higher asset values and growth of the community.

The project also officially established the corporate social responsibility (CSR) team to put into practice its management philosophy based on corporate social responsibility. That included associated activities such as the following:

*   Setting up a café run by people with different or limited abilities;
*   Sponsoring an orchestra of disabled people;
*   Holding a Korean pickle (Kimchi) – making and sharing event;
*   Carrying out an abandoned animal adoption campaign;
*   Running a therapeutic horse-riding centre.

These efforts have been highly regarded by all the media as well the government in its evaluation of the Incheon Bridge Project's operation, not to mention the nationwide love and support for the project.

The environment was included in the scope of the stakeholders. A joint analysis team was formed to conduct the preliminary environmental analysis. A post-environmental impact analysis was carried out after construction completion to secure and preserve the mudflat, pursuing an eco-friendly approach, without any land reclamation. The Incheon Bridge Company concluded an agreement with the environmental protection group and actively engages in preserving the mudflat through activities such as the ghost crab protection movement.

Strategic objectives and organization

The three main phases of the project (finance, construction and operation and maintenance [O&M]) were confirmed during planning. These phases reflected and confirmed all the stakeholders' dreams and expectations, including those of Incheon city. Execution of the project established detailed objectives managed by procedures and

Stakeholders	Expectations
Government	• Reinvigorate the economy to overcome the Asian financial crisis and improve national confidence through the attraction of foreign investment • Pursue a project symbolizing close cooperative ties between Korea and the UK, engaging a UK company in the process of product development and execution • Raise national competitiveness through conducting an international project • Facilitate growth of the private sector investment market with the introduction of a new paradigm of private investment projects • Set an exemplary open policy project case achieved in accordance with the Act on Free economic Zone, with building a core infrastructure connecting the Free Economic Zone
Incheon City	• Create the Free Economic Zone, full of vitality, which connects Chungra and Songdo districts and Youngjongdo • Develop the Songdo International Business District to be turned into a globally renowned area, ranging with Pudong, Hong Kong or Singapore • Become a logistics hub linked to harbour and airport (Incheon Harbour and Incheon International Airport) • Achieve the first successful case of a project jointly planned and developed by the public and private sectors • Develop the first project led by a foreign partner
Shareholders	• Secure stable financial status of the project with lowering construction costs (which impacts on toll reduction) • Establish a well-organized business structure, with advanced PM methodologies being introduced through involving a globally renowned company in the project • Build a stable business model to enable operation costs during the 30-year operation period to be secured • Secure stability in terms of project operation and maintenance with 30-year land use rights being obtained • Eliminate risk factors from potential construction of competing routes so that stable project earnings could be realized • Ensure project stability through construction liabilities being guaranteed by design and construction contractors
Lenders	• Enable the principal sum and interest to be paid back under stable circumstances • Ensure stable project earnings • Ensure project stability through the construction liabilities being guaranteed by design and construction contractors
People	• Anticipate an aesthetically well-designed bridge • Build a safe and solid bridge and roads • Lowered tolls
AMEC	• Agree on mutual benefits for stakeholders through a smooth process of negotiations with the government • Attempt to take the lead of the project as a global PM expert for the first time in Korea • Expand its business boundaries to the other industries in Korea
IBC	• Predict management stability under the 30-year operation circumstances • Obtain knowledge of advanced PM methodologies through working together with international experts, and strengthen individual competence
NGO (nature)	• Apply environment-friendly technologies (conducting environmental research on 23 sectors) • Expand the main span of the bridge
Design and construction contractor	• Observe the project completion date despite unpredictable weather conditions (offshore section) • Shorten the construction period • Reduce the total construction costs

Figure 14.2 Definition of stakeholders broadened to the nation, the people and nature

other means, and these procedures and means were confirmed by management methods specified in the execution plan. The objectives relevant to each of the three phases are set out in Figure 14.3.

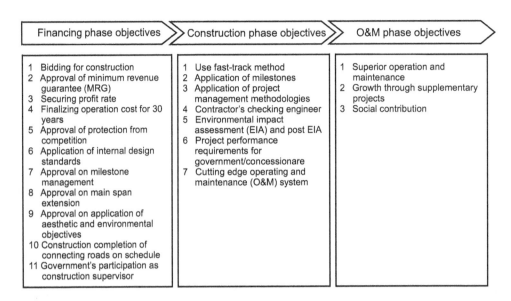

Financing phase objectives	Construction phase objectives	O&M phase objectives
1 Bidding for construction 2 Approval of minimum revenue guarantee (MRG) 3 Securing profit rate 4 Finalizing operation cost for 30 years 5 Approval of protection from competition 6 Application of internal design standards 7 Approval on milestone management 8 Approval on main span extension 9 Approval on application of aesthetic and environmental objectives 10 Construction completion of connecting roads on schedule 11 Government's participation as construction supervisor	1 Use fast-track method 2 Application of milestones 3 Application of project management methodologies 4 Contractor's checking engineer 5 Environmental impact assessment (EIA) and post EIA 6 Project performance requirements for government/concessionare 7 Cutting edge operating and maintenance (O&M) system	1 Superior operation and maintenance 2 Growth through supplementary projects 3 Social contribution

Figure 14.3 Strategic objectives in the three phases

As this was the first project in Korea conducted by both public and private sectors (as well as a foreign company), the Incheon Bridge Company created a workforce with various experiences and cultural backgrounds. It sought continually for operational strategies to increase task efficiency. In particular, because the government was the partner in this national policy project, both sides' employees were set to work interchangeably in order to create close task cooperation,

The members of the project (commercial, planning, engineering and quality managers) were recruited worldwide. Technical experts gave general advice on design and construction, commercial experts propelled negotiations and bidding, and financial experts propelled financing. For accounting, legal and insurance fields, the Incheon Bridge Project used separate advisory companies.

The number of people mobilized for project execution during the construction period ran to 230 000 per annum. The Incheon Bridge Project, the first PM management organization in Korea, overcame cultural differences between foreign professional project managers and Korean employees and actively introduced global standards in order to communicate effectively.

The organizational structure was divided into Korean at the working level, the foreign middle management, Korean executive decision-making and the investment decision body, which was the UK headquarters.

The project management office (PMO) comprised approximately 40 PM professionals under the construction director and the project director. Those people included the following:

- Coordination manager;
- Engineering managers for each construction zone;
- Progress manager;

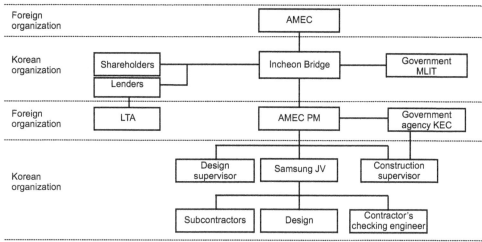

LTA = lender's technical advisor

Figure 14.4 The Incheon Bridge Project organizational structure

- Document controller;
- Project web engineer;
- Finance director; and
- Safety and environment officer.

Relevant suborganizations of the project included the following:

- Shareholders, lenders and their technical advisors (about 30 people);
- 17 design supervisors;
- 342 from design and construction contractors;
- 107 from Korea Expressway Corporation;
- 59 construction supervisors and advisors;
- 148 construction designers and contractor's checking engineers plus 104 from subcontractors.

The organization is charted in Figure 14.4.

PM-based execution process

As the project concessionaire, Incheon Bridge Company concluded a concession agreement, completed the financing process and supervised all construction companies during the construction phase, with the PM as the project operator. The Incheon Bridge Project pioneered advances in the programme, portfolio and project office (P3O) concept, which was strategically implemented in 2003 and is discussed in the following paragraphs.

After closure of the ARCA, the biggest concern was to apply the ASHITO load and resistance factor design standards (LRFD) to the project within a limited construction period, and ensure establishment of an aesthetically well-designed and solid bridge. In order for this to be achieved, AMEC PM proposed using the fast-track method to meet various expectations of the project stakeholders.

In order to manage processes successfully, facility-specific milestones were specified and quantified to enable progress to be measured against the timeline. The following key components of PM were identified:

1. Design management;
2. Construction management;
3. Planning and schedule management;
4. Quality/safety/health/environment/risk management; and
5. Contract management.

These five key management items were fulfilled using the fast-track method, reflecting the characteristics of the three processes of design, construction and reporting. The design structure participates in the process of designing a large number of stakeholders as shown in the business organization chart (Figure 14.4), and is divided into 20 design packages which included a total of 74 detailed design packages. It is a key component of successful construction to proceed with the design review and approval process with due diligence. In particular, the design review process was limited to complete the final design approval within 63 days of the initial design proposal, ensuring that the construction timeframe was free from disruption.

PM participated in the design validation and approval, and fulfilled the interests of the project executives, shareholders, lenders and governments. As the design approval was confirmed and executed in advance, completion of 20 packages within the time-frame of the construction would not have been possible without using milestone management through the PM.

The construction process involved the government, business operators, AMEC PM, construction supervisor (CS), design and construction contractor. The reporting process was structured so that AMEC PM would have timely business reports for each stakeholder.

AMEC PM transferred all information collected under the above-mentioned structure to the concessionaire after completion of the bridge construction. Currently, the Incheon Bridge Project, at the operation and maintenance phase, has developed its own asset management process by integrating all available information assets with the project facilities.

The Incheon Bridge Project put its value chain as a top priority in order to meet the expectations of project stakeholders, including shareholders, lenders and regional communities. The basic system to substantiate the company's value was established and is accordingly in operation. The core value was defined as 'best operation and maintenance, growth through supplementary projects and social contribution', and the company introduced the asset management process system to follow up on this, with tangible and non-tangible values being defined as company assets.

This means that project management know-how for the operation management period is designated as intellectual property, which can have a significant impact on the overall expected life expectancy and value growth of the facility. Therefore, in order to establish this, a step-by-step process owner was designated and a process management standard established. A standard task baseline for operation and maintenance was established, manuals were maintained and checkpoints for each step of the process were established.

In the course of developing the process, feedback from individuals in charge of separate tasks is gathered. Through this feedback process, the opinions of the individuals are reflected as much as possible, and this process is embodied in the development process through weekly reports.

Project results

The Incheon Bridge Project's PM resulted in realizing the objectives of the financial covenants in the financing phase and succeeding in non-recourse project financing for the first time in Korea. This also does not mention setting a precedent as a new model and, in the construction phase, the application of a fast-track method brought forward the completion of the phase by 19 months compared with the initial proposal, with no increase in the construction cost, unlike any other projects. The Incheon Bridge Project currently in operation is making ongoing efforts to lower the toll and grow into a social enterprise through additional projects, as shown in the projects described below. The key project achievements and features are summarized in Figures 14.5 and 14.6.

In recognition of its excellence, the Incheon Bridge Project has won many prestigious awards, including the Highest Order of Industrial Service Merit–Gold Tower Medal awarded by the President of Republic of Korea and the best management awards from seven different institutions. Its outstanding performance in achieving the objectives of each phase was acknowledged through winning very many awards, of which the following list is just a tiny selection:

- Ten Wonders in the Construction World in 2005 by the UK Construction News;
- The Best Project Finance Deal of the Year Award in Asia Pacific Transport Infrastructure by Euromoney;
- Top 25 Newsmakers in 2007 by ENR;
- Tanaka Award by the Japan Society of Civil Engineers in 2010;
- World's Top 5 Construction Projects by the American Society of Civil Engineers (ASCE) in 2011.

Conclusion: the Incheon Bridge Project is still in progress

The Incheon Bridge Company (Figure 14.7) is committed to achieving the following three future objectives:

1. Realizing perfect operation and maintenance management;
2. Conducting supplementary projects to increase traffic volume; and
3. Creating a model social enterprise that practises love.

The methods used are to establish annual objectives for the teams, good operation management and practising love, while resonating with the future generation and leaving philosophy behind.

	Objective	Achievements
Financing	ARCA	• Agreement made in phases to minimize risk of projects proposed by private sector (1st concession agreement and 2nd amended and restated concession agreement)
	Financial close	• Financial stability ensured by reaching agreement on MRG with government, removing financial risk factors at the same time • It enabled the financial agreement to be signed to borrow as much as USD 1 billion with no security and no guarantee
	Lower toll	• A toll was lowered given the application of international design standards and reduction in total construction cost caused by the tendering process applied to the selection of design and construction companies • The initial toll of US$8-10 for small-sized vehicles was reduced to USD 5.2
	Application of international design standards	• Aesthetically well-designed and solid bridge was constructed through the application of economical, eco-friendly and technically advanced design concepts • This offered an opportunity for domestic civil engineering skills to be upgraded to keep in step with the world's leading companies
	PM methodology	• Under the domestic circumstances of PM's role not being widely recognized, project led by PM through all phases was highly appreciated given the integrated concepts of planning and execution • Overall management of milestones, design and construction (design, construction, quality, health and safety, environment, milestone payment, risk management and so on)
	Lump-sum turnkey project for design and construction	• Fair and transparent process taken to select construction contractors, recognized as the first case among Korea's private investment projects. Independent evaluation was conducted to ensure proper assessment of technologies and estimate reasonable amount of construction costs • Fair and transparent tendering packages to select contractors were progressed. Construction cost reduction through the tendering process = US$270 million (79 per cent against the design cost)
Construction	Fast track	• PM competence was developed to integrate each stakeholder's expectations
	Milestone management	• Management of schedule, payment, safety, quality, design and risk factors to achieve construction completion on time
	On-time construction completion	• The bridge is an eco-friendly green structure with slender shape and graceful curves. Stiffness had to be strengthened further, making it the first exemplary case to offer a chance to get the domestic civil engineering standards. See Figure 14.6 for key construction features of the bridge
Operating and maintenance	Toll reduction and its effects	• Reasonably lowered tolls, estimated at about 77 per cent of of those for comparable projects. • MRG burdens reduced by narrowing a gap with the estimated traffic volume. Currently the lowest MRG level recorded among private investment projects and it is expected that no support of MRG will be needed after 2016 • Project confidence ensured by mobilizing advanced PM methodology • Activated regional economy - increased asset value of Incheon City by about US$250 billion USD in line with the development of Songdo international business district • Establishment of new tourism belt increased Yongjongdo asset values • Travel time from southern part of metropolitan area to Incheon airport reduced by 40 minutes • Carbon dioxide emissions reduced by 25,000 tonnes, equivalent to planting 833 pine trees • The Incheon Bridge is a significant contributor to greatly enhancing the national logistics network (innovative change in the logistics transportation structure for the mid and southern parts of Korea)
	Social contribution	• An agreement with environmental protection organizations was signed and environmental protection activities are in progress accordingly • The Incheon Bridge began its journey with a belief that people are the best client. Therefore it is making continued efforts to facilitate the growth of the city through the development of supplementary projects and keeps expanding its business areas, realizing increased traffic volume and reduced tolls

Figure 14.5 Key project achievements

Key features

- World's largest:
  - Dolphin-shaped impact protection (diameter 25m, height 38m, 44 units in total).
  - FSLM girders, length 50m, weight 50 tonnes.
  - Pile loading (compressed load more than 30,000 tonnes).
- Korea's biggest:
  - Scale (total length 18.38km, main span of the cable-stayed bridge 800m).
  - Height of pylon 238.5m.
  - Manufacturing and installation of PC house, pylon's foundation, (scale: 35m x 28m x 5.4m, weight 1,800 tonnes).
  - Application of large calibre in-site concrete pile, (diameter 3m, length 76m).
  - Large-scale expansion joint device (width 4m, maximum expansion 2m).

Figure 14.6 Some key construction features of the Incheon Bridge

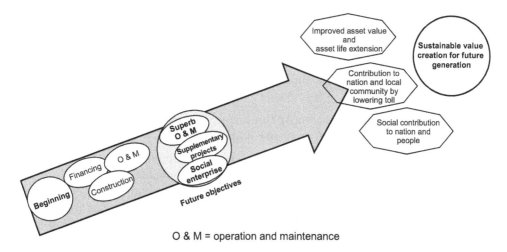

O & M = operation and maintenance

Figure 14.7 The Incheon Bridge Project in progress

Differentiated maintenance: turning processes into assets

The currently most importance process of the operation phase is defined as 'the asset management process'. This controls and manages project experience and know-how obtained during the operation and maintenance phase. This know-how is one of the company's intellectual assets, and it could impact on the expected lifecycle and values of facilities overall. Therefore, a process owner is designated at each stage, with process management standards being put in place. Manuals were organized with a set of standard operation and maintenance activities, and a checklist for each stage.

Staff opinions were collected for consideration when the processes were being developed, and this feedback process was a tool for making the best use of the viewpoints of people who were in charge of each process. This reporting was conducted on a weekly basis, to ensure that processes being developed took account of staff viewpoints.

For the benefit of smooth communication between the relevant people inside and outside the company, meetings take place on a regular basis, with necessary training programmes being offered. The feedback process is reflected back to the system, its procedures being formally notified as being in operation. A person in charge of measuring the outcome of the asset management process was appointed to monitor the following:

- Whether or not the process runs with no interruptions and in an efficient manner;
- Whether there is any need for improvements.

This outcome is to be used as basic information for performance management.

The additions of new processes or amendments of existing processes are being reviewed and discussed thoroughly between process owners and people in charge of execution. The system was established to agree on and implement the core standard items. A feedback process is in operation to see whether the results of new or amended processes run satisfactorily, which would all be monitored and recorded

Besides tangible facilities, these processes and knowledge obtained from the execution of such processes are all regarded as company assets. With definition of the value of an operation company, objective management items are listed and agreed throughout discussions between process owners and people in charge of execution. The feedback process for monitoring results, on a regular basis, is a key contributor to increasing the process users' level of satisfaction, minimizing unnecessary losses and boosting efficiency.

Social enterprise: rehabilitation of the differently abled and community engagement service to the community

The Incheon Bridge Company has been working on developing programmes to help handicapped and disabled people enjoy life to the fullest possible extent. A cafeteria is run together with the social welfare foundation, where adults with developmental disorders can learn and work, as well as providing a stage for performances arranged by the Young-Jong Art Company for differently abled people. Plans are also in existence to support these disabled people by offering a therapeutic horse-riding programme.

Also, the Incheon Bridge Company holds the Korean Kimchi-making event on a yearly basis to distribute to underprivileged individuals within its neighbourhood, which involves all employees and local communities. Provision of free legal services for local residents, provided in cooperation with the Legal Aid Foundation under the Korean Bar Association, is also a part of the company's efforts to serve the local communities.

In an attempt to preserve the Young-Jong mudflat in Incheon, which is one of the world's top five mudflats, the Incheon Bridge Company provides funds to protect the mudflat ecosystem, and hosts an annual event to raise awareness of mudflat protection to put more effort into removing the factors that threaten the mudflat and strengthening the monitoring.

References and further reading

International Project Management Association (IPMA) (2015), *Individual Competence Baseline for Project, Programme & Portfolio Management*, Version 4.0 (electronic document).
International Organization for Standardization (ISO) (2015), ISO 21504 *Project, Programme and Portfolio Management – Guidance on portfolio management*, Geneva: ISO.

Chapter 15

Portfolio management in public institutions

Silke Schönert and Michael Münzberg

Public sector organizations worldwide are under pressure to increase efficiency while delivering improved and integrated services. As in other industries, innovation or change is mostly driven by projects. The discipline of project management provides the structure, processes and tools to make changes happen. This chapter describes the characteristics of project portfolio management in public organizations and provides an example.

Introduction

With portfolio management the Federal Office of Administration in Germany is able to prioritize and track the progress of multiple ongoing projects, and determine where and when to invest the resources necessary to complete all of them. At a time when federal spending is under greater scrutiny than ever before, there is increased pressure for agencies to make sure that they are making the smartest investments. Portfolio management is a critical tool that helps them to achieve that goal.

The public sector and project management

Achieving project management success in the public sector has its challenges. Several of these are different from those that face projects in the private sector. Some of the typical success factors of project management and the characteristics of public organizations even seem to be contradictory. The purpose of public organizations is to create stability, whereas projects stand for innovation. In summary there are some influencing factors that seem to be compelling reasons for problems in public projects. We have listed these factors in Figure 15.1.

Nevertheless the importance of project and portfolio management capability in the public sector has been recognized in government initiatives in various countries. For example, the US government has invested significantly in project and programme management, notably in defence acquisition, the Department of Energy and NASA. In the UK, the Office of Government Commerce (OGC) was established to 'help government deliver best value from its spending' including the 'delivery of projects to time, quality and cost, realizing benefits' (Campagnac, 2012).

Public sector characteristics	Project success factors
• Hierarchical organization structure • Influenced by politics and political cycles • Contradictory goals • High interest from the public and media • Complex network of interest groups • Cooperation with other authorities • Political oppositions • Variety of administrative regulations • Given resources • Often low availability of project management expertise • Performance and output difficult to measure because of public welfare • Low fault tolerance and therefore cautious decisions • Rare possibilities for incentives in project work	• Stable and, at the same time, flexible project organization • Systematic planning and project controlling • Support from top management • Established fault/problem culture • Career perspective and incentives • Stable processes • Project management qualifications • High communication capability • Clear goals • Appropriate methodology • Stakeholder involvement • Competent project management and motivated employees • Proactive risk management

Figure 15.1 Public sector characteristics and project success factors

Portfolio management in public organizations

The implementation of strategy is a high priority for organizations. Project portfolio management (PPM) is recognized as a key method for achieving this goal. The mission of PPM lies in evaluating, prioritizing and selecting projects in line with the organizational strategy. Alignment of all ongoing projects with the overall business strategy is generally recognized as being very important for most modern organizations. The selection process involves identifying opportunities, assessing the organizational fit, analysing the costs, benefits and risks, and developing and selecting a portfolio.

The first major element of portfolio management is to identify opportunities and determine whether or not those opportunities are in line with the corporate strategic direction.

The second major element of portfolio management is to define each project further (if needed) and to analyse the details surrounding its utility. The utility of a project captures the usefulness of the project and its value. It is typically defined by costs, benefits and associated risks.

The third stage of portfolio management is the development and selection of the project portfolio.

Success factors of portfolio management at the German Federal Office of Administration

Throughout the last few years the number and complexity of projects conducted by the German Federal Office of Administration have increased rapidly. Owing to this development, the number of interrelationships of the projects has increased as well. This is especially true for the management of resources. All this has made it necessary to focus on centralized control, particularly to assign resources (which are not limitless) to those projects that mainly fulfil the strategic goals. Also, the high complexity associated with these projects means that many stakeholders are involved. These stakeholders have to be kept up to date with progress and other information on a regular basis.

The portfolio management of the German Federal Office of Administration distinguishes between portfolio planning and portfolio controlling. The question behind portfolio planning is 'Which projects should be started next and how can the resources be assigned most efficiently?'. Portfolio control focuses on deviations compared with the initial plan and how to overcome these. Over the past few years several success factors have been discovered from the application of portfolio management. These success factors can be summarized as follows:

- Involvement of major stakeholder groups from the early phase;
- Having an influential supporting team;
- Having an organization that had 'project affinity' from the start;
- Starting small, simply and quickly;
- Establishing organizational structures for the project portfolio;
- Having a process guide to give clarity over new processes.

The German Federal Office of Administration runs portfolio management by applying the following five phases.

Phase 1: initializing

After an application to approve a new project is received, a stakeholder negotiation is conducted to generate feedback about whether or not the project should be started. The actual decision is made by considering the following seven criteria (which are not necessarily listed in order of importance):

1. Strategic impact;
2. Urgency;
3. Resource requirements;
4. Availability of resources;
5. Insecurities, risks and complexity;
6. Time frame;
7. Legal necessity.

Phases 2–4

For each approved project, phases 2–4 are as follows:

- Planning;
- Conception;
- Realization.

During these phases, regular data collection and status reporting are established to keep all the stakeholders involved fully informed.

Phase 5: finalization

During this final phase, the project manager reports about goals, quality, and the impact made in solving the initial problem or need for the project. In addition the findings and consequences for future projects (lessons learned) are stated and recorded. If there is a need for more decisions or additional deliverables, this is pointed out as well.

Success factors

During the last few years, approximately 80 portfolio meetings have taken place. As a consequence about 120 projects were started and successfully completed.

A survey initiated in 2014 found that almost every employee agreed to the usefulness and importance of establishing portfolio management. Several key success factors that could be determined were as follows:

- Involving stakeholders from an early stage;
- Support from the influencer or sponsor,
- Starting quickly and simply;
- Using integrated processes (Brombach and Herfeld, 2016).

Conclusion

Portfolio management in the public sector increases operational excellence through the ability to get projects done according to specifications, in order to accomplish the desired outcomes. A key part of this is the ability to execute projects in a prioritized manner, according to rules and policies laid out in agency governance requirements. Risk mitigation is another essential benefit, because government agencies and their contractors are subject to more regulations than ever. The impact of government projects is undeniable. Finally, the proper implementation of portfolio management – from initial planning to ongoing project monitoring and measurement – can go a long way towards achieving standardized portfolio management.

In this chapter we have described an example of a successful portfolio management system. The best thing that federal organizations can do when it comes to portfolio management is to communicate honestly and frequently. Portfolio management should be a valuable tool in promoting interagency collaboration and efficiency, by creating and successfully performing projects that have high strategic impact.

References and further reading

Brombach, S. and Herfeld, J. (2016), 'Projektportfoliomanagement: Erfolgsfaktoren bei der Einführung', in: Schoenert, S., Muenzberg, M. and Staudt, D. (eds), Projektmanagement in der Öffentlichen Verwaltung, Symposion, S. 215–228.

Campagnac, E. (2012), 'Governance and knowledge management for public private partnerships', *Construction Management and Economics*, 29(2), pp. 211–213.

Schoenert, S., Muenzberg, M. and Staudt, D., eds (2016), Projektmanagement in der Öffentlichen Verwaltung, Symposion, Düsseldorf.

Chapter 16

Portfolio management in non-governmental organizations

Subas Subedi and Reinhard Wagner

Non-governmental organizations (NGOs) are regulated through government policies but they operate in a fairly independent way. They are not-for-profit or charitable organizations, usually funded by donations and run primarily by volunteers. Their activities span a wide field, for example:

- Supporting local communities;
- Responding to natural disasters such as earthquakes and floods;
- Improving the living standards of people in need;
- Mitigating the effects of climate change;
- Improving infrastructures.

NGOs usually perform their work through projects and programmes. Increasing demands of beneficiaries, a growing number of projects and challenging requirements imposed by donors all mean that the success of a typical NGO has become increasingly dependent on professional portfolio management.

The specific context for portfolio management in NGOs

There is a huge variety of NGOs, differing greatly in size, purpose, services and setting. So, it is difficult to generalize but there are trends and peculiarities that allow insights into the specific context of portfolio management. Before implementing portfolio management, an NGO needs to analyse its specific context and develop an approach for portfolio management that is fit for purpose.

NGOs depend on funds donated by private people, foundations, business organizations, agencies and governmental institutions. Every donor wants the NGO to maximize the impact of the money that they provide. Thus, it isn't primarily the project that is in the interest of the donor, but rather the impact created through the project. When stories highlight successful projects, donors will be encouraged to continue sponsoring projects and new donors can be attracted. In essence, portfolio management needs to support the continuous flow of funds for an NGO through the successful delivery of projects that make a positive impact.

The number and demands of the beneficiaries is steadily increasing. In response to this, the United Nations (UN) adopted 17 goals for sustainable development, including (but not limited to) ending poverty, protecting the planet and ensuring prosperity for all. Each goal is associated with a number of specific targets to be achieved over the next 15 years. NGOs focus on one or several of these targets and try to fulfil the needs of their beneficiaries through performing projects and programmes. Clearly the beneficiaries would like to benefit to the maximum extent from these projects and their impacts. However, an NGO has to balance the huge and various demands made on it with the funds that it can gather. Portfolio management is instrumental in this challenge.

The competences of the staff and volunteers working for an NGO are typically very specific. NGOs involved with environmental protection employ people with competences in that specific area. An NGO engaged in providing safe drinking water will use people with competences in water cleansing, and so on. The ability to manage projects or programmes is not necessarily a competence given a high profile in an NGO. Some NGOs apply international project management standards and invest in specific training but, unfortunately, in most cases maturity in managing projects, programmes and especially portfolios is rather low. However, the more projects and programmes that an NGO performs, the more dependent it will become on professional project and programme management (and eventually on portfolio management) in order to satisfy the needs of donors and beneficiaries.

There are instances where an NGO gains trust for its best performance in small-scale activities, and donors provide more funds over a relatively short timespan. However, projects that are not managed professionally will lead towards losing the trust of essential donors, and this could even lead to collapse of organizations. So, it is crucial for an NGO to demonstrate that it can achieve the desired impact by good management of its portfolio of projects and programmes. Otherwise the organization will inevitably lose credibility and support from its donors.

Governmental organizations also play a role in the work done by an NGO. First, they register each NGO based on its purpose and charitable work being done. They monitor and control whether each NGO complies with relevant laws, norms and regulations set by the government. Second, governmental organizations often support the work of NGOs (for example, through funding arrangements as one of the partners during project execution, or helping with logistics). An NGO could not operate in a country without the support of that country's national government. Engaging all stakeholders of governmental organizations is critical for the success of projects and programmes. The portfolio of projects and programmes performed by the NGO should be synchronized with the strategic goals and key activities of governmental organizations. Portfolio management gives the NGO the capability to provide the relevant feedback and information to all those government stakeholders.

Applying portfolio management in the context of an NGO

According to ISO 21504, 'portfolio management aligns the portfolio components with an organization's strategic objectives, stakeholder priorities, and values such as sustainable practices and ethical principles' (International Organization for Standardization [ISO], 2015). Therefore, an NGO needs to formulate strategic objectives before applying portfolio management. The strategic objectives guide NGO's decision-makers through the process of selecting and prioritizing projects and programmes (the portfolio components) as well as aligning the objectives of those components to the overall strategy. Portfolio planning, balancing the resources, and controlling the progress and impact of the components are dependent on the availability of strategic objectives – otherwise every result fits (or not)! The stakeholder priorities and values of the NGO should also be reflected in the strategic objectives of the NGO. The leadership of an NGO is directly involved in setting the strategic objectives and, in parallel, taking decisions within the portfolio.

Some NGOs have established steering committees in order to balance their decisions better, based on information from involved organizational functions, and to get more acceptance for those decisions. Only a few NGOs have formally established organizational roles such as a portfolio manager or a project management office (PMO). In some cases, portfolio management is performed by the leader of a specific service function – a leader responsible for a geographical area or a specific target group. Project and programme managers need to understand to whom they may escalate issues and file their (status) reports and whom to ask for support. In ISO 21504 it is stated that 'Portfolio management requires competent individuals applying their knowledge and experience. Executives and senior management should demonstrate leadership and commitment with respect to portfolio management' (ISO, 2015). The International Project Management Association Individual Competence Baseline (IPMA ICB), in version 4.0, outlines the competences necessary for managing portfolios (IPMA, 2015).

Some NGOs may have several portfolios running in parallel. There must be transparency about the basis upon which projects and programmes are grouped together and how the organization is managing potential interrelations between projects and programmes across the portfolios.

Identifying potential portfolio components

Identifying potential projects and programmes should be a continuous effort of any NGO. Projects and programmes may be proposed by beneficiaries, intermediaries, government agencies or donors. They may be triggered through events such as natural disasters, political changes, economic turmoil or social unrest. In some cases, projects and programmes may be initiated through the strategy of the NGO, based on a sound analysis of stakeholder needs, a strategic plan and international best practices. The potential portfolio components need to be described in a standard format (for example, a project charter, project canvas or business case). The description should outline resource needs, objectives, benefits and the impact of the potential project, as well as the alignment to the NGO's strategic objectives.

Assessing, selecting and prioritizing portfolio components

Based on the information available, the steering committee or leadership of the NGO needs to decide on the project proposals. Assessment of the proposed projects and programmes will take the following into account:

- Their strategic fit (to what extent the strategic objectives of the NGO are supported);
- Feasibility;
- Availability of resources, know-how and competences;
- Conformance with the requirements of donors, beneficiaries and other key stakeholders.

This assessment needs to be done in a systematic way, applying lessons learned from previous projects and programmes. It should ideally be done from a strategic (not operational) point of view in order to maintain objectivity. Research on complex projects and programmes suggests the need for comparison with external references to avoid a bias towards undue optimism. Involvement of an independent third party for assessing the project proposals is also useful.

Selection and prioritization of portfolio components should be done using a set of transparent criteria. These criteria could include (but are not limited to) the following:

- Contribution of the project or programme towards achieving strategic objectives;
- Exposure to risk;
- Impact on available resources;
- Extent to which key stakeholders' objectives will be achieved; and
- The opportunities for learning and advancing the NGO's capabilities.

The process of decision-making should be transparent to the stakeholders, to avoid any misunderstanding or conflict.

Planning the portfolio with its components

Planning the portfolio of an NGO focuses on aspects such as time, cost, resources and the interdependencies of the portfolio components. Based on inputs from all projects and programmes, all schedules or milestone plans are merged into a portfolio schedule. This schedule will show the start and end dates as well as all milestones of the projects and programmes. In this portfolio overview the relevant interdependencies could also be displayed. What is most important for NGOs is an overview of the available resources and how they are to be utilized in projects and programmes. From a portfolio point of view, any foreseen resource shortages or under-utilization should be made apparent. The forecast resource utilization, including materials, will enable calculations of cost estimates. Then portfolio cash outflow schedules can be calculated which display the forecast spending over the life of the portfolio. All this requires competent project and programme managers, who are capable of developing plans for their project and portfolio components (which is an essential prerequisite for portfolio planning).

Validating portfolio alignment with the strategic objectives

Projects and programmes should realize benefits related to the strategic objectives of the NGO and the various stakeholders. Maintaining alignment between organizational strategy and the intended benefits should be a continuous activity. ISO 21504 illustrates the sequence of necessary activities (Figure 16.1).

Evaluating and reporting portfolio performance

Evaluating and reporting portfolio performance is another key activity of portfolio management in NGOs. Donors, governmental organizations and other stakeholders

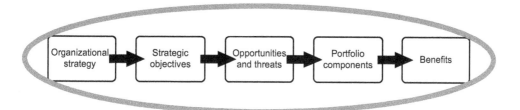

Figure 16.1 Continuous alignment

require the NGO to establish transparency of how it operates and how the money they were given is spent. Based on a set of KPIs (key performance indicators, described in Chapter 23) an NGO should be collecting information from all its projects and programmes, and evaluating them against the performance measurement baseline (as outlined in the NGO's strategy or the donor's requirements). Deviations must be detected and analysed. Then remedial actions have to be taken to reverse or minimize those deviations. Reports have to be made to all stakeholders and other interested parties.

Clearly such reporting is important (especially to donors) and requirements for reporting should be arranged and agreed in advance, before any expenditure is committed. This agreement should cover the content, format and frequency of reporting, as well as the distribution of reports. It might be decided that some stakeholders will receive fully detailed reports, whereas others can be given abridged or summary reports. We have already written that an NGO is also required to support the marketing activities of significant donors and its own organization. This is why an NGO needs to collect (in addition to performance information) information that could be used for marketing and public relations activities. This typically includes photos, videos, testimonials, case studies and lessons learned in projects and programmes.

Balancing and optimizing the portfolio

According to ISO 21504 a 'portfolio manager should balance and control the portfolio, including but not limited to, maintaining the portfolio pipeline, optimizing resources, managing portfolio risks and portfolio change, and optimizing the synergies among portfolio components' (ISO, 2015). For an NGO this is very important, because it will typically suffer from scarce resources (both financial and human) and is therefore required to balance projects and programmes with available resources. Risks and opportunities need to be managed from a strategic perspective, for example the risk of losing one of the key partners in a project could affect all the projects in a portfolio.

Synergy is another aspect that is success critical for NGOs. For example, using experiences and lessons learned from one project to plan and calculate another project is critical. Making know-how available from one project to another will help the NGO to develop in certain domains and grow with projects and programmes. This can be achieved only from the level of portfolio management – not from the rather operational level of projects and programmes.

Insights into the practice of portfolio management

With two short examples, we want to provide insights into the practice of portfolio management in an NGO. The first example will provide insights into the approach that the IPMA uses in a portfolio of projects to achieve its Strategy 2020. The second example reflects on what the Employment Fund in Nepal is doing to support the employment and development of people in need.

Performing strategic change through a portfolio of projects

The IPMA is a federation of about 70 national project management associations (www.ipma.world). It was established in Europe about 50 years ago and grew rapidly all over the globe. Member associations of IPMA develop project management competencies in their geographical areas of influence, interacting with thousands of practitioners and developing relationships with corporations, government agencies, universities and colleges, as well as training organizations and consulting companies. The IPMA is member driven, and volunteer staffed. As a geographically distributed organization, IPMA collaborates intensively on an ongoing basis, holding board and council meetings regularly around the world.

In 2014, the IPMA Council of Delegates approved the Strategy 2020 with an inspiring vision, mission and goals for a continued growth path towards 2020. For the Executive Board of IPMA it was clear that the strategic change could be achieved only by using professional project, programme and portfolio management. Two areas for change activities were identified:

1. For achieving the strategic goals of growth (qualitatively and quantitatively); and
2. For advancing the organizational setting in order to cope with the change in a professional way.

The first area covered (for example) projects to develop new standards, publications and services. In the second area, projects were launched to reorganize, change the budget structure and process, as well as improve the information technologies used. Based on Strategy 2020 and the annual budgets, the executive board developed a plan for activities to be performed within the next two-year timeframe plus a roadmap of all projects to be performed from 2015 until 2020.

The executive board acts as steering committee for all projects and programmes and performs the activities outlined above. A vice-president 'projects' is the 'chief project officer' (see http://blog.ipma.world/chief-project-officer-cpo-new-role-project-oriented-organisations) and leads all project-related activities. This includes (but is not limited to) the following:

- Selection, planning and prioritization of projects based on Strategy 2020 and the budget, as well as volunteer resources available;
- Collecting status reports via the executive director;
- Highlighting the major issues and decisions necessary;
- Ensuring the professional management of all projects (for example, chartering projects using a 'project canvas');

- Informing the council of delegates on a regular basis about progress and any decisions necessary; and finally
- Collecting the lessons learned.

As the IPMA is a truly global organization, project collaboration is done mainly on a virtual basis, using tools such as ProjectPlace. Another challenge is that projects are staffed mainly by volunteers, so it is difficult to get a commitment for time dedicated to projects (which is why sometimes schedules slip or projects are postponed). Portfolio management needs to take all of this into account by aiming high and encouraging the project teams to stick to the targets set. Graphic display of all project schedules in a roadmap helps people to understand how (or whether) the strategic goals are being achieved, where interrelations are in the portfolio, and what consequences might arise from postponing projects.

Reporting is another critical issue. The council of delegates, the executive board, the vice-president for 'projects' and all project sponsors (typically a vice-president responsible for a particular remit) want to be informed about the plans, the progress and any decisions necessary. Information can be collected and disseminated to specific target audiences through ProjectPlace. Standards for managing projects, programmes and the overall portfolio, as well as regulations such as an IPMA Code of Ethics and Professional Conduct, guide the people involved in performing their tasks. At the time of writing the next iteration of the IPMA Strategy is under way, and this will build on the experiences collected during recent years.

Ensuring the impact of projects through a portfolio supervision

Entering gainful employment remains a challenge for many Nepalese youth owing to low educational levels and limited access to vocational training (which often does not respond to market needs). With the aim of addressing these needs, the Employment Fund (see www.employmentfund.org.np) was established in 2007 and operated from 2008 in a joint effort of the Government of Nepal, the Swiss Agency for Development and Cooperation (SDC) and HELVETAS Swiss Inter-cooperation.

The Employment Fund Secretariat, which is operated by HELVETAS, is managing the employment fund programme. The employment fund is governed by a steering committee with representatives from the Government of Nepal and the donor agencies. These donor agencies include, for example, SDC and UKAid (Department for International Development [DFID]). The fund offers training for economically very poor and socially discriminated youths to ensure their entry into the labour market immediately after short-term market-orientated skills training in about 80 trades under the 'Path to Prosperity' component. It also facilitates youths who want to establish enterprises of their own creating additional jobs under 'Micro Enterprising' for the 'Job Creation' component.

HELVETAS is applying the Logical Framework (LogFrame), a simple methodology developed by the United States Agency for International Development (USAID) in 1969. LogFrame is commonly used by donors (including the European Commission, Deutsche Gesellschaft für Internationale Zusammenarbeit [GIZ] GmbH, DFID, and so on) for illustrating how projects or programmes will work in order to achieve the desired impact. What is the impact and how does it relate to input, activities, outputs and outcomes of a project? First, the terms used in that context are defined as follows and below, explained in case of the Employment Fund:

- Inputs: the financial, human, and material resources used for the development intervention, for example a well-equipped training venue, instructors, training materials, and so on;
- Activities: actions taken or work performed through which inputs, such as funds, technical assistance and other types of resources, are mobilized to produce specific outputs, for example instructors' training, technical training sessions to the youths in the plumbing trade, and so forth;
- Outputs: the products, capital goods and services that result from a development intervention; these may also include changes resulting from the intervention that are relevant to the achievement of outcomes, for example a youth certified in the plumbing trade;
- Outcomes: the likely or actually achieved short- and medium-term effects on the beneficiaries by using the outputs generated, for example gainful employment of the trained youth, meeting minimum salary requirement;
- Impact: positive and negative, primary and secondary long-term effects produced by a development intervention, directly or indirectly, intended or unintended, for example the plumber has achieved a better living standard, his children are attaining a better quality of education, and so on.

Thousands of people were killed in the devastating earthquake in Nepal during April 2015, and millions lost their homes. Thanks to generous donations a programme was launched to support the people of Nepal. One focus of the programme was to rebuild as many of the houses as possible, but also to support the people in making their living and having a better future. The inputs of the project were financial support from international donors, plus the experience and proven concepts of HELVETAS, which has been active in Nepal for more than 60 years, and a long-established network of partners working with HELVETAS. During the programme, other resources were made available.

The key activities of the core team at HELVETAS were as follows:

- Setting up an organization;
- Planning all activities (such as training programmes) with all partners;
- Monitoring and controlling progress; and
- Filing reports to the government and the donors.

Many other activities were also performed, including the following:

- Designing a train-the-trainer curriculum for earthquake-resilient construction of homes;
- Training the instructors themselves for this work;
- Providing 50 days training to 6500 masons and 1000 carpenters in house construction work;
- Finding employment for the trainees locally and in urban centres.

It is noteworthy that there was a major strategic shift from 'institution-based' training to 'on-site' training. This is the best example of how an NGO builds on its past experience while dealing with the emerging needs of the society. As a result, this approach has been adopted by the National Reconstruction Authority of Nepal.

Outputs of the Employment Fund Programme are the concepts for the train-the-trainers, the training curricula, earthquake-resilient homes reconstructed during the training, as well as job counselling and placement for the trainees. One outcome is the gainful employment of economically poor and socially discriminated youth. Another important output is increasing knowledge in how to build earthquake-resilient homes, which will help to avoid massive destruction during the next earthquake and a much stronger network of construction people in the community. The employment of the disadvantaged Nepalese youth will have great impact on their self-esteem, their wealth and social situation.

In essence, HELVETAS is monitoring and controlling the progress of portfolio components using a holistic approach (Figure 16.2).

Another issue is worth mentioning because the monitoring and controlling of the progress of projects were performed through an innovative electronic photo monitoring system. Using their smart phones, the supervisors could upload pictures to an application, which transferred them to a central database that provides the basis for project control.

Payment was based on progress. Of the fees 25 per cent were paid on signing the agreement (to allow preparation for the project activities). The next 25 per cent was paid on training completion. A further 25 per cent will be paid after three months' employment verification and the final 25 per cent payment become due after verification of six months' minimum wages earned. In addition, there are financial incentives

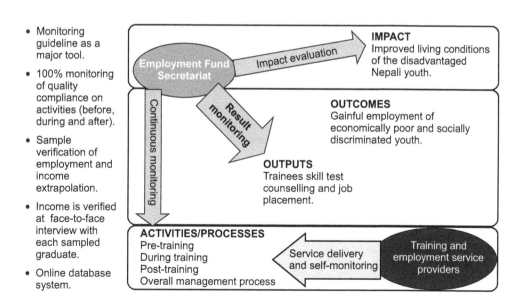

Figure 16.2 Monitoring and controlling of progress in portfolio components

for training and providing employment to underprivileged or discriminated people. Thus, the payment is focusing on outcomes rather than on output and activities. In summary, this can be called a 'best practice' for ensuring the impact of projects and programmes through portfolio supervision.

HELVETAS is also a good example for collecting lessons learned, case studies and testimonials in the scope of a portfolio. Taking photos, videos and interviews with people engaged in projects and programmes helps HELVETAS to spread the word of doing good for the society in Nepal. It helps all parties involved (HELVETAS, the donors and the international NGOs involved in the case) to explain what they do, what impact has been achieved and what their contribution to the success has been. Public relations work is done by collecting case stories through project reports and disseminating these via all available media (such as videos, audio messages, social media like Facebook and a website for the Employment Fund), communicating the portfolio of activities and reaching out to all stakeholders.

Conclusion

NGOs use portfolio management because they are performing the most of their activities through projects and programmes. Owing to the fact that NGOs operate in a specific context, their way of managing portfolios is different from business-orientated organizations. Especially, the staffing with volunteers, dependency on funds donated or generated through charitable activities, as well as the limited know-how in project, programme and portfolio management, require an NGO to adopt the good practices available in the domain of portfolio management. Scarce resources and funds are typically the main bottlenecks for an NGO, and these require a thorough selection of priorities and balancing of the available resources with the ambitions set out in the strategy.

The two short examples given here demonstrate that NGOs are starting to think beyond the application of tools, processes, methods and competences only to projects, but increasingly also to programmes and the portfolios. Portfolios help the NGO to align all its projects and programme activities to the organization's strategy, the stakeholder needs and the resources available. The active engagement of the NGO leaders is a clear success factor for portfolio management. It is those leaders who are in charge of providing strategic guidance and taking decisions based on the information provided from the operations, which are mainly projects and programmes for an NGO. An NGO is certainly interested in deliverables or outputs of projects. However, the outcomes, benefits and impact are more important for NGOs working in the field of society and helping to achieve the UN's Sustainable Development Goals.

References and further reading

International Project Management Association (2016a), *IPMA Individual Competence Baseline*, Version 4.0, Amsterdam: IPMA

International Organization for Standardization (2015), ISO 21504 *Project, Programme and Portfolio Management – Guidance on portfolio management*, Geneva: ISO.

Part III

Prerequisites for portfolio management

Chapter 17

Portfolio governance

Steve Butler

Governance of a portfolio is a key component of an organization's overall governance strategy. It may occur at various levels of the organization to support portfolio strategy, performance, communications and risk management, as well as to align with and support the organization's defined strategy.

Introduction

The key aim of governance in portfolio management is to ensure that processes are in place to define, align, authorize and control elements of a portfolio, as well as provide support for the overall governance decision-making activities. It should help ensure that investment decisions can be taken in a timely fashion to identify opportunities, assess changes, select activities to fund and achieve performance targets.

The Project Management Institute's (PMI's) *The Standard for Portfolio Management* (PMI, 2013) defines portfolio governance as 'a set of practices, functions, and processes within a framework based on a set of principles that are the fundamental norms, rules, or values that guide portfolio management activities in order to optimize investments and meet organizational strategic and operational goals.' Thus governance is the guide that shapes or bounds management practices, providing a structure for the execution of portfolio, programme and project management processes. It should reduce complexity to ensure that management processes can propagate throughout the portfolio management structure. Governance therefore operates at all levels of an organization.

Core principles

Distinction should be made between governance principles and management principles, because the two are often confused. Management principles address the question of how an organization delivers. Governance principles provide the structure to enable that to happen. Put simply, governance principles should ensure clarity about what decisions are made, where and when, and what criteria are used – with the following being taken into consideration:

- Care should be taken to ensure that governance structures, processes, escalation routes, tolerance/control limits and role descriptions are clearly defined and included in the portfolio management framework;

- There should be a vision for the portfolio that is shared and agreed by the management board, widely published within the organization, and included in a portfolio strategy and delivery plan;
- There should be a regular (ideally real-time) communications platform such as a portfolio dashboard report;
- There should be a regular review of continued business justification and strategic alignment – both at the individual initiative level (stage/phase gates) and for the portfolio;
- The portfolio management framework should be widely publicized and openly available throughout the organization.

Portfolio governance structure

Effective governance starts with leadership, commitment and support from the top. However, leadership, although crucial, is not enough. You must define appropriate organizational structure and roles and responsibilities for all participants. For example, the Association for Project Management (APM) defines four main organizational components in portfolio management, which are:

1. Executive leadership;
2. The portfolio management team;
3. Programme and project managers;
4. Resource management.

For large portfolios, tiered organizational structures, based on a hierarchy of programmes and portfolios, are common. It should be noted, however, that governing a portfolio does not necessarily require defining new functional positions at a senior level – people with the required responsibilities often already present in the organization. The basic responsibilities are not new; what is new is that these responsibilities are to be carried out in a formal, structured and organized way.

The following core principles apply when considering the components of portfolio governance:

- Role profiles should be prepared for key positions, and terms of reference are agreed for the portfolio governance forums;
- A portfolio management framework should be in place that includes a description of what portfolio management is designed to achieve (and the measures used to assess this), the key processes and governance structures;
- A clear and agreed portfolio strategy should be in place containing a vision of the portfolio's objectives;
- Governance oversight of initiatives should extend from start gate to post-implementation review;
- Escalation paths with control/tolerance limits should be clearly defined and agreed;
- An effective portfolio management office (PMO) should govern the operation of the portfolio processes and provide oversight, foresight and insight to the portfolio operation.

Governance roles according to The Management of Portfolios framework

The Management of Portfolios framework (The Cabinet Office, 2011, later renamed as AXELOS) defines the following key governance roles.

Portfolio direction group or investment committee

This is the governance body where decisions about inclusion of initiatives in the portfolio are made. No initiative should be included within the portfolio or funded without the portfolio direction group (PDG)/investment committee's (IC's) approval. The PDG/IC responsibilities are to:

1. Agree the portfolio management framework;
2. Agree the processes contained within the portfolio definition cycle and ensure that they operate effectively;
3. Approve changes to the practices within the portfolio definition cycle;
4. Approve the portfolio strategy and delivery plan;
5. Receive investment appraisal and portfolio prioritization reports, and decide on the scope and content of the portfolio;
6. Ensure that the portfolio is suitably balanced;
7. Ensure that resources are allocated appropriately;
8. Ensure that the portfolio development pipeline contains sufficient initiatives at the feasibility/concept stage and that initiatives progress through the pipeline at an adequate speed;
9. Undertake regular portfolio-level reviews to assess progress and confirm that the portfolio remains on course to deliver the desired strategic benefits and outcomes;
10. Review recommendations from the portfolio progress group (PPG)/change delivery committee (CDC) and make decisions accordingly;
11. Ensure that any conflicts between portfolio delivery and business as usual (BAU) that cannot be resolved by the PPG/CDC are addressed effectively;
12. Promote collaborative working across the organization;
13. Undertake periodic reviews of the effectiveness of portfolio management within the organization – and take appropriate action where required.

Portfolio progress group or change delivery committee

The PPG or CDC is the governance body responsible for monitoring portfolio progress and resolving issues that may compromise delivery and benefits realization. It has the following responsibilities:

1. Agree the processes contained within the portfolio delivery cycle and ensure that they work effectively;
2. Approve changes to the practices within the portfolio delivery cycle;
3. Ensure that all programmes and projects comply with agreed delivery standards, including the business change lifecycle;

4. Monitor delivery of the portfolio delivery plan (via the portfolio dashboard), including spend against profiled budget and revised forecast result;
5. Ensure that effective action is taken to deal with overspends;
6. Where underspends occur, take prompt action to consider reallocating the funds to other initiatives, including those in the portfolio development pipeline by referring the issue to the PDG/IC;
7. Review and resolve key portfolio-level issues;
8. Ensure that risks and dependencies are effectively managed;
9. Ensure that limited resources are managed effectively and efficiently;
10. Monitor and approve changes to the benefits forecast;
11. Approve communications on portfolio progress;
12. Where justified, make recommendations to the PDG/IC for the termination of initiatives;
13. Escalate issues that cannot be adequately resolved to the PDG/IC and/or management board;
14. Undertake periodic reviews of the effectiveness of portfolio delivery within the organization – and take appropriate action where required;
15. Approve communications on portfolio progress;
16. Where justified, make recommendations to the PDG/IC for the termination of initiatives;
17. Undertake periodic reviews of the effectiveness of portfolio delivery within the organization – and take appropriate action where required.

Business change director or portfolio director

This is the management board member who is responsible for the portfolio strategy, and provides clear leadership and direction through its life. This person has the following responsibilities:

1. Champions the implementation of portfolio management;
2. Secures investment to implement portfolio management, including a portfolio management office, if required;
3. Provides overall direction and leadership for the implementation and delivery of the portfolio;
4. Gains relevant management board approval for the portfolio strategy and delivery plan;
5. Promotes an energized culture that is focused on collaborative working in the interests of the organization;
6. Ensures that the portfolio evolves to reflect changed strategic objectives and business priorities and that resources are reallocated where necessary;
7. Ensures that the portfolio management practices are documented in a portfolio management framework and that they are amended in the light of lessons learned.

Portfolio manager

The portfolio manager coordinates the effective and efficient operation of the portfolio management practices and provides support to the business change/portfolio director,

PDG/IC and PPG/CDC. This includes ensuring that they receive the information they require to enable them to discharge their responsibilities.

The portfolio manager has the following responsibilities:

1. Drafts the portfolio strategy and delivery plan for the business change/portfolio director;
2. Prepares the regular portfolio dashboard for the PDG/IC and PPG;
3. Ensures that business case data (particularly costs, benefits and risks) are prepared on a consistent and reliable basis;
4. Establishes and maintains a framework (a conceptual and communicable structure of ideas) and methodology (a body of policies and procedures) for portfolio management within the organization;
5. Establishes and maintains relevant portfolio management processes (strategic management, governance management, communication management, performance management, risk management);
6. Guides the selection, prioritization, balancing and termination of portfolio components to ensure alignment with strategic goals and organizational priorities;
7. Undertakes investment appraisals and reports accordingly to the PDG/IC;
8. Coordinates portfolio prioritization exercises and reports accordingly to the PDG/IC;
9. Ensures that dependencies are effectively managed and. where required. escalates issues to the PPG/CDC for resolution;
10. Leads on the preparation and implementation of the portfolio stakeholder engagement and communications plan;
11. Identifies constraints within the portfolio and works to overcome them;
12. Identifies improvements to the portfolio management practices;
13. Establishes and maintains appropriate infrastructure and systems to support portfolio management processes;
14. Continuously reviews, reallocates, reprioritizes and optimizes the portfolio, and ensures continuing alignment with evolving organizational goals and market opportunities and threats;
15. Provides key stakeholders with timely assessment of portfolio component selection, prioritization and performance, as well as early identification of (and intervention in) portfolio-level issues and risks that are impacting performance;
16. Measures and monitors the value to the organization through portfolio performance metrics and targets, such as benefit ratios, return on investment (ROI), net present value (NPV), payback period (PP), internal rate of return (IRR) and scorecards. Government and not-for-profit organizations may have other measures and targets;
17. Ensure that legal and regulatory requirements are met;
18. Satisfies the information needs of current or future stakeholders;
19. Supports senior-level decision-making by ensuring timely and consistent communication to stakeholders on progress, changes and impacts on portfolio components;
20. Influences active executive sponsorship engagement for the portfolio and each portfolio component as it is initiated;
21. Participates in programme and project reviews to reflect senior level support, leadership and involvement in key decisions.

Portfolio benefits manager

The portfolio benefits manager ensures that a consistent 'fit for purpose' approach to benefits management is applied across the portfolio, and that benefits realization is optimized from the organization's investment in change. He or she carries out the following duties:

1. Develops and maintains the organization's portfolio benefits management framework;
2. Considers and advises the portfolio manager or director on changes to the portfolio benefits management framework;
3. Provides training and awareness-building sessions on the application of the portfolio benefits management framework;
4. Participates in investment appraisals, ensuring that business case benefits forecasts are consistent with the organization's benefits eligibility rules;
5. Works with the organization's (and programme-based) business change managers to promote more effective benefits management practices;
6. Facilitates benefits-mapping workshops;
7. Provides advice and support to PPM and business-as-usual colleagues on the development of initiative-level benefits forecasts and benefits management strategies;
8. Provides assurance on the effectiveness of benefits management practices at programme and project level;
9. Maintains the portfolio-level benefits forecast and ensures that double counting is minimized;
10. Updates the forecast to reflect approved initiative-level changes at stage/phase gates and portfolio-level reviews;
11. Coordinates production of the annual portfolio-level benefits realization plan;
12. Consolidates progress reports for the portfolio dashboard and for periodic portfolio-level reviews;
13. Escalates any benefits-related issues via the portfolio manager to either the PDG/IC or PPG/CDC;
14. Sets the standards for, and monitors post-implementation reviews to compare the benefits realized with the benefits forecast and identifies lessons learned in relation to benefits management for wider dissemination.

The portfolio management office

This portfolio management office (PMO) incorporates many of the standard programme and project management responsibilities across the organization. However, with a specific relationship to portfolio management, the PMO is responsible for the following actions:

1. Defining portfolio-wide PPM standards, processes and templates – to ensure that consistent approaches are applied and to provide a clear line of sight across the portfolio;
2. Providing assurance to senior management on effective and efficient management and delivery of change initiatives;

3. Providing a challenge or 'critical friend' role for individual initiatives;
4. Providing support, advice and guidance to individual change initiatives;
5. Preparing the portfolio strategy and delivery plan;
6. Coordinating and participating in stage/phase gate, investment appraisal, portfolio-level prioritization and progress reviews;
7. Preparing the portfolio dashboard;
8. Improving the links and feedback loop between policy/strategy formulation and PPM delivery.

Factors involved in portfolio governance

Portfolio authorization

Portfolio authorization processes should be defined and agreed as part of the portfolio charter process. Whatever the process or action, governance considerations should include portfolio authorization and modification elements. For example, governance considerations may state that new portfolios will be initiated as deemed necessary by senior executive management, using a process of engagement across the executive management suite and in consultation with projected portfolio management personnel. The actual process and procedure of portfolio authorization or modification is not part of the governance process and would be worked out separately, but within the above-mentioned governance guidance. These procedures are part of the senior board's operating procedure and may be codified in corporate policy or process documents.

Portfolio planning

Governance planning ideally should come before the actual implementation of a specific portfolio. The ideal is that portfolios are managed consistently across the enterprise. As such, senior executive management should have minimal governance guidance in place that will be used by the portfolio manager to develop and extend corporate governance practices to each portfolio. The portfolio charter should refer to this high-level governance guidance and task the portfolio team with developing supporting portfolio governance processes as needed to supplement the overarching enterprise guidance.

There is an axiom in the field of project management that says that, 'Project managers don't do anything unless there is a plan first'. Preplanning is even more critical at higher levels of management because of increased complexity. There are basically two approaches to planning:

1. Plan all actions ahead of time and then implement the plan;
2. Perform some level of incremental planning that can accommodate change over time. The plan is then implemented and updated as the effort progresses.

The type of planning process used at any level of management should be related to the complexity of the effort. The more complex an undertaking the more incremental planning should be used. Duration of the effort is also a consideration because long-term efforts have more uncertainty associated with them. Complexity and uncertainty are related due to the difficulty in projecting future events. Uncertainty is also associated with risk, although much of portfolio management involves dealing with risk.

Risk by itself does not imply a complex undertaking. For example, the safety certification process for a nuclear power plant may involve great risks because of legislative and public approval uncertainty. However, the actual process of certification is well defined by statute in most countries and, although complicated, does not involve the attribute of complexity as discussed here. Of course, I'm not saying that designing a nuclear power plant, and operating the interfaces between the various systems and subsystems, is not a complex process.

In most cases portfolio management is a complex endeavour. The grouping of multiple programmes and projects along with operations portends a systems structure in which component interrelationships are neither well known nor predictable. Further, portfolios tend to be long lasting, resulting in considerable uncertainty with regard to future events. As such, at the portfolio level incremental and iterative planning is recommended.

Change control

Effective change control is a well-acknowledged requirement at both the project and the programme levels of management. The same holds good for portfolios. However, as the success of a portfolio is measured by the aggregate of the investment performance and benefit realization of the portfolio, and portfolio managers manage the organization's strategic initiatives and objectives, a change management process must have a different focus from that at the programme and project levels. The focus should not be on specific product design requirements. There also must be a methodology to include changes that might occur in the operational environment because operations may also be a sub-element of the portfolio.

More than one system may be implemented within the portfolio for change control. For example, operational considerations could be sufficiently different from programme and project considerations to require a completely different process for managing operational changes. However, from a governance perspective, the same overarching principles of a good change control system must still be in place as at the project level. In brief a change control system should:

- Be comprehensive and include all change requests;
- Document all actions taken to include both approvals and rejections;
- Have processes that are open, well documented and timely;
- Involve all key stakeholders in the change control process;
- Include full funding for all approved changes.

Finally, clear lines of authority and responsibility must be defined between the portfolio and subordinate change control board. Subordinate change control boards do not necessarily roll up to the portfolio change control board. In fact, it would be unusual for a project change control board to roll up into a portfolio change control board owing to the difference in focus of these two boards.

Portfolio governance artefacts

The following should be in place as reference points to effective portfolio governance. They should be up to date, agreed and signed off.

The portfolio management framework

This portfolio management framework is simply a description of the agreed portfolio management practices adopted by the organization and its governance arrangements. Its purpose is to provide all stakeholders with a single, authoritative and up-to-date source of advice on the portfolio management practices adopted by the organization and its governance arrangements. A typical contents list is as follows:

- The objectives of portfolio management;
- The investment criteria and portfolio categorization/segmentation to be used;
- The business change lifecycle – timings of stage/phase gates and portfolio-level reviews;
- Regular performance reporting and change control;
- The governance framework – where, when and by whom key decisions are made and the role of the PMO;
- Terms of reference for the key portfolio boards;
- Role descriptions for the main portfolio positions;
- Overview of the portfolio-level strategies for benefits, finance, risk and resource management and for stakeholder engagement.

The portfolio strategic plan

The portfolio view of the strategic plan is produced using the organizational strategy and objectives – and the portfolio manager should collaborate with key stakeholders in developing the plan. Although not being part of portfolio governance, the portfolio strategic plan may address the organizational strategy for the corporate, organization unit, functional or department levels, and is therefore an important consideration in portfolio governance.

Typical contents will depend on the organization and the strategy. Note that the strategic plan will not be necessary in all cases – where the strategy is wholly managed by another group, this artefact may be unnecessary.

The portfolio delivery plan

The portfolio delivery plan (or roadmap) is a collection of tactical information about the planned delivery of the portfolio based on the overarching portfolio strategy. The portfolio delivery plan usually focuses on the forthcoming year in detail, in terms of schedule, resource plans, costs, risks and benefits to be realized. But it can also consider the medium and longer terms. Its purpose is to provide a basis for formal senior management approval of planned initiatives and the associated resource requirements, and to provide a baseline against which progress will be monitored via the portfolio dashboard.

Portfolio roadmaps are an output of high-level portfolio planning that graphically depict all portfolio elements needed to achieve organizational strategy and objectives.

The roadmap provides a high-level plan, which should then be used for identifying both internal and external dependencies. Portfolio roadmaps may contain both programme-level and project-level roadmaps included in the scope of the portfolio. Roadmaps might not provide details of all identified portfolio components at the onset but they can be used to build details later.

A roadmap shows alignment from the components to the strategic objectives. It can also highlight the gaps between the components and the strategic objectives that need to be analysed. In addition, it supports mapping of portfolio milestones, dependencies, and identifies the challenges and risks. It can be used to communicate the linkage between the organization strategy and portfolio management, and is used by the governance processes to determine when new components should be initiated. A roadmap example is shown in Figure 17.1. This is shown in greyscale but in practice the use of different colours enhances the value of the chart.

The portfolio charter

An agreed portfolio charter should always be present because it is the document that formally authorizes the portfolio manager to apply portfolio resources. The charter provides the portfolio structure, including the hierarchy and organization of the portfolio, sub-portfolios, programmes, projects and operations. Also, it forecasts how and when the portfolio will deliver value to the organization. Chartering a portfolio links

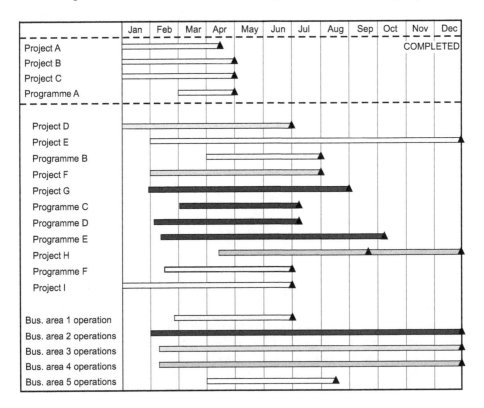

Figure 17.1 A portfolio roadmap example

the portfolio to the organizational strategy and describes how the portfolio will deliver value to the organization. The charter may include portfolio objectives, portfolio justification, portfolio sponsor(s), portfolio management roles and responsibilities, key and major stakeholders, stakeholder expectations and requirements, communication requirements, high-level scope, benefits, critical success criteria, resources, high-level timeline, and assumptions, constraints, dependencies and risks.

Thus the charter is a collection of top-level strategic information that provides total clarity to all the stakeholders with regard to the content and long-term objectives of the portfolio. The contents of a typical charter are as follows:

- Vision and longer-term objectives for the portfolio endorsed by senior management;
- Overview of the strategic priorities;
- Management roles and responsibilities;
- High-level terms of reference for governance forums;
- Key and major stakeholders;
- Stakeholder expectations and requirements;
- Communication requirements;
- High-level scope;
- Constraints, dependencies and assumptions;
- Top-level information about benefits to be realized and how they link to the strategic objectives;
- Key strategic risks;
- Key dates, measures and success factors;
- Key resource and cost information;
- Motivational team-work statement from senior management.

The portfolio stakeholder engagement/communication plan

The Portfolio Stakeholder Engagement/Communication Plan provides the framework for coordinated and consistent communications across the portfolio, without which effective governance would be impossible.

Typical contents include the following:

- A statement of the objectives of portfolio stakeholder engagement and communications;
- Description of the key stakeholder groups analysed by interest and influence;
- Media to be used for each individual or group, together with timings and content

Governance with an agile portfolio

One of the biggest challenges for those involved in managing portfolios in an agile environment is the struggle to have a strong focus on long-term planning. Agile teams are typically not asked to create detailed plans, traditional timelines or cost estimates in the planning phase. Instead, resource requirements and timelines are measured using sprints, story points and velocity for their respective products. Releases are based on a 'cut-off' date and not around meeting well-defined requirements; development work is based on incremental advances and iterative feedback from customers and stakeholders.

Visibility requirements increase as you move up agile work levels and across organizational stakeholders, and typically can become inadequate. Indeed, this lack of visibility creates huge gaps between the different stakeholders, causing disconnects and increasing tension throughout the organization.

Providing the right level of visibility in an agile environment is a difficult and challenging task. The requirements will vary from organization to organization and should ultimately be designed to provide insight into project alignment against strategic objectives – answering the question, 'Are we working on the right things?'.

In addition to visibility difficulties, release and progress reporting for agile projects also fall short of executive management expectations. Once an organization is comfortable that the right priorities are being acted upon, the natural question to ask is, 'When will these features or projects be delivered?'.

This requirement can be built into the methodology described in this handbook, but requires additional thought and consideration. For example, it is critical to bridge the gap between the different layers in the organization. Every agile organization needs a single 'front door' where all stakeholders have instant access to the relevant and applicable data to make the correct business decisions quickly – making the organization truly agile. Best practice includes the following (note that this also applies to traditional organizations):

1. Keep everybody aligned with organizational priorities. Focus resources on the right things at the right time. Putting portfolio governance in place as described in this chapter prevents rogue work from making its way to the delivery teams. Crucially, do not let projects 'get the green light' simply because somebody had the political clout to push them through;
2. Create a pre-backlog to keep everyone on the right path. Prioritization is difficult to do – requests and bugs pile up in the backlog and can get stuck in an endless queue. Agile portfolio management solutions can provide a pre-backlog for agile projects, letting you move tasks into the agile development arena only when they are ready to be worked on. Developers will no longer dive into work that hasn't been prioritized or approved, such as work that is waiting for a signed customer commitment;
3. Track time and costs: senior managers want to know about resources' (people's) time for analysis and financial metrics. Enterprise cost accountants want to capitalize labour related to building products so they can cost it over the correct time period. An agile portfolio management solution can give everybody a clear picture of how people are spending their time, even enabling accountants to differentiate between capital and non-capital labour costs;
4. Consistent reporting for all projects: this is crucial. It is rare to have total agile adoption (in fact recent studies show that 53 per cent of organizations practising agile claim to have a 'hybrid' agile plus waterfall approach). Consistent reporting can therefore be difficult, but is none the less still vital.

References

Cabinet Office, The (2011), *Management of Portfolios*, Norwich: The Stationery Office.
Project Management Institute (2013), *The Standard for Portfolio Management*, 3rd edn, Newtown Square, PA: PMI.

Chapter 18

Portfolio management roles and responsibilities

Afshin Farahmandlou

Nowadays more and more companies use projects and programmes to realize their business strategy and achieve their goals. In addition to the traditional roles of project management and programme management, the new managerial role of portfolio management has evolved. This new role (which needs to be understood better) is pivotal in planning and controlling complex project structures more effectively and efficiently. This chapter gives an overview of the main roles and responsibilities in portfolio management, alongside the project lifecycle and in interaction with other key roles and stakeholders at different organizational hierarchical levels.

Projects, programmes, portfolios and their management

I must start by describing the relationship, commonalities and differences across projects, programmes and portfolios (three words that are sometimes used synonymously. According to *A Guide to the Project Management Body of Knowledge* from the Project Management Institute (PMI, 2013) 'a project is a temporary endeavor undertaken to create a unique product, service, or result, while a program is a group of related projects managed in a coordinated way to obtain benefits and control not available from managing them individually. A portfolio is a collection of projects or programs and other work like sub-portfolios or operations grouped together in order to facilitate the effective management of that work to meet the strategic business objectives.' Figure 18.1 shows an example of a portfolio structure.

Based on the PMI definition above, projects, programmes and portfolios all have one common goal, which is to contribute to the fulfilment of the strategic business objectives of the organization. It is just the manner of that contribution that differs according to the particular organization, and the different knowledge, skills, tools and techniques applied by project, programme and portfolio managers to achieve those objectives. Therefore it is important that the organizational strategy and business objectives derived from the vision and mission of the organization are clearly defined and communicated to the organization. In addition to the strategic objectives, stakeholder priorities, values such as sustainable practices and ethical principles can also become a priority according to ISO 21504 (International Organization for Standardization [ISO], 2015). Figure 18.2 shows a general relationship between the strategy, and portfolios, programmes and projects.

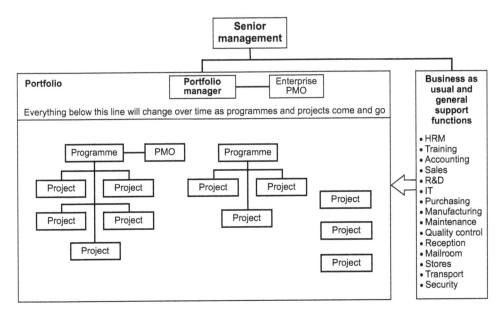

Figure 18.1 Example of a portfolio structure within a company organization

Portfolio management plays a major role in planning and successful implementation of the strategy in order to maximize the benefits for the organization. It aligns with the strategies of the organization by the following activities:

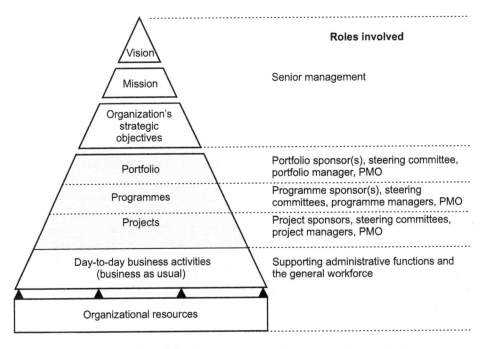

Figure 18.2 Typical place of portfolio(s), programmes and projects in the organization

- Selecting and including the right projects and programmes in the portfolio;
- Terminating projects and programmes that are putting the organizational goals at risk;
- Prioritizing the work among the active projects and programmes;
- Providing the proper resources.

This is a continuous decision-making process with an organizational scope. Figure 16.1 depicted the ongoing process of validating portfolio alignment to the strategic objectives according to ISO 21504.

Programme management is applied to manage the deliverables and interdependencies among a group of projects or programmes with the objective of maximizing the benefits to the organization and achieving the organizational goals.

Project management focuses on achieving everything defined within the scope of a single project in time, quality and budget, based on the clearly defined requirements and objectives of the organization or customer.

Principal roles and responsibilities in portfolio management

In order to implement successful portfolio management several roles need to be established. The responsibilities and level of authority of each role need to be defined, with the objective of achieving the goals of portfolio management. The main roles in this context are as follows:

- The portfolio governance body;
- Portfolio sponsor;
- Portfolio manager;
- Programme managers;
- Project managers;
- Portfolio management office (PMO; see Chapter 20).

Portfolio governance body

The portfolio governance body is normally represented by business executives or business managers, with the purpose of providing guidance and making decisions on investments and defining priorities for the portfolio. They make sure that the portfolio is aligned with the organization's strategic objectives and have the authority to make strategic portfolio decisions. Here is a list of the portfolio governance body's most important responsibilities:

- Definition of the framework, rules and guidelines for supervising and controlling the portfolio;
- Control of the allocation of resources and assets according to the organizational strategy and priorities;
- Definition of the key performance targets and limits of tolerance;
- Establishment and communication of criteria for selection, prioritization and approval of portfolio components;
- Determination of the risk and reward, including the financial investments, return and portfolio value;

- Review and definition of measures to solve issues and mitigate risks;
- Performance reviews and application of any adjustments needed to maintain progress towards the portfolio's goals.

Portfolio sponsor

The main role of the portfolio sponsor is to act as an interface between the portfolio governance body and the portfolio components, programmes and projects in order to do the following:

- Facilitate the required changes;
- Resolve escalations;
- Ensure the fulfilment of the portfolio goals and benefits;
- Ensure that the goals are aligned with the strategic objectives of the organization.

In the case of escalated issues, the portfolio sponsor steps in where necessary to remove obstacles and enable portfolio success. This role is normally represented by a business manager or functional manager within a business unit in the organization.

Portfolio manager

A portfolio is managed by a portfolio manager who looks for various ways to apply processes and techniques for optimizing the organizational returns from project investments, by improving the alignment of projects with the strategy and ensuring that resources are made available in sufficient quantity and necessary quality. The portfolio manager's aim is to optimize the results from project investments across a portfolio. This can also be considered as the method of choice for evaluating, selecting, prioritizing and authorizing new projects or programmes.

Organizations that do not align their portfolio with the organizational strategies and governance tend to increase the risks of running projects that are low priority initiatives, or to waste their management time and use of highly specialized resources on less profitable activities. Therefore, providing guidance and applying processes and techniques of portfolio management within the context of organizational governance provides reasonable assurance that the organizational objectives can be achieved. As shown in Figure 18.3, according to ISO 21504, portfolio management may also be described as a continuous decision-making process where new opportunities and threats are evaluated, selected, prioritized and authorized. To build and manage a portfolio effectively, the portfolio manager needs to apply certain processes, activities and tasks to get the required oversight over the portfolio, in order to control and support the decision-making process to the maximize benefit for the organization.

The portfolio manager is responsible for aligning with the portfolio governance body to manage the portfolio, and get the return on investments from programmes and projects and meet the organizational strategic goals. The most important responsibilities of the portfolio manager are as follows:

- Supporting the processes concerning selection, prioritization, balance and termination of portfolio components to ensure alignment with the strategic goals and priorities;

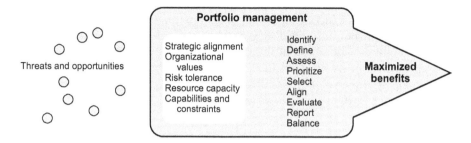

Figure 18.3 A view of portfolio management according to ISO 21504

- Screening and analysing the portfolio and making corrective recommendations to optimize the portfolio in alignment with the evolving goals of the organization and varying environmental business conditions;
- Conducting portfolio assessments and providing regular portfolio performance reports to stakeholders and decision-makers;
- Identifying risks and other issues at the portfolio level that could have implications for portfolio performance;
- Evaluating and monitoring portfolio performance based on unified metrics or key performance indicators;
- Supporting the decision-making process within the organization by timely and consistent performance reporting of portfolio components to the executive management or other decision-makers within the organization;
- Selection and proposal of programmes or projects with high-risk exposure for review by senior management;
- Evaluation of critical risks and issues, and escalating these to the portfolio governance body;
- Provision of relevant information to the programme and project managers in order to support the lessons learned, and process and facilitate learning among other portfolio components.

Programme and project managers

The programme manager interfaces with the portfolio manager, the portfolio governance body and the portfolio sponsor to manage the programme, such that the intended benefits are achieved. This includes ensuring that programme risks and issues are under control. Regular and proper monitoring and reporting of the critical risks, issues and programme performance must be established, with the results being made available to the portfolio manager.

The project manager interfaces with the portfolio manager and programme manager to manage the project deliveries, thus contributing to the goals and results of the portfolio. The main contribution of the project manager is the proper assessment, reporting and escalation of critical risks and issues to the portfolio manager and the programme manager, together with proper management of the internal and external dependencies of the project.

Project or portfolio management office

Depending on the size and structure of the organization, many portfolio management support activities might be centralized in a project or portfolio management office. These activities might consist of establishing a standardized governance process and providing aggregated reports on portfolio progress, in addition to the oversight of portfolio components and escalation of risks and issues to the portfolio manager. For more on the enterprise PMO, please see Chapter 20.

References and further reading

International Organization for Standardization (2015), ISO 21504, *Project, Programme and Portfolio Management – Guidance on portfolio management*, Geneva: ISO.
Project Management Institute (2013), *A Guide to the Project Management Body of Knowledge (PMBOK® Guide)*, Newtown Square, PA: PMI.

Chapter 19

Alignment with organizational structures, management systems and processes

Elvira Molitor

Portfolio management does not happen in isolation and will never be more mature than the organization as a whole. As a means of strategy execution, it presents itself as a core strategic business process, closely interlinked with other key business processes. Portfolio definition depends on a well-articulated mission, vision, goals, strategy and targets. Portfolio delivery relies on the organization's structure, culture, people and execution skills. A full understanding of the organizational context is vital for the success of portfolio management.

Context and environment

The type of organization (such as public or private sector), type of industry and the size of the organization determine organizational influencers directly affecting the portfolio process. Equally influential is the environment in which an organization operates, specifically the boundaries applied through regulations, norms, standards or polices (Figure 19.1).

Management systems

Management systems comprise coherent combinations of managerial processes, practices and procedures used by an organization to achieve a particular purpose, function or objective. They qualify as systematic if opportunities for evaluation, sharing and improvement are built in, allowing the system to improve continuously. Their role is to align the purposes of individual parts of the organization with the larger environment. Consequently, they are described in two ways: integrated as a whole as well as in parts.

Since the late 1970s, consultancy companies have developed models to help organizations create, enhance, change or describe their management system in an integrated way. McKinsey (see www.managementstudyhq.com/mckinsey-7s-framework.html) developed the 7-S framework dealing with people (skills, staff, style and shared values), systems, structure and strategy.

In the 1990s, Kaplan and Norton (1992, 1996) began to investigate the effectiveness of strategy execution and developed the balanced scorecard system. This early work assumes the existence of a strategy and treats strategy development as a 'black box'. In response they filled the gap and created a three-step strategic management system approach (Kaplan and Norton, 2008). Morgan et al. (2014) formulated a strategic execution framework of six imperatives with an explicit focus on project portfolio management.

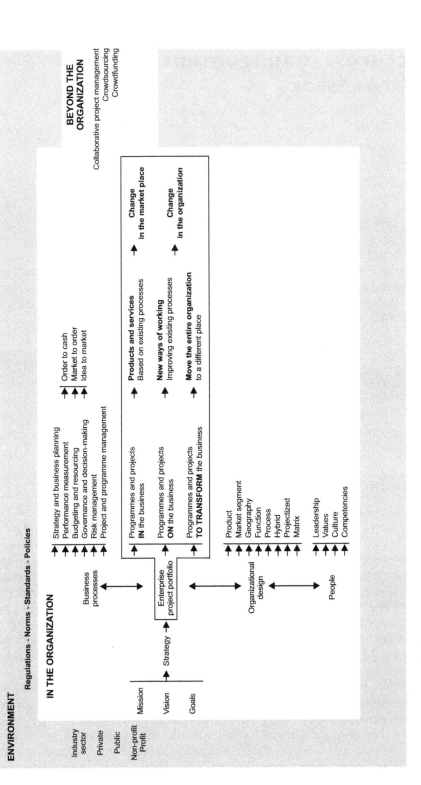

Figure 19.1 The organizational context of portfolio management

In contrast to the aforementioned holistic systems, the International Organization for Standardization (ISO) publishes norms for managing specific aspects of company systems (particularly ISO 9000 *Standard for Quality Management* – ISO, 2015a).

The relevance of the company's management systems for the discipline of portfolio management is twofold. First, portfolio management must align to the organization's existing management systems. Second, management systems design can help to create the appropriate portfolio management system. By nature, the portfolio management system is characterized as 'knowledge based' and 'creative'. Therefore, it should result in a rather flexible framework, based on principles and understandings, as opposed to a rigid specific procedure. When creating the portfolio management system, look out for T-shaped people who combine depth in project portfolio management with the breadth to span cross-functional thinking, appreciative enquiry, systems and design thinking, sociology or psychology (Latham, 2012).

Mission, vision and strategy

Any organization needs to define at the outset its collective 'why', 'what' and 'where'. The mission statement articulates its basic reason to exist, and defines the fundamental purpose and identity. A concise vision statement explains the high-level journey and the long-range intention. In order to become executable, mission and vision need translation into a strategy, including specific goals, strategic objectives and metrics (Morgan et al., 2008). The strategy can then be brought to life through an artfully defined portfolio of programmes and projects. As outlined above, portfolio management is heavily dependent on the mission, vision and strategy – all well articulated and communicated. It is important to note that the main portfolio management standards (described in Chapter 7) presume the existence of mission, vision and strategy, and see executive management in charge of their delivery. Consequently, any portfolio management can only be as good as the strategy. In case the strategy does not deliver the necessary depth or detail, a dialogue has to start with the executives. An agreement needs to be achieved to either fill the gaps or live with the consequences of lower portfolio management maturity.

Business processes

> If you can't describe what you are doing as a process, you don't know what you are doing.
>
> (W.E. Deming, 1986)

In order to manage the complexity of a modern organization, a solid understanding of how it works is needed. Business process management can provide this transparency as well as helping to improve processes. It emerged at the start of this century and builds on a strong heritage that started much earlier with the theory of Adam Smith, followed by scientific management (Taylorism), operations management, Lean (1950–1990), total quality management or TQM (1970–1980), six sigma (mid-1980s), business process re-engineering (1990s) and workflow management (1990s). Today's business processes management 'inherits from the continuous improvement philosophy of TQM, embraces the principles and techniques of operations management, Lean and

Six Sigma, and combines them with the capabilities offered by modern information technology, in order to optimally align business processes with the performance objectives of an organization' (Dumas et al., 2013).

A business process is a logical chain of events, activities and decisions. It involves actors and objects, is triggered by an event and has an outcome. Every business process has a customer and an owner. Business processes can be categorized into core processes, support processes (Porter et al., 1985) and management processes (Dumas et al., 2013). Core processes include the essential value creation of the organization, from the production of goods and services to selling them. Aghina et al. (2014) came up with a compelling, simplified model of three core processes: idea to market, market to order and order to cash.

Management processes provide direction, rules and practices. Examples of relevance in the context of portfolio management are as follows:

- The strategy and business planning process;
- Performance management;
- Budgeting and resource management;
- Governance and decision-making; and
- Risk management processes.

Supporting processes help to execute the portfolio and provide resources. They can include the following:

- Project and programme management;
- information technology (IT);
- Accounting;
- Human resources management (HRM);
- Communications; and so on.

Exactly how the process architecture is set up and what process falls into which category are specific to the particular organization and can be a heavily disputed topic.

Another important aspect of business processes is their complexity as defined by the organizational sub-units involved in the process. Davenport and Short (1990) distinguish the following processes:

- Inter-organizational (between two or more organizations);
- Interfunctional (within the organization, but across several functional or divisional boundaries); and
- Interpersonal (within or across small groups).

The portfolio management process can be described as an interfunctional management process sitting within the strategy and business planning process family. It is closely linked to the 'idea-to-market' core process, and all other management processes (including the project management processes). For an organization to deploy its strategy effectively, these processes need to be connected seamlessly, and ideally should be at the same stage of maturity.

Below I now outline some processes that are closely linked to portfolio management.

Idea to market

Any project portfolio that entails initiatives targeting the creation of new or improving existing products or services has a close connection to the organization's 'idea-to-market' processes. These processes are also known as the product development processes (PDP), Stage Gate® (Cooper et al., 2002) or more generically can be referred to as the business change lifecycle (Cabinet Office, 2008). Sources for new ideas can be anything from product portfolio reviews, to idea campaigns within the company or even inviting stakeholders, clients and customers to participate. The 'idea-to-market' processes feed into and influence the development project duration, the frequency of the portfolio reviews and even the portfolio structure. As an example, idea-to-market cycle times of three months in the fast-moving consumer goods industry require more frequent portfolio reviews than development cycle times in the pharmaceutical industry which are closer to 5–10 years.

In a portfolio of projects that sets out to improve existing ways of working or organizational set-up (often referred to as the change portfolio), the same principles apply as described for the idea-to-market processes. Various change methodologies provide standard processes, which vary in line with the size and complexity of the change in scope.

Budgeting and resource allocation

A chosen portfolio of projects is not much more than an intent, unless executive management approves the budget for its execution. This means that portfolio and finance processes require synchronization to produce good results. As portfolio management is about resource allocation, another influencing factor is the ownership of the budget and the various models that exist to manage budgets. If the organizational budget can be divided and held in individual directorates, each of the directorates might run its own portfolio process, resulting in an independent sub-portfolio for this entity. When dealing with a portfolio of change initiatives the budget is often held centrally and kept separate from the operational budget. This can enable very effective portfolio management, but managers may feel that their individual autonomy is undermined. A third model is to leave the budget in the operational units, but run a central portfolio process with enterprise-wide governance.

Performance management

How will the organization know if it is on track to deliver the project portfolio and how will it learn whether it took the right portfolio decisions so that the expected portfolio value is realized? This can happen only when performance management processes exist that can measure the appropriate parameters and provide reports. For this, portfolio management needs to work closely with performance management and agree on performance targets, parameters, metrics, timing and reporting. Finally (but importantly) the messages to senior management must be aligned, credible and consistent.

Governance and decision-making

Portfolio management both supports and relies on corporate governance. It supports effective corporate governance because it enhances accountability for the portfolio

Decisions	Organizational conditions	Methods and outcome
Data driven	– high discipline – fact based – high data quality and completeness – tools and systems in place – for bigger organizations or (sub)portfolios – central portfolio management	– artificial intelligence – mathematical models – portfolio optimization methods ⟶ reduced bias
People driven	– high confidence in experts – experience based – no consistent data set available – no or limited tools and systems – small organizations or smaller portfolios – decentralized subportfolios	– one-over-one decisions by individuals accommodating decision-makers – peer review and challenge rounds ⟶ increased personal accountability

Figure 19.2 Aspects influencing the portfolio decision process and methods illustrated by the extremes

definition and delivery through clarity, transparency and data. On the other hand, it depends on the existing governance and decision-making methods because an organization is unlikely to apply a different approach to portfolio decisions than it would use for all other decisions. An organization that believes in facts and data will find it easier to collect and maintain the required database to run sophisticated portfolio analyses and consider the results of such analyses in decision-making. A culture that has a strong belief in individuals' expertise may find a data-driven approach hard to support or even unacceptable (Figure 19.2).

As an approach to portfolio management is developed for a certain organization, the existing environment needs to be taken into account. Less sophisticated portfolio management methods might gain better results because they are more in line with existing, established, decision-making methods and therefore fully supported by the organization. Even within an organization, different sub-portfolios in different business units might be based on different approaches. Other factors to take into consideration are the level of consensus required or levels of influence from outside (political changes in the public sector or legal changes in highly regulated areas).

Project management process

The maturity of the portfolio management process cannot be higher than the programme or project management maturity, and the quality and completeness of the data provided by the projects and programmes.

Other support processes

In addition to the above-mentioned processes portfolio management relies heavily on organizational change management processes, communication, knowledge management and the HRM processes.

Organizational structures

Effective organizational structures support strategic objectives, improve overall organizational performance and reduce cost. To be effective they should include five principles: work, task, results, performance and relationships (Drucker, 1974). The most common generic organizational structures include: product, market segment, geography, function, process or project dimension, as well as a matrix or hybrid thereof (see Figure 19.1).

The *product* structure (for example, pharmaceuticals, nutritional products and animal health products) is most often used for companies that maintain multiple, clearly differentiated, product lines.

Organization by *market segment* is suited for companies with operations in multiple countries and significantly diverse service offerings (corporate clients, small business clients, commercial clients).

The *geographical structure* suits very large global players with operations in multiple countries and regions requiring service delivery on-site and benefit from the perception of a local vicinity (Asia Pacific, Europe, Middle East and Africa, Latin America and North America).

Organization by main functions (production, sales and services) has benefits for smaller entities present in few locations that wish to maintain consistent policies and scale expertise.

Process-based structures are more recently evolving and most suitable for industries where the strategy focuses on achieving a sequenced workflow, or can help to harness the specialized capabilities of distributed business partners (partnering networks – see Aghina et al., 2014).

Often hybrids of two or more of these organizational models are used when (for example) alignment of corporate and divisional goals is required.

Projectized and matrix organizations

A fully projectized (team) structure can be effective in organizations that pursue a project business and where most resources are involved in project work. In the projectized organization, the project manager has the ultimate authority to make all project decisions, including budget, application of any predesignated resources and assuming the line management role for project teams. Organizational structures are described in PMBOK (PMI, 2013a) and Chapter 9 of Lock (2013).

Organizations often choose a matrix organization structure, because this combines the need for functional excellence with the focus on the product, service or output. Most large projects and programmes are cross functional. They draw employees from different functional disciplines from within or even outside the organization, assigning them to a project team but without removing them from their respective positions.

Such matrices are described as weak, balanced or strong, depending on whether the functional (weak) or the project (strong) dimension has the primary influence over the project team members. For organizations with a product leadership strategy the weak or balanced matrix is often the model of choice. The weak matrix does not have direct formal project management, allows experts to acquire technical depth, splits their time supporting multiple projects and has limited idle time. Functional managers gain a powerful influence on the project through coordination of activities, ownership of the budget and performance appraisals. In a balanced matrix, a formal project manager role is established, reporting into the function.

In a strong matrix organization, employees receive their primary direction from the project managers who also own the budgets.

In the context of portfolio management, the type of matrix or projectized organization, and specifically the assignment of budgets, can have a significant influence on the portfolio management process. In the projectized organization or strong matrix, budgeting and resource management are straightforward and easily aligned with portfolios and sub-portfolios because there is with little interdependence across projects.

Attention needs to be paid to the potential for idle capacity. In a weak matrix, however, where the same resources are assigned to multiple projects, resource management and budgeting require more sophistication to prevent overbooking of resources and ensure that portfolio priorities are executed as planned.

Link to portfolio categories

The link to the organizational structure is of relevance in the context of portfolio management because it has a direct link not only to the portfolio structure and portfolio categorization, but also to portfolio decision-making (Figure 19.3). Portfolio categories enable tailored portfolio management activities. They help to segregate and segment the portfolio into groups of projects of similar nature that decision-makers can compare and trade off against each other. Categories have a purpose, are clearly defined, described and attributed, and are aligned with strategic parameters. A one-to-one relationship between different project attributes and the category is required. The portfolio guidance allocates the investment in different proportions to categories.

Categories should correspond to the organizational structure to enable deployment of resources, effective governance and decision-making. It is vital for an effective decision-making process to assign an accountable owner to a portfolio or sub-portfolio. For this to happen the category must reflect the organization, and be linked to budget and a senior decision-maker. As a prerequisite for portfolio investment decisions not only within but also across categories, a clear hierarchy between portfolio categories is required.

People

Another important element of the organizational context of which portfolio management must be aware as it designs and executes is the human element. The culture, values, organizational agility and leadership systems of an organization determine what portfolio management can achieve (Cabinet Office, 2011). Research (Cooper et al., 1998) has shown that management's satisfaction with portfolio management is highest, when it fits the organization's management style.

Likewise, the level of skill in project, programme and portfolio management and the connected business areas are key to its success. Portfolio management cannot deliver more than the organization as a whole. In addition, skills managing the people and human side of change are crucial for success. This might be one of the reasons why *Management of Portfolios* (MoP) advises taking a continuous improvement approach rather than using a 'big bang' when implementing portfolio management.

Organizational structure by	Relevance for the design of portfolio categories	Example	Advantages	Potential drawbacks to be dealt with
Product or market segment	Often applied in product development portfolios Centralized portfolio is possible Portfolio category = product category or = market segment	By disease in the pharmaceutical industry	− Intuitive − Widely understood without additional communication efforts − Easily aligned to product strategy or customer base − Aligned with existing governance structures − Comparisons and trade-offs relatively easy within product category − Product- or segment-specific resources and expertise available	− Perpetuates investment in existing product lines or market segments − Difficult to maximize value across categories − Shifting to new lines or segments requires a cross-category decision-maker or structure − Local needs might become de-emphasized or compromised in favour of global initiatives − Difficult if abstract strategic objectives need to be pursued in order to manage change − Budget often sits in the function
Geography	Often applied in product develop-ment and change portfolios Decentralized portfolios	Regional portfolio 'APAC' portfolio	− Widely understood without additional communication efforts − Local sponsorship − Aligned with local needs − Aligned with established gover-nance structures − Local trade-off can be made across product function or market segments in line with local (market) needs − Decisions are taken close to the customer	− Perpetuates re-investment in existing geographical patterns − Difficult to maximize value and shift investment across geographies − Shifting to new lines or segments requires a cross-category decision-maker or structure − Global needs might get de-emphasized or compromised in favour of local initiatives − Difficult if abstract global strategic objectives need to be pursued in order to manage change
Function	Often applied in portfolios of change initiatives IT portfolios Decentralized portfolios	The HR portfolio The IS portfolio	− Active functional sponsorship − Strong link to functional strategies − Little extra comm-unication efforts − Aligned with existing governance and decision-making − Aligned with functional budgets	− Difficult to prioritize, maximize value and shift investment across functions − Difficult to mobilize and gain support: cross-functional priority may be ignored − Siginificant communication and mobilization effort for anything cross-functional − Need to create a specific governing body for cross-functional initiatives
Process	Not relevant in the context of investment or change project portfolios			
Hybrid	In order to establish an enterprise portfolio for a hybrid organization several subportfolios of diverse nature might be constructed			
Projectized	Straightforward link into portfolio structure, budget, process and governance			

Figure 19.3 Organizational structures and their relationship with the portfolio structure and portfolio categories

Beyond organizational boundaries

In today's world of increasing collaboration, project portfolio management is applied even beyond single organizations (see Figure 19.1). Collaboration across company boundaries has become the norm rather than the exception. Organizations find ideas for new products or solutions to problems via crowdsourcing. They raise funds to support projects through crowdfunding. Co-development happens between private companies but also takes the shape of public–private partnerships. The agreements, contractual designs and rules for such agreements are manifold and the design of the cross-company project portfolio can therefore be challenging.

In collaborations, the portfolio management process may take shape of an inter-organizational process. The collaborative aspect can influence each partner company's portfolio governance and decision-making, resourcing and budgeting processes, and might even require the design of a new inter-organizational portfolio management process. Collaboration is an important consideration in the design of the portfolio structure. A specific portfolio category or specific attributes to indicate the 'collaborative' segment in a portfolio will be required to provide transparency and ensure the right level of control.

The business process for 'Collaborative Project Management', which was developed with and for the automotive industry with research institutes (ProSTEP iViP, 2007) focuses mainly on day-to-day project management issues. However, some ideas about governance and decision-making can help to manage cross-company portfolios.

Outlook

Portfolio management is a core business process that must reflect the essence of the organization that it serves. An overall understanding of the organization allows the portfolio manager to identify what organizational prerequisites are required, which of them are not (yet) in place or what elements may even be conflicting with portfolio management principles. Only then can the portfolio manager reach an agreement with the executives on changes to the organization and the pace of the journey. Portfolio management practitioners therefore need to look beyond the standard portfolio management methods, and must understand business context, strategy creation, strategy deployment, management systems, organizational design and key business processes. Only then will they be able to design and implement efficient portfolio management processes. From my perspective the current portfolio management frameworks do not emphasize these links and practices enough. Moreover the clear lines that used to exist between the aforementioned adjacent practices and portfolio management are disappearing as practitioners apply best practice to help organizations to change and adapt with the required agility at fast pace.

References and further reading

Aghina W., DeSmet A. and Heywood S. (2014), 'The past and the future of global organisations', *McKinsey Quarterly*.

Bayney, R.M. (2012), *Enterprise Project Portfolio Management*, Plantation, FL: J. Ross Publishing.

Benko, C. and McFarlan, F.W. (2003), *Connecting the Dots: Aligning Projects with Objectives in Unpredictable Times*. Boston, MA: Harvard Business School Press.

Cabinet Office, The (2008), *Portfolio, Programme and Project Offices*, Norwich: The Stationery Office.

Cabinet Office, The (2011), *Management of Portfolios*, Norwich: The Stationery Office.

Cooper, R.G., Edgett, S.J. and Kleinschmidt, E.J. (1998), *Best Practices for Managing R&D Portfolios Products*, 2nd edn, Cambridge: Perseus Publishing.

Cooper, R.G., Edgett, S.J. and Kleinschmidt, E.J. (2002), *Portfolio Management for New Products*, 2nd edn, Cambridge: Perseus Publishing.

Davenport, T. and Short, J. (1990), 'The new industrial engineering: information technology and business process redesign', *Sloan Management Review*, Summer 11–27.

Deming, W.E. (1986), *Out of the Crisis*, Cambridge, MA: MIT Press.

Drucker, P.F. (1974), 'New templates for today's organizations', *Harvard Business Review*, January.

DuBrin, A.J. (2007), *Fundamentals of Organizational Behavior*, Mason, OH: Thomson South-Western.

Dumas M., La Rosa M., Mendling J. and Reijers H.A. (2013), *Fundamentals of Business Process Management*, Berlin, Heidelberg: Springer.

International Organization for Standardization ISO (2015a) 9000, *Quality Management Systems – fundamentals and vocabulary*. Geneva: ISO.

International Organization for Standardization (2015b), 21504 Project, *Programme, Portfolio Management – Guidance on portfolio management*. Geneva: ISO.

Kaplan, R.S. and Norton, D.P. (1992), 'The balanced scorecard – measures that drive performance', *Harvard Business Review*, Jan–Feb, 71–79.

Kaplan, R.S. and Norton, D.P. (1996). *The Balanced Scorecard: Translating Strategy into Action*. Boston, MA: Harvard Business School Press.

Kaplan, R.S. and Norton, D.P. (2008), *The Execution Premium: Linking Strategy to Operations for Competitive Advantage*, Boston, MA: Harvard Business School Press.

Latham, J.R. (2012), 'Management system design for sustainable excellence: framework, practices and considerations', *Quarterly Journal of Medicine*, 19(2), 7–21.

Lock, D. (2013), *Project Management*, 10th edn, Farnham: Gower.

Lowell, D.D. and Pennypacker, J.S. (1999), *Project Portfolio Management: Selecting and prioritizing projects for competitive advantage*, Glenn Mills: Center for business practices.

Morgan M.M., Levitt R.E. and Malek W. (2008), *Executing your Strategy: How to break it down and get it done*, Boston, MA: Harvard Business Review Press.

Peters, T. and Waterman, R. (1982), *In Search of Excellence*, New York, London: Harper & Row.

Porter, M.E. (1985), *Competitive Advantage: Creating and Sustaining Superior Performance*, New York: Free Press, pp. 11–15.

Project Management Institute (PMI) (2006), *The Government Extension to the PMBOK® Guide*, 3rd edn, Newtown Square, PA: PMI.

Project Management Institute (2013a), *A Guide to the Project Management Body of Knowledge (PMBOK Guide)*, Newton Square, PA: PMI.

Project Management Institute (2013b), *The Standard for Portfolio Management*, 3rd edn, Newton Square, PA: PMI.

ProSTEP iViP (2007), Recommendation. Collaborative Project Management (CPM). Reference Model; PSI 1-1. Version 2.0.

Rowe, A.J., Mason, R.O., Dickel, K.E., Mann, R.B. and Mockler, R.J. (1994), *Strategic Management: A methodological approach*. 4th edn, Reading, MA: Addison-Wesley.

Chapter 20

The enterprise portfolio management office

Emma-Ruth Arnaz-Pemberton

This chapter provides a path for a company that is establishing a PMO for the whole organization. In that case the resulting PMO will become known as the 'enterprise PMO'. Confusingly, the 'P' in PMO can stand for project, programme or portfolio. In this chapter PMO is used generally as the abbreviation for portfolio management office and I have used EPMO for enterprise portfolio management office. The chapter includes real-life examples that provide a number of key lessons gleaned from the experience of others.

Definitions

Reference sources listed at the end of this chapter give various helpful definitions of a PMO. A PMO reports to top management and is established centrally to manage the following for projects and programmes:

- The investment process;
- Strategic alignment;
- Prioritization and selection;
- Progress tracking and monitoring;
- Optimization and benefits realization.

Portfolio, programme and project management offices provide decision-enabling information and support for all business change within an organization and for projects undertaken by the organization externally.

The EPMO can include single or multiple physical or virtual structures (permanent or temporary offices), which provide a mix of central and localized functions and services. These integrate with governance arrangements and the wider business such as other corporate support functions.

The Project Management Institute (PMI) says that a portfolio PMO 'exists in the space of a portfolio of programs and projects. If the projects have separate goals, are not characterized by synergistic delivery, and are only related by common funding, technology, or stakeholders, these efforts are better managed as a portfolio' (PMI 2013a).

Even though the functions used in this office are called the same in other offices, the benefits and results are different. Consider, for example, the work selection process. In a portfolio PMO, this function is used to select the appropriate projects and programmes that comprise the total portfolio. For example, the head of a *portfolio* PMO might reject a project owing to its high-risk rating. In a *programme* PMO, the selection process is used to choose the components that are expected to be best for fulfilling the programme's objectives and provide the greatest benefits.

The Association for Project Management's (APM's) *Body of Knowledge* (APM 2012) does not define a PMO as you would expect, but instead advises that the large scale of portfolios makes a support function (such as a portfolio office) essential. This function will perform the data collection, analysis and reporting that enables the portfolio to be controlled. In many cases, the portfolio office might perform the same functions for the component programmes and projects. The APM states that portfolio planning will identify activities for the management of risk, communication, quality, procurement and so on that should be managed at portfolio level. These activities will form part of the portfolio management plan and are not delegated. Therefore, they will be directly tracked and controlled by the portfolio management team.

Portfolio management must also ensure that control methods are implemented consistently across the portfolio. If this is not done it can be difficult to aggregate data for the whole portfolio and construct an overall picture of progress.

Now I would like to expand on the meaning of the word 'enterprise' in the PMO context. Is this a magical term added to PMO to make ourselves feel more clever and important? That would make this chapter far easier to write, but it actually means something more significant. In the context here it refers to a company or business organization with all its business activities. As a venture it helps us to define an undertaking (or maybe a project). In the realm of initiative, it represents innovation and creativity ('get up and go').

Michael McCormick wrote a paper a few years ago which advises its readers that a PMO that is structured to manage projects across departments, locations and regions is best implemented on an enterprise-wide basis. This is because it will hold the responsibility for ensuring consistency in the management of all elements of each of these projects, and will also be able to assess and prioritize each project for alignment with the corporate strategy. The goal of an enterprise PMO is to help the organization effectively manage projects in today's complex, global marketplace. The successful management of these projects has a direct impact on the organization, its customers and resources. (see www.mccormickpcs.com/images/Enterprise_Project_Management_Office_ePMO.pdf).

In addition to this, Wipro published a white paper detailing the challenges of traditional PMOs and defining an EPMO as a centralized business function which operates at strategic level with the enterprise executives and provides enterprise-wide support on governance, project portfolio management best practices, mentoring, tools and standardized processes. It reads that an EPMO ensures strategic alignment between business objectives and projects executed (see Wipro.com).

The EPMO does not eliminate the need for project, programme or department level PMOs; it simply complements these traditional PMOs. Although the traditional PMOs operating at the tactical and operational level focus on doing things right, organizations with an EPMO and traditional PMOs get the right things done the right way. So the EPMO helps the overall organization achieve its strategic goals and in the process also helps better support the project teams.

Even technology organizations are getting in on the act! Oracle defines enterprise project portfolio management (EPPM) solutions as those that enable project-driven organizations to manage their programmes and projects intelligently (from small and simple to large and complex). They say EPPM solutions drive better portfolio management decisions by providing end-to-end, real-time visibility into all relevant information. EPPM solutions also help companies evaluate the risks and rewards associated with projects and programmes by providing project management, collaboration and control capabilities necessary to manage change and successfully deliver projects on time, within budget, and with the intended quality and design.

Lessons to be learned

In the following sections I discuss some of the lessons to be learned from the various definitions given above.

Lesson 1: there is no 'one size fits all

I'm sorry to disappoint if you expected this chapter to give you the answer to building your (E)PMO similar to all those successful ones that exist. What I can promise is that, after reading this chapter, you should be able to understand the questions to ask of your organization to enable you to create its appropriate PMO.

The theory and definitions that I have explored so far indicate that an EPMO should be the steward and gatekeeper of all change across an entire organization. It should be the organization's conscience and be recognized as an innovative business partner for bringing value to the organization. It will achieve that through the change and support it initiates towards enabling the achievement of strategic objectives. I shall now break that theory down:

- A steward and gatekeeper needs to have the authority to ensure that all change is initiated through any agreed processes, as well as providing recommendations to the organization on its investment decisions;
- All change across an entire organization effectively means that the EPMO is known to be the single source of truth and the pathway to obtaining investment for change;
- Being the organization's conscience, and recognized as an innovative business partner, assumes that the EPMO is promoted as a source for good around the organization. It is listened to and respected in all walks of organizational life;
- Bringing value to the organization to support achievement of strategic objectives means that benefits realization management is in place and facilitated by the EPMO. The EPMO will then have the ability to feed into the strategy discussions of the organizations.

Ask yourself if the points listed above reflect your current reality. They probably will not. Organizations that live in that perfect world are few and far between. But this is no reason to be disheartened.

Just because these might all seem like insurmountable changes to the culture in your organization, it does not mean that you cannot begin the journey towards achieving these objectives. But that journey will probably not be the same as the one your peers have followed.

The person asking . . .	wants to know . . .	so that . . .
CEO	A better understanding of the change going on in my organization	I can make more informed investment decisions in the future
Financial director	The benefits derived from the change, expressed or presented in a clearer way	Our collation of reports for the CEO is consistent and valuable
Line manager	To see what change will happen that might affect my people	I can support individuals better through changing the way in which they work

Figure 20.1 Examples of questions that arise when setting up an EPMO

Lesson 2: the journey must always start with the question 'why?'

Why does your organization need an EPMO? There is always a trigger for an organization to start talking about any kind of PMO. This often stems from a lack of visibility or understanding of the changes happening around the organization. Sometimes it's a desire to know whether resources are being used effectively. Less often, it could be a top-down-driven initiative, perhaps following a change in leadership. Identify and ask your potential EPMO customers what their triggers are. Use every day language instead of blinding them with technical project terms. Figure 20.1 gives some examples.

Fact: if what your customers want is a reporting team, an EPMO is not what they need It always sounds great when a leader asks you to set up any kind of PMO and gives you carte blanche to do that how you see fit. For a PMO manager this is nirvana! So, you will spend their money and build the perfect EPMO that has an answer for every aspect of change. But when you deliver it you may well disappoint despite your efforts. Why try to build a Ferrari when a horse and cart is all that is needed. You can build up to the Ferrari!

Lesson 3: value is in the eye of the beholder

Once you understand the 'why?' for your customers, make sure that you understand the 'value thread' of your organization. Every organization has a purpose for its existence. Sometimes that's a profit line, but often it is not. When asked what 'value' meant to their organization, 40 people in a workshop scenario identified over 30 different types of value. These included reputation, safety, profit, customer experience, and cost savings. Whatever your EPMO brings to the organization, it needs to align to that value thread (Figure 20.2).

Fact: you will be able to sell your proposal, recommendations and views much easier if you can talk their language. Get into the value piece properly. Don't half do it with your elevator pitch having all the right words in, but then get your PRINCE2 book out to show them how to 'do' change. Tailor your metrics, reports, language and even your way of working to demonstrate your belief in that value.

Kind of organization	Value means . . .	Reason
Private equity firm	Profit	That is how we grow our business
Fire authority	Safety	We put fire engines on roads
Food manufacturer	Traceability	Quality is paramount for our customers
Consultancy firm	Customer experience	We acquire contracts by word of mouth
Bank	Compliance	Consequences might mean that we cannot safeguard our customers' savings

Figure 20.2 The meaning of value for different organizations

Lesson 4: you are a salesperson

Don't be alarmed: this lesson is not about cold calling! Any kind of PMO structure needs to be seen consistently as adding value to the organization. It must not be regarded as a blocker. The entire team needs to sell the idea continuously – the output that is created and distributed, the behaviours displayed by the team, the relationships built and maintained, right down to the preparedness in meetings. All of this helps to 'sell' the EPMO to the organization.

It is widely accepted that PMOs typically last for only four years. This number is moving up, but, when you take out the programme or project specific functions, the fact remains. The reasons for this are well documented and can largely be tied back to a failure in selling the concept continuously (see Figure 20.3).

Fact: if you start to see your stakeholders as customers, you suddenly re-frame the relationship into that of a partner who is delivering a set of services. So selling is important. If you don't your 'customers' may well go elsewhere!

We failed because . . .	Could be attributed to . . .	We could have . . .
Lack of support from leadership'	Sponsors not getting what they expected to see	Treated them as customers and checked on their needs
Perceptions of PMO differ	Lack of education	Sold and worked to a public service catalogue
Change in strategic direction	Not being a business partner	Added to strategic movements through information
Methods not embedded	Not bringing the customer along on the journey	Developed everything with the end users
The PMO is not adaptable	Not seeing what the organization needs at a point in time	Been effective change agents and realizing the need for pragmatism

Figure 20.3 Some reasons for the short life of a PMO

Metric	Result	Tells us ...	Action needed
Training sessions offered this month	3	EPMO is delivering to its service level agreements	None. The EPMO is great!
Registrations for training	25	The business is engaged	None. The EPMO is still doing great
Attendance at training	12/48 per cent	The business is not engaged	The EPMO is reluctant to arrange valuable courses New courses are required
Feedback scores from training	4.8/5	Those who attend love the courses	The EPMO needs to find a way to get more people to attend. Review the marketing strategy
Reason for non-attendance	85 per cent unexpected work took precedence 1 per cent absence 1 per cent role change 3 per cent forgot 10 per cent sent to another site	Line managers are allocating work that does not allow team members sufficient time for development	Line managers must allow their teams time for development. One-to-one forms and the process need to be reviewed

Figure 20.4 Changing the perception of a PMO by combining measures

Lesson 5: metrics are important

Elsewhere in this handbook you can read more about the kind of metrics that help to focus your organization on the performance of the portfolio and those managing it. From an EPMO perspective, build your metrics as part of the work you do on value. Don't be scared to measure the 'scary stuff' that seems difficult. It's not impossible to measure your customer experience if you think 'outside the box' – you might have to use three or four different measures that together tell a story. The example in Figure 20.4 shows how the perception of training offered by an EPMO can change if you combine a few measures.

Fact: a story is often more powerful than a bottom-line number. The example in Figure 20.4 demonstrates that with real information it is possible to re-frame a conversation around metrics. Taken separately, each metric tells a different story. Thinking 'outside the box' is hard work but don't shy away from it. This can really work and make a big difference to the perception of your EPMO.

Lesson 6: build a model that allows for differentiation in your services

Most mature EPMOs aim to support three key areas, an approach that I encourage. Identification in detail of what your organization needs in each area can help to sell the product, build a roadmap and show progress. It defines what you are there to do – and

Portfolio	Delivery	Centre of excellence
Capacity planning and resource management	Monitor, review and report	Standards and methods
Portfolio build and prioritization	Quality	Project and complementary skills training
Benefits management	Information management	Coaching and mentoring

Fact: publishing your service catalogue will help people to see all the good things you do that don't ever get talked about: sometimes they have no idea!

Figure 20.5 Examples of EPMO activities for supporting each of the three key areas in the organization

as with projects (most importantly) what you are not going to do. These three key areas are as follows:

1. Portfolio: supporting the organization to define, monitor and implement its strategic change portfolio, while maintaining a view on doing the right thing for the business;
2. Delivery: providing tools and support to the management teams delivering change while assuring the leadership that things are being done in the right way;
3. Centre of excellence (CoE): providing the capability to the change community in order that organizational priorities are successfully delivered according to their defined criteria.

Some examples are defined in Figure 20.5. Note that it is not advisable to have more than seven or eight services in each function.

Fact: publishing your service catalogue will help people to see all the good things you do that don't ever get talked about – sometimes they have no idea!

Lesson 7: enterprise should mean all aspects of change, including capability

Creating a journey for your change community is really important. If you want to support all aspects of change across the organization, handing your up-and-coming project people to a third-party training provider is not always the way. If you can, create a training and career path dedicated to the learning and development of those interested in a career in P3 (projects, programmes and portfolios). Across all EPMO areas this will help you to become recognized as belonging to a team of experts and internal champions, because you will be helping other people in your organization to move ahead in their careers. Consider the different audiences you have around you and tailor the package to what they need. Training sponsors and team members so that they know what is expected of them can be very insightful for people!

Fact: many skills from the P3 world are very transferable, so don't be afraid to open your events up wider than the change community. You will be surprised how much interest you get!

Lesson 8: the people in your PMO are not always the people who should be in your EPMO

EPMO roles, as for any kind if PMO, have (and continue to be) varied over time. Traditionally the 'tick in the box and report' skillset is still very important. But organizations and the industry expect more from the structures of today. All the 'dark arts', such as benefits realization, prioritization, earned value management, various methodologies and capability building, can be part of the remit now.

An EPMO needs to tackle all facets of change and organize itself into the three key service areas that can answer all the requests that they get in one form or another (although) maybe not all in one go. Hard decisions must be made sometimes when creating an EPMO, just as, when change occurs in the organization, people need to be positioned to work to their strengths (if someone is a natural process person, perhaps it could be unwise to put them in a training role).

The roles of any kind of change office can and should vary depending on the situation. The APM's PMO Specific Interest Group completed some work on the types of roles people play in real terms. These are tabulated in Figure 20.6.

Conclusion

In conclusion, remember what an EPMO is trying to achieve.

The EPMO should be the steward and gatekeeper of all change across an entire organization. It should be the organization's conscience, and be recognized as an innovative business partner for bringing value to the organization through the change and support it initiates to enable the achievement of strategic objectives.

Role	Activities
Doctor	Diagnoses problems Prescribes and monitors remedial action Offers prognosis
Handyman	Assists in a crisis Undertakes quick repairs Highlights underlying problems
Librarian	Classifies and stores documents Tracks issues and risks Change control
Nurse	Attends to day-to-day needs Provides encouragement Provides a sounding board
Policeman	Ensures compliance Offers advice and guidance Reports deviations from plans
Teacher	Educates and mentors Promotes use of learnings Enables learning

Figure 20.6 Roles identified by the PMO specific interest group of the APM

It is important that, if you are starting on your journey, or if you are endeavouring to move your PMO into the enterprise space, you take on board all these lessons that have been learned by professionals through the years. Don't try to boil the ocean. Do share your successes so that others can learn and improve too.

References and further reading

Association for Project Management (APM) (2012), *APM Body of Knowledge*, 6th edn, Princes Risborough: APM.

Association for Project Management https://www.apm.org.uk/body-of-knowledge/delivery/integrative-management/control

AXELOS (2012), *Best Management Practice Portfolio: Common glossary of terms and definitions*, Version 1, Norwich: The Stationery Office.

AXELOS (2013), *Portfolio, Programme and Project Offices*, Norwich: The Stationery Office.

International Organization for Standardization (2015), ISO 21504 *Project, Programme and Portfolio management – Guidance on portfolio management*, Geneva: ISO.

Project Management Institute (PMI) (2013a), *The Standard for Portfolio Management*, 3rd edn, Newtown Square: PA, PMI.

Project Management Institute (2013b), *A Guide to the Project Management Body of Knowledge (PMBok Guide)*, 5th edn, Newtown Square, PA: PMI.

Taylor, P. and Mead, R. (2016), *Delivering Successful PMOs: How to Deliver the Best Project Management Office for your Business*, Abingdon: Routledge.

Chapter 21

Portfolio communications and management data

Dennis Lock

Hartman (2000) wrote (paraphrased) that the only reason for project failure is bad communications. He made a good point. This chapter begins by outlining what should happen in a perfect portfolio world. It ends by outlining some of the risks and threats that could delay or even prevent successful delivery of the expected portfolio benefits. Note that the enterprise portfolio management office or PMO (discussed in Chapter 20) should play a leading role in designing and maintaining the database and communication structure.

Data codes and breakdown structures

Clearly the accurate and rapid communication of management data is an essential part of control, whether for business-as-usual operations, for a single project or for a combination of work in programmes and portfolios. Access to data from past projects, programmes and portfolios is also useful for many reasons including (but not limited to):

- Generally benefitting from past management experience (lessons learned);
- Revealing solutions previously found to recurring technical problems (this is sometimes known as retained engineering);
- For legal reasons, in resolving post-project disputes.

Pooling data in a managed and accessible database is the ideal way for making data available to all those who manage or work on portfolio tasks or who are otherwise stakeholders (Figure 21.1). But for sorting, editing (filtering), updating, merging and retrieving data some system protocols have to be observed. One essential feature is that every item in the database has to be given an address or code so that it can be retrieved, updated, sorted, merged, filtered, deleted or otherwise accessed.

All people working in projects should be aware of the various breakdown structures from which project, programme and portfolio codes are derived. The three essential breakdown structures are as follows:

1. Work breakdown structure (WBS);
2. Organization breakdown structure (OBS);
3. Cost breakdown structure (CBS).

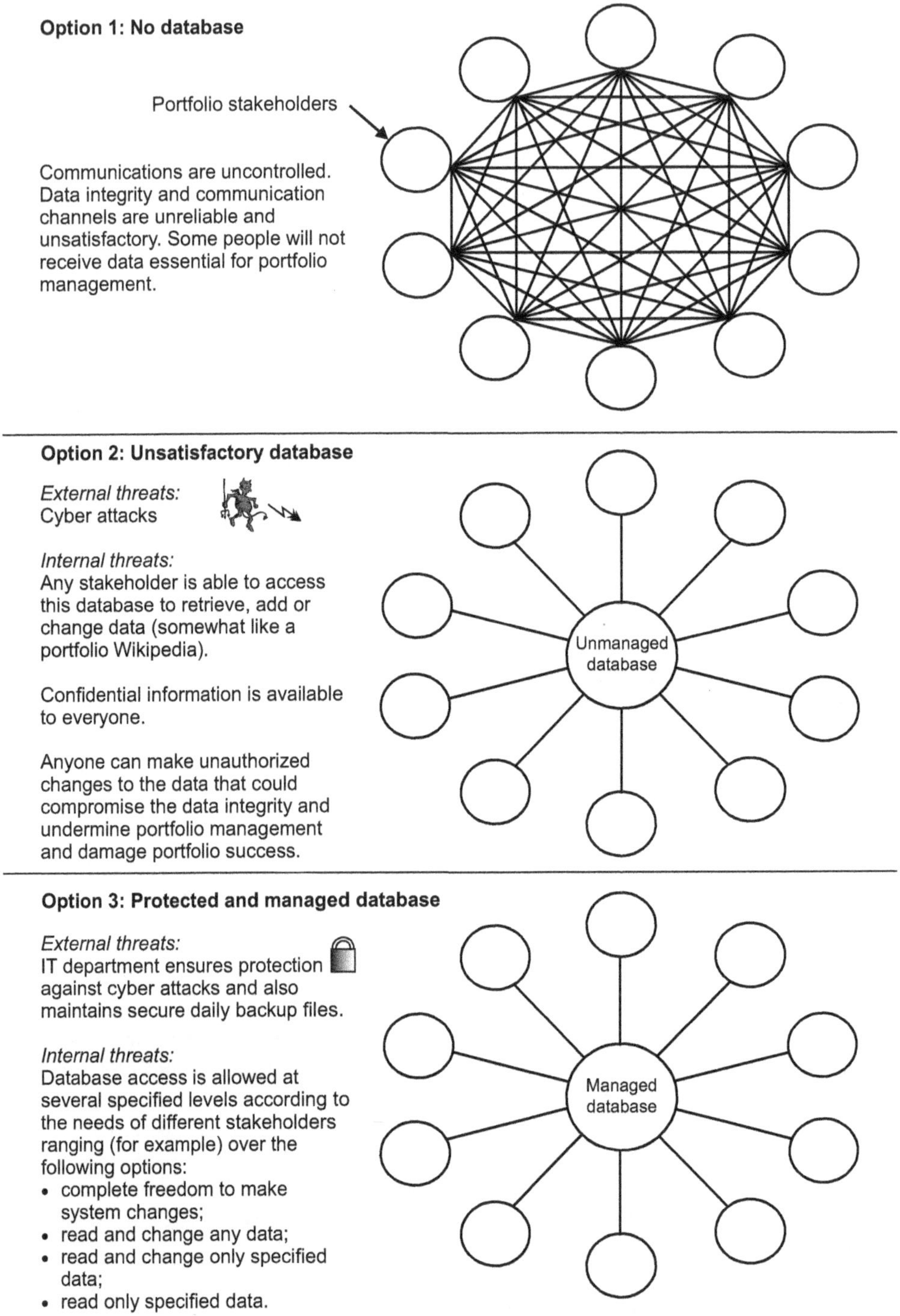

Option 1: No database

Portfolio stakeholders

Communications are uncontrolled. Data integrity and communication channels are unreliable and unsatisfactory. Some people will not receive data essential for portfolio management.

Option 2: Unsatisfactory database

External threats:
Cyber attacks

Internal threats:
Any stakeholder is able to access this database to retrieve, add or change data (somewhat like a portfolio Wikipedia).

Confidential information is available to everyone.

Anyone can make unauthorized changes to the data that could compromise the data integrity and undermine portfolio management and damage portfolio success.

Unmanaged database

Option 3: Protected and managed database

External threats:
IT department ensures protection against cyber attacks and also maintains secure daily backup files.

Internal threats:
Database access is allowed at several specified levels according to the needs of different stakeholders ranging (for example) over the following options:
- complete freedom to make system changes;
- read and change any data;
- read and change only specified data;
- read only specified data.

Managed database

Figure 21.1 Three different options for handling and communicating portfolio data

Figure 21.2 shows how internal codes from the WBS and OBS for a small single project can be combined to produce codes that identify individual tasks and their cost account codes. This is a greatly simplified view. In practice, each code shown in Figure 21.2 would be prefixed with higher-level codes to identify the programme (and possibly also the portfolio) in which the project is located.

Some organizations also need to sort data according to which external company or client is involved, so that can add yet another prefix. Other task codes are often used to identify resource skills (for task and departmental resource scheduling). Higher-level codes identify external companies or other companies within a group, clients and so on. Examples of coding systems can be found in Lock (2016), and more discussion of code structures is given in Harrison and Lock (2004).

It is clear that, without common sense and ingenuity, every single item of data within a portfolio could be burdened with an identifier code comprising a long string of digits, well beyond the limits of what is practical for people to use in everyday life.

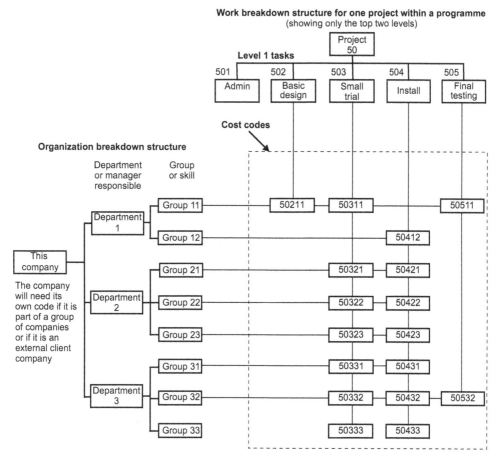

Figure 21.2 Upper levels of possible breakdown systems and coding for a single project within one portfolio

I remember from my own project management experience that people working at exposed sites on mining engineering projects were expected to use complex 16-digit task codes on timesheets – and those people not surprisingly simply refused to use them. So some ingenuity is needed when designing coding and control systems to keep the numbers simple for users.

Further complication is introduced when it is realized that departments, such as purchasing and (especially) finance, also use codes for some of the same tasks and items that appear in project, programme and portfolio management codes. It is desirable, but usually difficult to achieve compatibility across all these departments and functions. I once carried out a consultancy assignment for an engineering company that was running a portfolio of around 150 constantly changing projects, and we discovered that there were no fewer than 10 different systems in current use for numbering drawings (a different system for every design department). None the less, a common coding system, or at least one that has logical compatibility, is very sensible. So the design and allocation of codes is an important precursor to having a reliable and useful portfolio database. Responsibility for designing the coding system (and for changing it when necessary) needs to rest with those who have the necessary appreciation and skills, and that usually means a PMO. In a large organization there might be more than one PMO, so here responsibility for the coding system should be given to the most senior PMO, which is often called the enterprise PMO. Designing the coding system should be done in conjunction with the design, finance and procurement departments to obtain as much compatibility as possible.

Managing portfolio communications

Immediate access to information from the portfolio database is usually technically possible by everyone in an organization, whomever and wherever they may be. Obviously that could introduce risks including the following:

- Unauthorized access to confidential data;
- Entering incorrect data (such as declaring better results than those actually achieved);
- Changing and corrupting the database system itself.

So a database will usually have more than one level of access authorization, depending on the seniority and needs of the individual users. Changes to the system itself will probably be restricted to the enterprise portfolio management office (EPMO) or the information technology (IT) department.

Responsibility for securing the data against loss through system failure or cyber attack is usually an IT department responsibility, but it is a matter that should concern anyone who relies on having accurate and reliable data readily accessible. Too often we hear of instances where large organizations (including banks, major retailers and even the UK's National Health Service) have had data stolen or corrupted, even to the extent of having an entire system rendered useless, possibly with demands for payments of ransoms before operation can be resumed.

Providing user access to the database

Data have to be protected from unauthorized changes. Also, some portfolio data will be confidential. Senior management need access to data at summary level, but should not need access to the day-to-day details of task schedules, progress and so on. Managers of functional departments need access to receive work schedules and find out how they are performing against planned times and costs. Some relatively junior staff will be expected to enter timesheet and progress information at task level.

So classifying data into the categories suitable for different users at all levels inside and outside the organization has to be done, to avoid overloading anyone with detail that is irrelevant to their function or seniority and to protect organizational confidentiality. The EPMO can (in association with the IT department) arrange for the various database users to have access only to data that are relevant to them. Designing such a system can be a difficult task. One tool that can help decision-making in this process is an adaptation of a responsibility matrix, the principles of which are shown in Figure 21.3. This works well and easily for a single project, is far more difficult for a programme, and will require considerable ingenuity when applied to storing, updating and communicating data internally and externally across a portfolio.

Regular reports

It is not appropriate to say much here about reporting methods and the nature of and distribution of regular periodical reports to the stakeholders of projects, programmes and portfolios. Every organization will have its own needs and choices. However, there are one or two principles that should govern all regular reporting, namely the following:

- Reports must always be factual, even if (for proprietorial reasons) they do not always contain all the facts;
- Reports should be issued on time, and before the items reported in them become out of date;
- It must always be remembered that reports to clients and other external stakeholders are windows into the reporting organization, so they should be well organized, well presented, well written, suitably concise and, above all, accurate.

Irregular reports

Elsewhere in this handbook you will find reference to the practice of 'escalating issues'. This means telling an appropriate manager at a suitably high level in the organization that something, somewhere in a portfolio, programme or project, is not meeting the expected cost, progress or quality level, and that senior intervention is needed to correct the situation, or at least to prevent it from becoming worse.

There was once a school of thought that claimed that a successful senior manager should have everything within his or her command under such perfect control that the manager could relax, read a newspaper or spend time profitably working out future strategy. Above all, it should not be necessary to burden any manager at any level with

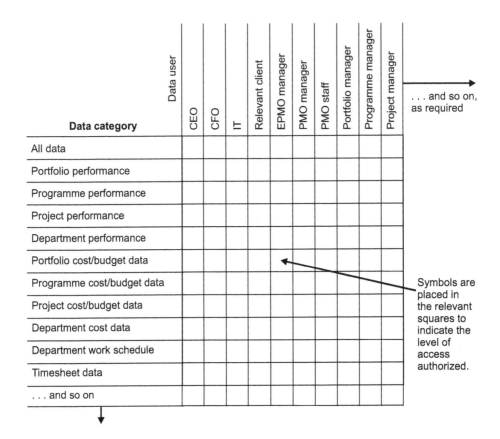

Examples of access categories and symbols

■ Responsible for database integrity and security
O Authorized to make system changes to the database
+ Authorized to add, delete or change portfolios, programmes and projects
A Access to client-specific reports, suitably edited by the EPMO or PMO
C Authorized to make changes to prespecified programme/project content
N Receives notifications that specified data have been updated and
    can access those data at any time
T Authorized to input timesheet data

Figure 21.3 Principles of a responsibility matrix adapted for managing portfolio, programme and project communications

reports containing volumes of data and progress descriptions about matters that are running well, needing no management intervention. This led to the expression 'reporting by exception', which is another way of saying that the emphasis in reports to senior managers should be on those things that are at risk of falling out of plan.

'Escalating issues' is the current description of this process of reporting by exception. Everyone at any level in the portfolio should be encouraged always to communicate any foreseen or actual risk to any task to their appropriate manager. That manager, in turn, might have to escalate the issue further by reporting to a more senior manager, if that is the only way to resolve the issue (for example, if more expenditure or additional resources have to be authorized).

There have been cases in public organizations where so-called whistle-blowers have either not escalated issues within their organization, or their appeals to senior managers have been ignored. Whistle-blowers have even been punished for daring to 'speak out' or for breaching confidentiality. In portfolio communications it is important that people know how and where to report issues, and know also that, far from being penalised, they should be commended for seeking help or action in averting or reducing the severity of risks.

Software tools

Chapter 24 deals with this subject, but I want to emphasize that a senior project management professional in the organization should have a significant (preferably deciding) role in the choice of the system. IT professionals will most likely not be suitably qualified to know which software tools are best suited to the management and reporting of work and performance in complex multiproject or portfolios.

Portfolio management software has to tick many boxes – not least its effectiveness for the PMO's use in planning, scheduling, progressing and reporting costs and progress for all portfolio elements. PMOs have to rely on effective and reliable software, so it follows that the EPMO or PMO manager is usually the person who is best able to specify what is needed and choose the best tool. There is some advice on using a checklist in the search for management software at project level in Lock (2016). When buying new software it is always best to begin with a checklist of what you actually need, and then approach the sellers (rather than adopting the weaker approach of allowing the vendors to tell you what they think you need).

Risks and threats

Database security

A database will not manage itself. It requires constant attention to ensure that it contains only data that are relevant and accurate, and that access to the data is allowed only for valid reasons by authorized people. The EPMO is a clear candidate for making sure that data entries and changes are valid and free from errors. But there are also some serious considerations to be given to the stability and security of the database system, in particular guarding against external intrusions (cyber attacks) and system malfunctions. So the IT department will ensure that security applications are installed and kept up to date, and that adequate steps are taken to save and store data in backup files on a frequent and regular basis.

The dynamic nature of programmes and portfolios

Figure 21.4 illustrates the dynamic nature of a portfolio. Nothing is constant in a large and thriving organization. When each new project is introduced, it might be the

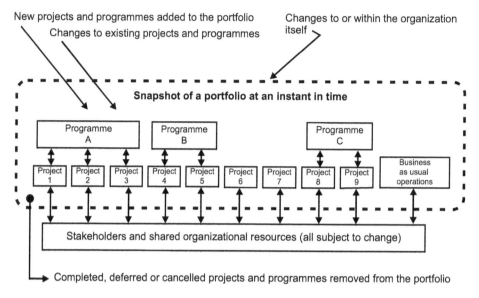

New projects and programmes added to the portfolio

Changes to existing projects and programmes

Changes to or within the organization itself

Snapshot of a portfolio at an instant in time

Programme A	Programme B		Programme C	

Project 1 · Project 2 · Project 3 · Project 4 · Project 5 · Project 6 · Project 7 · Project 8 · Project 9 · Business as usual operations

Stakeholders and shared organizational resources (all subject to change)

Completed, deferred or cancelled projects and programmes removed from the portfolio

Figure 21.4 Nothing is constant in a portfolio environment

subject of a 'kick-off meeting', which is designed to inform and motivate those who will work on the project. When projects are cancelled while they are in progress, this can demotivate all staff in the organization and communicating the change to those affected must be handled responsibly, especially if redundancies are going to follow.

There are some specific risks when the portfolio includes projects that are intended to change systems within the organization. One important rule is that, where a project is in progress to change an established and familiar system or part of the organization, that project should be allowed to finish and begin producing its benefits before any other project is allowed to change the same system or part of the organization. This is a commonsense rule for obvious reasons.

Communicating a forthcoming change that will affect any part of the organization or its systems has to be planned carefully and sensitively. One danger is that information leaks about a project proposal, so that it generates false rumours, leading to apprehension and worse. Here is a courageous experiment for you to conduct. Hire two actors, dress them in formal business suits, equip them with notepads and cameras, and then let them tour the offices during working hours, taking measurements and photographs. Now watch productivity plummet as the apprehensive employees form little ad-hoc discussion groups and harbour unwarranted fears about their fate.

When a change project or programme is likely to affect people in the organization, the timing and way in which that change is communicated are clearly very important. Communication has to be planned, and then handled with sensitivity. There is more on the subject of communicating and handling change in Fowler and Lock (2016), where the importance of emphasizing the benefits and creating a positive outlook is stressed, and where there is also some discussion about handling redundancies and changed roles.

Organizational instability

Imagine a portfolio management system that is running perfectly. The EPMO has a well-established and logically coded system, which ensures that all data can be associated with the appropriate managers responsible across the organization. But what happens if one or more projects in the portfolio will change the organization itself, possibly with departments being merged, added or removed? Even one or more PMOs might be affected. This will change the database reporting and control structure itself, so managing the change will itself have to become part of the change programme.

Lack of senior management support

Portfolio management and its satellite components of programme and project management are intended to ensure that planned benefits are realized. But those management functions incur costs that are very often overhead costs, which have to be borne by the organization itself. Most organizations strive to keep their overhead costs low compared with their direct costs, and failure to do so can damage the organization's position in a competitive market. So there has to a balance between how much is spent on the EPMO and PMOs in a group. Spend too little, and the strategic and other intended benefits will be put at risk. Spend too much, and market competitiveness could suffer. So senior management have to recognize the value of portfolio management and support its funding at sensible levels.

Harold Kerzner (2000) conducted a survey of several hundred organizations to examine how well project management was implemented in each organization. Many questionnaires were completed and returned. The book gives telling accounts of the results. One case concerned a company where projects were not performing particularly well until one woman managed to communicate her enthusiasm across the organization. She created a small PMO and productivity throughout the organization improved. Order replaced the former chaos. Then the company changed hands. The new incoming management slashed overheads, among which they included the PMO and its competent manager. The former chaos returned. So there is a lesson for senior management.

References and further reading

Fowler, A. and Lock, D. (2006), *Accelerating Business and IT Change: Transforming Project Delivery*, Aldershot: Gower.

Harrison, F. and Lock, D. (2004), *Advanced Project Management*, 4th edn, Aldershot: Gower.

Hartman, F.T. (2000), *Don't Park Your Brain Outside: A Practical Guide to Improving Shareholder Value with Smart Management*, Newtown Square, PA: Project Management Institute.

Kerzner, H. (2000), *Applied Project Management: Best Practices on Implementation*, New York: Wiley.

Lock, D. (2016), *Project Management*, 10th edn, Farnham: Gower.

Chapter 22

Portfolio management competencies

Alistair Godbold

The competencies of a portfolio manager are wide-ranging. They cover leadership, business management and project management. There are also many kinds of portfolio manager, working in many types of business. Portfolio managers operate at the organization level or manage a sub-portfolio. These businesses may focus on operations or on project delivery only.

Introduction

Describing the competencies required by a portfolio manager is a complicated business, not least because the definition of a portfolio has not yet been universally accepted among industry professionals. One firm I have worked with spent over six months trying to agree the internal definitions of *project, programme* and *portfolio*. The *Management of Portfolios* (MoP – AXELOS, 2014) guidance defines portfolio management as the better coordination of investment in programmes and projects, improving the management of risk, encouraging collaborative working and by providing accurate, timely information that enhances management decision-making, such that organizations are able to do the following:

- Invest in the 'right' programmes and projects in the context of the current environmental conditions and the organization's strategic objectives; and
- Ensure successful delivery in terms of time, quality, budget and, most significantly, benefits realization.

MoP goes on to say that it can provide a view of priorities to help with informed allocation (or removal) of resources, and to manage dependencies.

In my experience I have never seen a pure portfolio management role as described in ISO 21504 (International Organization for Standardization [ISO], 2015) and MoP (AXELOS, 2014). To address this I describe some of the different types of portfolio to set the context for the description of the skills and competencies needed by the portfolio manager to deliver successfully. The most significant point made in MoP that is relevant to all types of portfolio is that the portfolio manager facilitates collaborative working to realize the organization's strategic objectives. The most important task is to ensure that the projects and programmes under the manager's control have the right environment and resource levels for success. Balancing resources between projects and programmes is best done at this portfolio level, where a more holistic view can be taken.

Portfolio management is a dynamic process in which new projects and programmes are evaluated, selected, prioritized and balanced alongside existing projects and programmes within the portfolio. This ensures that their phasing and resource allocation is continually adjusted such that the resources are used efficiently and outcomes are achieved. With a holistic view, the portfolio manager is well placed to implement an organization's strategy top-down through the implementation of projects and programmes. The portfolio manager is similarly able to inform the continual development of strategy bottom-up, identifying new opportunities and risks that may influence objectives, altering existing projects or initiating new ones.

A competent manager is one of the most important factors influencing the success of a business initiative. In this chapter competence in its widest sense will be discussed as a generic quality. Portfolio competencies are independent of the type of portfolio (for example, rail, construction, nuclear, information technology [IT], pharmaceutical and so on). However, there may be a number of contextual or industry-specific skills necessary to be able to operate successfully in the organization – or even to be credible among other leaders; these are not discussed here.

Portfolio management

Types of portfolio

When portfolio management is discussed in professional texts, they tend to refer to the whole investment cycle. Most people employed in the role of portfolio managers find themselves managing a section of the portfolio. This section of the portfolio may be a subset of a larger investment that is ultimately managed by the executive leadership of the business or, for some key investments, the board of directors. The political and business environment in which these investments are made is rarely simple. For many public sector organizations the investments are to implement policy and have political kudos attached. Even in private sector organizations, the projects may be sponsored by an executive with significant influence whose motives encompass not only the financial return to the business and shareholder value, but also serve wider personal and political agendas.

As previously discussed, many organizations have portfolio managers who manage a subset of the total portfolio (IT, business change, human relations and accommodation). With these portfolios there is some element of choice and value judgement to select projects that are going to give the best return to the business. Other portfolios exist to maintain the business, either through regulatory compliance or by asset replacement (where the choice is how this should be done, not if it should be delivered).

For some project-orientated companies in the business of delivering projects for clients. there is little choice. Here the work is how to balance the portfolio and deliver all, and to maintain the margin needed to make an adequate financial return on the contract.

Portfolios frequently include the operations of the business as well as the projects and programmes needed to change them. These types of portfolio can be grouped into the following;

- Strategic (to achieve an overall outcome);
- Operational (to cover an area of the business);

- Project (a collection of similar projects and programmes); and
- Resource (to optimize the use of common resources or suppliers across a number of projects and programmes).

Each of these portfolios may be nested inside others, further adding to the complexity and richness of the competencies needed by the portfolio manager. Sponsors and users may be more concerned with effective delivery; they want the outcomes as soon as possible and are not as concerned with the cost of delivery. The portfolio manager has to balance *effective* with *efficient*, developing and maintaining the 'big picture'.

Managing complexity in portfolios

As with other 'real-world' project and programme tasks portfolios do not operate in a purely logical and rational world. They are complex, as well as complicated, with many moving parts. This includes the business environment, changes to the funding they have in order to deliver, and the emergent properties of individual projects and programmes as they gather more information to understand what they must do to deliver. Further complexities may also emerge from the outputs of projects as they interact in unexpected ways. The manifestation of risks, uncertainties and developments in the business environment, or strategic priorities in the portfolio, may also require adjustments to the way in which projects are delivered and, in some cases, what is delivered (Cooke-Davies, 2011).

This means that, as well as the technical skills of project delivery, resource, finance, risk, baseline and schedule management, a key competency for a portfolio manager is leadership in dealing with complexity (Rayner et al., 2013).

Portfolios involve many different stakeholders, sponsors of change, users and delivery teams. All of these will have different perspectives on the objectives. In order to manage these groups and lead them in the shared environment towards achieving a shared objective for the organization, the portfolio manager needs to bring them together. This is done by lots of 'co'-type actions (collaborate, cooperate, co-design, co-create). Many of these actions will involve right-to-left organizing to be able to deliver right-to-left planning. The portfolio manager must bring together and harness the skills, creativity and energy of all stakeholders.

Becoming a portfolio manager

There are two main ways in which people become portfolio managers. The first is through the project delivery route. These people are project managers who progress to programme management and then to portfolio management.

The second route is through a general management route. These individuals are managing an area of the business in which a number of changes are going on, and so they find themselves managing a portfolio. At the highest level, managing directors of businesses can be considered to be portfolio managers, because they are ultimately accountable for the performance of the business and its development.

People who develop as project professionals acquire the title and recognize that they are portfolio managers. Those who come through the general management route may not recognize that this is in fact the role they are fulfilling.

Competencies for portfolio management

Portfolio managers will either have a number of project and programme managers working directly for them, or have to influence a number of their peers through formal governance processes or informal networks. They must create the right environment for the projects to succeed. They must ensure the following:

- Others have the right skills, structures and governance, for the projects to have the right scope (balanced with all of the others); and
- The projects are all initiated correctly with the right scope, resources, plans, sponsorship and so forth.

Competencies for portfolio management are by their very nature generic. There will be competencies that are specific to some industries or types of portfolio and there will be some of the generic portfolio competencies that are needed in different degrees for different types of portfolio.

Sources of standards

Standards from professional bodies are available at the national and international level. These standards and guides for portfolio management include:

- Management of Portfolios (MoP) (AXELOS, 2011);
- Australian Institute of Project Management (AIPM) Professional Competency Standards for Project Management – Part F Certified Practicing Portfolio Executive (AIPM, 2014);
- International Project Management Association: *Individual Competency Baseline*, Version 4.0 (IPMA, 2015);
- UK Association for Project Management (APM) Competence Framework (APM, 2015);
- AПM *Body of Knowledge* (6th edn) (APM, 2012);
- AПM *Praxis Framework* (Praxis, 2014);
- International Organization for Standardization, ISO 21504, Project, Programme and Portfolio Management – Guidance on portfolio management (ISO, 2015).

As well as these standards and guides aimed at portfolio management, the International Centre of Complex Project Management (ICCPM), in their *Complex Project Manager Competency Standards*, Version 4.1 (ICCPM, 2012), describe many of the attributes needed by a portfolio manager for dealing with the complexity of a portfolio.

Portfolio competencies shared with project and programme management

The role of the portfolio manager has, as you would expect, many of the same competencies needed for project and programme management. As with the other roles in project delivery, what makes the difference is the relative levels of competency in each one of the attributes. As the portfolio manager is more of a leadership role, the competencies focus more on the behavioural aspects and less on the technical elements.

For people who develop into portfolio managers through the project and programme route, the behaviours and characteristics needed for each of the roles are different. Those who are successful as project or programme managers may not be successful as portfolio managers. The reverse is often not the case, because if people have not been successful in project or programme management they will not have the opportunity to become portfolio managers.

In general project managers are focused on delivering to time, scope and cost: they drive out ambiguity and seek certainty. The programme manager achieves an outcome and is a lot more comfortable with the ambiguity, driving it out and commissioning projects at the right time. The portfolio manager still has the ambiguity of the outcomes and the changing business environment, and also has to balance the portfolio of projects, programmes and operations, taking into account the following:

- The business environment;
- The change in technology;
- The capacity of the business;
- Competitors; and
- The funding arrangements.

In this regard portfolio managers will often have to make decisions in complex environments based on incomplete information. Those decisions might not be optimal, but will be satisfactory for producing the desired outcome. In this respect their characteristics and competencies are similar to those of a business manager balanced with those of a project professional.

More emphasis on these competency elements:	Less emphasis on these competency elements:
Ethics, compliance and professionalism **Team management** **Conflict management** **Leadership** **Contract management** **Resource management** **Risk, opportunity and issue management** **Consolidated planning** **Financial management** **Resource capacity planning** **Governance arrangements** **Stakeholder and communications management** **Reviews** **Change control** **Independent assurance** **Business case** **Benefits management**	Procurement Requirements management Solutions development Schedule management Transition management Frameworks and methodologies Quality management Asset allocation Capability development

Figure 22.1 Table showing which competencies require more or less emphasis

Using a blend of the competence standards for project and programme management, a comparison of the shared technical competencies that require different emphasis are given in Figure 22.1.

Portfolio management competencies

The IPMA has published a competency standard for portfolio management as part of its *Individual Competence Baseline*, Version 4 (ICB V4 – IPMA, 2014). The ICB divides the competencies into people, perspective and practice (Figure 22.2).

The 'people' aspect covers the competencies of individuals in managing themselves. The 'perspective' aspect covers some of the more technical aspects of strategy and governance. The 'practice' aspect covers the technical skills of managing a portfolio. In particular these competencies cover the following:

- Perspective:
  - Strategy – to be able to translate the organization's vision, mission and strategy into a set of projects and programmes to initiate and govern them. Individuals must be able to influence the strategy from the top down and through their insights into projects and programmes, and from the bottom up making the necessary adjustments in the portfolio.
  - Governance, structures and processes – to be able to integrate the management of the portfolio into the overall governance processes of the organization including those for: finance, human resources (HR), legal, asset management, engineering and so on. They must make sure that the processes serve the portfolio and that the portfolio does not end up serving the governance.

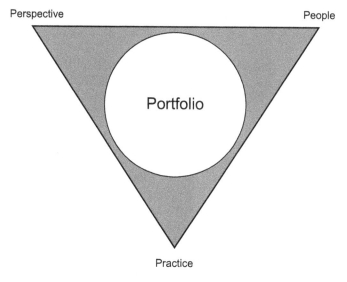

Figure 22.2 Triangle of portfolio management competencies

Many processes can become a burden, not adding value where people blindly follow those processes and are maliciously compliant. Individuals must also be able to set up the necessary governance within their portfolio to ensure that it is set up and managed to succeed.

- o   Compliance, standards and regulation – companies operate in a regulated environment to a greater or lesser extent. At the lowest level this will be complying with legal, financial and accounting regulations through to safety and market regulation. The portfolio manager needs to be aware of these and any internal regulations to be able to make decisions in this context.
- o   Power and interest – the portfolio manager operates in a political (with a small 'p') environment where there will be informal personal and group interests that influence the portfolio. The manager must be aware of these and be able to operate building alliances and using formal and informal networks to achieve the outcomes.
- o   Culture and values – the portfolio operates in an environment where multiple sets of values and cultures exist. These might range from the different cultures in the same organization and from department to department in the same location, through to different locations in the same country. The supply chains they use or the scope of implementation may span many countries with different value sets which have to be recognized and managed. Portfolio managers need to have a strong sense of their own internal values to anchor themselves and to ensure that these values are promulgated throughout the portfolio. They also need to be able to articulate all the different values clearly with reasoning, even when others do not agree.

- •   People:
    - o   Self-reflection and self-management – being able to learn from oneself and reflect on what has occurred and how you have reacted to that is a key skill. As part of being a leader you need to ensure that you behave in a consistent way to other members of your team and stakeholders; this will help to develop trust, because they know how you will be likely to behave in any given situation.
    - o   Personal integrity and reliability – as with any leadership position the manager will be making commitments to stakeholders, team members and sponsors. It is essential that managers can deliver against these commitments and that they are in line with society's moral values and their own ethical codes. The portfolio manager, as with any project professional, needs to be aware of ethical systems to be able to reason and articulate a position to others.
    - o   Personal communication – this involves both verbal and written communication to local and virtual teams. The portfolio manager needs to be able to communicate complex issues and the status of the portfolio to a wide range of stakeholders in ways that the messages are understood and acted on. They need to be able to gain feedback to ensure that these messages have been understood. Communication is not only a transmit skill, but even more of a receiving skill, and the most important part of this is to be able to listen and understand a person's perspective by what they say, by the way in which it is said and, perhaps more importantly, by what they do not say.

o   Relations and engagement – building trusting and durable relationships with your stakeholders and team members is the foundation of productive collaboration. The portfolio manager needs to have the emotional intelligence to demonstrate empathy and develop trust. If operating internationally, the manager must be able to understand the different cultural norms to be able to operate in these areas.

o   Leadership – this is perhaps the most important competency of all for any project professional. There are many definitions of leadership and whole books are devoted to defining and understanding it. In this context, at its most simple, it is the ability to provide direction and guidance to individuals and groups using appropriate and authentic styles. This is needed to motivate and guide the people who are delivering the portfolio and enhance their performance. This is particularly important when there is change or uncertainty within the portfolio.

o   Teamwork – all projects, programmes and portfolios are delivered by teams. The portfolio manager must be able to select and bring people together to deliver this common objective. Once they have selected the team, the manager must be able to take the team through the full lifecycle of forming, storming, norming and performing (Belbin, 2003) as fast as possible.

o   Portfolio managers may even have to use techniques to develop people into a 'high performing team' where little direct management is needed.

o   Conflict and crisis – in the delivery of any project, programme and portfolio, there will be times when there is conflict between team members, sponsors and contractors, and maybe even crises when things do not go as planned. This is normal and the portfolio manager must be able to take action to deal with these difficulties in a constructive, timely and direct way. Ideally the manager should be able to anticipate situations and times where there could be conflict – and then take steps to deal with each case in advance. Dealing with conflict might not be a case of making an either/or decision, but the portfolio manager must have the courage to recognize and manage each case.

o   Resourcefulness – the portfolio will contain many uncertainties and unknowns. There will be changes in scope, requests for changes in budgets, and demands to do things faster, better and cheaper. In response the portfolio manager must be resourceful, solving these challenges in creative and different ways. Portfolio managers must be able to harness a team's imagination and creativity as well as their own. They must be able to do this by continuously searching for new ways to deliver the portfolio – and not just as a response to an external request or event.

o   Negotiation – this is traditionally thought of in the commercial sense, where a price or contract terms are being agreed. The portfolio manager must also be able to apply the full range of negotiating tools and techniques to internal departments, sponsors and teams with the aim of achieving a 'win–win' solution. As well as some of the more technical negotiation skills the portfolio manager must have the patience, tenacity, resilience, integrity, empathy and creativity to develop new solutions that will work and endure for both parties. Too often I have seen agreements where one party thinks they have won the negotiation, only for the contract or agreement to come undone at the expense of the project.

o Results orientation – portfolio managers are project professionals who deliver. They are there to deliver outcomes and outputs, not just to manage a process and create the right environment for their teams. They must be able to hold people to account, making sure that the outcomes are agreed with the stakeholders and sponsors. They must do this in line with the shared values of the portfolio and the stakeholders.

- Practice:

  o Portfolio design – the portfolio manager must structure the overall architecture of the portfolio. In the literature a portfolio is used as a vehicle to say how the organization will implement its strategy. However, many operate below this level and may be structured around common areas of resource or outcome such as IT, business change or asset management. Other portfolios for project-orientated companies manage the allocation of scarce resources such as key skills, equipment, demands on the supply chain, lay-down areas for heavy equipment or access to areas of the site, and so on. Designing the portfolio will depend on the context and may be best achieved by a set of coordinated or subservient portfolios, the design of which is driven by what is important to the organization.

  o Goals, objectives and benefits – the projects and programmes in a portfolio are there to achieve benefits for the organization. The portfolio manager must ensure that these benefits are delivered in the most effective and efficient way, recognizing that there may be relationships between some of these projects and programmes. These relationships may be dependencies, they may build on others to create new benefits or they might even conflict. It is the role of the portfolio manager to ensure that they remain aligned with strategy and respond appropriately to the business environment.

  o Scope – the projects and programmes within the portfolio operate within a defined scope. The portfolio manager must manage these areas of scope, ensuring there are no overlaps and that gaps are understood and managed appropriately. During the execution of the portfolio there will be changes in the scope of their projects and programmes. The portfolio manager must use a variety of tools and techniques under a governance structure to manage these and ensure that they continue to deliver benefit for the organization.

  o Time – this is known to project professionals as one of the key parts of Martin Barnes's 'triangle of objectives' (time–quality–cost), now also commonly known as the iron triangle. All the projects and programmes must be delivered to their schedules, with their dependencies managed.

  o Organization and information – there will be many teams and lots of information generated. Information will flow between (and be used by) many parties as part of the operation of a portfolio. Governance structures and teams will need to be formed and then changed as projects and programmes move through their lifecycles. The portfolio manager must ensure that these governance structures are appropriate, robust and being used effectively. As part of the delivery and operation of the portfolio there will be a lot of information and documentation generated that needs to be stored and managed. It is the role of the portfolio manager to ensure that this is controlled.

- o Quality – the second part of the iron triangle is quality. The portfolio manager must put in place the standards and processes necessary to ensure that the quality of all of the outputs and outcomes are managed and consistent. This is in the same way that a programme or project manager would have to do for their projects.
- o Finance – the final part of the iron triangle is cost. As part of the portfolio, it might be more efficient to have this conducted at the portfolio level rather than at the project or programme level. This will include not only the cost management, but also the estimating, contingency provisions, planning, approval, cash flow management and funding.
- o Resources – many portfolios, as discussed above, are designed to manage the demands on common sets of resources. The portfolio manager must have the right competencies to be able to define those resources that are common, and then acquire, control and develop them. These resources can take the form of physical assets (such as specialist plant or machinery) or they might be specific skills that are in short supply. It could be the case that the portfolios impact on the business, community or market, which might have a finite capacity for change. It could be the coordination of new products and the capacity for sales that need to be managed.
- o Procurement – many projects and programmes will use the same parts of the supply chain. Relationships with these suppliers will be more effectively managed at the portfolio level, where greater control and better commitment can be given. This will also allow for the implementation of common terms and conditions, tendering rules and market engagement.
- o Planning and control – a typical portfolio consists of many projects and programmes. The portfolio manager must maintain a plan to show how these relate to each other and interact, maintaining a portfolio view. The planning standards, cost, organization and work breakdown structures should be common to allow shared learning and estimating improvements, as well as understanding the demands on other parts of the organizations' resources and the supply chain. This will also help with the flexibility of project controls, enabling resources to be moved between projects and programmes, understanding the structure and form of plans, and thus being able to add value immediately.
- o Risk and opportunity – much of the risk management will be conducted at the project and programme level. However there will be risks that are best managed at the portfolio level owing to their size, or to the fact that they impact a number of projects or programmes across the portfolio. The portfolio manager must set the standards for these, the risk appetite of the organization and the common tool sets to be used.
- o Stakeholders – there are multiple stakeholders associated with the delivery of a portfolio. Some of these will be common across the projects or programmes. In order to present a common interface, a strategy should be formulated, identifying the common stakeholders and putting in place actions to ensure that they are influenced appropriately for the benefit of the whole portfolio.
- o Change and transformation – as part of the delivery of a project (be it an asset or a transformation) people will have to change the way they work to deliver the intended outcomes and benefits. Having been involved in organizations

where this is not done in a coordinated way, I know that this can be frustrating for the individuals impacted by these changes to be subjected to many different methods while trying to continue with operations and 'do their day jobs'. Transformation needs to be coordinated across the portfolio to ensure that it is optimized as far as possible, with synergies exploited and conflicts eliminated.

o   Select and balance – it is the role of the portfolio manager to ensure that the portfolio contains the right mix of projects. This means projects that can be implemented and deliver the strategy for the organization. There are very few types of portfolio where this is possible and most of the time the portfolio manager must work out the dependencies between projects and programmes to ensure that they all can deliver. This can be done by issuing change requests to speed up or slow down projects, to procure extra resources, or to alter scope or phasing for the greater good.

As discussed above the portfolio manager is more of a business leader in a project context. There will be a strategic approach to translating the company strategy (or, in government circles, its policy) into a set of projects and programmes. The manager's implementation of the strategy will be through the projects and programmes, which is how the organization drives forward. This is not a mechanical process, because the portfolio manager will be dealing with the agendas and interests of other members of the leadership team, as well as operating in the dynamic nature of the business. The portfolio manager must be able to understand and sense the political environment of the organization, and so be able to negotiate and persuade others of the benefits of managing the portfolio in the way that they are doing. This will inevitably mean that some sponsor's projects are not top of the list or given the priority that all sponsors feel they should be given. As well as the competencies described above, portfolio managers must have some qualities in greater abundance than many of their fellow programme and project professionals. These include the following:

- Emotional intelligence: to understand how others will feel about the decisions they are making and so how to respond accordingly;
- Gravitas: to command the respect of others and allow them to follow the decisions made and cooperate with plans;
- Resilience: during delivery there will be inevitably be a number of issues and obstacles. These will have to be overcome to maintain energy and keep on going;
- Creativity: many of the complexities, opportunities and issues faced by the portfolio manager will have no obvious solutions, so he or she will have to find new and novel ways to join projects and programmes, to exploit synergies and optimize their delivery;
- Ambiguity: portfolios are dynamic and uncertain. Portfolio managers must be able to operate in this environment and feel comfortable in dealing with this situation, knowing when to drive to a solution;
- Complexity: portfolios are also complex and non-deterministic. Portfolio managers must be able to manage this and spot the weak signals of issues arising in the portfolio. They must be familiar with the tools and techniques for dealing with this and know when to take action (Heaslip, 2014);

- Business: the portfolio manager needs to be a business person to be able to understand the context of the portfolio, what the organization is trying to achieve, and the pressures and opportunities that it faces. The portfolio manager must be able to react accordingly, presenting options and not waiting to respond to requests;
- Networking: portfolio operation will involve people from across the business and supply chain. Some of the operating information will flow through formal channels. However, much information will be through trusting relationships that the portfolio manager has developed and maintained with their colleagues (McChrystal, 2015).

The AIPM has developed a standard for portfolio management and classified the competencies into a number of units in their AIPM *Professional Competency Standards for Project Management – Part F – Certified Practicing Portfolio Executive* (CPPE) (Young and Conboy, 2013; AIPM, 2014). The AIPM standard was developed as a generic standard that would be appropriate for a range of businesses. The details of these competencies are similar to those outlined in the IPMA standard, albeit from a different perspective, using slightly different language and grouping. This shows a general agreement on the competencies needed by the portfolio manager and how they deliver.

Conclusion

The competencies of the portfolio manager are numerous. Many of them come from the project profession, consisting of the common skills for managing time, cost, quality and risk. These competencies are enhanced and supplemented with those needed for leadership, influencing, business and strategic management. Project professionals will come to be portfolio managers from a number of different backgrounds and they will have wide ranging experience. In summary these people will be the following:

- Experienced in business and/or project management delivery;
- Experts in project and programme management principles, concepts and techniques;
- Experienced in managing large operations or projects across organizational or industry boundaries;
- Senior managers and part of the leadership team; and
- Experienced in evaluating and reviewing project or programme performance.

Like all roles in the project profession, being a portfolio manager is challenging and exciting but never dull. It is a vital strategic leadership role that allows the organization to implement its strategy and drive itself forward. The routes to becoming a portfolio manager are more open than those to being a project manager, as people can come from a project or a business route. If so desired, the routes from portfolio management to more mainstream business roles are also more open.

References and further reading

Australian Institute of Project Management (2014), *Professional Competency Standards for Project Management – Part F, Certified Practising Portfolio Executive* (CPPE), Version 2.1, AIPM.

Association for Project Management (APM) (2012), *APM Body of Knowledge*, 6th edn, Princess Risborough: APM.

Association for Project Management (2015), *APM Competency Framework*, 2nd edn., Version 1, Princess Risborough: APM.

AXELOS (2011), *Management of Portfolios*, Norwich: The Stationery Office.

Belbin, R.M. (2003), *Management Teams: Why They Succeed or Fail*, 2nd edn, Oxford: Elsevier Butterworth-Heinemann.

Camilleri, E. (2011) *Project Success: Critical Factors and Behaviours*, Farnham: Gower.

Cooke-Davies, T. (2011), *Aspects of Complexity: Managing Projects in a Complex World*, Newtown Square, PA: Project Management Institute.

Geries, R. (2012), 'Professional project portfolio management', 26th IPMA World Congress, Crete, Greece.

Heaslip. R.J. (2014), *Managing Complex Projects and Programmes – How to improve leadership of complex initiatives using a third-generation approach*, Hoboken, NJ: Wiley.

International Centre for Complex Project Management (2012), *Complex Project Manager Competency Standards*, Version 4.1 (August), Deakin, ACCT: ICCPM.

International Project Management Association (2015), *Individual Competence Baseline*, Version 4.0, Amsterdam: IPMA.

International for Organization Standardization (2015) ISO 21504: *Project, Programme and Portfolio Management – Guidance on portfolio management*, Geneva: ISO.

McChrystal, S. (2015), *Team of Teams: New Rules of Engagement for a Complex World: Portfolio*, London: Penguin.

Praxis (2014), *Praxis Framework: An integrated guide to the management of projects programmes and portfolios*, Princes Risborough: Association for Project Management.

Rayner, P., Reiss, G. and MacNicol, D. (2013), *Portfolio and Programme Management Demystified – Managing Multiple Projects Successfully*, Abingdon: Routledge.

Young, M. and Conboy, K. (2013), 'Contemporary project portfolio management: Reflections on the development of an Australian Competency Standard for Portfolio Management', *International Journal of Project Management*, 1091.

Chapter 23

Key performance indicators and their role in portfolio management

Stuart Dixon

Portfolio managers use key performance indicators (KPIs) to judge how their portfolios are performing. Typically included on a one-page document (referred to as a dashboard), KPIs allow the reader to have control and oversight of the portfolio performance. The indicators are usually represented visually, using charts, dials or other graphics. A well-designed KPI can help the portfolio manager, providing direction to make appropriate decisions to control the portfolio effectively. Conversely, a badly designed KPI can confuse or obscure the decision needed, leading to incorrect or invalid actions.

Definition of KPIs

Each KPI is defined as a business metric used to evaluate factors that are crucial to the success of the organization. KPIs can and do differ by organization. A business may already be using KPIs in its organization, sometimes without realizing that it is doing so.

Some organizations already use a set of KPIs, provided in a dashboard, to help run their business. A balanced scorecard, first introduced in the early 1990s, is used in companies to monitor how the business performs across its operational areas. Because businesses differ in what each is trying to deliver, so the contents of their balanced scorecards will differ.

A portfolio is made up of programmes and projects that are about changing the organization, whereas a balanced scorecard is all about monitoring the operational side (known as business as usual in the portfolio world). This means that the balanced scorecard cannot be used as it currently stands to monitor the success or otherwise of the portfolio.

Before starting to work out what should appear as a 'key performance 'indicator', perhaps it is best to understand exactly what each of these words really means:

- *Key: anything that is important.* In portfolio management, key indicators are relevant to the decisions that are to be made about the portfolio;
- *Performance*: this is something that describes whether or not the portfolio is being executed (delivered) as intended; and
- *Indicator*: a measure or something visual that shows the state of the portfolio.

Anything can be (and sometimes is) used as a portfolio KPI. However, before choosing a set of KPIs to be shown together on a dashboard, it is useful to understand the drivers for the portfolio – that is, to understand what is important or key for the portfolio.

Displaying KPIs on a dashboard – an analogy

The dashboard of a typical modern car provides a set of indicators, all of which are perceived as key by the manufacturer of the car (otherwise they wouldn't be there). A look at indicators on that dashboard shows the different levels of importance at different times:

- *Speedometer*: this is useful for indicating the speed at which the car is travelling. However, to make it truly useful it is important to understand what the speed limit is on the road. An indicator without a limit (or target) is only of partial use.
- *Revolution counter*: this has a red line or segment that shows when the maximum recommended engine revolutions per minute are being exceeded, indicating that a higher gear should be chosen. This is a good example of a KPI. It allows the driver to make a decision (to change gear) based on the information displayed. This is then reflected in the indicator after the relevant decision has been taken.
- *Fuel gauge*: this is useful for seeing whether the car has enough fuel to keep going. However it becomes really significant for decision-making only when the gauge is showing low or nearly empty – otherwise it is generally ignored by the end user (car driver).

These examples illustrate that it is important to understand what each indicator shows and (probably more importantly) the decisions that are relevant to make based on the indicator.

KPIs for a portfolio

There are three main parts to a portfolio: a beginning, middle and end. The beginning of a portfolio is where new ideas get added into the portfolio. The middle of the portfolio is where the projects and programmes are delivered. The end of the portfolio is where the benefits of the project are obtained (or not). To find out how the portfolio is performing it is important to identify those performance indicators that allow the organization to track the individual parts of the portfolio. The following sections outline some of the indicators that can be considered.

KPIs at the beginning of a portfolio

These indicators allow the organization to understand how good (or bad) it is on converting ideas into projects. This allows the organization to see whether the correct projects are coming through. It is not enough just to have lots of projects approved if they do not align through to the strategy.

These will then allow the portfolio manager (or approval board) to make decisions on how to improve the quality of the ideas coming through and to improve the portfolio induction process. Remember that new ideas can come into the portfolio at any time, even if the approval process is only quarterly.

Examples of KPIs to consider at the start of a portfolio

- *How many ideas are being submitted from each area of the business?* This indicator tells the organization whether or not one part of the organization is dominating the ideas process. Will there need to be some balance inserted? For areas, which have not been submitting ideas, will they need some education on how to submit their ideas? This report is probably better if it shows the numbers of ideas by size of the department. It might be expected that a larger department would submit a larger number of ideas.
- *How many ideas are transferred into projects and programmes?* This indicator tells the organization how good the selection process has been. Most organizations are resource constrained in some way, so just approving every idea is a sign of an immature organization. A high performing organization might approve only 40 per cent of the ideas suggested.
- *How much of the available budget has been assigned to committed projects?* This indicator tells the organization whether there is money available to deliver the project, before approving a new idea. This metric can encounter problems of definition, because an idea will have a cost to deliver, but the finance department will have the budgets split into years. Care needs to be given to ensure that the committed effort in the current year is compared with the budget for that year, rather than try to fund the entire project cost out of the current year's money. For projects that span multiple years, ensure that there is funding available to continue the project in subsequent financial years. If the budget has been split down by department or strategic intent, for example, then the presentation of this indicator should be split by the same divisions. This will allow the organization to see whether they can reassign money to where it is required to deliver existing projects, or promote the department or strategic intent that has not committed as much money as would be expected to put forward some more ideas.
- *What is the alignment between the ideas and the strategy?* This indicator tells the organization whether or not they have been successful in turning their strategy into execution. There are many organizations that provide a strategy with a top three items, only to find that most of the actual project delivery is in a category of 'other'. The organization should use this information to ensure that the correct ideas get approved and ensure that the strategy gets delivered.
- *What is the current backlog of ideas – how many ideas have been outstanding and for how long?* This indicator tells the organization how good their pipeline process is; are they wasting effort introducing new ideas that then don't get developed into projects? Once the portfolio has been running for some time (over a year) there will be ideas that have been raised that were not deemed to have sufficient priority to be delivered. Without a pruning of the older ideas there can be a lot of deadwood within the portfolio. After about six months without progression, any estimate of cost and benefit (and the need for the idea) becomes out of date. This will have to be revisited before the idea is reconsidered. Any idea over one year old may be aligned with needs that the organization had with a different strategy in mind; this idea will need to be revisited to ensure that it still aligns with current strategic aims.

KPIs during the middle of a portfolio

Indicators during the middle of a portfolio allow the organization to understand how well it is delivering the ideas that have been turned into the projects. How many of those projects are actually going to be delivered? When will the organization get the benefits that they have signed off as part of the portfolio approval and initiation process? If there are any issues with the delivery, the organization will need to take appropriate action to ensure that these are resolved (which might, of course mean cancelling a project). The following are some indicators to consider during this middle period of the portfolio:

- *RAG indicators*: RAG (red, amber or green) indicators can be used to show the status of ongoing projects. RAG indicators tell the organization how well the delivery of the portfolio is going. Are all the projects going to be delivered as expected (green status)? Are there potential problems (amber status)? Or is intervention required (red status)? In a normal organization, there would be a balance of all these statuses. Having all green on the portfolio could mean that someone is hiding the truth, because all projects can be expected to encounter issues. Most of these can usually be dealt with, but at least one or two projects in a portfolio will encounter something that cannot easily be dealt with. So these need flagging up a level so that they can be resolved.

    Having a portfolio with red and green, but no amber, would indicate that there is no early warning system in place to flag problems. Therefore the organization becomes very reactive to the issues that occur. This might indicate that the organization needs to review the settings for those status definitions that do not flag problems early enough. A view that shows a high proportion of red projects would indicate that the organization is not in control of the delivery and more focus is needed on getting the basics of project delivery right before focusing on portfolio management.
- *When are the portfolio's projects and programmes being delivered?* This indicator tells the organization about the expected delivery times for changes authorized in the portfolio. Good portfolio management would balance the amount of change that is hitting the organization in one go, and the areas that this is impacting. The indicator allows the portfolio manager and relevant senior management to see whether there might be any issues arising from the volume of change that could have an impact on the running of the business? Could, for example, there be a risk from project deliveries happening during a busy period (such as delivery of projects into the finance department at year end, or delivery of shop store refits at Christmas)? It could be necessary to show not only the volume of changes, but also the size of those changes. One large programme being delivered could have the same impact as 10 smaller projects.
- *Number of projects by stage.* This indicator tells the organization about the throughput of projects. Is there a glut of projects that are going to be delivered at once? Different resources will be needed at different stages of a project. If most projects are at the same stage, then they will be consuming the same resources. What will happen when those stages end? Will there be resources available, but

no work for them? If the organization is resource constrained, then more projects could be delivered each year by staggering the project deliveries.

- *How much of the available budget has been assigned to committed projects?* This indicator tells the organization how much money it has committed and, therefore, how much remains available to commit to new projects. The indicator should divide the committed money into the amounts already spent (actuals) and the remaining expenditure forecast.

  Early in the financial year it could be expected that there would be some money left uncommitted, so the organization can react to events and approve new projects. If there is no uncommitted money, then the only way of funding new projects would be to stop an existing one (which would be wasteful of resources because the organization will have spent money for no return). Later in the financial year it could be expected that most (if not all) of the money would be committed to projects. If not all the money has been assigned, then the organization could end up approving projects just to 'use the money up' rather than spending it on important projects. Towards the end of the financial year this may be extended to show how much of the following year's budget has been utilized by projects carrying over into next year, thereby reducing the available budget for next year.

- *Information on risk and issues that will stand in the way of portfolio delivery.* This indicator tells the organization the items that will need resolving to smooth out the delivery of projects. When considering at the portfolio level across all the projects and programmes, themes can be seen when looking at each of the risks and issues. If there are common themes (normally cost, resource, scope, timescale) these can be brought out and looked at across the whole organization. If a theme is spotted, then some analysis will need to be done to see if there is a root cause. For example, if the theme is cost, this might mean that work needs to be done to ensure that estimating is improved, either at initial stages or perhaps revised at each stagegate as more detail becomes known.

- *Information on cross project/programme dependencies that are impacting delivery.* This indicator tells the organization which projects have the biggest impact on the delivery of the entire portfolio. A small project might have a key dependency on several other larger programmes because they are relying on it to deliver something that they need. Or, possibly, those other programmes might need resources that will not be available until the project finishes. Just because a project has a low priority does not mean it is not important. With all this information, the portfolio manager can look to see whether to change the priority of projects or focus attention to prevent the dependency becoming an issue.

- *Resource capacity.* This indicator gives a view on the resource capacity, highlighting the issues that will prevent the delivery of the portfolio. It tells the organization whether there are any resource issues that are impacting the smooth delivery of the projects. It is important to include consideration of physical resources as well as people. For instance, an IT department might be able to deliver more projects if it had more technical environments available for use at one time. A construction portfolio could be limited by the number of delivery trucks that can access the site at one time to deliver materials. If a portfolio has a particular resource that is constantly overcommitted, the organization should consider investing in more of that resource. If people of a particular skill are in short supply, it may be a matter of retraining. If it is a physical resource shortage, then perhaps a purchase is required (a project might be required to deliver this). Under-utilization of a resource can indicate a different problem. Cost is being incurred, but the full value of the resource is not being exploited. Should the portfolio be changed so that resource can be used? Or does the organization need that amount of resource – could the capacity be reduced? When looking at resource decisions, remember that it can take considerable time to ramp resources up and down. It is therefore good to look at the impact over several quarters, rather than restrict attention to immediate issues.

KPIs at the end of a portfolio

Indicators at the end of a portfolio allow the organization to show whether it has managed to achieve its intentions for portfolio delivery. Benefits management is an area with which many organizations struggle. KPIs in the business case can become eroded gradually and finally forgotten as the project progresses. Paying appropriate attention to KPIs will enable the organization to measure success and build monitoring into the fabric of the portfolio. Over time this can lead to better business cases, including potential benefits that the organization knows can be tracked. Examples of KPIs to consider at the end of the portfolio include the following:

- *What benefits have been achieved this year?* This indicator tells the organization whether it has achieved what it expected from the projects. Where benefits are tracked, this is typically done only for a discrete period after the project is delivered (usually for six months or a year). Depending on the organization structure, it can be easier to track actual benefits rather than expected benefits (because the latter would necessitate a review of the business case each time to build up the information). Actual benefits can be monitored using existing measures. Non-financial benefits (such as customer satisfaction) can either be shown separately or converted into a pseudo-financial cost and shown with the financial benefits.
- *What benefits will be achieved this year?* This indicator tells the organization the benefits expected from projects that are running and from those that have finished. Where benefits are tracked, organizations have targets for the expected benefits that are due. Those benefits can then be offset against the cost of delivering the project.
- *How many projects have been cancelled or put on hold?* This indicator tells the organization how good it has been at selecting the right projects. Cancellation of too many projects could show that the project selection and approval process needs improvement. If too many projects are put on hold, this can show that the approvals process might need to be more 'drip-fed', preventing too many projects being implemented at the same time.

Displaying KPIs

Having decided what KPIs are required for the portfolio, the next step is to display them. This needs some kind of gauge (as in the example of a car dashboard) that can

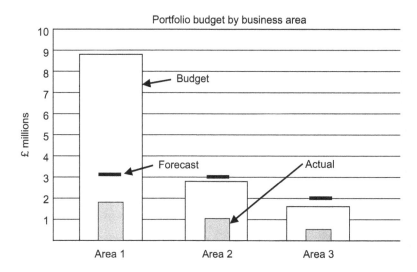

Figure 23.1 Gauge showing budget spend

display the current value of a KPI. It is helpful to display each KPI so that it can be compared with a target. This is useful in displaying KPIs where historical information is not relevant (for example, how much of the budget has been spent). Figure 23.1 shows how this might be done.

A pie chart (as shown in Figure 23.2) is the next step up, because this is effective in allowing the current value of multiple items to be displayed. This is useful when comparing items against each other (for example, which strategic items have the most projects or have had the most money spent on them?).

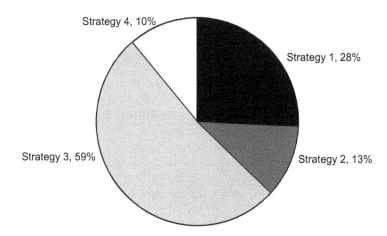

Figure 23.2 Pie chart showing spend by strategic category

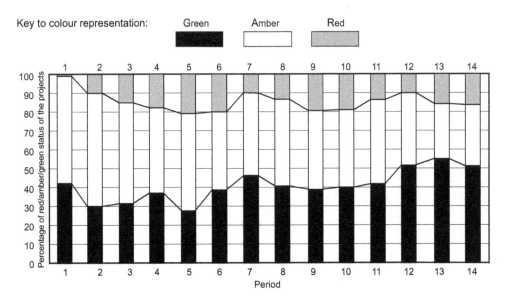

Figure 23.3 Chart showing RAG status over time

A column chart (histogram) allows for trends to be shown. This can be a simple view of the data, such as the number of projects contained in each stage. Or, it could be a stacked column graph, with different time periods on the horizontal axis (such as project delivery times). It could also be a 100 per cent stacked column graph, with different time periods on the horizontal axis, showing the red/amber/green status of the projects. This concept is illustrated in Figure 23.

Using the appropriate visual representation allows the user to understand the KPI and take the appropriate action. A bad choice of visual can ruin a good KPI. Imagine trying to interpret a car speedometer where the visual is a 100 per cent stacked column chart showing the percentage of time spent driving under 30 mph, between 30 and 60 mph and over 60 mph.

Responding to a KPI

KPIs give a high-level view on where the extent and location of problems. They do not show the detail level. It is important to have that greater level of detail available so that a problem seen at the higher level can be investigated, by drilling down into the detail (when, hopefully, the causes can be identified and resolved).

Suppose, for example, that the portfolio manager sees many projects with a red status, the next level of detail would be to list those projects, with the names of the people involved (such as the project managers and sponsors, along with the reasons for the status and the actions required to return this to green). Without drilling down into the detail, the KPI display just becomes a pretty picture.

For any indicator, it is important to be able to answer the simple question: 'So what?' If this question cannot be answered satisfactorily then it is not important enough to be a KPI.

Each of these indicators needs to be current. Consider using a tool and/or automation to provide an up-to-date view of each status. This does not need to be 'real time', but if the organization reports weekly only to have information that is six weeks old before it is viewed, this is useless because decisions are made with out-of-date information. Conversely if there is a quarterly approval process, then this information does not require updating between the approval cycles.

Understand what decisions the organization is being expected to make, and look at what information will support that decision. Understand what data will support that information, who will provide it and at what frequency. Then collate these into easy-to-understand views so that the decisions can be made. At that point it is possible to create the one-page portfolio dashboard. If the people receiving this information demand to have this and complain when it arrives late, then the organization has succeeded in providing the necessary KPIs to run and control the portfolio.

Chapter 24

Portfolio management software

Mey Mark Meyer

Today's market for project portfolio management software offers such a variety of products that it can be difficult to figure out the benefit of a solution for your own portfolio management. Specific software for portfolio management is far superior to the typical Excel lists that many organizations still use to plan and monitor their project portfolios. The functions provided today by mature software suites make it technically easy to integrate project management and project portfolio management. Therefore, the key challenge is to avoid too much integration in order to prevent creating a chaotic project management environment (in which even the smallest change in one project would immediately affect other projects). This chapter describes the most important functions of today's software tools and shows how they can help in integrating project and project portfolio management.

Why portfolio management software?

Specialized software for project portfolio management might seem to be superfluous at first thought. Isn't there the omnipotent Microsoft Excel just a few clicks away on the desktop, waiting for project data to be entered, pivoted and visualized in all the ways you can think of? It is simple to create project portfolio overviews based on data provided by the project managers in their monthly status reports. So, doesn't special portfolio management software force project managers to comply with the software's processes and concepts, and thereby make their lives more difficult?

Portfolio management can, of course, be done without specialized software. In that case, portfolio pipelines are often managed by means of Excel. Excel templates for project proposals might get sent around when someone wants to start a new project. And, at some point, a few macros will be programmed to condense information quickly from these proposals. But there it is: we have established specialized software for project management! So, instead of creating an Excel-based individual solution, why not choose a professional solution, such as many software providers offer?

Integrating project and project portfolio management

Project portfolio management is not just only about handling project proposals, checking them for plausibility, strategy compliance and profitability, and ensuring a proper approval process. Instead, state-of-the-art portfolio management also has to deal with strategic budgeting and resource management. Those making portfolio decisions need to consider both project proposals and ongoing projects to get the full picture.

Separate lists for portfolio management work well as long as they get filled with the latest project data. Therefore, project managers constantly need to provide information about their projects. Usually they do this by filling out status reports, which summarize each project's situation using a handful of key performance indicators (KPIs) and red, amber, green (RAG) status lights. A key benefit of a separate portfolio list is that project managers are free to use any tool they like to keep track of their projects. It doesn't matter which tools they use as long as they manage their projects properly and can provide reliable forecasts.

Having to copy data from their project management tools to a status report just to enable the project management office's (PMO's) portfolio management is something of which many project managers disapprove. The long-term forecast of resource demands, however, requires even more. An up-to-date schedule and agreements between project and resource managers based on that schedule are necessary to predict the organization's overall resource situation. Status reports do not usually contain such detailed information. To make solid portfolio decisions the portfolio manager thus needs access to the existing projects' resource planning and their schedules. This becomes difficult if each project manager uses his or her own, individual way of planning.

An integrated software solution that supports project management as well as portfolio management solves the problem. It helps project managers to create status reports without having to re-enter data that they already have in their project plans. Portfolio managers can condense resource and budget information across different projects to get their forecasts.

Of course, portfolio management does not only include bottom-up project reporting and project proposal management. It also requires project managers to be aware of the top-down set project targets and monitor those using standardized methods and processes. Just as portfolio management needs current data from the projects, so the project managers require up-to-date budgets and resource grants. If all this information is held in one software suite, it is much easier to provide everyone with the information they need. This is especially true as web-based software has become a standard, allowing easy access from everywhere to one single source of information. Sending Excel lists by e-mail, not being completely sure whether the file is really the latest version, should be a remnant from the past.

Consistently, project portfolio management software is in high demand in organizations that have already established basic portfolio management methods and aim to get to a higher maturity level.

The M Model (Figure 24.1) is a conceptual software architecture that embraces all tasks related to the initiation, planning, execution and termination of projects. The model describes enterprise-wide project and project portfolio management and explains the management levels involved. It is used in the market report *Project Management Software Systems* (Meyer and Ahlemann, 2016) to assess software products and describe their functions in a standardized way. The M Model covers different management levels throughout the whole project life cycle. It considers these levels to be fully integrated. The management levels and project phases constitute the model's

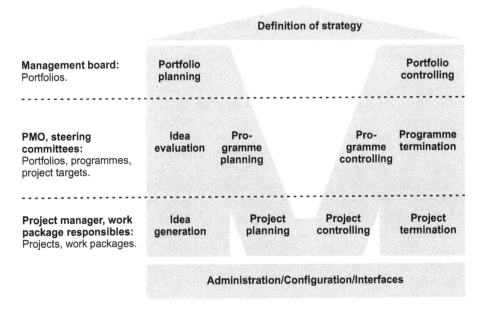

Figure 24.1 The M model

dimensions. Information between portfolio management and project management flows in both directions:

- Project targets and their tolerances (regarding, for example, schedule as well as financial and resource budgets) are set by the project owners. These are then planned accordingly in portfolio management and provided as baselines for project management. Reports and performance indicators can refer to these targets.
- Changes in the schedule and resource planning are reported automatically upwards to portfolio management. In this way, portfolio decisions can reflect the real resource demand and need not use numbers proposed or estimated when the project was initially requested.
- Project status reports are a key aspect of information flow. In an integrated system, it is possible to access a project's data directly, using the latest version of a project plan and actuals for portfolio management purposes. However, this leads to highly unstable portfolios in which even minor changes in a project immediately change the portfolio perspective. This can be avoided, if portfolio reports use data from the status reports instead of pulling the latest information directly from the database. In this way, portfolio reporting shows information that has been deliberately published by the project managers, while project managers can work with the latest data for internal project planning.

The PPM software market

A Google search for 'Project Portfolio Management Software' results in an almost endless list of competing products. For the market survey 'Project Management Software

Systems', which focuses on products being supported on the European market, we checked hundreds of search results, briefly reviewed about 100 products and conducted detailed analyses for about 30 high-end project portfolio management (PPM) solutions.

Many solutions offer only project portfolio reporting. It is important to distinguish between functions that support portfolio decision-making and strategic alignment, and a software's mere capability to group projects by any kind of filter condition and create aggregated reports on these groups. The latter is useful for portfolio reporting to keep track of portfolios.

In the M-Model portfolio, reporting is covered by the portfolio controlling section at the top right of the M. Portfolio controlling consolidates the status of individual programmes and projects and compares them with the current strategic direction of the enterprise. If necessary, the programme's and the project's objectives are corrected, and new programmes and portfolios are created so that the corporate strategy and project management are again harmonized. This can also lead to an immediate termination of current projects or programmes that no longer correspond to corporate strategy. But only if the software helps scoring projects based on strategic benefits, analyses different portfolio configuration scenarios and ensures a systematic pipeline management, does it really support strategic PPM.

The following sections in this chapter describe functions that can be found in most of today's portfolio management tools and help to design the information flow.

Typical functions of modern PPM software

Portfolio planning includes all running projects and project programmes as well as all potential projects and project ideas. Top management, usually assisted by a PMO, attempt to identify and select those projects and programmes that best implement the business strategy, considering the time, cost and human resource constraints placed on the organization. The result is a portfolio of programmes and projects to be implemented in the following planning period.

Most software functions are based on simple decision models: each project's strategic relevance and benefit are assessed using several assessment criteria to calculate a project score. The overall objective is to maximize the strategic benefit of the portfolio by selecting those projects with the highest scores. Of course, this is not sufficient. To obtain a realistic portfolio, resource and financial constraints must also be considered. Sometimes it is also desirable to maximize financial performance indicators such as net present value or other objectives. In professional service companies, this process step is often irrelevant, because a project's foremost objective is to generate revenue rather than implement the company's business strategy. As a result of this some tools focus on handling project offerings and invoicing project services rather than strategic portfolio management. This chapter does not, however, cover the corresponding functions but focuses on strategic portfolio management. This is mainly the initial phase in the M Model, where software is used to collect project ideas, evaluate them, and use ideas and project data for portfolio decision-making.

Project proposal management

Enterprises usually generate far more project ideas than they can implement. Some ideas might also not meet the basic requirements defined for new projects; for example, they do not comply with the strategic orientation of the enterprise, are not at all profitable (in today's words they have a 'negative benefit'), or they are not feasible because of financial and personnel constraints. Each new project idea must therefore undergo a comprehensive examination, including an estimate of the work involved, profitability analysis and risk analysis. Based on the work estimation, resource needs are specified and the budget is planned.

Many software functions in this context relate to calculating score values and indicators from project attributes. This can also usually be performed by designing adequate reports. However, mature software will offer more. It provides, for example, an input form for cost estimations and immediately sums the cost items and displays the totals. Using only the software's reporting functions, users would have to run a report to obtain the results, check these results and navigate back to the place where the values can be edited. Modern software shows the results of any changes immediately, making it easy to analyse different options.

Project scoring

A project proposal assessment aims to ascertain and define the strategic impact of a single project or programme by applying a scoring model. A scoring model generally contains several assessment criteria that reflect the major strategic objectives of the organization or organizational unit for which portfolio planning is being performed. The project or programme is assessed using each criterion, and the result is documented as a numeric value (for example, on a scale between 1 and 10). The assessment criteria are usually weighted so that the score of a project can be calculated as the weighted sum of all assessment criteria. To assess the strategic benefit of a project, the project is usually rated using the organization's strategic goals and objectives. Some systems support a scoring model that can be adapted to the organization's needs (for example, assessment criteria and weightings can be defined).

Visualization

Assessment results are usually displayed in tabular data grids. Indicators such as RAG traffic lights illustrate the results. However, this might not be sufficient if many projects and project programmes are assessed or the results must be presented in meetings. Many software products offer flexible assessment result visualization (for example, using bar, radar or bubble charts), which can ease portfolio analysis.

Must-have and thresholds

A basic decision model of weighted criteria does not always adequately satisfy the decision-makers' preferences. Some software systems therefore offer enhancements such as 'must-have' assessment criteria and thresholds for criteria values. In this way, projects not only can be ranked by their score, but can also be excluded from further consideration if they do not fulfil some basic criteria.

Portfolio budgets

Budgeting organizational units are normally not associated with project management in a narrow sense. However, it is an efficient way to make sure that the organization spends money on those projects that serve the strategic goals best. An increasing number of project management software systems support this planning process to prepare portfolio planning. Organizational budgeting is part of the organization's regular strategic planning process, which is usually performed once a year. The total budget is top-down distributed to organizational units, such as business units, departments and finally portfolios. To prepare this budget allocation, some organizations first perform bottom-up planning. In this phase, the organizational units communicate their estimated budget demands, calculated from basic estimations for their projects, up to the next level.

Organizational budgeting is an indispensable precondition for portfolio planning because it determines the amount of budget available to execute projects. In portfolio planning, only as many projects as considered financially feasible can be selected and prioritized, even if there were more profitable project ideas. Typical functions of PPM software in portfolio budgeting include the following.

Overall budget

Some project management software systems only allow the overall budget available for portfolio planning to be defined. The sum of budgets from all projects can then be compared with this limit to ensure that there is a sufficient budget for a portfolio.

Periodic budgets

The next level of functionality is reached when the software also allows time-dependent or periodic budgets to be defined. For example, three different yearly budgets may be considered in three-year portfolio planning.

Budget categories

Any advanced software can handle different budget categories (for example, items such as external IT services and travelling costs).

Top-down/bottom-up

High-end systems offer functionality for a mixed top-down and bottom-up organizational budgeting process. This includes budgeting functions at any level of both the organizational and project breakdown structures. Moreover, many products support the project budget, planning, requesting, approving and modifying processes with workflows functions.

Workflow support

Workflow management functions help to execute project management processes efficiently by letting the software control the process steps and inform the roles involved. Workflow engines are used for many tasks in project and project portfolio management. Modern software can be configured to support different workflows according to an organization's needs. Typical workflow support functions of PPM software are listed below.

Notifications

The simplest form of workflow support is given when a software system can send notifications or alerts each time a certain event occurs. For example, the software might send an e-mail to a resource manager each time a resource request has been created. The problem of such a rudimentary functionality is that workflows managed like this can easily be left unprocessed without anybody noticing.

Basic workflows

A growing number of project management solutions have a built-in workflow management engine. A workflow management engine is a software module used to define processes. This definition includes process steps, the roles involved, decision points, transitions, and sometimes even input forms and document templates for process-related data. When such a process definition is available, the software can control the entire process. It can automatically inform staff members who are responsible for the next process step, create necessary documents and provide staff members with the relevant information. As all currently running processes (process instances) are stored in the database, it is possible to monitor process execution, identify problems and automatically escalate these when necessary. System administrators, project management experts and consultants usually define the processes together.

More sophisticated workflow engines even allow model processes including loops and decision points as well as 'and/or' connectors. Such engines can even support complex approval workflows for project charters, which might require parallel approval by various decision-makers, depending on the project's attributes.

Supporting portfolio decisions

Automated portfolio optimization

With project proposals thoroughly evaluated and ongoing projects properly controlled, an integrated software system holds all the data needed for portfolio decisions. To support portfolio decisions, most software tools allow the user to compose portfolios of projects and project proposals and analyse the consequences on the organization's limiting resources. Some tools can automatically optimize the portfolio configuration.

Frequently, this optimization uses the project scoring data created in the previous planning step. In this case, the software endeavours to maximize the portfolio score, while considering the various resource and financial constraints. Other decision models concentrate on maximizing alternative performance indicators, such as the net present value.

From a theoretical perspective, several algorithm classes are available for optimizing the project portfolio. Deterministic algorithms such as 0–1 integer programming can be used for smaller project portfolios. In more complex scenarios with dozens of projects, heuristic approaches such as genetic algorithms are more promising. In real life, however, these algorithms often have little relevance. Apart from very complex portfolio decisions (such as those that need to be made when investing largely in pharmaceutical projects), the effort to create the necessary input is rarely justified by the benefit compared with a manual portfolio configuration.

Project portfolio configuration

Although modern project management systems can calculate an optimal project portfolio, it is often unlikely that management will accept such theoretical portfolios. Project portfolio planning is a process of balancing interests; the portfolio is thus adjusted continuously until all project portfolio stakeholders agree on its projects. This can be performed either by a planning department or at a management meeting.

Software supports this process by offering tools that help to configure the portfolio manually and immediately analyse the impact on portfolio KPIs, budgets and the resource situation.

Software is well suited for portfolio configuration when changes in a portfolio scenario are interactively reflected in grids and charts (for example, rescheduling a project should show the resulting capacity demand immediately). If it is necessary to run a report, this might be a workaround, which is likely to annoy users after some time. Of course, real portfolio management does not deal only with project proposals. It handles active projects too, because their resource demands also need to be considered and portfolio decisions include the option to stop active projects. Typical functions of PPM software for project portfolio configuration include the following items.

Scenario sandbox

A key requirement for sound project portfolio management is that the software has a separate scenario environment (sandbox) for portfolio planning and portfolio analysis. Portfolio planners can modify projects to see immediately the consequences of portfolio decisions on capacities and budgets without affecting the ongoing projects. For example, if a portfolio manager puts a project on hold to see whether this would allow a newly proposed project to be executed instead, this simulation must not affect the ongoing project unless the consequences are fully analysed and the portfolio decision has been approved. This is important in an integrated software suite, because other users could otherwise be irritated by supposed changes in their projects, even though the portfolio management simulates only some variants to aid decisions. If there is no scenario level available, users will really need to modify the projects and projects proposals and then run multiproject reports – just to assess the consequences of their changes. This is complicated.

Overview of scores and budget

A basic requirement for portfolio planning is a function that helps to determine which projects are included in the portfolio and which have been rejected. Users can interactively add projects to the portfolio or remove them from it. The software immediately calculates the resulting overall portfolio score. This is a very basic, short-sighted approach: the budget and other restrictions must also be considered. Most systems can thus also make budget spending transparent.

Capacity analysis

As mentioned above, advanced decision models are based on several scarce resources. Aside from the budget the available resources often limit the portfolio configuration.

Mature PPM software thus shows how a modified portfolio impacts the resource utilization of several resources and resource types. This might be performed by displaying the resource demand for a given portfolio in a table, and comparing it with the available capacity. This analysis can usually be made by departments and skill groups as well as by individual key resources.

Visualization

Visualization of the portfolio's characteristics supports decision-making. Many systems offer business charts, such as resource utilization histograms, efficient frontier graphs and budget consumption overviews. Risks and strategic benefit of projects can usually be shown over time and budget spending can be analysed in charts. The strategic benefit of the portfolio is often presented in bubble or radar charts. As business chart functions also help when the software is presented to a potential customer it should not be surprising that many of tools are well positioned on this score.

Scenarios

Some systems can be used to create multiple portfolio configurations as scenarios and then compare these scenarios with each other. Users can save different portfolio configurations and restore them later (for example, to plan one portfolio that adapts a market growth strategy and another focusing on projects that support product innovation).

Advanced decision support includes predefined analyser functions for scenario comparison. Two or more scenarios can then be compared with each other to find the optimum portfolio configuration. The few products that offer high-end scenario management allow the creation of reports and dashboards for any given scenario. Users can quickly compare the consequences of each scenario. Once a scenario has been chosen, its configuration can be activated by approving the respective project proposals and modifying the affected ongoing projects.

General functions for portfolio management

In addition to specific functions for PPM, modern software also comes with many useful functions that were not especially designed for portfolio management. These include the following.

Web-based software

Web-based software has become the *de facto* standard. Users can access the software from anywhere; all they need is a web browser. Deploying the software is therefore easy. Even more important, every user has access to the latest information and there are no concurring different versions of the data. Interfaces to other enterprise software, especially to financial data from enterprise resource planning (ERP) software, have also become a standard and can provide project and portfolio managers with the latest numbers without them having to learn the ERP software.

Reporting and dashboards

Almost every software package comes with sophisticated reporting functions. Many of the products even support interactive business intelligence (BI). Reports are usually designed by the PMO and made available to the users. They then apply the report to whichever project they want. This results in standardized reporting, which is a key requirement if a large number of projects are to be managed.

User permissions

Today's permission concepts virtually always follow a role-based approach in which project-related roles (such as project managers, team members and portfolio managers) are combined with organizational roles (controlling, PMO, line management). Projects are assigned to organizational units, which automatically gives the users access permission depending on their organizational roles. Users are furthermore assigned to projects, for example as project managers or work package owners, and thereby also get permissions according to these roles. Permissions can affect the functions accessible in a project as well as the possibility to view and modify data. All in all, modern tools can handle even complex permission concepts in a manageable way. Permissions not only ensure confidentially where needed, but also prevent accidental data changes and simplify the user interface, because functions can easily be removed from menus and dashboards by simply revoking permissions.

Conclusion

Modern PPM software offers a wide set of functions to support basic portfolio reporting as well as a sophisticated PPM. Modern tools also allow project managers to manage their projects. Quite often this can be done using different methods such as Scrum or Kanban, as well as classic Gantt chart or critical path planning. As a result of this, it is technically no problem to manage both projects and the portfolio in an integrated system. However, it makes sense to start small and extend the software's functions step by step. Piloting a PPM concept using Excel can be a good start. As soon as the basic PPM methods and processes are established, an integrated software system, if carefully configured and implemented, can help to standardize the PPM process and provide a single source of truth for the project landscape.

Reference and further reading

Meyer, M.M. and Ahlemann, F. (2016), *Project Management Software Systems*, 8th edn, Würzburg: Business Application Research Center.

Part IV

Managing portfolios

Chapter 25

Defining the portfolio

Robert Buttrick

Defining the portfolio is the first and most critical step in portfolio management. This is where the objectives are set. Everything that happens afterwards depends on this being right.

Doing the right thing the right way

You have probably heard about 'doing the right thing' and 'doing it right'. The former is about undertaking activities to further your strategic aims and the latter is about doing them in a consistent way. 'Doing the right thing' is related to effectiveness, whereas 'doing it right' is more about efficiency. An effective organization is more likely to survive and thrive than one that is merely efficient. If you are both effective and efficient you are in a good position to succeed as an organization.

This handbook is about 'doing it right'; it provides you with the procedures, tools and mind-sets to undertake portfolio management. It cannot, however, tell you what 'the right things' are for your organization. Setting the strategic direction is a fundamental responsibility of the senior leadership team and no handbook, consultant or observer can relieve them of that accountability. If you are a senior leader, this handbook can only prompt you to ask yourself the questions that will provide you with useful answers.

Defining a portfolio depends on having a thorough understanding of your organization, its aims and how it works. This is as true for a government department as it is for a multinational corporation, private company, partnership, non-government organization (NGO) or charity, regardless of size. If you do not understand the purpose and aims of the organization and how it is currently performing, you cannot hope to be successful.

Without a clear strategic direction, the following will happen:

- Business plans will not be aligned;
- Short-term focus is likely to prevail, to the neglect of the long-term one;
- Projects and other work might conflict;
- Priorities might be confused or conflicting;
- Decisions might be contradictory.

Without a 'right way' of working, the following will happen:

- There will be inadequate information for decision-makers;
- Too many projects might be started;

- Resources might become overstretched;
- Processes might be incompatible;
- Roles and accountabilities might be confused, overlap or be missing.

Any of the above problems could lead to organizational failure (Buttrick, 2009).

What is your portfolio? Context is everything

Process context

This chapter is concerned with defining the portfolio and is the first of five portfolio management activities covered in this handbook. These are shown diagrammatically in Figure 25.1. These five activities mirror the portfolio management activities in ISO 21504 (International Organization for Standardization [ISO], 2015), and in AXELOS (2013) *Management of Portfolios*, shown in Figure 25.2. An organization's managers

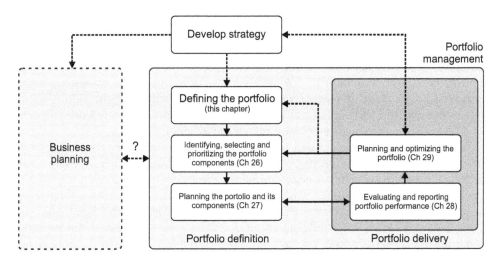

Figure 25.1 Context of defining a portfolio

ISO 21504 processes	Management of Portfolios Defining practices
Defining the portfolio Identifying potential portfolio components Selecting portfolio components Defining the portfolio plan Assessing and selecting portfolio components Validating portfolio alignment to strategic objectives Estimating and reporting portfolio performance Balancing and optimizing the portfolio	Understand Categorize Prioritize Balance Plan

Figure 25.2 Portfolio management practices in ISO 21504 (ISO, 2015) and AXELOS (2013) *Management of Portfolios*

can determine the equivalent practices or activities they want to use by tailoring published standards and methods (such as those in Figure 25.2) and creating their own organization-specific portfolio management process or method.

Strategic and business planning context

Generally, the development of a strategy is treated as external (and hence an input) to portfolio management. The development of strategy and the defining of the portfolio can, however, be part of the same strategic development process. The reasoning for this is that, if 'definition' is about setting objectives to support strategy, it is for those who set the strategy also to set the objectives for a portfolio. The setting of a strategy and objectives is generally done by the senior leadership team.

A strategy is pointless unless communicated in a way that is understood and actionable. Strategic alignment (a key tenet of portfolio management) is impossible without a clearly defined and communicated strategy. The interface between those who develop strategy and those who set portfolio objectives and their respective accountabilities must be clear. If business strategy and objective setting are undertaken in isolation by separate teams, they are less likely to be aligned, with all the confusion, crossed accountabilities and cost that this involves.

Organizational context

There are many different views on what a portfolio is. Many configurations of portfolios are covered in Chapter 5 and various definitions are discussed in Chapter 6. As a portfolio director or manager, you need to understand where 'your portfolio' sits in an organizational context. Does the portfolio cover the whole organization or a part of the organization? Is it simply the work undertaken by one function? Does the portfolio include 'business as usual' as a component, as well as programmes and projects? It is vital to understand the context because the management level above the portfolio should set the objectives (or as a minimum approve those objectives) and define any constraints. Furthermore, accountabilities should be traceable down and across the whole organization. For example, if the portfolio covers an entire company, the objectives would be set and approved by the senior management team. If the portfolio covers a division or region in a company, the objectives would be set by the 'parent' company. If the portfolio is part of a higher-level portfolio, the objectives would be set by the director of that higher portfolio.

When a 'portfolio' might not be a portfolio at all

If the portfolio is the collection of work being done by a particular function (say information technology [IT] projects undertaken by an internal IT department) the question of who sets objectives becomes more problematic. Effective portfolio management as defined in ISO 21504 and *Management of Portfolios* is value driven for the benefit of the organization as a whole. An IT portfolio, as described here, is simply a collection of tasks undertaken by IT specialists for other parts of the business. The objective of 'portfolio management' in such cases is usually to optimize the use of IT resources. IT specialists should not, however, be setting objectives for (say) customer services, manufacturing or financial processing. IT specialists should be providing capabilities to meet the needs of those groups, each of which should have its own business objectives. The danger of treating this type of IT portfolio as if it were a value-based portfolio makes it likely to be driven by costs and efficiency, rather than by business effectiveness. This would deflect the direction of the organization away from what really needs to be done. It is best not to call such an entity a 'portfolio' at all and avoid any confusion; it is simply the work that the IT department does. Although 'IT' has been used as an example here, the same logic applies to any functional group.

The importance of vision and values

In order to set a portfolio's objectives, you need to understand your organization's vision and values.

The *vision* is the lynchpin. It guides the whole organization towards a clear outcome. If well written, it will ensure that you focus on the right things to take your organization forward. Everything done within an organization should be aligned with and traceable to its vision.

Values influence the way in which you achieve the outcome defined in your vision. They influence and constrain the behaviours of the people within the organization and stop 'the end justifying the means'. Simply complying with the law and regulations is often not enough. There are many activities and practices that leaders choose not do because they consider them unethical, even if legal. Values not only might be stated in 'value statements' but also could be reflected in other documents (such as policies and working practices).

The clearer the vision and values, the easier it is to set a portfolio's objectives. However, a vision doesn't usually include enough detail to provide explicit direction. The vision should be broken down into a number of 'focus areas' (four or five is usually about right). These often relate topics found in the various strategy frameworks, such as the Ansoff matrix (Ansoff, 1957), McKinsey's strategic horizons (McKinsey & Co., 2009) or Treacy and Wiersema's value disciplines (Treacy and Wiersema, 1993). The following are examples, but you can create others, which could be more appropriate to your organization:

- Compliance, which is what you have to do simply to stay in business, as driven by any relevant legal or regulatory requirements;
- Market expansion – taking your products or service to new geographical areas or customer groups;
- Product leadership, by providing new products and services, through either innovation or 'me-too' approaches;
- Stakeholder engagement, for example through improving customer satisfaction by engaging your customers, or encouraging preferred suppliers to want to do work with you;
- Customer intimacy, say encouraging customer loyalty and repeat business for the same or new products and services; people love you, despite any shortcomings;
- Operational efficiency, by providing your services or products at a cost that enables you to achieve the required margins or stay within a predefined cost envelope;
- Employee relations, such as providing an environment or package to retain staff.

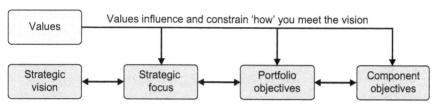

There should be two-way traceability from the vision to each portfolio component's objectives

Figure 25.3 Vision, values, focus and objectives

If you succeed in *all* your focus areas, you should achieve your vision. If this isn't true, you'll need to challenge and revise the focus areas until, as a whole, they cover the whole vision. You can now start considering the portfolio's objectives. Each objective should be aligned with and traceable (via a focus point) to the vision, influenced and constrained by the values, and be the source for the objectives of the portfolio's component parts (such as projects) (Figure 25.3).

There are countless books and papers on setting strategy and objectives as well as numerous supporting tools. All aim to help you channel your thinking. Some (such as Cascade) use a tool to draw on a range of different approaches, allowing you to tailor the approach to suit your needs and then track progress. Other tools, such as BusinessOptix (see References and further reading), enable you to model your organization and see through the layers of complexity to what really matters.

Understanding your organization's current performance and prospects

Very rarely is a portfolio defined from nothing as a totally new venture; there is usually an operational organization with a history of performance. Poor performance (or performance that is below that expected in your sector) is an indication of where action is needed and new or revised objectives need to be set. Similarly, you need to understand the possible futures for your organization. Will your services or products still be in demand? What are competitors doing? Are there entrants to your market with radically different offerings or operating models? Are technically disrupting innovations emerging or likely to emerge? Are there any social, environmental or legal issues that will impact you?

Poor performance and a negative outlook might be an indicator that you should withdraw from a particular activity and concentrate on other priorities that will take you towards your vision. A key problem with any ongoing organization is that it just keeps 'doing what it has always done' with little thought to whether or not this is still valid. Each year's budget is simply the previous year's budget plus (or minus) 5 per cent. This is particularly evident in organizations that concentrate more on keeping costs down as a priority over other objectives. It is true that everything must be affordable but affordability relies just as much on the revenue or benefit as it does on costs.

An ongoing organization will also have a number of programmes, projects or initiatives under way that are already absorbing resources which, when they come to fruition, should move the organization forward. Again, just because they have been started, it does not mean that they have to be completed. If an initiative no longer aligns with the strategy, there is no point in carrying on spending more money with little chance of any return; carrying on might even be detrimental to your other products or services. You need to understand how each initiative, project or programme serves the vision and the aspect on which it focuses. Organizations seldom fail because one project went awry; they fail when the totality of the change does not make sense or is unachievable.

Recognizing your organization's constraints

Although objectives should not be too constrained, some attention should be paid to business realities. There will not be unlimited funds, resources and energy. So a totally unconstrained objective could be ridiculed by those tasked with meeting it; we have all heard stories about strategists having their heads in the clouds. On the other hand, objectives should require people to think and plot a new course if the one they are on will not achieve the aims. Just because something is difficult does not mean that it is unrealistic. Lord Rutherford once said: 'We've got no money, so we've got to think' (Capri, 2007). Those who set the objectives need to be cognisant of the following:

- Availability of funds and resources;
- Overall risk across the portfolio and how it relates to the organization's risk appetite;
- The organization's capability and capacity to ensure that the portfolio can be delivered;
- The impact on those affected by the outcomes and whether or not they are able to take on the changes.

It is also important is to make sure that both short- and long-term objectives are covered. Generally the 'short term' should feed and fund the 'long term'. Early benefits are good, but neglecting the long term is usually bad, as emphasized by Carl-Peter Forster, when he was Group CEO at Tata Motors (including its British unit, Jaguar Land Rover): 'In my opinion, if you always take the short term view, you are always in trouble' (Hutton, 2013).

Choosing the portfolio's scope and boundaries

Portfolio objectives must reflect the portfolio's scope and boundaries. There is little point in giving a portfolio director an objective over which he or she has no influence. If yours is a simple organization it is likely that you will have just one portfolio, so there is no need to decide which parts of the operation are in one portfolio and which are in another. You will, however, still need to select the extent of the activities to be included within the portfolio (and hence managed as a portfolio) and what activities should be run in traditional ways. For example, Figure 25.4 shows an organization with five units (departments or functions, depending on your terminology) where the portfolio (A) includes just the programmes and projects. All of unit V and the rest of the other units' activities (B) are run separately by the respective unit heads on traditional cost centre lines.

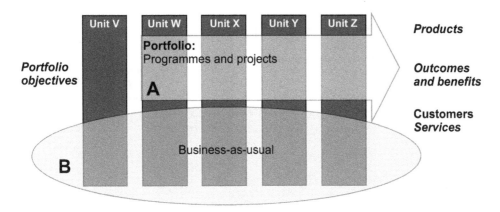

Figure 25.4 A portfolio that covers an organization's programmes and projects only

By managing the programmes and projects as a portfolio you can make sure that they are aligned, determine the scope of each to minimize interdependencies, and make effective and efficient use of your resources. Such programmes and projects will, however, be delivering into 'business as usual' (BAU), for which accountability is under the separate leadership of each unit head. The portfolio on its own would not include everything needed to ensure that the organization's vision is realized. You might also find that some resources have to be shared between projects and BAU – if so you will need to decide who sets the priority or makes decisions when these come into conflict.

AXELOS's *Management of Portfolios* includes the following definition of portfolio management:

> Portfolio management is a coordinated collection of strategic processes and decisions that together enable the most effective balance of organizational change and business-as-usual.
>
> (AXELOS, 2013)

Notice that this definition includes BAU, implying that BAU should be included within the portfolio. By including BAU in the scope of a portfolio, the portfolio director is able to manage them together, balancing resources and funding across both elements, and reacting to any sudden downturns or changes in the volume of BAU work.

Figure 25.5 illustrates a portfolio (A) that includes BAU (labelled as 'processes and other work in the diagram). The processes would be cross-functional, focused on customer needs; they would also be 'joined up' and represent the flow of work across the units needed to operate the business. This approach is more responsive than one in which each unit has its own targets and processes and 'coordinates' (or not!) across unit boundaries. The portfolio is run on the horizontal dimension of the organizational matrix, driven by customer need and value.

Note that the portfolio still covers only part of the activities for four units; all of unit V and some parts of units W to Z (B) are still outside the portfolio and these would be run on traditional cost centre lines. The portfolio's funds would be allocated on a

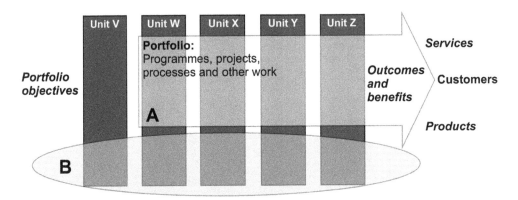

Figure 25.5 A portfolio that covers programmes and projects as part of an organization's business-as usual (BAU) operations

project-by-project and process-by-process (or portfolio component-by-portfolio component) basis rather than to each separate unit's cost centre (according to ISO 21504, a portfolio is a collection of portfolio components grouped together to facilitate their management to meet, in whole or in part, an organization's strategic objectives; a portfolio component is a project, programme, portfolio, *or other related work)*.

Direction would be given by a portfolio director and project sponsor (or business lead for a process) rather than divided between each unit manager. By doing this you avoid the tendency of unit managers to suboptimize their part of the operations to meet their budget targets and what they see as their objectives. That approach is found where central services (such as human resources [HR] and finance) are managed as traditional cost centres, or where the portfolio covers only part of the operations (such as one product line).

Figure 25.6 goes one step further and shows an organization in which the portfolio covers the entirety of its operations. Organizations might move to this complete model in which the central services share common ERP and finance service platforms, which is increasingly the case in today's connected businesses.

An organization will always have at least one portfolio. If it is a large and diverse organization it is often convenient to have more than one portfolio (which are effectively subportfolios), each of which is directed towards one or more of the focus points within the vision. For example, one large multinational company had five portfolios. Three were targeted at different market segments, one at service development, because most of the services in the customer segments were built on the same platforms, and one for the central services, such as finance, facilities and HR, as follows:

- Multinational organizations;
- Small and medium enterprises;
- Consumers;
- Service and product development;
- Central services, such as HR and finance.

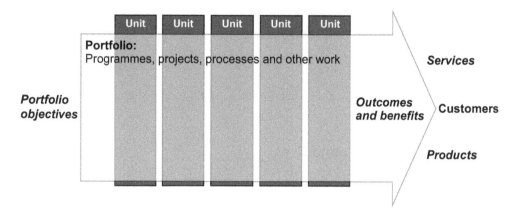

Figure 25.6 A portfolio that covers the entirety of an organization

Each of these had subportfolios, reflecting the objectives (outcomes) with which they were targeted. The scope of the portfolios was such that interdependencies between them were eliminated or at least minimized. The service development and central services were separated out because it was not cost-effective for each of the three market segments to have its own. Figure 25.7 illustrates an organization with multiple portfolios (three in this example). Note that in Figure 25.7 you could just as easily treat it as a single portfolio with three subportfolios – as long as the relationships and accountabilities are clear and traceable, how you label the levels is your choice.

There is no set pattern for defining a portfolio's scope and boundaries. Each needs to be designed to suit its circumstances and the permutations are limitless. The aim, however, is to run the organization driven by customer needs and value, rather than on a purely cost-constrained basis. Each portfolio or subportfolio should be as independent as possible (with minimum interdependencies), bearing in mind the cost-effectiveness of shared services. By taking this approach, direction and decisions should be focused

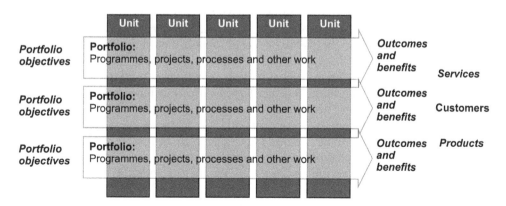

Figure 25.7 An organization with three portfolios

on value and benefits. This avoids the situation where decisions made by the head of a unit are driven by each unit's manager based on cost centre budgets and annually determined objectives. Such decisions are:

- not necessarily aligned;
- frequently suboptimal;
- based on objectives that can become out of date, especially in fast-moving environments.

Describing portfolio objectives

Most people are familiar with 'SMART' objectives. These have a few variations (some of which are shown here in brackets):

- **S**pecific (significant, stretching);
- **M**easurable (meaningful, motivational, matter of fact);
- **A**greed (attainable, achievable, acceptable, action orientated);
- **R**ealistic (relevant, reasonable, rewarding, results orientated);
- **T**ime bound (timely, tangible, trackable).

'SMART' can be a good basis for writing portfolio objectives but be careful not to mix up its different interpretations. For example, 'agreed' simply means what it says: the objective is *agreed* between the person who is accountable for meeting the objective and the person who sets the objective. This is very different from 'attainable', which is similar to 'realistic', because something that is not attainable can hardly be called realistic!

In practice a portfolio should have about two to five portfolio objectives. If you have too few they will not have sufficient coverage. Too many objectives might risk you losing attention and not meeting them all.

Portfolio objectives need to be described as 'outcomes', not 'outputs. They should describe a changed state for the organization – something that the business will be doing differently in the future. An output is simply a deliverable and is not enough, for example a portfolio aimed at providing a seamless customer experience, which delivers a customer service platform that is not used, hasn't actually achieved anything. What happens as a result of the platform being used is what matters – and if that platform doesn't work, then another way has to be found to meet that objective.

Do not dwell too deeply on 'measureable'. If you do, you might simply do what you can measure, rather than what you need to do. If something is hard to measure, think of other means to verify that the change has happened. For instance, some changes can simply be observed and don't need measuring at all.

There will always be financial constraints and targets but these should happen as a result of doing the right things. Setting objectives solely in financial terms does not help anyone align to anything, because the numbers could be achieved by any means. Financial targets should be considered more as constraints or rules. Anyone can simply set a budget of £1m or demand a cost cut of 15 per cent; it takes a true leader to set a vision and determine *how* that vision can be met.

Do it all over again

Whether you are working in a new organization or in one that is already running, defining a portfolio is not easy. But unless the portfolio is defined and objectives are set, the organization will lack direction. All organizations are constrained by the practicalities of cash flow and resources, and the objectives should reflect this. This means that there is likely to be some iteration in defining objectives before they are finalized. Furthermore, because all organizations operate in a real and changing world, the vision, values, focus and objectives might need to be reviewed to reflect this, as well as the current operational performance. This is why Figure 25.1 has a feedback loop from portfolio management to strategy development.

References and further reading

Ansoff, I. (1957), 'Strategies for diversification', *Harvard Business Review*, 35(5), 113–112.

AXELOS (2013), *Management of Portfolios*, Norwich: The Stationery Office.

BusinessOptix, Enterprise-wide business modelling software, available at: www.businessoptix. com (accessed August 2017).

Buttrick, R. (2009); *The Project Workout*, 4th edn, London: FT Prentice Hall.

Capri, A.Z. (2007), *Quips, Quotes, and Quanta: An Anecdotal History of Physics*, London: World Scientific Publishing Co. Ltd.

Cascade strategy software, available at: https://www.executestrategy.net (accessed August 2017).

Hutton, R. (2013), *Jewels in the Crown: How Tata of India transformed Britain's Jaguar Land Rover*; London: Elliott & Thompson Ltd.

International Standards Organization or ISO (2015), ISO 21504 *Guidance on Portfolio Management*, Geneva: ISO.

McKinsey & Co. (2009), 'Enduring ideas: the three horizons of growth', *McKinsey Quarterly*, December.

Treacy, M. and Wiersema, F. (1993), 'Customer intimacy and other value disciplines', *Harvard Business Review*, January–February, 84–93.

Chapter 26

Identifying, selecting and prioritizing the portfolio components

Knut Kämpfert and Alexander Schwarz

Identifying, selecting and prioritizing the portfolio components are the first steps in the project portfolio management process. In this chapter you will learn about these first steps and what is important for their practical usage.

Introduction

A mandatory prerequisite for the identification and selection process is that the strategy of the organization is clear and that strategic goals are defined. If the organization uses a structured way to find opportunities there are usually many opportunities with many different characteristics. This makes it difficult for one to manage them in one large combined portfolio in a proper way. Instead it is helpful to split the portfolio into subportfolios, examples of which might be as follows:

- One or more business-related portfolios;
- Supporting portfolios, such as information technology (IT), production technology, and so on.

This is illustrated in Figure 26.1.

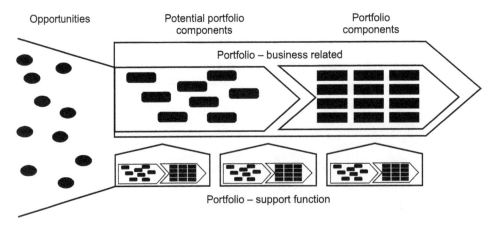

Figure 26.1 Developing opportunities in potential and finally accepted components for business-related and support function portfolios

In order to come to an objective selection of the different opportunities, the organization needs transparent selection criteria based on key performance indicators (KPIs) and risk definitions. With this procedure, we should be able to find the right mix of opportunities to support the organizational strategy, minimize risk and maximize benefit. The organizational environment is driven by change. It is important that the organization regularly adjusts the strategic objectives and checks whether the defined opportunities bring the defined output or still fit the strategic goals.

Identifying the portfolio components

Identifying the portfolio components is the beginning of the portfolio management process. A basic question in this step is: where and how does an organization find opportunities and identify whether these opportunities are relevant for that organization? Relevant means that there is a need to spend minimum resources to evaluate (and in the best case execute) these opportunities. If an opportunity is relevant, it must become part of the organizational portfolio. Once it has arranged this, the organization has defined how it would transfer an opportunity into reality. This can be done with a project, a programme or another kind of action. These actions together form the portfolio components. An important prerequisite for this and for making the right decisions is to know all the potential and actual portfolio elements.

Finding the opportunities

Spontaneous ideas and opportunities for implementing the strategy are always welcome, but for an organization it would be very difficult and risky to base the expectation of success only on spontaneous upcoming ideas. To support long-term success it is usual and seems important to implement a structured process and provide the necessary environment in which to find and develop opportunities for reaching the defined strategic goals.

Examples for the opportunity-finding process

The voice of the customers

Good relationships and regular communication with your customers give you the chance to find out what your customers expect in the future. You should listen very carefully to what your customers tell you. Then you should think about how you can help or support the customer's development plans. But, conversely, always keep in mind the truth of Henry Ford's statement: 'If I had asked people what they wanted, they would have said faster horses!'

Analysis from benchmarking

To survive in the market a competitor must have unique selling points, where he or she is performing equally or better than you. To find out the strength of that competitor, you should conduct a benchmarking programme. The competitor's unique selling points are usually protected by patents, but the benchmarking process can give you a lot of ideas, helping you to improve your own product and business model, and usually creating opportunities. For more on benchmarking, see Stapenhurst (2009).

Legal regulations

Any kind of change in business-related legislation brings a chance (or the need) to create new opportunities. For example, suppose that (for environmental protection) a government prohibits the use of certain alloys that you are currently using because of their resistance to corrosion. Clearly, to be able to continue to deliver your existing product, you will need to find an acceptable alternative method of corrosion protection. To achieve this change you will have to set up a project that will enable you to solve the problem and introduce the new corrosion protection into the market.

Input from suppliers

Suppose that a supplier already has an innovative solution on the market. With this innovation you are able to improve or create a new product.

Process and technologies

There are new production processes and technologies available on the market. With these new processes, you can improve your production or your product. An example is Industry 4.0, where you combine manufacturing processes with modern IT and communication technology.

Solutions from other industries

Suppose there is a problem with your product, for which you can find no solution. In this case, it is worth checking to see whether you can find similar problems in other industries. If you can find out how those problems were solved, you might be able to use the solution principles to solve your problem. This approach can create new opportunities.

Expert input

If the appropriate experts discuss a topic, they will probably find many opportunities. In addition, creative tools may be used to support the team flow, thus achieving greater efficiency and effectiveness. After such kind of a creative session, you will probably find that you have too many opportunities. You immediately know that many of these would never be successful. To go one step further, you have to identify those opportunities that have potential for success, and you need to map them with your strategic objectives. All these opportunities have to be brought into your portfolio process and aligned with your strategic targets. With this step, each opportunity will become a potential portfolio component. It is a 'potential' component because, at this stage, it will still not be clear if the element will become successful, and in which way (project, programme, own portfolio or other activity) it could be implemented in the organization.

Specifying the portfolio components

You should define the team (or person) responsible for a potential portfolio component and that team or individual will then be able to produce the specification. Decision criteria (key performance indicators [KPIs], business case description, risk criteria, and so on) should be well known and transparent for everybody. But, for a successful portfolio, it is not only the decision criteria that are relevant. It is also important to know where the dependencies between different components lie, and which portfolio components are mandatory, before you can start the selection process.

Selecting the portfolio components

Defining the portfolio and boundaries

A typical organization will have many portfolio components. To be able to handle these in a proper and effective way organizations use several different types of portfolios. Typically each portfolio will be managed by one specific group of deciders who have the experience and empowerment to do so.

Consider, for example, investment, research and development (R&D), IT or customer project portfolios. Such portfolios may be treated as a cluster of parallel portfolios, which are not directly integrated but rather connected by sharing a limited number of resources (budget, project managers, specialists, and so on).

It is rather rare for all activities in an organization to be covered in one integrated portfolio. For example, it would be quite difficult, to compare a general IT software upgrade project with an innovation initiative covering both R&D activities and CapEx investments within one combined portfolio. These two options are shown in Figures 26.2 and 26.3.

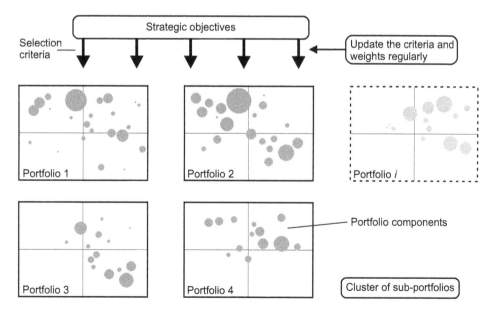

Figure 26.2 Cluster of subportfolios with selection criteria for components derived from strategic objectives

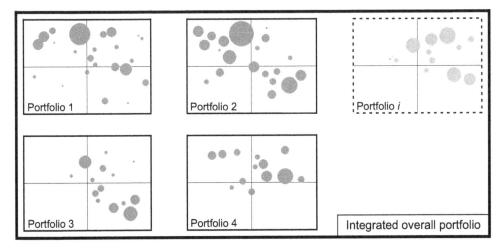

Figure 26.3 Integration of all subportfolios into one overall portfolio

Defining the selection criteria

Criteria for selecting portfolio components should be chosen so that:

1. They are useful for measuring the fulfilment of strategic objectives (strategic fit); and
2. The portfolio components can be evaluated and prioritized according to the strategic objectives.

As an example of selection criteria, there could be a score indicating how sustainability is supported with a component (sustainability score). Another example is how a contribution to business drivers or a technology score might well be taken to differentiate CapEx projects in an investment portfolio, or innovation projects in an R&D portfolio.

Regular updating and recalibration of selection criteria and their weighting factors (for example, during annual strategic planning cycles) could lead to shifts in the ranking of portfolio components from year to year.

Overall scoring of portfolio components might come from some balanced weighting of fulfilments in the different criteria (combined score).

Combination of selection criteria

The scheme in Figure 26.4 shows a model that distinguishes between strategic and economic criteria. Decision-makers may wish to see the portfolio components' contribution to strategic criteria and economic targets separately (for example, using a 2-dimensional way of illustrating the components' economic fit ϕE and strategic fit ϕS separately. The bubble size indicates the magnitude of required resources.

The left-hand side of Figure 26.4 (option A) may be used to select components in preferred quadrants II, I and IV. Another option (B) combines economic ϕE and strategic fit ϕS in one overall score ϕK, allowing simple ranking of all components in a portfolio.

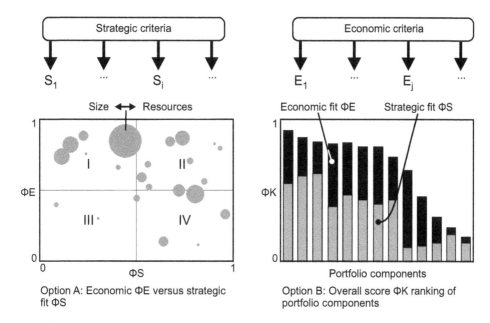

Figure 26.4 Cluster of subportfolios with selection criteria for components derived from strategic objectives

Interdependencies of portfolio components

Before moving from the selection phase to prioritization of portfolio components, it is quite valuable to look at interactions between or interdependencies of different portfolio components (even if they are not in the same portfolio). This will help to identify portfolio risks.

For example, take a portfolio of investment projects, in which some components comprise installing machines for a new production technology in connection with attractive business cases. One prerequisite for developing that new technology is, however, successful piloting and up-scaling beforehand, which is described in another portfolio component. If that prerequisite project fails, all machine investments will not make sense. Best practice to manage such interdependencies is to combine such related projects into a programme.

Another example of possible interdependencies could be the special technological know-how of a few experts in a company. Obviously, those scarce expert resources can support only a few selected projects, and this limits the number of corresponding portfolio components. We should be well area of such constraints before going into the prioritization phase. Methods for identifying interdependencies can be found in Hirzel et al. (2011) and Wagner (2016).

Prioritizing the portfolio components

Assigning priorities to portfolio components should result in the best-balanced outcome to maximize the overall portfolio benefit. In practical usage, different viewpoints and criteria are applied, such that a good mix of components is achieved, to satisfy the targets outlined in the following sections.

Strategic objectives

The components should be selected so that the strategic objectives are best fulfilled possibly by both of the following:

1. The sum of the components' contribution to the strategic objectives (for example by ranking the best components; and also
2. A good balance of the components' contribution to different or all strategic objectives.

Example: even if R&D activities into a new printing technology are strongly supporting a strategic objective of growth in that field, not all portfolio components will support exactly that direction, but may well contribute to further strategic objectives even if ranked a little bit lower. A balanced mix of portfolio components is needed here – not just mathematical optimization.

Risk exposure

According to known risk models (Cleary and Malleret, 2007), each portfolio component may exhibit single risks in terms of project, operations, financial and strategic risk. Cleary describes risk such that some evaluation is possible. However, other than risk there are so-called uncertainties, including, for example, 'unknown unknowns' according to the Cynefin framework (Snowden, 2005). Other approaches apply for these, which we do not elaborate further in this chapter. Ranking risk components according to the type and size of risk will give an idea of the average and/or summarized risk.

However, in addition some comprehensive portfolio risk might exist that is more than the sum of the components' single risk contributions. For example, in a portfolio of customer projects, suppose that one material supplier is needed to provide parts for a bunch of projects. If that source of supply were to be threatened, say owing to the supplier experiencing financial difficulties, there might be a severe portfolio risk owing to a shortage of various components. This is an example of a *portfolio clump risk*. This kind of clump risk is often a big problem for an organization. It can be an even bigger problem for a whole industry branch. As an example, the big Tsunami in Japan in 2011 caused big problems in the supply chain, not just in the automotive industry. But even smaller accidents at suppliers affected sensitive supply chains. Reference to Figure 26.5 shows a possibility of pointing out visually the impact of single risk factors on several portfolio components.

We have already mentioned a type of risk, where the limited availability of some critical (technical expert) resources might prevent execution of more than a limited number of portfolio components at the same time. However, such observation could trigger a long-term planning decision to recruit adequate personnel resources.

In the end, the selected components should result in a portfolio that not only maximizes potential benefits, but also provides a portfolio that is robust and not over-dependent for success on avoiding a few highly sensitive risk factors.

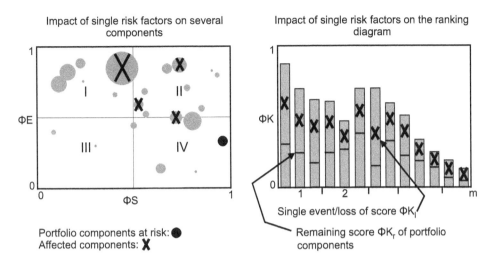

Figure 26.5 Schematic representation of the impact of single risk factors

Portfolio transformation

Each planning cycle's portfolio with its balance of components will vary whenever:

- new components are integrated;
- the weighting of existing components is changed;
- some components are removed;
- other components are completed.

However, portfolio transformation from cycle to cycle might exceed the limits of an organization's capacity and capability for handling the many new and different components. Whereas smaller, start-up type companies might appear to be more flexible and dynamic, some global-player organizations could exhibit higher resistance and inflexibility to crucial changes in their portfolio components. In such cases it could be worthwhile to review the overall picture of the prioritized portfolio components and check them in terms of the company's capability for handling them.

Iterative process and general aspects

A typical portfolio selection and prioritization process will go more than once through all steps and perspectives. The process is rather iterative in its nature owing to complexity and interdependencies. For example, a first selection of components that best meet the strategic objectives may need to be performed again after looking at risk, resources and the identification of non-acceptable project set-ups. In practice, a need to rework parts of the strategic planning and objectives will be necessary if no suitable result is being achieved.

In some cases, the overall budget for the selected portfolio components should be adapted (increased or decreased). At the end of the selection and prioritization process, a good balance between short-term goals, often offering more economic attractiveness, and the support of strategic objectives should be reached. Another aspect is that the overall size of the portfolio and the number of components should be aligned in a right way. It is often overlooked that, corresponding to new projects or initiatives, old ones or those with lower priorities should be pushed to completion, stopped or taken out in order not to overload the organization.

Summary and key messages

- Strategy: the basis for project portfolio management is a clearly defined and measurable strategy for the organization. First portfolio project management (PPM) process steps are identification, selection (with evaluation) and prioritization.
- Identification: there is a wide range of different systematic and intuitive ways and viewpoints from which to find relevant opportunities (besides unstructured ideas). These include: voice of the customer; analysis from competitor benchmarking; consequence of legal regulations; input from suppliers, process and technologies evaluation; and solutions from other industries or expert input. Specifying the relevant opportunities with success potential and mapping them to strategic objectives are then a prerequisite before they become portfolio components.
- Selection: evaluation of economic and strategic fit of portfolio components requires criteria and weight factors. These might vary from a previous to the current strategic planning cycle and need to be regularly recalibrated. The right and up-to-date balance of criteria for selecting portfolio components according to strategic objectives is crucial for successful application of PPM. Another essential check is to see if there are interdependencies of portfolio components before starting with the prioritization process.
- Prioritization then balances strategic and economic fit, critical resources, and the risk contribution of both single portfolio components and the overall portfolio (for example, to identify and avoid clump risks).
- The newly obtained portfolio(s) might be significantly different from previous portfolio(s). The organization's capability for mastering change in many portfolio components between two planning cycles has to be considered.
- A good PPM prioritization process may additionally trigger resource planning (for example, experts) after identification of critical resources. It may also help to find the critical aspects (for example, dependency on a few important suppliers). Related components should be identified that might be better lumped into programmes.

The use of several subportfolios has the advantage of easier handling in selection and prioritization steps, with each portfolio managed by a dedicated group of involved deciders, instead of using one large combined portfolio for the whole organization. In practical application, selection and prioritization steps are carried out iteratively and may be reworked several times, before the desired portfolio output is reached.

References and further reading

Cleary, S. and Malleret, T. (2007), *Global Risk: Business Success in Turbulent Times*, Basingstoke: Palgrave Macmillan UK.

Hirzel, M., Alter, W. and Sedlmayer, M. (2011), *Projektportfolio-Management: Strategisches und operatives Multi-Projektmanagement in der Praxis*, Wiesbaden: Gabler Verlag.

Snowden, D. (2005) 'Multi-ontology sense making: a new simplicity in decision making', *Informatics in Primary Health Care*, 13(1), 45–54.

Stapenhurst, T. (2009), *The Benchmarking Book*, Abingdon: Routledge.

Wagner, R. (2016), *Erfolgreiches Projektportfoliomanagement*, Düsseldorf: Symposion Publishing.

Chapter 27

Planning the portfolio and its components

Jörg Seidl

Planning a single project can be a complex affair, with questions such as time and resource constraints, task priorities, allocated responsibilities, and so on to be resolved. That process becomes more complicated when several projects are combined into a programme, and even more complex when a portfolio containing a changing pattern of programmes and projects has to be planned.

Before planning the portfolio

Planning a portfolio presents many challenges. The planning results will have to answer many different questions about the portfolio and its contained programmes and projects. Figure 27.1 lists the most important of those questions. This can help you to prepare a written checklist, which you should use as a basis for designing or acquiring your planning system. Your project management office (PMO) should have

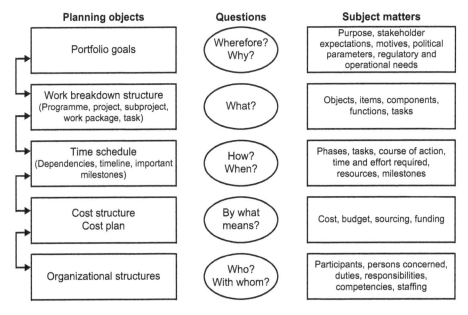

Figure 27.1 Questions to be answered by the portfolio plan.

at least one expert person who can help in this process, once you have considered and set out what you need the system to do.

Portfolio planning needs to be orientated to satisfying high-level goals which are typically set by the enterprise management or the management of the business area to which the portfolio belongs. For a planning period (for example, one year or for the next three years) a portfolio vision should be defined that contains the main goals and the expected major results. It is also recommended that a kind of portfolio vision should be defined, which will probably contain statements on how the portfolio should be controlled and managed. The focus of the portfolio management might be a maximized output generated by given resources or, alternatively, the focus could be to minimize project activities as far as possible.

As projects always bear specific risks, a portfolio planning and management guideline should also include principles on how the portfolio management will handle those risks. It must be assumed that the enterprise has a risk strategy, and this will have to be adopted within the planning methods (for example, the ability to respond rapidly to unexpected events or changes). One important key performance indicator (KPI) of a project portfolio is the total risk exposure, which has to correspond to the willingness of the enterprise to take risks.

After the goals for a planning period have been defined the portfolio has to be structured. The options for doing this are very versatile. The major components of a project portfolio are a mix of projects and programmes. Programmes, on the other hand, contain projects that support the overall programme goals. In practice there is much more variety: besides programmes and projects you will find things to plan such as large-scale projects, project bundles, project clusters, and so on. Furthermore the most detailed level of a project portfolio plan is not the single project but could be subprojects or single work packages. All these objects form a hierarchical structure, which is typically and essentially represented as a work breakdown structure (WBS). The methods for designing, coding and using a WBS have long been known to project managers and PMO staff and are well described in the literature (see, for example, Lock, 2013). The WBS for a portfolio simply takes the WBS to a new upper level. So you will need a WBS, and it must be capable of being changed as the portfolio evolves with time.

The next major challenge of a portfolio plan is to define how and when the major expected results can be achieved. Within a portfolio timeline, this can be expressed by identifying significant milestones, on the one hand, and important portfolio phases (for example, business periods, release cycles or frozen zones), on the other.

Planning a portfolio within an enterprise implies dealing with budgets and resources. The authority and ability to direct the use of money and people are an important indicator of the power of a manager or a management team within an enterprise. Besides the daily business-as-usual work, the project portfolio is the second area where major decisions on money and people are taken. So the most crucial tasks of portfolio planning may be to work out the overall cost plan and the planned resource allocation for the portfolio.

As the portfolio is also an arena in which very different stakeholders fight for their interests, it is also a big challenge to define and approve adequate organizational structures and responsibilities for the programmes and projects within the portfolio and the portfolio management (for example, having steering committees at the portfolio and/or subportfolio level).

Actors and interests

Planning a project portfolio is very difficult, not least because of the various stakeholders involved (some of whom are shown in Figure 27.2). The planning process is permanently subject to events and decisions that change or completely redesign the work and objectives. So plans have to be flexible and capable of change.

At this point it seems to be meaningful to look at specific interests and the surroundings that should be considered in order to plan a portfolio of programmes and projects. As already mentioned there are many different players involved in the process of project portfolio planning. The most important target group is the responsible management of the enterprise, division or management area that owns the projects of the particular portfolio.

The person principally responsible for planning may be a kind of portfolio manager or portfolio coordinator (a staff function, reporting to line management) or a manager of a corporate function (for example, the head of controlling operations or the head of business development).

Very important stakeholders are of course the project sponsors (the 'customers' for whom the project plans are made). They will naturally want to optimize the priority ranking of their 'own' projects within the portfolio. During the planning process they promote the priority of their favourite projects and try to ensure that sufficient resources are allocated. For each project manager, the portfolio plan bears career opportunities and risks. If their project achieves high management attention, offers a long-term perspective, has been allocated a significant budget, uses its many resources

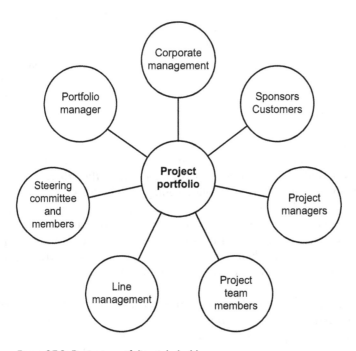

Figure 27.2 Project portfolio stakeholders

efficiently and is completed successfully (contributing to the goals of the enterprise and the portfolio), clearly these factors will be important for the project manager.

Even though project team members are not usually involved in the project portfolio planning they are very important stakeholders. A range of very different skills is demanded for the realization of a portfolio, and how those skills are allocated is important for the motivation of the project teams and for success. After the baseline of the portfolio has been planned, line managers may need to be consulted about which people should be involved, which skills are needed, and how those should be developed or engaged. It might be necessary to involve human resources management (HRM) at this stage if it is realized that additional resources will be needed to perform the work identified by the plan.

Line managers have to provide skilled team members for the project realization. They face goal conflicts between managing their business-as-usual work and supporting the projects adequately. Projects may be appropriate instruments for personnel development, on the one hand, but they reduce capacities for the daily business as usual, on the other.

Several of the above-mentioned stakeholders may be members of one or more steering committees, which have to approve the portfolio plan(s), supervise the progress of the projects and programmes, and approve major results. They also have to discuss and decide major changes. Steering committee decisions can cover budgets, project priorities, resource allocation and go/no-go decisions based on stage gates and other important milestones.

Level of detail in the planning process

Planning can take place at one or more levels of detail, which can result in two or more plans (which clearly must not conflict with each other). So, should portfolio planning aim at the highest aggregation level or the greatest level of detail? In the first case (highest aggregation level) the planning covers all programmes, plus all projects that are not part of any programme. In this case the programme planning may be more important and the programme managers will be more independent from the portfolio management. The second option is portfolio planning that includes every single project – whether or not it is part of a programme (which would indicate a strong position of the portfolio management averse to the programme and project managers). Figures 27.3 and 27.4 illustrate some of these options. To be complete, planning should encompass the portfolio and all its components (subportfolios, programmes, projects and tasks).

Planning goals

An important aim of portfolio planning is to find out which projects and programmes should be conducted within a specific planning period. As the number of project initiatives normally exceeds the necessary financial and personnel resources and management capabilities by far, the biggest challenge of portfolio planning is to select the right projects and programmes. The second challenge is to allocate the necessary resources. Resource allocation should follow project priorities, ensuring that the most important and urgent work takes place on time.

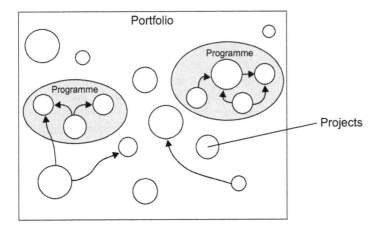

Figure 27.3 Components of the portfolio management

Planning dimensions

The number and the granularity (level of detail) of the planning dimensions determine the extents and efforts for any planning activities. A complete portfolio plan includes all the planned objects (the components of the portfolio), the necessary resources, a timeline and several value types for cost and efforts, as shown in Figure 27.5. In addition to these common dimensions a complete portfolio plan includes the well-known trio of goal perspectives of the magic triangle (scope/performance, time and cost).

As one of the most important functions of a portfolio management is an accurate allocation of the resources needed to fulfil the projects, it seems appropriate to treat resources as a separate planning dimension.

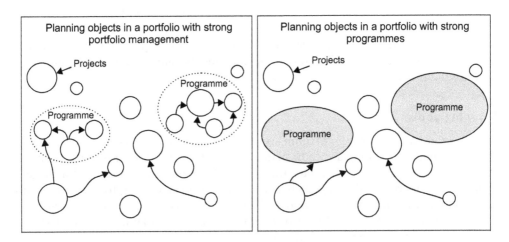

Figure 27.4 Planning objects of a strong/weak portfolio management.

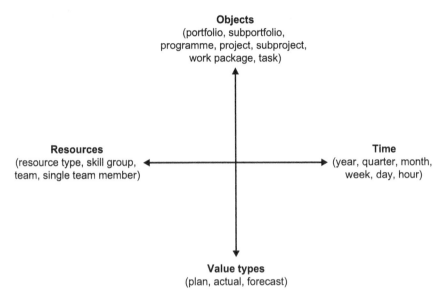

Figure 27.5 Typical planning dimensions

Planning parameters

The planning of a project portfolio can be characterized by a set of important parameters, which are discussed next.

Top-down versus bottom-up planning

Planning activities in general are directed either from the whole planning object to its components (top-down) or the other way around. Behind this there are different management philosophies (for example, if budgets or resources are limited, it is perhaps better to distribute them top-down to the projects and programmes within the portfolio).

If projects get budgets and resources depending on their business cases it may be better to calculate the projects and programmes first, and then aggregate the figures to subportfolios and the overall portfolio (bottom-up). Very often the first planning is done following a top-down or bottom-up approach, but is then adapted (so that you mix the top-down or bottom-up planning directions).

Planning periods

Portfolio plans are normally divided into fixed, equal time periods (which might be, for example, years, quarters or months). These plans tend to be continuous, extending into the future as new programmes and projects are added. On the other hand, each constituent project or programme of projects usually has a finite life, with a recognizable start and an end. So a plan for an individual project, or a programme of projects, can cover the entire lifespan of the project or programme. So one very important factor for the entire portfolio plan is how it is made up: will it include only whole programmes, or will it also include every single project whether or not it belongs to a programme?

Planning focus and strategy

The planning methods chosen differ very strongly, subject to focus and overall goals. Typical focal points of portfolio planning may be:

- Business value of the projects and programmes;
- Minimization of costs;
- Resource-based planning.

If the portfolio management is focused on business values, the portfolio plan will aim at maximizing the return on investment from the project and programme candidates. In this case it is very important to establish a value-orientated project evaluation process to select those project proposals with the highest expected return on investment. To avoid embellished business cases, it is also necessary to review the business cases at the end of the project lifetime, and also at major milestones or stage gates during the project lifecycle. The biggest challenge of this approach is a realistic evaluation of the project benefits. As the benefits will appear a certain time after the project end, in most cases the portfolio management has to use more or less realistic estimations. Cost reduction will cause similar planning activities without the necessity to estimate project benefits. This makes this approach much easier and more reliable. Last (but not least) a resource-based plan focuses on the maximization of results that can be achieved with a given team or given means of production.

Planning granularity

The granularity of planning (level of detail) reveals the biggest variety in practice. As shown in Figure 27.4 there are many options that can determine the granularity of planning. Many people tend to choose the most detailed information because they associate more detail with more quality. In real life this assumption is often not true. For the quality of portfolio planning it is better to choose a granularity that can be supported by all projects in the portfolio, in such a way that it can deliver reliable figures that can be compared with all others.

The portfolio planning process

A portfolio is a living thing. While new projects are being added, others will be finished and removed. Other projects may be frozen, with work on them stopped for a definite or indefinite time. The projects within the portfolio are living things as well. Their scopes may be amended. Budgets, resource allocations, timelines and priorities are always subject to change. Figure 27.6 shows the several stages that a project or programme can take while running through the portfolio process.

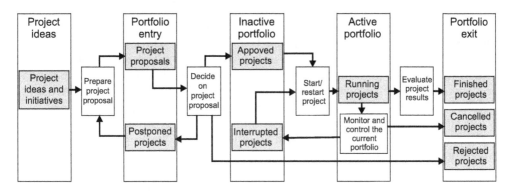

Figure 27.6 Stages of the portfolio planning process

Initial portfolio planning

Portfolio planning usually begins by defining the project portfolio for the next portfolio management period (for example, for the next year or the next quarter). A major challenge is to join projects and programmes in their different stages (project ideas, project proposals, already approved projects and already running projects). A second challenge may be defining the scope of the projects and avoiding overlapping or redundant project tasks. Last (but not least) it is necessary to define clear and objective criteria for including or excluding projects.

Supervision of each portfolio entry

After the initial portfolio planning it is crucial to control the portfolio entries. New project ideas and proposals will appear and have to be handled according to the evaluation criteria mentioned above. Figure 27.7 presents a simple model that depicts how the portfolio project entries can be filtered and processed.

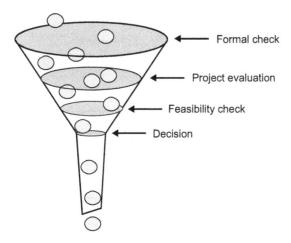

Figure 27.7 Filters at portfolio entry

Prioritization of programmes and projects within the portfolio

If you have asked important stakeholders to put priorities on projects, you will probably find that every project has been rated as 'Priority A'. Obviously this will not be helpful when it becomes necessary to resolve competition for scarce resources among two or more projects. Putting priorities on projects means having to resolve potential conflicts or considering several options for action in advance. As a result, there is no need for escalations or additional management decisions that require extra time.

On the other hand, priorities will be helpful only if they can differentiate between (two) projects where a conflict appears. So, if you want to be prepared for every possible situation, the result of the prioritization must be to allocate a distinct ranking to every project within the portfolio. Figure 27.8 shows one useful way of coming to a distinct ranking of the projects and programmes within the portfolio.

At the first stage, the portfolio is divided into enforced projects and the rest. Enforced projects can be classified at the next level in regulatory and operational needs. The other projects can be divided next into strategic and non-strategic projects.

After this the resulting subportfolios may be sorted by a suitable indicator. In Figure 27.8 such indicators may be calculated for the acuteness, urgency, contribution to strategic goals or returns on investments. Of course, you can choose similar indicators for use in your own context. As a result, you get a distinct project ranking.

Resource allocation within the portfolio

The benefits of a distinct ranking become apparent when you look at a resource allocation chart, such as that shown in Figure 27.9. If you collect the project plans

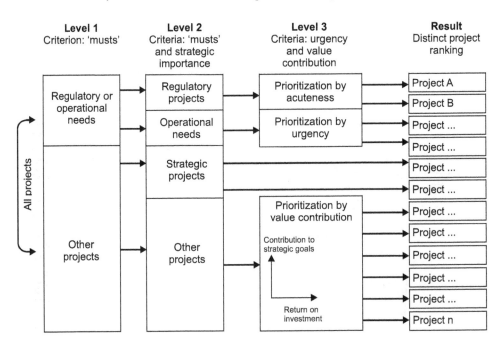

Figure 27.8 Stages of the portfolio process

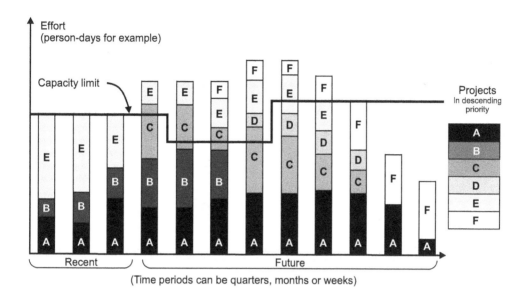

Figure 27.9 Resource allocation corresponding to project priority ranking

of the single projects and programmes you will be able to arrange the demand for resources in a staple-diagram like this. The *x* axis is divided into the reporting respectively planning periods (for example, months). On the *y* axis, you show the resource levels. As the most important resources are usually the people working in the projects, you may choose personnel weeks, days or hours. If the portfolio planning is more budget and cost orientated you can choose currency units such as €, £ or US$ instead. If it is very difficult to collect all the figures needed for every project, I advise you to focus on the key resources, or the resources for which there will be the greatest competition.

Monitoring the current project portfolio

As I wrote earlier, a project portfolio is a living thing. Projects and programmes come and go, and the components within the portfolio will change in status with progress and as priorities are changed. All in all, it will be necessary to adjust any initial portfolio plan after a short period, and then at intervals thereafter. If you have established a portfolio board that gathers at monthly or quarterly meetings, one option is to monitor the current project portfolio using a Kanban board, as shown in Figure 27.10. Using Kanban cards to represent the projects enables you to visualize the changes that have occurred in the portfolio since the previous meeting. When the current meeting begins, the portfolio board members see the Kanban board as they left it last time. The portfolio manager or coordinator will show what has changed since that time by shifting the existing cards from column to column, while explaining the principal facts. In addition, change marks can be added to the relevant cards.

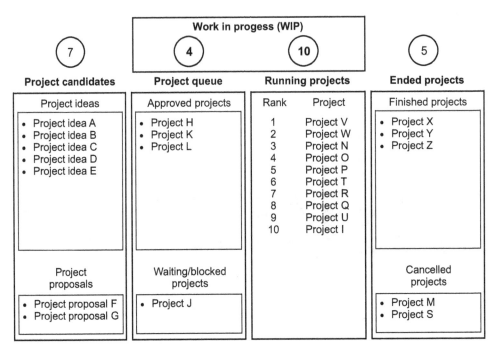

Figure 27.10 Project portfolio board (Kanban)

After the project cards on the board have been updated, the portfolio manager will lead the portfolio board on to a discussion of needs for action and to make any necessary decisions – for example, decisions on project proposals or decision memoranda from the projects or programmes. The portfolio manager will also present any important new project ideas, which could lead to further discussion and proposals in future meetings.

If projects can be finished, the board will accept the results and then have to discuss which projects out of the queue can be started or restarted. If the portfolio board decides to start one or more projects from the queue, they can simultaneously discuss and decide on the new ranking of the running projects by shifting the projects into the new ranking. Every board member can see the consequences of the discussion and the decisions made directly on the Kanban board.

At the end of the meeting, the Kanban board will show the new situation. It can be photographed and sent as part of the meeting minutes to the participants and also to the programme and project managers.

Controlling the value contribution at portfolio exit

This chapter deals with portfolio planning, so you may ask 'What has planning a portfolio of projects to do with benefits management?'. There is very simple answer to that question. If you don't care about the real benefits that result from the projects, there will be no sanctions if any project applicants brighten their business cases. That's why a proven benefits control is also a precondition for establishing portfolio plans.

Recommendations

Give management attention to prioritization and expected results

Programmes and projects are very important instruments for managing change within enterprises. In consequence, they tie up large amounts of capital and allocate resources on a large scale. Senior management has to give serious attention to the portfolio management to avoid major risks and achieve the overall goals.

Define commonalities and differences in treating programmes and projects

Programmes are a specific form of managing multiple projects. If both portfolio management and programme management have been established in the same organization, they will come into conflict at certain points (for example, during the portfolio entry process).

Portfolio management tends to require evaluation of the business case for every single project. Programme management, on the other hand, will claim the right to start projects within a programme without an additional decision from the portfolio board. Similar conflicts will occur on resources and budgets. To avoid conflict between portfolio management and programme management, it is therefore necessary to define clear rules and responsibilities with regard to each of the above-mentioned topics.

Prioritize projects by ranking them

The classic meaning and purpose of project prioritization is to save time in cases of conflicting situations between projects. A prerequisite is therefore that the result of the prioritization is to give every project its own distinct ranking. If two or more conflicting projects have the same priority (whatever that might be) someone has to decide or arbitrate and this will take some extra time. Giving projects their own distinct rankings, on the other hand, may cost some more time and effort initially, but has great advantages and the situation will be easier to maintain within a running portfolio.

Allocate resources according to the given priorities

When the management of an organization puts priorities on projects and programmes, they do this for good reasons. As discussed above it is necessary to allocate the resources (especially those that are scarce or in high demand) according to the decided priorities if the overall objectives are to be achieved.

Review the portfolio plan at frequent intervals

Business and its environment are changing faster and faster, so that a portfolio plan that is not regularly reviewed and adapted will in time become inadequate for the practical needs. In order to use project portfolio management as an effective strategic instrument for achieving enterprise goals and to master change, the portfolio should be reviewed (and if necessary replanned) at frequent intervals. Those intervals should possibly be every 4 weeks (and certainly no longer than 12 weeks).

References and further reading

Cronenbroeck, W. (2008), *Projektmanagement*, Reihe Training International, Berlin, Cornelsen.

Hirzel, M, Kühn, F. and Wollmann, P. (2002), *MultiProjektManagement. Strategische und Operative Steuerung von Projektportfolios*, Frankfurt: Frankfurter Allgemeine Buch.

Hüsselmann, C. and Seidl, J., eds (2015), *Multiprojektmanagement – Herausforderungen und Best Practices*, Dusseldorf: Symposion.

Lock, D. (2013), *Project Management*, 10th edn, Farnham: Gower.

Pennypacker, J. and Dye, L. (2002), *Managing Multiple Projects – Planning, Scheduling and Allocating Resources for Competitive Advantage*, New York: Basel.

Seidl, J. (2004), 'Projekte als Instrument der Strategieumsetzung', in: Frick, A., Kerber, G., Lange, D. and Marre, R. (eds), *Dokumentationsband zur inter PM 2004, Konferenz zur Zukunft im Projektmanagement*, Stuttgart: GPM, pp. 243–258.

Seidl, J. (2007), 'Konvergentes Projektmanagement (KPM). Konzepte der Integration von Projektportfoliosteuerung und operativem Programmem- und Projektmanagement', Dissertation, University of Bremen.

Seidl, J. (2011), *Multiprojektmanagement. Übergreifende Steuerung von Mehrprojektsituationen durch Projektportfolio- und Programmemmanagement*, Berlin/Heidelberg: Springer.

Seidl, J. (2016), 'Multiprojektmanagement in der öffentlichen Verwaltung', in: Schönert, S., Münzberg, M. and Staudt, D. (eds), *Projektmanagement in der öffentlichen Verwaltung*, Dusseldorf: Symposion.

Seidl, J. and Ziegler, T. (2008), 'Management von Projektabhängigkeiten', in: Steinle, C. and Eichenberg, T. (eds), *Handbuch Multiprojektmanagement und -controlling – Projekte erfolgreich strukturieren und steuern*, Berlin: Erich Schmidt Verlag.

Seidl, J. and Baumann, D. (2009), '3.03 Projektportfolioorientierung', in: GPM Deutsche Gesellschaft für Projektmanagement (ed.), *Kompetenzbasiertes Projektmanagement (PM3), Handbuch für die Projektarbeit, Qualifizierung und Zertifizierung auf Basis der IPMA Competence Baseline*, Volume 4, Version 3.0, Nuremberg: Deutsche Gesellschaft für Projektmanagement, pp. 2205–2242.

Chapter 28

Evaluating and reporting portfolio performance

Jörg Floegel and Helene Metoui

This chapter focuses on the following key aspects of evaluating and reporting portfolio performance management:

- Establishing the portfolio performance measurement baseline;
- Managing portfolio performance
- Reporting portfolio performance; and
- Integrating the benefits (ISO 21504: 2015-07(E) – International Organization for Standardization or ISO, 2015).

The chapter highlights the challenges and provide recommendations for overcoming them.

Introduction

Research reveals that, on average, 95 per cent of the workforce are unaware of their organization's strategy (Kaplan and Norton, 2015). The vast majority of executives have no real-time insight into how their organizations' projects are aligned with overall business strategy. More than three-quarters of project managers question if their execution is aligned with business objectives and 17 per cent are confident that it is not aligned at all (Changepoint Press, 2016). 'The rubber' (ideas, mission, vision, values and strategy) is disconnected from 'the road' (the day-to-day operations of an enterprise) (Maltzman and Shirley, 2016). As a result, employees struggle to understand how their actions and behaviours can help or detract from creating value for their organization. Communicating effectively with employees about strategic goals, and the ways in which their behaviours and actions can help to achieve those goals, is crucial (Kohl, 2016). Leading global companies illustrate that their success is dependent not only on seeking the most innovative and new talent, but also on supporting, driving and reinforcing the things that everyone knows they are supposed to do but frequently overlook. This pragmatism also extends to communication (Price and Toye, 2016).

The ability to improve communication and align strategy across business areas is provided by portfolio governance (Project Management Institute [PMI], 2016). Portfolios change with the strategic objectives of the organization. The success of a portfolio is measured by the performance of the portfolio and the optimization of investments. A portfolio is designed to achieve one or more organizational strategies and operational goals (PMI, 2013). By establishing a structured relationship between strategy and actions, effective portfolio management becomes a fix for the failure to connect between 'the rubber' and 'the road'. The portfolio is where strategy (the action-orientated stepchild of mission, vision and values) meets operations (Maltzman and Shirley, 2016). Strategic clarity and coherence set successful companies apart from their competitors (Couto et al., 2017).

In executing its corporate strategy, an organization can only be as mature as the development of its portfolio management process. Portfolio management can lead to competitive advantage only when a coherent strategy is in place. Without portfolio management, the strategic direction is more a 'feeling' that flows top-down through the structure, sometimes mentioned here and there (Romano, 2017), rather than a method that produces measurable results. Portfolio management truly brings strategy to life. Project portfolio management should therefore do the following:

1. Target projects that are key elements for the strategic objectives;
2. Make sure that the portfolio of projects fulfils project success criteria and delivers value according to the project objectives and;
3. Manage the portfolio proactively in line with any changes in the strategy.

Three key factors in meeting these objectives are selecting the projects that best support strategic objectives, monitoring performance during implementation to ensure that the portfolio remains on track to deliver strategic benefits, and adjusting strategy (and the portfolio) when changes in strategy or performance dictate (Bivins and Bible, 2012).

However, the link between the actual board strategy direction and daily operations may need to be amplified because the portfolio could be a mix of many strategies (declared, hidden, deduced, unreal) coming from many 'business-as-usual' years (Romano, 2017). Moreover, those strategies may be complicated by several organizational silos following their own budget-driven agendas. To find out where your company will be in three to five years from now, we recommend that you look not at your stated strategy but at your project portfolio and ask two questions:

1. In which projects do you invest?
2. What is the performance of those investments?

The answers to these questions will determine your company's direction (Benko and McFarlan, 2003).

There are several signs that indicate whether or not the portfolio management requires improvement and that the strategy is yet to be fully realized. These signs include the following:

• Many former strategic objectives projects are still active, with resources still working on them;
• Some projects are still active, but stopped somewhere and neglected;
• Most projects are late compared with their baseline completion dates;
• Resources are multi-utilized, overbooked and overworked;
• Readiness to start new projects based on the new strategic objectives is limited;
• New ideas are not assessed and not linked to any strategy;
• Most strategic objectives are missed or not aimed at all.

Establishing the portfolio performance measurement baseline

Before measuring the portfolio performance, the baseline has to be defined and set up in the existing systems. Establishing the baseline creates the ground for measuring the benefits and the value to strategic objectives. Thus, the baseline should contain metrics that reflect strategic objectives of the portfolio and the organization. Special attention should also be paid to the quality of the information (ISO 21504 – ISO, 2015).

The main challenges in this area arise because many organizations already have a certain management structure and processes in place. Thus, portfolio management evolution maturity must be considered. The extent to which the portfolio component success framework has to be enhanced should also be determined. In particular, the non-operational performance baseline has to be taken into account and it has to be ensured that the defined performance metrics are relevant.

Considering the portfolio management evolution maturity

When starting to establish project portfolio management (PPM), the current level of PPM evolution maturity should be assessed and taken into account. There is a set of tools and relevant indicators that can support organizations to analyse and shape their evolution towards PPM implementation. This uses past experience to anticipate problems and avoid pitfalls. Methods range from such aspects as change spread, top management sponsorship, organizational extent, process and software, to prioritization and selection criteria, external connection and completeness. For example, in the course of implementing project portfolio management, an organization will be moving from creating 'handmade' software based on MS Office to using professional PPM software (Romano, 2017; see also Chapter 24).

Resource skills play a key role in successful portfolio management. Portfolio managers need to have specific competences to run portfolios and programmes appropriate to their organization's guidelines. According to the International Project Management Association (IPMA) Individual Competence Baseline, the key contributors need to have perspective competencies that allow an appropriate understanding of the portfolio, people management competencies that allow the individual to handle personal and social challenges in a portfolio, as well as practice competencies as the core element to handle portfolios properly (IPMA, 2015; see also Chapter 37).

Enhancing the portfolio component success framework

Projects are the main vehicle in achieving and maintaining competitive operations. In short, a successful project is likely to support a successful business. However, the perception of success continues to mean different things to different people (Barclay, 2016). The 'iron triangle' of schedule, budget and scope is commonly used as the key driver for managing projects (Kloppenborg et al., 2014). Although these success dimensions are a common method of evaluating project success, they represent only the organization's minimum expectation of the project (Pinto, 2004). Organizations must expect more than efficient projects; they need impactful results (Romano, 2017).

By evaluating strategic performance (Jugdev and Müller, 2005), the organization can evaluate the change benefits resulting from the completed project. For instance, a project may deliver the entire scope within the budget and schedule expectations, but the outcomes might not contribute significantly to the long-term organizational goals. The efficiency of the project alone does not determine the effect that the project outcomes have on the organization. When the project does not provide strategic value, the success of the project has to be questioned. Clearly a project cannot be considered as successful if its outcomes fail to achieve the desired benefits and strategic value.

Rather than simply considering project efficiency as a means for evaluating project success, a common expanded framework of the measures for project success has been proposed (Kloppenborg et al, 2014; Malach-Pines, et al 2009; Pinto, 2004; Shenhar and Dvir, 2007; Shenhar and Levy, 1997). This framework expands the dimensions of project success to include the impact on the customer, contributions to business success and preparation for the future. In addition, it includes impact on the team (Shenhar and Dvir, 2007). Together, these dimensions represent a more complete evaluation of a project's success (Romano, 2017).

Formalization of single project management has a strong impact on the quality of PPM. So the transparency in a project portfolio increases owing to the increased availability and comprehensiveness of information (Teller, et al., 2012). Therefore, we suggest that formalization of single project management should be applied, because this significantly improves the quality of the portfolio management.

Establishing a non-operational performance baseline

A common approach when establishing a baseline is to consider such operational dimensions as:

- The portion of the project scope delivered (progress made);
- Difference between the planned and actual budget; and
- Difference between the planned and actual schedule.

Elaborating a non-operational performance baseline can be much more challenging for many reasons. According to the enhanced project success framework mentioned above, the non-operational baseline components are customer impact, team impact, organizational success and future preparation.

For instance, measuring the effectiveness of project outcomes with respect to customer impact requires a baseline of the customer's current business standing and technical specifications (Romano, 2017). With regard to the team impact, it is well known that employee engagement (commitment) has a direct impact on the success of projects. Establishing employee engagement as a project performance metric not only benefits the project performance, but also promotes the sustainability of the company's strategy throughout the organization. Sustainable strategy is a lever for attracting, engaging and retaining the workforce (Kohl, 2016).

Making performance metrics relevant

Indicators and controls are key prerequisites for managing project portfolios. Preferably these indicators and controls will be represented in a portfolio dashboard, with traffic lights and metrics. Performance metrics are a vital mechanism for managing and controlling the project portfolio. A focus on these measures is, for example, achievement of strategic goals of the programme, financial contribution, stakeholder satisfaction, risk profile and resource utilization (Project Management Institute [PMI], 2009). Examples of performance metrics according to Pennybacker (2005) are:

- The completeness of requirements;
- The extent of rework;
- The number of key milestones completed;
- The number of key milestones missed;
- Use of a work breakdown structure to develop project plans;
- Use of a team charter for managing conflicts;
- Resource utilization versus the plan;
- Expected results and actual results in testing;
- Effectiveness of risk–response strategies in mitigating risks;
- Vendor progress in meeting schedule, cost and performance; and
- Extent of requests for information outside of regular communications.

To be relevant, performance metrics must add value to an organization. This value comes from the usability of the metrics in supporting the organization to manage and drive the project portfolio according to the organization's strategic goals. According to (Pennypacker, 2005) the set of metrics will differ according to the organizations and industries. Nevertheless, within an organization the measures should be recorded and indexed for projects conducted over several years. This enables the organization to establish a solid base from which to compare metrics and take appropriate decisions.

Managing portfolio performance

Project management activities necessary to ensuring the performance of the portfolio include the following:

- Tracking portfolio performance at both individual component and overall levels;
- Maintaining the baseline record;
- Evaluating the contribution of portfolio benefits and comparing them with strategic objectives;
- Forecasting future performance;
- Assessing the impact of various portfolio components on each other; and
- Reviewing the priority of strategic objectives (ISO, 2015).

These tasks should be performed consistently over time, and should also be applied to a wider range of projects and portfolios, to allow comparison or calibration of several portfolios over time (to put this in familiar terms, making sure that 'apples are compared with apples'). Doing this enables the organization to compare its projects and portfolios.

The education and training of the portfolio managers are a key factor for effective and efficient portfolio management. The portfolio manager has to cover several domains of knowledge and experience to run a portfolio effectively. These competencies have to cover the portfolio perspective, people and practice competences that deal with personal and social topics, and portfolio competences that address the specific practice (IPMA, 2015). Research unveiled several reasons for ineffective portfolio management. For example, the decision-making on project and portfolio selection is more political and less planned and rational. Also the competencies and activities of the portfolio manager play a crucial role in the portfolio management. Furthermore, portfolios need adjusted management processes – not one size fits all (Martinsuo, 2013). See Chapter 37 for more on the subject of competencies.

Changing the mind-sets at various levels

Projects guided by the operational performance metrics are managed to optimize performance according to the operational goals. This means that measures, decisions and actions are focused on achieving these operational goals. The operational goals of the project therefore influence the project stakeholder's behaviours and drive the project processes. An excessive focus on operational goals may force the projects to make decisions that are counter to the goals of portfolio performance management (Romano, 2017).

Targeting to achieve operational success, project teams and project stakeholders may make decisions or take actions that improve project operational performance, but have a negative impact on non-operational performance: customer, team and organizational success, and preparation of the organization for the future. This not only diminishes project benefits, but also drives strategic misalignment of the project with the company's strategy.

To ensure strategic alignment, it is imperative that project stakeholders act as sponsors of non-operational performance management, convince project teams to keep their non-operational performance goals at all times and drive implementation of according actions. To be truly sustainable, the project portfolio management process must be embedded not only into operations of the organization, but also into the culture. Culturally, change has to be viewed as something you do together *with* people, not *to* them. It has to be recognized that 'the soft stuff' is really the hard stuff (Price and Toye, 2016). When the entire organization has to change, leading the change effectively is challenging, but can be much easier when you understand how change intelligence works at different levels of the organization (Trautlein, 2013). Last but not least, finding a change agent who will be championing non-operational performance metrics in the C-Suite is the key (Kohl, 2016).

Integrating sustainability

Continuous progress requires a clear ownership. In addition to a chief operating officer (COO) role focused on running an organization's ongoing operations, it is recommended that organizations appoint a chief project officer (CPO) with similar responsibilities for the organization's projects, programmes and portfolio. The CPO has to become the champion of non-operational performance metrics in the C-Suite. For example, Steve Jobs was truly the CPO of Apple and propelled Apple with his direction by driving innovation through project management (Archibald and Archibald, 2016).

However, it is not recommended to establish a PMO overnight. As the maturity of the project management grows, PMOs must evolve its responsibilities gradually. An evolutionary plan must be established that builds on the existing situation, and in a series of steps or phases extends the PMO responsibilities (Archibald and Archibald, 2016). According to research, PMOs are performing increasingly more functions, especially portfolio management (PM Solutions, 2014). Building a process for linking organizational strategy to project outcomes, along with increasing alignment of project management and business strategy to the benefits of the organization, belongs to the top 10 PMO trends (ESI International, 2015).

Reporting portfolio performance

Reporting portfolio performance means providing appropriate information to stakeholders, at appropriate intervals, and integrating the data across the portfolio components. All activities of the portfolio manager should serve the goal of providing valuable and timely information to stakeholders (ISO 21504 – ISO, 2015). A vital feature of reporting progress through metrics is gathering accurate, valuable and current data without undue delay. The quality of the portfolio management framework can be judged by the quality of the data and adherence to the reporting guidelines.

ISO 8402-1994 (ISO, 1994) defines quality as 'the totality of features and characteristics of a product or service that bears its ability to satisfy stated or implied needs'. Reported information should be validated and include data related to achieving the portfolio key performance indicators (KPIs). Any potential performance failure or issue must be highlighted and reported as early as possible, so that there is still time in which to make decisions or take corrective action. Industry standards (for example, ISO/IEC 25000 Software Engineering) should be used for guidance in defining the appropriate metrics. Independent consulting organizations can provide research and guidance on appropriate metrics as well as guidance on best practices (TSIA, the Technology Services Industry Association, is one example).

Reporting incomplete, faulty or old data will most probably lead to ineffective or bad management decisions. Low-quality data reporting diminishes the potential benefits (such as risk mitigation, partnership opportunities and employee engagement). To ensure data compliance, the data-gathering and reporting structure has to be designed so that it contributes data credibility. The process of data gathering has to be disclosed to all involved parties to promote transparency (Kohl, 2016).

In today's fast-paced economy, transparency into real-time business insights (both from the top down and the bottom up) is no longer a luxury: it is a requirement. Moreover, it is a game-changer for businesses that are striving to achieve operational excellence to drive a healthy bottom line, gain a strong competitive advantage and/or target exponential growth. Despite all these insights, the field research shows that 80 per cent of executives have no real-time visibility of their portfolio performance and how that is aligned with the overall business strategy (Changepoint Press, 2016).

Guidelines for setting up the appropriate portfolio reporting management processes can be found in industry standards such as ISO/IEC 25000 (ISO/International Electrotechnical Commission [IEC], 2014). In addition, reference metrics and analysis can be provided by independent organizations like the TSIA.

Managing the integration of benefits

To ensure that benefits are realized and to enable future actions, the portfolio manager should verify the identification of benefits and their realization timeframe, as well as forecast future investment gains and losses to track them in comparison with actuals and identify gaps where forecast benefits will not meet expectations (ISO 21504 – ISO, 2015). When performing these activities, several challenges may have to be overcome such as the following:

- Resistance to evaluating projects by the delivered benefits;
- Pairing project management with benefits managements;
- Ensuring acceptance of the outcomes by the organization; and
- Making portfolio rationalization a routine and a capability.

Overcoming resistance to evaluate projects by the delivered benefits

The expanded success metrics demonstrate that projects can be evaluated beyond their operational efficiency. These additional metrics evaluate the benefits that result from executing the project and the project's outcomes (Romano, 2017). However, despite an accepted framework for enhanced project metrics (Kloppenborg et al., 2014; Malach-Pines et al., 2009; Pinto, 2004; Shenhar and Dvir, 2007; Shenhar and Levy, 1997) and a clear connection between projects and business strategies, organizations continue to evaluate projects by efficiency (Romano, 2017). Despite the assumption that project managers are in the approximately 45 per cent of the population that is open to change (Maltzman and Shirley, 2016), two aspects are known to be the main drivers of resistance. First, measuring project benefits is considered as difficult (Zwikeal and Smyrk, 2012). Second, measuring benefits has to be done after the project has been completed (Yu et al., 2005).

In addition to taking the lead in change management, for example by applying the 'sense, scout, synthesize and steer' model (Scott and Esteves, 2013), and reinforcing the purpose that drives an organization (Mourkogianniss, 2016; Price and Toye, 2016) the proposed solution is benefits realization management (BRM). BRM can be applied to projects to clarify the value and strategic relevance (Serra and Kunc, 2015). It is known to increase the overall success of projects in achieving the planned benefits, especially when paired with effective project management practices (Badewi, 2016; Serra and Kunc, 2015).

Pairing project management with benefits management

The later in the project lifecycle the benefits management begins, the more challenging it becomes. To implement effective benefits management, a governance framework has to be established to pair project management with benefits right from the start and during the entire project lifecycle (Badewi, 2016). This governance framework requires assignment of two key roles: project manager and benefits manager. The project manager is responsible for driving the project through all its phases, from initiation to closure. The benefits manager is responsible for realizing the benefits of the project by identifying the potential benefits, planning for the benefits, building a business case for the project, implementing the benefits and auditing the actual benefits gained from the project.

The benefits manager role is the same role as the executive sponsor who improves visibility of the project (Chandler and Hall, 2016). Research indicates that high-performance organizations that actively engage sponsors have a higher percentage of projects meeting their goals (PMI, 2015). The benefits manager ensures that the project is viewed as strategic effort associated with targeted business value, and communicates this to the project team and stakeholders in a clear way to support decisions about changes to the project scope, schedule and budget. This ensures that the organization evaluates projects through the lens of organizational value and not only from operational performance metrics (Romano, 2017).

Ensuring the organization's acceptance of the outcomes

If the project is evaluated on its ability to produce the deliverables, but not to ensure that the deliverables are adopted, then acceptance of the outcomes by the organization may be challenging. The operational performance metrics of the project do not address the organization's acceptance and application of the deliverables. The project output may meet the organization's expectations but the value goals cannot be achieved if the organization is unable to adopt or apply the project output (Romano, 2017).

To overcome this, it is important that the project management be obliged to demonstrate to the organization the benefits realized as a result of the project completion. This can be achieved by making benefits demonstration a mandatory part of the project delivery methodology. These benefits may be in two forms:

1. Operational: these can be in form of reduced expenses, increased revenue and profit margin;
2. Non-operational: these can include the following:

   - increased customer satisfaction;
   - extended headcount;
   - improved employee engagement;
   - improved skill sets;
   - lessons learned;
   - expanded services and products and;
   - compliance with regulatory requirements and policies.

Making portfolio rationalization a routine and a capability

Managing the integration of benefits may become more challenging as portfolios become more diverse. The diverse portfolios mean higher complexity, increasing costs and driving inefficiencies. For this reason, making decisions about the portfolio is fundamental to the company's success. Rationalizing the portfolio not only helps to cut costs, but also refocuses the company on its differentiating capabilities. However, it can be challenging to identify an underlying portfolio complexity problem.

There are various symptoms that can help to verify whether portfolio complexity creates an issue:

- Time to market is slower than competition;
- Failure to respond to changes in the market;
- Trying to reduce costs across the products;
- Labelling projects as strategic even where their profitability is not high;
- Doing many small-scale different things;
- Too many products are generating diminishing returns as sales increase;
- Decision-making takes too long with, multiple iterations.

Recognizing any of these symptoms signals that portfolio complexity should be analysed. Although most companies rationalize their portfolio only when they have a problem, best-practice companies are known to monitor and clean up their portfolio by identifying and discontinuing underperforming portfolio elements continuously (Couto et al., 2017; Price and Toye, 2016).

References and further reading

Archibald, R.D. and Archibald, S.C. (2016), *Leading and Managing Innovation: What Every Executive Team Must Know about Project, Program, and Portfolio Management*, 2nd edn, New York: CRC Press.

Badewi, A. (2016), The impact of project management (PM) and benefits management (BM) practices on project success: towards developing a project benefits governance framework', *International Journal of Project Management*, 34(4), 761–778.

Barclay, C. (2016), A dialogue on the diversity in the constituents of project success,' in: Barclay, C. and Osei-Bryson, K.M. (eds), *Strategic Project Management: Contemporary Issues and Strategies for Developing Economies*, New York: CRC Press.

Benko, C. and McFarlan, F.W. (2003), *Connecting the Dots: Aligning Projects with Objectives in Unpredictable Times*, Boston, MA: Harvard Business School Press.

Bivins, S.S. and Bible, M.J. (2012), 'Evaluating strategic project portfolio performance', *PM World Journal*, I(III), October.

Chandler, D.E. and Hall, P. (2016), *Improving Executive Sponsorship of Projects: A Holistic Approach*, New York: Business Expert Press.

Changepoint Press (2016), 80% of execs have no real-time visibility, available at: https://www.changepoint.com/press/know-new-research-finds-80-execs-no-real-time-visibility (accessed 23 February 2016).

Couto, V., Plansky, J. and Caglar, D. (2017), *Fit for Growth: A Guide to Strategic Cost Cutting, Restructuring, and Renewal*, Hoboken, NJ: John Wiley & Sons.

ESI International (2015), 10 Project Management Trends Watch 2015, available at: www.esi-intl.co.uk/blogs/pmoperspectives/index.php/10-projectmanagement-trends-watch-2015.

International Project Management Association (IPMA) (2015), *Individual Competence Baseline for Project, Programme and Portfolio Management*, Version 4.0, Amsterdam: IPMA, pp. 1–432

International Organization for Standardization (1994), ISO 8402, *Quality Management and Quality Assurance Vocabulary*, 2nd edn, Geneva: ISO.

International Organization for Standardization (2014) ISO/IEC 25000, *Systems and Software Engineering – Systems and software quality requirements and evaluation (SQUARE)*, Geneva: ISO.

International Organization for Standardization (2015), ISO 21504:2015-07 (E), *Project, Programme and Portfolio Management – Guidance on Portfolio Management*. Geneva: ISO.

Jugdev, K. and Müller, R. (2005), 'A retrospective look at our evolving understanding of project success', *Project Management Journal*, 36(4), 19–31.

Kaplan, R.S. and Norton, D.P. (2015), *The Office of Strategy Management*, Boston MA: Harvard Business Review.

Kloppenborg, T.J., Tesch, D. and Manolis, C. (2014), 'Project success and executive sponsor behaviors: empirical life cycle stage investigations', *Project Management Journal*, 45(1), 9–20.

Kohl, K. (2016), *Becoming a Sustainable Organization: A Project and Portfolio Management Approach*, Boca Raton, FL: Auerbach Publications.

Malach-Pines, A., Dvir, D. and Sadeh, A. (2009), Project manager-project (PM-P) fit and project success,' *International Journal of Operations and Production Management*, 29(3), 268–291.

Maltzman, R. and Shirley, D. (2016), *Driving Project, Program, and Portfolio Success: The Sustainability Wheel*, Boca Raton, FL: Auerbach Publications.

Martinsuo, M. (2013), 'Project portfolio management in practice and in context', *International Journal of Project Management*, 31(6), 794–803

Mourkogianniss, N. (2006), *Purpose: The Starting Point of Great Companies*, New York: Palgrave Macmillan.

Pennypacker, J.S. (2005), *Measures of Project Management Performance and Value*, Chadds Ford, PA: Center for Business Practices.

Pinto, J.K. (2004), 'The elements of project success', in Cleland, D.I. (ed.), *Field Guide to Project Management*, Hoboken, NJ: Wiley & Sons.

PM Solutions, (2014), *The State of the PMO 2014*, PM Solutions Research, available at: www.pmsolutions.com/reports/state_of_the_pmo_2014_research_report_final.pdf

Price, C. and Toye. S. (2016), *Accelerating Performance: How Organizations Can Mobilize, Execute, and Transform with Agility*, Hoboken, NJ: Wiley & Sons.

Project Management Institute (2009), *The Standard for Portfolio Management*, 2nd edn, Newtown Square, PA: PMI.

Project Management Institute (2013), *The Standard for Portfolio Management*, 3rd edn, Newtown Square, PA: PMI.

Project Management Institute (2015), *PMI's Pulse of the Profession: Capturing the Value of Project Management*, Newtown Square, PA: PMI.

Project Management Institute (2016), *Governance of Portfolios, Programs, and Projects, A Practice Guide*, Newtown Square, PA: PMI.

Romano, L. (2017), *Project Portfolio Management Strategies for Effective Organizational Operations*, Hershey, PA: IGI Global.

Serra, C.M. and Kunc, M. (2015), 'Benefits realization management and its influence on project success and the execution of business strategies', *International Journal of Project Management*, 33(1), 53–66.

Scott, S. and Esteves, T. (2013), *Leadership for Sustainability and Change*, Oxford: DoSustainability.

Shenhar, A. and Dvir, D. (2007), *Reinventing Project Management*, Boston, MA: Harvard Business School Press.

Shenhar, A. and Levy, O. (1997), 'Mapping the dimensions of project success', *Project Management Journal*, 28(2), 5.

Teller, J., Unger, B., Kock, A. and Gemünden, H.G. (2012), 'Formalization of project portfolio management: the moderating role of project portfolio complexity', *International Journal of Project Management*, 30(5), 596–607

Trautlein, B. (2013), *Change Intelligence: Use the Power of CQ to Lead Change That Sticks*, Austin, TX: Greenleaf Book Group Press.

Yu, A.G., Flett, P.D. and Bowers, J.A. (2005), 'Developing a value-centered proposal for assessing project success', *International Journal of Project Management*, 23(6), 428–436.

Zwikael, O. and Smyrk, J. (2012), 'A general framework for gauging performance of initiative to enhance organizational value', *British Journal of Management*, 23(1), 6–22.

Chapter 29

Balancing and optimizing the portfolio

Claus Hüsselmann

This chapter deals with balancing the project portfolio (PP). This process follows on from calculating 'project scores' (or project ranking) and improving the portfolio and the underlying management system in a continuous improvement process (CIP). Aligning the portfolio primarily involves optimizing the list of selected projects based on project score rankings, although not so rigidly as to become deterministic (see Chapter 26). Each project score is based on a cost–benefit analysis. Balancing thus seeks to achieve a project landscape that is balanced with regard to risk aversion as well as to the company's capacities capabilities, possible synergies, target allocation of benefits and costs, and so on. However, alignment and optimization of the portfolio are also a continuous task of project portfolio management (PPM) that follows the familiar plan–do–check–act (PDCA) cycle shown in Figure 29.1. Continuous project portfolio optimization is the only way in which PPM can be transformed into a flexible process that is experienced and accepted at all levels of the organization. It is also the only way in which PPM can realize its full potential, by maximizing the benefits and adding value to the company through the use of its resources in projects.

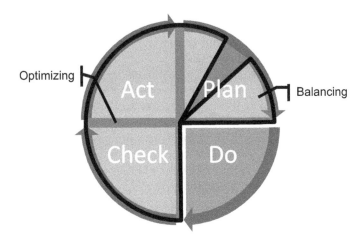

Figure 29.1 Continuous portfolio optimization

Context and classification

Goals

The goal of PPM in general (and balancing and optimizing the portfolio in particular) is to establish a workable system that best reflects the following:

- The company's (project) reality;
- The kind of direction-setting the company requires; and
- The company's overall strategic orientation.

Optimization, as used here, should not be understood in a mathematically precise sense, but rather in the sense of striving for improvement as seen with a 'proof of concept'. This is the only way that PPM can achieve acceptance and inspire confidence, because it makes it possible to objectify the 'gut feeling' for priorities and master the complexity of what can be a very extensive project landscape.

Clearly the balance of the selected project landscape plays a significant role (see Figure 29.2). Balancing and optimizing are thus a concrete application of the PDCA cycle. Although balancing should be classified as a quasi-final step before approval of a new project landscape, optimization within the CIP context serves the 'check', 'act' and parts of the 'plan' components of the cycle.

Benefits and necessity

As a rule, project portfolios are assembled and put into effect while creating a plan for the business year ahead. The big picture results from setting the overall corporate strategy and the resulting measures (projects, project bundles or programmes). This results in a primary cycle of applying for and approving projects that either run annually or at even longer intervals. In a dynamic environment, however, such rigid intervals can often prove to be too inflexible and can mean that some project proposals will have to wait for up to a year before a positive decision can be made to move forward. Although this provides a certain degree of stability and reliability, it no longer does justice to the increasing demands for agile leadership of companies. Figure 29.2 shows the underlying influences of portfolios that require continuous evaluation and adaptation of their make-up and systematic as part of CIP.

The project portfolio brings together projects and company strategies into a cause-and-effect relationship, with the goal of selecting projects so that they make the highest possible contribution to the company (both strategically and otherwise) and cover the strategies adequately (see Chapter 27). If this results in changes to priorities and framework conditions (for example, new management) or simply realizing the actual cost or benefit of the projects (for example, project xy becomes more expensive), it must be possible to make a strategic correction. The main factors influencing the need for a dynamic adaptation of the portfolio are as follows:

- Misguided first version: there is always room for improvement. The design elements of the PPM system and the components of the portfolio itself are based on assumptions that may be erroneous. This includes, for example, the usefulness of individual projects, but also the reality (practicability, acceptance) of defined criteria and weightings, and so on.

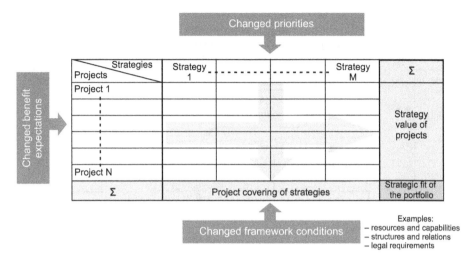

Figure 29.2 The portfolio in a changing environment

- Updates to the company strategy: the contribution of individual projects to the company strategy may change and thus affect how well the overall portfolio covers the strategy.
- Dynamics of the environment: this includes market developments (politically induced, for example), technological developments (such as Industry 4.0), changes in legal and regulatory requirements (such as tariffs, regulation of competition), and so on. In particular given the current developments in information technology (IT), which is increasingly present in all sectors of the economy and society (digitalization), dynamism of the environment is reaching a fevered pitch. In many cases, technologies change before individual, complex projects can be completed (for example, smart devices and their role in the automobile product development process).
- Demands for flexibility and agility: the dynamic environment and efforts towards innovation and greater efficiency make it necessary to subject the portfolio to a fundamental, continuous critique. An annual review of the company's project landscape, with an eye only on the budgeting process for the following financial year, has increasingly proved to be insufficient. New projects and insights into ongoing projects must not be shelved until the annual project review process is ready to kick in; instead, they need to be addressed as soon as possible.
- Development of active projects: progress in current projects is necessary in order to evaluate the expected cost and benefit of the individual projects in terms of the knowledge gained, progress, cost and effort involved, as well as forecasts for what will be required to complete each project, timing for its completion, and so on.

The story so far

Figure 29.3, following the scheme of a process-orientated quality management system (cf. DIN EN ISO 9000 – Deutsches Institut für Normung e.V. or DIN, 2005),

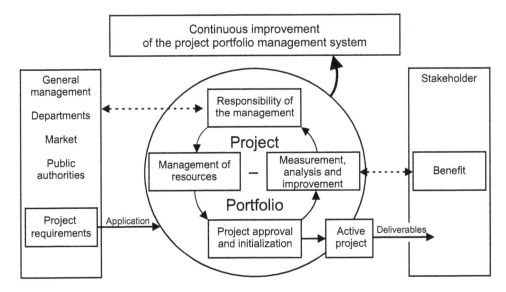

Figure 29.3 Managing the project portfolio system.

summarizes the overall approach. In summary, balancing and continuous optimization of the portfolio is an important aspect of professional and systematic PPM. Establishing this process is evidence of a significant, more mature PPM (stages 4–5) using the known discrete maturity models of *Project, Programme and Portfolio Management* (PMMI – Kerzner, 2017) or PfM3 (Project Management Institute or PMI, 2013).

Subprocesses and methods

ISO 21504 assigns to the process of balancing and optimizing the portfolio the following tasks:

- Optimizing portfolio components (5.8.2);
- Maintaining the portfolio (5.8.3);
- Optimizing resources (5.8.4);
- Managing portfolio risks (5.8.5); and
- Controlling portfolio change (5.8.6) (see ISO 21504 – International Organization for Standardization or ISO, 2015).

These activities are considered below in the subprocesses 'Balancing the portfolio', 'Continuously assessing the benefit of the portfolio' and 'Reviewing the portfolio configuration', excluding substantial considerations of topics such as risk management, defining assessment criteria, resource management, and so on.

Balancing the portfolio

Aligning or balancing refers to the make-up of the portfolio (selecting and prioritizing the portfolio components), especially projects and programmes (see ISO 21504 – ISO, 2015).

Portfolio alignment includes 'manual intervention' into the ranking of listed projects determined by project scoring. In this sense, each calculated score is to be understood as an analytical basis to be optimized by the balancing process, with an eye to the complex situation of the company and the decision-making abilities of management. The aim is to select a project landscape that is balanced with regard to the factors mentioned above. Alignment thus creates the list of projects that will ultimately be approved. Important influences include in particular the following:

- Available capacities and capabilities;
- Factual/logical contexts of the projects;
- The company's risk aversion or affinity;
- The strategic formation of standard project budgets (subportfolios);

but also:

- The individual requirements of top management.

Figure 29.4 summarizes these basic principles of portfolio alignment. This results in the final prioritization of the projects. It preserves the score calculated for each individual project, which can later be used as a decision-making tool for comparing and contrasting projects as needed. Methods for analysing the portfolio include THE following:

- Diagrams: portfolios/matrices, web diagrams, roadmaps;
- Analytical methods: dependency and synergy matrices;
- Quantitative methods: project portfolio-specific key performance indicators (KPIs).

Of course, all of the other methods typically used to prioritize portfolio components are also used. These include, for example, cost–benefit analysis, AHP (the analytical hierarchy process, described, for example, in Saaty and Vargas, 2013), pairwise comparison, monetary cost–benefit calculations, and so forth.

Matrix diagrams

Depicting project landscapes in the form of portfolio diagrams is the most commonly used method, in addition to the pure list. When trying to balance the project landscape, a suitable chart representation can help management to discuss the projects to be approved. Figure 29.5 shows one example. In this case, the two axes of the portfolio chart can, in principle, be chosen arbitrarily, but purposefully. The shading (or colour) and size of the bubbles allows other dimensions to be added easily. For example, a particular shade might indicate an IT project. A larger diameter could be used to indicate a greater budget. However, with a larger number of projects (say more than 30) this visualization can lose its effectiveness.

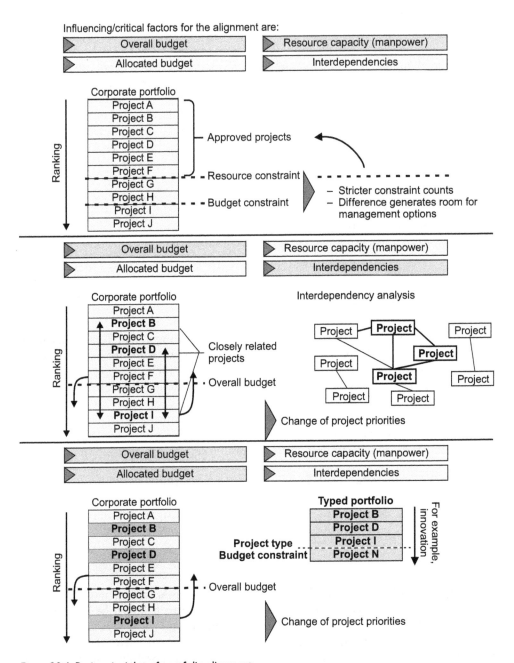

Figure 29.4 Basic principles of portfolio alignment

Depending on the specific design of the PPM system in the company, dimensions such as contribution to strategy, project risk, urgency, monetary or process benefit, burden on resources, strengthening of resources, and so on, are often depicted on the chart axes. An economical arrangement can provide a clear picture, allowing multiple dimensions to be displayed at the same time. Figure 29.6 shows charts after Kunz

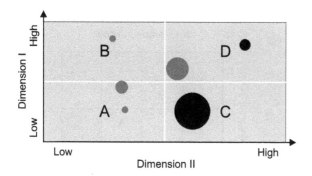

Figure 29.5 A schematic portfolio chart

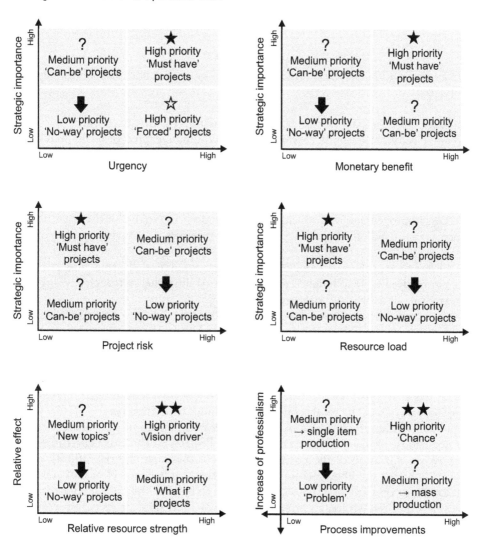

Figure 29.6 Project portfolio charts

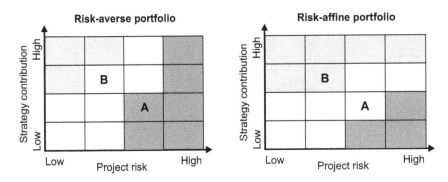

Figure 29.7 Risk-averse and risk-affine portfolios

(2007) and Seidl (2011). The following explanation of the chart axis labels might be helpful here:

- Relative effect: impact of core competencies within the organization;
- Relative resource strength: existing resources (human, capital or technology) with regard to their availability, ease of acquisition or ability to be controlled;
- Increased professionalism: externally orientated improvement of the competitive position. For example, decision quality, order processing, direct competitive advantage, impact on the market;
- Process improvement: that which constitutes success internally for the organization, such as improved efficiency, direct increase in revenues, cost savings, and so on.

Using the example of the 'risk' dimension, it is now possible to illustrate how portfolio charts can be used to help balance the project portfolio. The matrix charts in Figure 29.7 relate to risk-averse and risk-affine portfolios.

In many cases, the scorecard designed to quantify the benefit of a project includes the project risk as one of its criteria, possibly divided into risk categories such as monetary or temporal risks, and so on. Risk is therefore generally included in the evaluation of the project, but it also 'disappears' in the overall score. For example, Project A and Project B in Figure 29.7 may both have a score of 70 (and are thus equally ranked), but Project A has a risk score of 40, whereas Project B's risk score is only 20, making the former twice as risky. The total score, however, hides this difference.

Depending on how risk-averse or risk-affine the organization is, it will either certainly not choose Project A or certainly choose Project B. The two charts in Figure 29.7 show the variation of the portfolios and how they map the risk affinity of the organization by the shading (or colouring) of the fields. It becomes clear how portfolio design can map company preferences and be used to balance the project landscape. Of course, the usual risk strategies are also applied to individual projects, for example, risk transfer and reduction in order to improve a project's risk classification before being put up for final scrutiny.

Web diagrams

The web diagram can take the portfolio chart described above and expand it from just two dimensions to include any number of dimensions. However, the application is less suited to the classification of individual projects, and more to the project landscape as a whole (Rietsch, 2015).

First, criteria groups are formed. These may arise, for example, from the company strategy, but they might also reflect operational aspects, such as the project planning risk. Examples can include increasing productivity, digitalization, internationalization, and so forth. These form the dimensions (the main axes) of the web diagram and need to be prioritized with a target score, for example on a Likert scale from 1 (less important) to 5 (very important). A target line (shown as bold in the example in Figure 29.8), with corresponding priorities, is then drawn.

Evaluating projects using the scorecard quantifies their contributions to the criteria groups (see Chapter 26). The total score indicates the contribution of the project landscape as a whole to the respective strategies (the total line Σ in Figure 29.2) and other criteria groups. These values are now inserted into the web diagram (grey line), resulting in an image as shown in Figure 29.8.

The impact of balancing the portfolio in this fictitious example is clear: digitalization and increased productivity are not yet adequately covered, although there is too much value placed on (for example) the project risks and return in investment (ROI) for existing projects.

Dependency and synergy matrices

Dependency and synergy matrices are used for the systematic identification and documentation of causal relationships between projects within the project landscape.

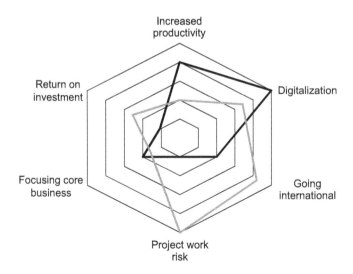

Figure 29.8 Web chart for portfolio alignment

Projects	A	B	C	D	E	F	G	H	Σ
Project A		0	1	0	1	1	0	0	3
Project B	0		0	0	0	0	1	0	1
Project C	0	1		1	1	1	1	0	5
Project D	1	1	0		0	0	0	0	2
Project E	0	0		1		0	0	1	3
Project F	0	1	0	0	1		0	1	3
Project G	0	0	0	0	0	0		0	0
Project H	0	1	0	0	0	0	0		1
Σ	1	4	2	2	3	2	2	2	18

Figure 29.9 Schematic representation of a dependency matrix

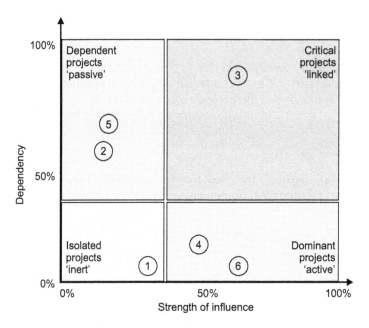

Figure 29.10 Visualization of interactions

They serve to identify conflicts as well as the possibilities for meaningful bundling of projects, even to the point of establishing programmes. The context 'Project A affects Project B' is plotted, usually from the vertical to the horizontal axis of the matrix (Figure 29.9 and also see DIN 69909-3 – DIN, 2015a).

By converting the identified context into a Likert scale, the totals across the rows or columns of the matrix can indicate the extent to which either Project A is dependent on other projects (column total) or the project affects other projects as a whole (row total). Row and column totals, when multiplied, give an important indication of the interconnectedness and integration of Project A into the project landscape. The higher the value, the more interconnected the project (in which case, the values are normed as necessary). This can be transferred to a portfolio chart for illustrative purposes (Figure 29.10). The projects can thus be classified according to their classification within the portfolio (see Kunz, 2007; Seidl, 2011):

- Dominant (active or determinant) projects are those that have a strong impact on other projects in the portfolio without themselves being affected to any significant extent;
- Critical projects have as much of an effect on other projects as they themselves are affected. They have very strong interactions with other projects;
- Dependent (reactive) projects depend very strongly on the results of other projects;
- Isolated projects are only marginally interlinked with others and can be run relatively independently.

Depending on the desired or required complexity of the evaluation, the strength of the dependency can also be expressed using a Likert scale, such as '1' for little influence to '5' for a great deal of influence. Furthermore, the relationship can also be typed to illustrate the type of dependency between the projects. Typical flavours are the use of shared technical systems (such as test environments) or other infrastructure, the need for the participation of the same employees (for example, IT developers with specific skills), or simply the application of Project A results in Project B (for example, outsourcing the redesign of an ERP system). Additional dimensions are then added to the dependency/synergy matrix (Figure 29.11).

As a result of its two-dimensional representation, the dependency/synergy matrix is basically very consistent in providing an overview, even in large project landscapes. It does not become more complex like web diagrams; instead, only additional rows and columns are added. It may be necessary to reduce the number of projects, clusters or subportfolios viewed at a time. For the reverse instance of viewing dependencies within a focused subportfolio (IT projects, for example) there are other more or less practical applications of dependency/synergy matrices (see, for example, Kunz, 2007).

Reviewing the portfolio configuration

As shown in Figure 29.12, however, alignment and optimization also include the structural configuration of the portfolio itself.

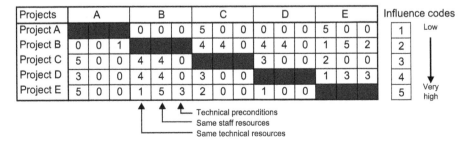

Projects	A			B			C			D			E		
Project A				0	0	0	5	0	0	0	0	0	5	0	0
Project B	0	0	1				4	4	0	4	4	0	1	5	2
Project C	5	0	0	4	4	0				3	0	0	2	0	0
Project D	3	0	0	4	4	0	3	0	0				1	3	3
Project E	5	0	0	1	5	3	2	0	0	1	0	0			

Influence codes

1	Low
2	
3	
4	
5	Very high

Technical preconditions
Same staff resources
Same technical resources

Figure 29.11 Typed dependency and synergy matrix

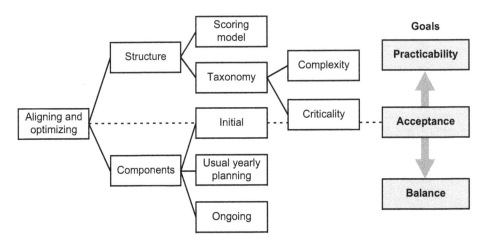

Figure 29.12 Purpose of aligning and optimizing the portfolio

Typical structural components of the portfolio are the scoring model, that is, the systematic evaluation of the projects by assessing and weighing various criteria. This also includes project taxonomy, the systematic classification of projects by such factors as size, project purpose, importance for the company, and so on.

Finally, the question turns to strategic buckets that define the strategic allocation of overall budgets to a specific type of project. Typical for this are buckets for IT projects or research and development (R&D) projects. (Note: ISO 21504:2015 describes other elements under 'Balancing and optimizing the portfolio' (ISO, 2015, Ch. 5.8) such as defining the evaluation system, or processes such as reviewing the benefits, risk management and resource management. These are treated in this handbook in the chapters of the same name. For this reason, they are not explained in further detail here. It goes without saying, of course, that the above aspects are part of the continuous improvement process of the portfolio and are also cyclical.

Continuous assessment of the portfolio benefit

Benefit reviewing

The criteria for portfolio inclusion are also used to assess the value of the portfolio. This primarily involves the quantitative and qualitative value contribution of the individual projects in relation to their costs and risks. This is typically shown in the corresponding scoring model.

Inherently, both the costs and the benefits are identified *a priori* initially based only on assumptions, which, however, make a substantial contribution to the decision on whether or not to pursue a project. As the project progresses, the uncertainty about these assumptions is reduced, because, for example, actual cost information becomes available that could change the cost–benefit ratio previously calculated. Projects originally accepted as feasible may, in some instances, prove otherwise.

However, strategic aspects can also be incorporated into a changed cost–benefit analysis. These include external developments that can potentially overwhelm long-term projects. This becomes acute when unexpected events occur – for example, a political upheaval that affects the regional market for a sales project.

A systematic and regular review of the continued applicability of the assumptions underlying cost–benefit calculations is therefore an important part of professional PPM.

Even where actual cost analyses and ongoing cost projections are continuously updated, the actual and projected benefits of a project often are not. This is largely due to the fact that the value actually achieved can be determined only *post facto*, because the benefits are often only clearly available once the project is complete (Seidl, 2011). In many cases, the only remaining option is to validate and possibly adjust the assumptions underlying the expected benefits.

Depending on the project requirements, however, the actual benefits realized can as well be measured relatively early, possibly while the project is in progress. The push for so-called quick wins or 'low-hanging fruit' (project results that can be achieved in the short term and implemented effectively together with the increasing use of incremental development as part of agile project management, such as sprints in scrum projects) allows the desired benefits to be achieved early – or at least the underlying foundations of the goals to firm up with the knowledge gained over time.

A *benefit review plan* is a tried and tested means for operationalizing the often non-trivial measurement of benefits achieved – refer to the PRINCE2-PM approach (AXELOS, 2009). It describes what benefits should be determined by whom, when, how and in relation to which reference parameters. The benefit assessment plan should be drawn up at the outset of the project because it provides significant support to the management of the project in question, in particular with regard to assessing proposed changes mid-stream. This important artefact of individual project management therefore also serves for the systematic and dynamic examination of expected benefits within PPM.

Change requests can affect the evolving expected usefulness of projects. (Note: at the time of writing this can be observed, for example, in constantly shifting plans for the Berlin–Brandenburg Airport. A constant flow of massive change requests has delayed completion and exploded the costs for this project exponentially.) It is therefore essential within the framework of PPM to monitor project development at the assignment level and evaluate what should happen with the help of a *change journal*. The change requests are systematically documented and traceable in this record.

A number of selected KPIs are used to provide an efficient evaluation of the structure and quality of the project portfolio. Some of these are presented below.

Portfolio-related KPIs

There is probably no perfect system of KPIs for portfolios; the objectives and framework conditions of PPM are simply too variable in practice. In literature and in multi-project management systems there is a series of more or less practicable KPIs, which are relevant through their explicit reference to the analysis balancing of project portfolios. These include the project's contribution to the organization's strategy and the portion of the strategy covered by the portfolio. There are also some special KPIs that, for example, consider the remaining time before projects are completed (Rietsch, 2015).

- SAI – strategic alignment index: this is used to measure the contribution of projects in the portfolio to the organizational strategy. The starting point is an evaluation matrix (as shown in Figure 29.2). Typically, the strategies are also prioritized and weighted. The row total quantifies the strategy contribution of the individual project, potentially normed to a maximum value in order to make them more comparable.
- BVI – NPV budget index: the budget value index (BVI) is the monetary counterpart to the SAI and represents the relative, purely financial contribution of a project. It is the quotient of the net present value (NPV) and the total cost of the project: BVI = NPV/total cost. The BVI thus represents the ratio of the NPV to the total project costs and balances one of the weaknesses of NPV analysis, namely the failure to take into account the amount invested, which is a key risk factor. Input variables, such as the discount rate, the term and cost rates, are generally provided by the company's finance department. As these variables have a decisive influence on the calculation of the NPV, they must be used carefully, transparently and uniformly. The BVI can be applied to both the total value of the portfolio and the individual projects themselves. A variant of the BVI puts the total development and operating costs and benefits in the denominator. Another variant does not put the (original) total project budget in the denominator, but instead uses the budget unspent at the reference date. This can provide a more valid, purely forward-looking view and it takes into account the sunk-cost effect. In general, the larger the BVI, the better the project assessment. The comparison of the BVI and SAI in a portfolio presentation (see Figure 29.5) provides a balance between monetary and qualitative strategic aspects.
- PPV – portfolio value: the PPV combines the SAI and the BVI: PPV = SAI × BVI. It thus expresses the total value of the project landscape, taking into account the monetary and the strategic benefits in relation to the total costs. Further indicators for the simple quantification of the state of the portfolio (see also Kütz, 2016) more methodologically related to the balancing and operational management of the portfolio are, however, portfolio structure and portfolio status, both of which are described in the following paragraphs.
- Portfolio structure – this includes, for example, KPIs such as the number of elements in the portfolio including project lifecycle status, the extent to which the portfolio budget has been spent, and the distribution of projects by project taxonomy (type, size, and so forth).
- Portfolio status – which includes, for example, key figures such as the number of projects in red, amber or green status, possibly differentiated by output, time or costs; the overall portfolio risk status; the number of change requests; and so on.

For more on KPIs, see Chapter 23.

Integration and establishment within the organization

Roles and organizational anchoring

The process of balancing and optimizing depends on the roles and committees defined during the configuration of the PPM system and their tasks, competencies and responsibilities (and it possibly enriches these further). The central process responsibility lies with the portfolio manager, whereas strategic accountability lies with the general manager (or is delegated to the project portfolio board). The portfolio manager is responsible for collecting and preparing the data for decision-making, whereas the portfolio board makes decisions or approves changes.

Integration into other management processes

Balancing and optimizing the portfolio cannot take place independently of the other relevant management processes within the company. This includes, in particular, the budget planning process (which is frequently done on an annual basis), but also processes such as controlling, direction setting and procurement, as well as creating and updating the company strategy (see Rietsch, 2015). Figure 29.13 presents one such process against the directly related processes of financial year planning and portfolio controlling. In particular, it is advisable to synchronize with the established processes of portfolio control, including the general reporting system within the PPM in order to ensure efficient data collection from the bottom up.

Risks and obstacles

The task of terminating unprofitable current projects ('dead horses') is a major cultural challenge in many organizations, often requiring courage. People and organizations alike are predisposed to the sunk cost bias, making them reluctant to cancel projects into which they have already put a lot of effort. Even the need to deprioritize can run into a number of problems.

Overly frequent changes to the PPM system (such as the evaluation criteria) can overtax the organization. So can constant shifts in the company strategy, which can certainly lead to disorientation. Therefore, sufficient long-term stability must be sought

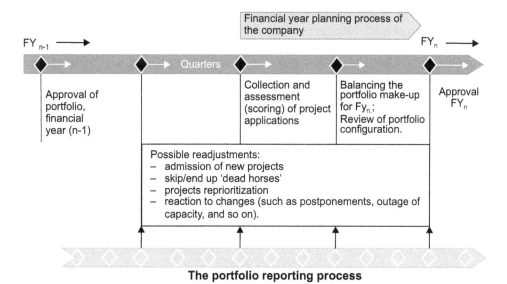

Figure 29.13 Process integration during the business financial year

and accepted. However, the system must, of course, be capable of correcting its mistakes such as incorrectly prioritizing projects.

Organizational lack of perseverance or willpower is another risk. Consistent application of the process, a systematic PDCA cycle as part of PPM, requires taking many a deep breath. Often PPM systems are introduced in emergency situations when projects fail. Even though they soon deliver good results, it can take some time for their full potential to develop – even several years and over several planning cycles. Especially when there are changes in the top management, there is often pressure to short-circuit a centralized PPM, primarily out of cost reasons, because its benefit is often only indirectly justifiable. The decisive factor here is the volume of the project landscape, its value contribution and the current resource situation within the company. The larger and more important the project landscape and the scarcer the resources, the more significant the PPM and its continuous optimization become.

Success factors

The process of balancing and optimizing the portfolio expresses a high degree of maturity in the PPM. Therefore the typical success factors include the following:

- Support by top management: top management needs to want and promote the process. They must embody the process themselves with consistency and not attempt to bypass it by wielding their own authority/competence.
- Integration into existing target setting, planning and budgeting processes: the need should be self-evident for the establishment of mechanisms that, for example, allow for changes during the year, even if they affect the (overall) budget. The right cycle needs to be found, but it will have to be specific to the organization because the framework conditions such as cyclical nature of other internal processes, the dynamics of the environment, the company's culture and flexibility, the criticality of the project for the organization, and so on, all need to be included.
- Up-to-date, correct, and complete input data: 'No valid input, no meaningful output.' In this sense, this success factor also applies to the process of balancing and optimizing. As, by definition, the process questions and re-evaluates existing decisions and systems, a valid foundation for decision-making must be established in order to achieve acceptance.

These success factors reflect the treatment of the risks and obstacles discussed above. In this sense, the following success factor is also worth mentioning:

- Creating the cultural prerequisites within the organization by establishing a corresponding change management system: target groups include top management, department managers and project leaders. A culture of readiness to change, willingness to move beyond long-term investment of time and energy and overcome the sunk cost bias, and acceptance of fallibility are important required factors.

Conclusion

The measures described in this chapter will ultimately lead to a changed project roadmap – to changed strategic project schedules (Figure 29.14). When revising

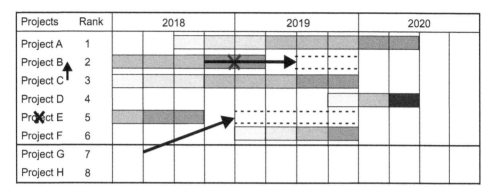

Figure 29.14 Impact on the project roadmap

the portfolio, the re-evaluation of each project may have consequences that can be divided into the following four groups (based on Kunz, 2007):

1. Continue the project: non-intervention, expansion or reduction of the project scope, as well as a budget increase or decrease;
2. Suspend the project: maintain the project framework, postpone project realization, suspend project implementation with the option of subsequent restoration. Project resources are released for other projects;
3. Terminate the project: leading to total cancellation with full release of project resources;
4. Initiate a new project: use the resources freed up to take a project not previously approved.

Figure 29.14 shows these measures schematically. It becomes clear once again that a consistent implementation of portfolio realignment requires a high level of management maturity within the organization. This conclusion is worthwhile and is becoming increasingly important.

The project landscape of a company is subject to the influence of the dynamics of the environment. The digitalization of processes within business and society plays a role here. This IT-driven development is moving at an incredibly fast pace (the first smartphone with touchscreen only appeared in 2007!) and this will also have an effect on the lifecycle of the project. These developments sometimes happen before complex projects can be completed. Non-linear dissemination effects through social media also accelerate the time-to-market requirements, for example for innovative products and services. These do not adhere to once-a-year business planning cycles.

Thus I conclude that there is an increased demand to react quickly and flexibly in the project landscape (agility) and for rapid-fire adaptation of portfolios. This requirement for agility is also reflected in the changing approach to project implementation and management. With origins in IT development, agile methods such as Scrum are increasingly finding their way into project landscapes (see Komus and Kuberg, 2005). There are increasingly bimodal multiproject situations that require adapted control mechanisms (Müller and Hüsselmann, 2017). Characteristic, in particular, is the principle of continuous benefit optimization (and achievement through incremental results) within projects, strict project management based on objectives and overall benefits, and requirement specifications that are not predefined. So there is a need to integrate classic, hybrid and agile project approaches into PPM.

References and further reading

AXELOS (2009), *Directing Successful Projects with PRINCE2*, Norwich: The Stationery Office.

Dammer, H. (2008), *Multiprojektmanagement*, Wiesbaden: Gabler-Verlag.

Deutsches Institut für Normung e.V. (2005) DIN EN ISO 9000:2005 (D/E/F), *Qualitätsmanagementsysteme – Grundlagen und Begriffe*, Berlin: DIN, Beuth Verlag.

Deutsches Institut für Normung e.V. (2013a) DIN 69909-1:2013: *Multiprojektmanagement – Management von Projektportfolios, Programmen und Projekten – Teil 1*, Grundlagen, Berlin: DIN, Beuth Verlag.

Deutsches Institut für Normung e.V. (2013b) DIN 69909-2:2013: *Multiprojektmanagement – Management von Projektportfolios, Programmen und Projekten – Teil 2*, Prozesse, Prozessmodell, Berlin: DIN, Beuth Verlag.

Deutsches Institut für Normung e.V. (2015a) DIN 69909-3:2015: *Multiprojektmanagement – Management von Projektportfolios, Programmen und Projekten – Teil 3*, Methoden, Berlin: DIN, Beuth Verlag.

Deutsches Institut für Normung e.V. (2015b) DIN 69909-4:2015: *Multiprojektmanagement – Management von Projektportfolios, Programmen und Projekten – Teil 4*, Rollen, Berlin: DIN, Beuth Verlag.

GPM and Gessler, M., eds (2012), *Kompetenzbasiertes Projektmanagement (PM3). Handbuch für die Projektarbeit, Qualifizierung und Zertifizierung*, 5th edn, Nürnberg: GPM Deutsche Gesellschaft für Projektmanagement e.V.

Hirzel, M., Kühn, F. and Wollmann, P., eds (2006), *Projektportfolio-Management. Strategisches und Operatives Multi-Projektmanagement in der Praxis*, Wiesbaden: Gabler Verlag.

Hüsselmann, C. and Seidl, J., eds (2015), *Multi-Projektmanagement. Herausforderungen und Best Practices*, Düsseldorf: Symposion Publishing.

International Organization for Standardization (2015), ISO 21504:2015(E) *Project, Programme and Portfolio Management — Guidance on portfolio management*, Geneva: ISO.

Kerzner, H. (2017), *Project Management: A Systems Approach to Planning, Scheduling, and Controlling*, 12th edn, Hoboken, NJ: Wiley.

Komus, A. und Kuberg, M. (2015), *Status Quo Agile. Studie zu Verbreitung und Nutzen agiler Methoden*, Nürnberg/Koblenz: GPM Deutsche Gesellschaft für Projektmanagement e.V. und Hochschule Koblenz.

Kunz, C. (2007), 'Strategisches Multiprojektmanagement', in: *Konzeption, Methoden und Strukturen*, 2nd edn, Wiesbaden: Deutscher Universitäts-Verlag.

Kütz, M. (2016), 'Projektportfoliosteuerung mit Kennzahlen', in: Wagner, R. (ed.), *Erfolgreiches Projektportfoliomanagement*, Düsseldorf: Symposion Publishing pp. 101–122

Lomnitz, G. (2004): *Multiprojektmanagement. Projekte erfolgreich planen, vernetzen und steuern*, 2th edn, Frankfurt am Maine: Redline Wirtschaft.

Müller, P. and Hüsselmann, C. (2017), 'Agilität im Projektportfoliomanagement. Auswirkungen und Potenziale agiler Methoden', *projektManagementaktuell*, 2, 57–66.

Office of Government Commerce (2008), *P3O: Portfolio, Programme and Project Offices*, Norwich: The Stationery Office.

Project Management Institute (2013), *The Standard for Portfolio Management*, Newton Square, PA: PMI.

Rietsch, J. (2015), *PMI Projektportfolio-Management*, Freiburg: Haufe.

Saaty, T. and Vargas, L. (2013), *Decision Making with the Analytic Network Process: Economic, Political, Social and Technological Applications with Benefits, Opportunities, Costs and Risks*, 2th edn, Pittsburgh, PA: Springer-Verlag.

Seidl, J. (2011), *Multiprojektmanagement. Übergreifende Steuerung von Mehrprojektsituationen durch Projektportfolio- und Programmmanagement*, Berlin/Heidelberg: Springer-Verlag.

Wagner, R., ed. (2016), *Erfolgreiches Projektportfoliomanagement*, Düsseldorf: Symposion Publishing.

Chapter 30

Portfolio-level benefits management

Stephen Jenner

Benefits can be defined as 'The measurable improvement from change which is perceived as positive by one or more stakeholders, and which contributes to organizational (including strategic) objectives' (Jenner, 2014).

Introduction

Benefits are realized from projects and programmes (putting aside the debate about whether projects deliver outputs and only programmes deliver outcomes that result in benefits). Therefore, one might legitimately ask why benefits need to be considered at the portfolio level. If we have chosen the initiatives that deliver the greatest strategic 'bang for our buck', surely all we need to do is monitor delivery against schedule and expenditure against budget to ensure that those forecast benefits and the anticipated return on investment are actually realized? The reality is, however, somewhat different and a portfolio perspective is crucial for three main reasons:

1. A portfolio-level approach to benefits management enables more effective investment appraisal and portfolio prioritization because the benefits included in cost–benefit analyses are categorized, quantified and valued in a consistent manner.
2. Research suggests that the track record of projects and programmes in realizing the benefits they were set up to deliver is not good – failure rates typically range from around 50 per cent to between 70 and 80 per cent. The Project Management Institute's (PMI, 2014) *Pulse of the Profession* report noted: 'Change initiatives are time consuming and costly, significantly impacting an organization's drive toward success. And nearly half of them fail.' Change management 'guru' John Kotter has a more pessimistic view: 'Up to 70% of change initiatives fail to deliver on the benefits that they set out to achieve' (quoted in www.apm.org.uk/sites/default/files/APM_BenefitsManagement.pdf). The root causes of this failure include factors such as the following:

   - Projects starting without a clear view on the benefits anticipated;
   - Overly optimistic forecasting;
   - Double counting of benefits where more than one initiative claims the same benefits;
   - In many cases benefits realization occurs after closure of the project; and
   - If benefits realization is not actively managed then potential value remains just that – potential.

3. As the Association for Project Management (APM) BoK states, the portfolio life cycle encompasses 'consistent portfolio-wide approaches to benefits management' (APM, 2014). Applying consistent approaches to benefits management is more efficient. It saves time and money. The benefits management process is then repeatable so individual initiatives don't waste time 're-inventing the wheel'.

The bottom line is that benefits, in terms of costs savings, revenue generation, risk reduction or some measurable contribution to the organization's strategic objectives, are the rationale for investment of taxpayers' or shareholders' funds in change initiatives. It is therefore crucial that we monitor and manage benefits realization at least as rigorously as we manage spending against budget and delivery against schedule.

However, despite the above, it appears that many organizations struggle to apply benefits management effectively at the portfolio level. Brian Hobbs, for example, identified 27 functions of multiproject project management offices (PMOs) and found that benefits management was third from bottom (Hobbs, 2006). Research in the UK and Australia found a generally low maturity level of portfolio management of projects and programmes – with benefits management being the lowest scoring area (Jenner and Byatt, 2011–12).

Why, if portfolio-level benefits management is so important, do so few do it well? The answer lies in three interconnected factors, as follows:

1. Benefits management is an emerging discipline and, as such, organizations often struggle to apply it to their projects and programmes. Research by the PMI and the Boston Consulting Group or BCG (2016) found that 'Interest is high but few are doing it well'. So it should not be surprising that organizations struggle to apply benefits management at the portfolio level.
2. Second, as Santiago says, 'Governance structures for portfolios, programs and projects in most organizations have been designed to execute projects and deliver outputs, not deliver benefits or business results' (see www.projecttimes.com/articles/why-is-benefits-management-so-hard-to-do.html). At its heart effective governance is about decision-making. But to make informed benefits-led decisions, portfolio governance bodies need reliable data – and this leads to the next (third) factor.
3. Informed decision-making at the portfolio level depends on accurate summary-level information. Progress against budget on individual initiatives can be measured and consolidated in financial terms to provide an overall portfolio-level view. Similarly, performance against schedule can be consolidated in terms of the time ahead or behind schedule, or the number of initiatives that are ahead or behind schedule. However, there is no standard metric for assessing and consolidating improvements in benefits such as risk reduction, customer experience, financial savings, staff engagement, and so forth. So obtaining a clear and consolidated view on benefits forecast and benefits realized to include in our portfolio dashboard can be problematic. Consequently there is a tendency to measure what is easy to measure rather than what is important.

Despite these obstacles, the most successful organizations have made significant progress in applying a portfolio-level benefits management approach. The key components of this approach are as follows:

- Governance with a benefits (rather than a delivery) focus. As the old management adage says, 'What gets measured gets done'. The focus of senior management's attention sends clear messages about what they regard as important;
- A disciplined approach to investment appraisal and portfolio prioritization that treats projects and programmes as *investments*, that is, we expect to see a return on investment where the benefits realized have a value (not necessarily financial) that exceeds the costs incurred;
- A focus on monitoring and managing continued strategic contributions and benefits realization across and beyond the project lifecycle, to ensure that performance matches the promise and that we learn from experience.

I now address each of these factors in turn.

Governance of benefits at portfolio level

Managing benefits effectively requires a shift from a delivery-centric culture, where the focus is on delivering capability to time, cost and quality standards, to a value-centric culture, where the primary focus is on realizing benefits.

(Change Management Institute or CMI, 2015)

Achieving this shift from a delivery to a benefits focus requires that portfolio governance bodies take an active and continued interest in benefits across (and beyond) the project lifecycle – including the following:

- The portfolio investment committee (or equivalent body) – the governance body that decides which initiatives should be included in the portfolio. Such decisions should be based on achieving the optimum strategic contribution (as determined by scale of benefits), subject to risk, from the available resources.
- The portfolio delivery committee (or equivalent body) – the governance body that monitors benefits realization against the portfolio benefits realization plan. This body takes appropriate corrective action to deal with emerging threats to benefits realization, and ensures that lessons learned are captured, disseminated and applied to improve the management of benefits.
- A PMO also has a key role to play in developing and managing the portfolio-wide benefits management processes, producing portfolio-level summaries of benefits realization, providing support to the governance bodies, and supporting change initiatives in their benefits management activities. Beyond this there is another crucial role that the PMO can play – that of a 'critical friend'. I wrote above that the track record of change initiatives in terms of benefits realization is not great. The causes include:
  - o Optimistic bias. According to Lovallo and Kahneman (2003), business case writers suffer from: 'Delusional optimism: we overemphasise projects' potential benefits and underestimate likely costs, spinning success scenarios while ignoring the possibility of mistakes.'
  - o Strategic misrepresentation. Flyvbjerg et al. (2005) define this as: 'The planned, systematic, deliberate misstatement of costs and benefits to get projects approved.'

One solution is the development of a benefits eligibility framework. I discuss this further below. Another solution is to subject benefits forecasts to rigorous challenge before investment – as Armor and Taylor say in Gilovich et al. (2002): 'the very awareness that one's predictions will be publicly tested motivates people to try to be more accurate when making predictions; people in this view, feel accountable to their own performance and then respond to this accountability by critically evaluating the basis of their predictions.' The PMO has a crucial role to play here in challenging the biases and self-interest that compromise effective portfolio investment management. Key questions to ask when reviewing project proposals include the following:

- What is the sponsor's track record in terms of benefits forecasting?
- What is the business case writer's record in terms of benefits forecasting?
- Have all potential benefits been identified?
- How confident are we that the benefits forecast will be realized?
- Could the required benefits be achieved by some other, more cost-effective, means?

One idea is to include a front page in all business case submissions comparing the cost–benefit result with the original forecast in the last three projects with which the sponsor and business case writer were involved. Do they have a track record of delivering on their commitments, or do costs tend to escalate and benefits decline – and, if so, by how much?

One cannot over-estimate the role of the PMO in developing portfolio-level benefits management. Indeed, Santiago (ibid.) argues: 'Success in this area can naturally position a PMO to evolve into an SMO or Strategy Management Office, focused on the execution of strategy, not just delivery of projects.' This mirrors John Thorp's concept of a value management office that provides a portfolio-wide, full business change lifecycle focus on benefits and value management – which, 'acts as an advocate of change in the organization in the way people think about value' (Thorp and Fujitsu's Consulting Centre for Strategic Leadership, 2003).

It is also important that responsibility for benefits realization is clearly assigned in all initiatives included within the portfolio. A good example of this is the formal appointment letters now being issued to senior responsible owners (SROs) in the UK Government's Major Projects Portfolio (see https://www.gov.uk/government/publications/cabinet-office-major-projects-appointment-letters-for-senior-responsible-owners). These letters refer explicitly to the SRO's responsibility for benefits realization and detail the steps they need to take in discharging this responsibility.

Although not part of the formal governance structure, consideration should also be given to establishing a benefits management forum that brings practitioners together from the strategic planning, change delivery and operational business areas, to share experiences and improve the planning and delivery of change. This can be an effective means of raising stakeholder commitment to, and engagement with, the development of portfolio-level benefits management.

One final point on governance – research for the US Federal Government concluded that: 'Large private organizations such as GE Global eXchange Services, Oracle and Lockheed Martin noted that having a governance structure that is well documented, effectively communicated, and understood throughout an organization is critical in implementing portfolio management' (Best Practices Committee of the Federal CIO Council, 2002). So, document the portfolio-level benefits governance structure in a *benefits management framework*, and ensure that all key stakeholders understand it. Just as most organizations will have a financial manual and chart of accounts (defining how the organization manages costs), so a benefits management framework should be prepared providing guidance on the benefits management practices applicable to all initiatives included within the portfolio.

Benefits-led investment management

Project benefits can be considered synonymous with positive strategic impacts.
(PMI, 2013)

As resources are limited it is crucial that we apply consistent, benefits-led approaches to investment appraisal and portfolio prioritization – to ensure that we invest in the change initiatives that optimize strategic contribution (as measured by the benefits realized) and return on investment. This is turn requires that we give consideration to the four factors described below.

1. Start gates to control setting up projects and programmes

Project success depends on many factors, but starting a project off on the right foot (project initiation) is clearly one of those factors. This includes being clear about the benefits that we are 'buying'. Do we understand what is required to ensure that those benefits will be realized?

2. Investment appraisal on the basis of attractiveness and achievability

Portfolio management is based on the concept of appraising potential investments on the basis of risk and return (where return equates to the balance between benefit and cost) in the context of the portfolio as a whole. Change initiatives should therefore be appraised on these twin dimensions, incorporating a benefits perspective:

- Assessments of 'attractiveness' (or return) need to demonstrate clearly the benefits to be realized and all the costs required to realize them;
- Assessment of 'achievability' (or risk) should extend beyond consideration of whether the initiative can be delivered on time and to budget, to an assessment of how likely it is that the benefits included under the 'attractiveness' heading will actually be realized.

Furthermore, both these dimensions relate to the incremental portfolio impact, that is, what benefits will be realized over and above those already planned from the portfolio, and how achievable are they given the demands of other initiatives?

3. Portfolio-wide benefits categories

Establishing expected benefits requires a systems view of the portfolio where each expected benefit is aligned with the vision and its contribution to the change purpose at the organizational level.

(PMI, 2013)

What this means is that a standard set of benefits categories is derived from the organization's strategic objectives which enable initiatives to demonstrate their strategic contribution in measurable terms. There are a number of approaches to achieve this including:

- Root cause modelling (the root causes of problems to be addressed are identified);
- Balanced scorecard (Kaplan and Norton, 1996), with KPIs under the four dimensions of: financial, customer, internal business process, and learning and growth; and
- Driver-based analysis.

Driver-based analysis identifies the factors that drive improvements in each element of the organization's business model. Driver-based analysis thus enables change initiatives to be designed to deliver improvements in the factors identified as influencing strategic success.

Another approach is to map benefits at the portfolio level. We start with the organization's strategic objectives and ask 'What measurable improvements would demonstrate achievement of, or progress towards, those objectives?' Commonly identified benefits categories include the following:

- Customer/user benefits (time saved, money saved, improved customer experience, less frustration);
- Improved output (service quantity and quality);
- Financial benefits (cost reduction and increased revenue); and
- Risk reduction (reduced exposure to the organization's strategic risks).

These benefits categories and subcategories are then used for all initiatives included within the portfolio.

4. Benefits eligibility guidance

In addition to the benefits categorization to be used, the benefits management framework should include guidance on which techniques should be used to forecast benefits. For example:

- Single point forecasts or three point forecasts (optimistic, pessimistic, most likely);
- Group expert judgement;
- Analogous or reference class forecasting – where forecasts of costs and benefits are derived from what actually occurred in a reference class of similar projects. This approach has been found to produce more accurate forecasts, by avoiding both the optimism bias and strategic misrepresentation identified above.

The guidance should also consider the issue of validation. I wrote at the beginning of this chapter that benefits are 'improvement from change, which is perceived as positive by one or more stakeholders'. So, wherever possible, quantified benefits should be validated or agreed with the stakeholder receiving the benefit. These benefits recipients can include the following:

- Financial benefits – the budget holder or finance director;
- Measurable contributions to strategic objectives – the relevant strategy owner;
- Increased output quantity or quality – the operations director;
- Risk reduction benefits – the relevant strategic risk owner; and
- User benefits – with the user by direct engagement, focus groups, and so on.

The question of benefits validation also includes the extent to which the benefits should be 'booked', that is, recorded in organizational performance targets, budgets, headcounts, and so forth.

Such guidance on benefits categorization and quantification has a number of significant advantages in that it:

- Enables change initiatives to be appraised on a consistent basis;
- Helps prevent double counting by enabling benefits to be consolidated across the various initiatives in the portfolio; and
- Facilitates tracking and reporting of benefits realization at portfolio level.

Monitoring and managing benefits realization

Successful execution of the change can only be measured through benefits realization.
(PMI 2013)

The objectives here are to ensure that the portfolio remains aligned with strategy, that potential benefits are actually realized, and that lessons learned are captured, disseminated and applied. This is facilitated by regular reviews of performance against a portfolio benefits realization plan using a portfolio benefits dashboard report, regular stage/phase reviews, periodic portfolio-level reviews and rigorous post-implementation reviews.

I deal with each of these in turn below, but one point should emphasized first. I regularly ask people on my training courses – 'What happens in your experience to costs and benefits over time on projects and programmes?' They almost always reply, 'Costs go up and benefits go down'. And then I say 'Why, surely if the forecasts on which we base our investment decisions are reliable, shouldn't the cost–benefit position improve as our knowledge grows and we mitigate risk and uncertainty – surely that's why we come to work: to make things better?'

A key objective of portfolio-level benefits management is therefore to embed the expectation that cost–benefit ratios should normally improve over time. But this will happen only if senior management clearly communicate that they expect this to occur, and if they follow this commitment up by checking to see that it actually happens in practice (see Fowler and Lock, 2006, for example). One example of this in practice comes from Dubai Customs, where a 'benefits quadrant' with a drill-down facility

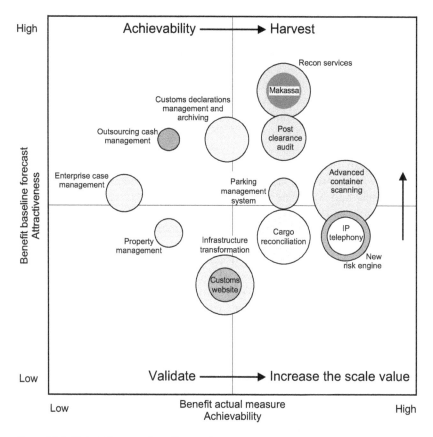

Figure 30.1 Dubai Customs benefits quadrant

to a benefits dashboard (encompassing a project benefits realization overview and a detailed benefit analysis) is used to maintain a benefits realization focus after project closure (see Figure 30.1).

Tracking performance using a benefits dashboard

The portfolio benefits dashboard report can be a stand-alone document or an integral part of the portfolio dashboard. It is used by the portfolio delivery committee to monitor progress against the portfolio benefits realization plan, which is designed to show the expected impact of the portfolio (including closed initiatives) on each of the portfolio benefits categories referred to above.

When I deal with executive briefing sessions, I say that within a matter of days (if not hours) I could find out how much money their organizations are spending on projects and programmes. But how many of them can answer the question 'What benefits will your organization realize in the next year from its accumulated investment in change?' So we know the costs (a constraint) but not the benefits (the rationale for our investment in change). I therefore recommend that they commission their PMOs to produce a portfolio benefits realization plan. In many cases the base data needed to complete such a plan will not be immediately available – but it's crucial that we start monitoring benefits immediately and (where necessary) leave the relevant sections on the plan and dashboard report blank. There will then be a very visible reminder that further action is required.

It was noted at the start of this chapter that one of the barriers to portfolio-level benefits management is the absence of a standard metric with which to consolidate initiative benefits data. There are a number of ways in which this can, at least partly, be addressed. These include the following:

- One option is to assign a monetary value to all benefits, financial and non-financial. This is the approach adopted by HM Treasury using econometric techniques such as willingness to pay and willingness to accept;
- A common approach is to track financial benefits in monetary terms and then use the RAG method (allocating red, amber or green ratings) to illustrate progress on non-financial benefits;
- Another approach is to use a normalized scale where a value of 1 is assigned if benefits realization matches plan, with the values proportionate to the level of realization. Values >1 indicate that realization exceeds plan. Values <1 apply where a benefit is below plan. Alternatively, the scale rating can be expressed as a percentage (where planned benefits = 100 per cent). Individual benefits can also be weighted to reflect their relative importance to the achievement of the initiative's investment objectives. Similarly individual initiatives can be weighted to reflect their relative importance to the organization's strategic objectives. In this way, a weighted benefits realization metric for each portfolio benefits category and for the portfolio as a whole can be calculated; and
- Rather than seeking to consolidate benefits data bottom-up, one can take a top-down approach – monitoring the impact of the portfolio as a whole on the standard benefits categories and/or KPIs linked to strategic objectives.

The above approaches are not mutually exclusive. They can be used in combination to provide a more informative view on benefits realization status. Commonly used portfolio-level benefits KPIs include:

- Benefits realization progress against a profiled plan (trajectory) for each category of benefit;
- Changes to the total forecast for each benefit category since the last report;
- Percentage of change initiatives with benefits realization ahead, on track or behind plan;
- Scale of emergent benefits identified by type; and
- Overall cost–benefit position.

Regular stage/phase-gate reviews

Regular stage-gate or-phase gate reviews should be undertaken on all initiatives included in the portfolio. These are undertaken by, or on behalf of, the portfolio governance bodies. They seek to ensure that the initiative remains the best use of available funds, considering changes in the environment in which the organization operates, current business priorities and the initiative's performance to date. From a benefits perspective the key questions to ask at such reviews include:

- Have required actions from the last review been completed and what actions are required before the next review?
- Have all significant benefits been identified?
- Is treatment of benefits consistent with the portfolio benefits management framework?
- What changes in benefits forecast and assessments of achievability have occurred since the last review?
- What progress has been made in realizing forecast benefits, have emergent or unplanned benefits been identified, and are disbenefits being effectively mitigated?
- Does the initiative still represent value for money?

Ideally, stage or phase gates should also be linked with the technique of 'staged release of funding'. Funding for change initiatives should be released only on passing each stage/phase gate, and should be limited to the funds required to take the initiative through to the next review. In this way initiative funding can be linked to regular confirmation that the benefits will be realized and that they continue to represent value for money.

Portfolio-level reviews

Although stage/phase gates occur at the initiative level, there should also be portfolio-level reviews at least annually. These will be undertaken by the portfolio investment committee and:

- assess the portfolio performance as a whole;
- the continued balance of the organization's portfolio;
- seek to ensure that the allocation of resources continues to represent the optimum return from available funds and other constrained resources, in the context of current strategic objectives, business priorities and initiative performance.

From a benefits perspective, the questions include:

- Has there been any change in the strategic objectives to which benefits from initiatives in the portfolio contribute?
- Are the benefits forecasts used to inform investment appraisal and portfolio prioritization accurate?
- Does performance in terms of benefits realization at least match that included in the portfolio benefits realization plan?
- What emergent benefits have been identified, and can these be further exploited?
- Are disbenefits being effectively mitigated?
- Does performance confirm or disconfirm the assumptions underpinning the business model?
- What lessons have been learned in relation to benefits management and is any action required?

Rigorous post-implementation reviews

The requirement to undertake post-implementation reviews (PIRs), to compare the out-turn cost–benefit position with that originally forecast, is a standard feature of most project management methodologies. Yet research consistently finds that PIRs are poorly done. A key feature of portfolio-level benefits management is ensuring that such reviews do take place and, at least, seek to answer the following questions:

1. Have adequate handover arrangements been agreed to ensure appropriate owner-ship of benefits management activity after initiative closure?
2. How did the initiative perform in terms of outcome against original forecast for budget, schedule and the benefits realized? (These data can then be added to the organization's reference class database and be used to improve forecasting accuracy.)
3. What improvements to the benefits management practices have been identified? Where appropriate the benefits management framework should be revised.
4. What lessons have been learned in relation to the assumptions underpinning the organization's driver-based business model?

The focus is therefore very much forward looking, emphasizing the applications of lessons learned as part of a cycle of continuous improvement.

Conclusion

The benefits of a portfolio approach include, 'increased realization of forecast benefits and the identification and realization of unplanned benefits to create additional value' (APM, 2012). Given that realization of benefits is the rationale for investments in change, a portfolio-level approach to benefits management is of fundamental impor-tance in:

- Ensuring limited resources and funds are allocated to those initiatives that collec-tively offer the greatest strategic contribution;
- Maintaining that contribution in response to organizational and environmental change, and initiative performance;
- Ensuring good practice is repeatable across all initiatives in the portfolio; and
- Optimizing the realization of benefits, both planned and emergent.

Fundamentally this is about ensuring that we lay the foundations for continuous improvement, based on realism in forecasting, with a commitment to ensuring that benefits realization and value for money are optimized in practice.

References and further reading

Association for Project Management (2012), *Body of Knowledge*, 6th edn, Princes Risborough: APM.

Best Practices Committee of the Federal CIO Council (2002), *Summary of First Practices and Lessons Learned in Information Technology Portfolio Management*, March, Federal CIO Council.

Change Management Institute or CMI (2015), *The Effective Change Manager's Handbook*, London: Kogan Page.

Flyvbjerg, B., Metter, K., Skamris, H. and Søren, L.B. (2005), 'How (in)accurate are demand forecasts in public works projects', *Journal of the American Planning Association*, 71(2).

Fowler, A. and Lock, D. (2006), *Accelerating Business and IT Change: Accelerating Project Delivery*, Aldershot: Gower.

Gilovich, T., Griffen, D. and Kahneman, D., eds (2002), *Heuristics and Biases: The Psychology of Intuitive Judgment*, Cambridge: Cambridge University Press.

Hobbs, B. (2006), *The Multiproject PMO: A Global Analysis of the Current State of Practice*, a white paper prepared for the Project Management Institute.

Jenner, S. and Byatt, G. (2011–12), 'Project portfolio management coming of age', *Project Manager*, December–January.

Jenner, S. (2014), *Managing Benefits*, London: The Stationery Office.

Kaplan, R.S. and Norton, D.P. (1996), *The Balanced Scorecard*, Boston, MA: Harvard Business School Press.

Lovallo, D. and Kahneman, D. (2003), 'Delusions of success – how optimism undermines executives' decisions', *Harvard Business Review*, July.

Project Management Institute (2013), *Managing Change in Organizations: A Practice Guide*, Newtown Square, PA: PMI.

Project Management Institute (2014), In depth report 'enabling organizational change through strategic initiatives', in: *Pulse of the Profession*, Newtown Square, PA: PMI.

Project Management Institute and the Boston Consulting Group (2016), *Connecting Business Strategy and Project Management*, PMI Thought Leadership Series, Newtown Square, PA: PMI.

Thorp, J. and Fujitsu Consulting's Centre for Strategic Leadership (2003), *The Information Paradox – Realizing the Business Benefits of Information Technology*, Whitby, ON: McGraw-Hill-Canada.

Chapter 31

Portfolio-level risk management

Martin Haberstroh

All projects are new ventures that contain an element of the unknown, and thus projects carry risk. Risks are usually regarded as damaging, but they can also be positive occurrences. From my point of view a focus just on complexity is too narrow – I have seen small projects with a very high risk for a company. In general the potential for risk becomes even greater when we consider project programmes and portfolios.

Introduction

Any project without at least the possibility of risks is almost unthinkable. Raz et al. (2002) state: 'With today's rapid dynamic change and increased competition, it is not enough to have a good plan, or even a proper monitoring and controlling system. Organizations have to be prepared for project risks and be ready to do something about them.' Therefore an 'early warning system' is clearly desirable which can detect potential incidents that could lead to negative (or positive) deviations from the project or portfolio goals. Risk management can be part of an 'early warning system', because it tries to capture early warning signs (Williams et al., 2012; Haji-Kazemi et al., 2013).

Risk management should improve project management because possible negative (or positive) incidents are detected earlier, allowing more time for improved decision-making, including the efficient implementation of steering activities (Haberstroh, 2007; Haji-Kazemi et al., 2013). The relevance of risk in projects is also reflected in project management research – Padalkar and Gopinath (2016) report that 39 studies have researched the topic.

In the first part of this chapter I describe the basic concepts of risk and risk management at the single project level and the portfolio level. Then, various approaches to risk management at the portfolio level are covered. In the final main section I summarize key results of empirical studies with regard to the success implications and contingencies of project portfolio management.

Basic concepts for risk management at portfolio level

The foundation: risk and risk management at the single project level

For the management of single projects, risks and risk management are elements in major international project management standards. Two typical definitions of the PMBoK (Project Management Institute or PMI, 2013a) and ICB (Individual Competence Baseline) 4.0 (International Project Management Association or IPMA,

2015) are shown in Figure 31.1. According to the PMBoK, a risk can have a positive or negative impact. According to ICB 4.0, risks have negative effects, but they are closely related to opportunities (positive effects). In both of these standards risk management is described as a stepwise approach for dealing with risks (and opportunities).

The degree of risk in a single project can depend on several factors (for example, the uniqueness of the project). Less experience has been gathered for unique or non-routine projects, which leads to higher uncertainty and resulting risks (Rohrschneider and Spang, 2009). Projects with very ambitious goals have higher risks than projects with less difficult goals. Furthermore, the outcomes of projects with longer durations are more difficult to predict compared with those with shorter durations and this leads to increased uncertainty. In the same way, larger projects (for example, with more funding and more project team members) are exposed to greater uncertainty

The basic concepts of risk and risk management at portfolio level

Often companies manage not only single projects but also a collection of projects. Therefore, a holistic view of risk management – portfolio-level risk management – has also been proposed. This level of risk management can also be found in major international project management standards (see Figure 31.2 for selected descriptions of risk and risk management at the portfolio level).

These descriptions are similar to the definitions at the single project level, but they are related to the portfolio level; the possible effects through interdependencies among projects and programmes are also mentioned. It is important to add that, compared

Single project risk

Source	Characteristics and definitions
PMI (2013a) page 310	Project risk is an uncertain event or condition, Which, if it occurs, has a positive or negative effect on one or more project objectives such as scope, schedule, cost and quality
IPMA (2015): ICB 4.0 page 141	Risk (negative effects) and opportunity (positive effects) are always viewed in their relation to and consequences for realizing the objectives of the project

Single project risk management

Source	Characteristics and definitions
PMI (2013a) page 310	Project risk management includes the processes of conducting risk management planning, identification, analysis, response planning and controlling risk on a project. The objectives of project risk management are to increase the likelihood and impact of positive events, and decrease the likelihood and impact of negative events in the project
IPMA (2015): ICB 4.0 page 141	Risk and opportunity includes the identification, assessment, response planning and implementation and control of risks and opportunities around projects. Risk and opportunity management helps decision-makers to make informed choices, prioritise actions and distinguish among alternative courses of action

Figure 31.1 Selected descriptions of risk and risk management at the single project level

Project portfolio risk

Source	Characteristics and definitions
PMI (2013b) page 119	Portfolio risk is an uncertain event or condition that, if it occurs, has a positive or negative effect on one or more project objectives. A risk may have one or more causes and, if it occurs, the corresponding effects may have a positive or negative impact on one or more portfolio success criteria
IPMA (2015): ICB 4.0 page 376	Risk (negative effects) and opportunity (positive effects) are always viewed in their relation to and consequences for realizing the objectives of the portfolio

Risk management at the project portfolio level

Source	Characteristics and definitions
PMI (2013b) page 119	Risk management is a structured process for assessing and analyzing portfolio risks with the goal of capitalizing on the potential opportunities and mitigating those events, activities and circumstances which can adversely impact the portfolio. Risk management is critical where interdependencies exist between high-priority portfolio components, where the cost of portfolio failure is significant or when risks from one portfolio raise the risks in another portfolio component
IPMA (2015): ICB 4.0 page 141	Risk and opportunity includes the identification, assessment, response planning and implementation and control of risks and opportunities around projects, programmes and portfolios. Risk and opportunity management helps decision-makers to make informed choices, prioritise actions and distinguish among alternative courses of action
ISO 21504 (2015) page 12	To manage portfolio risk, the portfolio manager should use the defined risk policy for the portfolio to: (a) determine the level and tolerance of risk that is acceptable within the portfolio; (b) develop or adapt an analysis technique for risks held at the portfolio level; (c) identify risks at the portfolio level based on identified risks for each portfolio component; (d) analyse and prioritize the portfolio risks considering such items as priority of strategic objectives, goals, benefits and the relationships among components; (e) evaluate the risks over time including changes that should be monitored for risk impact and changes in portfolio composition

Figure 31.2 Selected descriptions of risk and risk management at the project portfolio level

with the risk management of single projects, risk and risk management at the portfolio level are more strategic (Olsson, 2007). If negative risks occur they become issues. If positive risks are not realized, they will be missed opportunities (PMI, 2013b).

In relation to the organization in which a project portfolio is situated, it is possible to distinguish between internal and external sources of project portfolio risk (PMI, 2013b). Internal sources of risk can be 'management decisions, bankruptcy, corruption, lack of integrity, shifting priorities, funding reallocation, and corporate/organizational realignments' (PMI, 2013b, p. 122). External sources of risk can be 'competitors, the competitive market, the financial market, political events, legal requirements, natural events, technological advances, environmental concerns, regulatory requirements, and globalization pressures' (PMI, 2013b, p. 121).

Risks can occur at project, programme, portfolio and organization levels. According to the PMI, risk management at the portfolio level is crucial 'where interdependencies

Possible effects	Difficulties
Supports prioritization of resources (for example alignment and redistribution) among projects	Low consciousness of portfolio risks and of the need to view risks holistically
Considers additional portfolio risks	Challenge to evaluate risks at the portfolio level
Transparency regarding problem transferences among projects	Is time-consuming and involves costs: do the benefits justify the costs?
Identify risks that emerge in multiple projects simultaneously	Portfolio managers may lack expertise and time, or have a problem of cost justification
Information for improved decision-making (including planning and coordination)	Pressing tasks/issues often have higher priority than risks ('reactive approach')
Enhances the capacity to cope with risks	Is rarely implemented: are existing methods good enough?
Improved identification and handling of early warning signs	
Greater visibility to senior management	
Improved risk (and opportunity) management within the organization	

Figure 31.3 Advantages and difficulties of project portfolio management

exist between high-priority portfolio components, where the cost of component failure is significant, or when risks of one portfolio component increase the risks in another portfolio component' (PMI, 2013b, p. 17). Components of a project portfolio can be projects, programmes or other work. Clearly those responsible for the portfolio should have their focus on portfolio risks, whereas risks at the other levels should be handled by the respective responsible people.

The possible positive effects and the difficulties of portfolio-level risk management are summarized in Figure 31.3. The positive effects can be achieved if portfolio-level risk management lives up to its promise. With regard to the difficulties, portfolio-level risk management seems to require that people working in the project portfolio should have current, high-quality risk information. Obtaining this risk information can create a lot of work for an organization. I should add that people in projects (particularly the 'top experts') often have many pressing tasks and issues to deal with and it can be difficult to motivate them to identify risks or potential issues. This is most probably also the case at the portfolio level. Therefore, portfolio risk management must deliver on the possible positive effects (not only the negative issues) to establish its 'proactive approach'.

Approaches for portfolio-level risk management

Risk–reward relationship for project portfolio management

At the project portfolio level, the 'classic' risk–reward relationship is important and is often mentioned in the literature (for example, Cooper et al., 2001; Shenhar and Dvir, 2007; Cooper, 2011; Patzak and Rattay, 2014; Hab and Wagner, 2017). According to financial portfolio theory, high rewards are usually associated with higher risks.

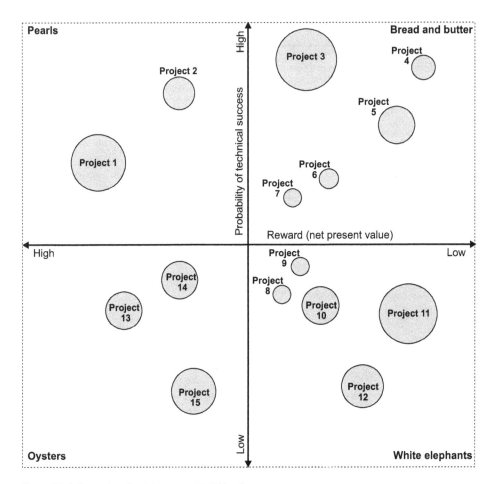

Figure 31.4 Example of a risk–reward bubble diagram.

AS projects can be interpreted as investments, this might also be the case for projects. There is empirical evidence concerning new product development projects that many companies have too many small and routine projects in their project portfolios. They do not have enough higher-risk projects with the potential for breakthroughs that could enable future profitability and growth. In other words, companies neglect the future with their tendency to pick too many small and routine projects in their portfolios (Cooper, 2011). Therefore, portfolio-level risk management is helpful in creating transparency about the risk–reward profile for the overall portfolio (improving decision-making to reach a well-balanced project portfolio). There is no best risk–reward profile. The risk profile chosen depends on the company's strategy (see Figure 31.4 for an example of a risk–reward bubble diagram).

Another example with which to analyse the risk–reward relationship is the approach from Shenhar and Dvir (2007). To assess the overall risk and benefit of an entire project these writers suggest the following four dimensions:

1. Novelty (market uncertainty);
2. Technological uncertainty;
3. Complexity;
4. Pace.

Projects scoring high on these four dimensions are riskier than projects scoring low. The scoring for each of these four dimensions could be from 1 (low) to 4 (high). For aggregation, Shenhar and Dvir (2007) suggest using a weighted average, which allows different weights for different dimensions. Each of these dimensions has specific benefits and opportunities as well as potential risks or difficulties. Projects with high novelty (market uncertainty) might have innovative ideas, and address new markets and new customers. The potential downside is that customer needs are wrongly assessed and market opportunities missed. Projects with high complexity may have benefits if the scope of the business is based on size. If complex projects falter or fail, they lead to substantial losses. Complexity may lead to coordination and integration difficulties during the whole project duration.

High technological uncertainty can lead to improved performance (of products or processes, for example) and new uses of technology. The potential risks or difficulties are technical failures or the lack of technical skills of the people involved. Working at a high pace might result in a timing advantage, but speed could also lead to the risk of errors, which themselves could cause the risk of delays. The scores in these four dimensions can be aggregated to receive the overall benefit and opportunity and the risk or difficulty for each project (ibid.). Of course, alternative approaches for calculating the benefits for a single project include financial figures (for example, the project's net present value). Regarding the risk calculation, Shenhar and Dvir (ibid.) suggest the following as typical weightings:

- 0.2 for risk of market uncertainty (higher than for technology or pace);
- 0.15 for technological uncertainty;
- 0.5 for complexity (higher expenses compared with the other risks might be possible); and
- 0.15 for pace.

To explain how this works, here is an example. The project to develop the first Segway had a very high novelty for the market (rated at 3), a very high technological uncertainty owing to significant new product engineering required (again rated at 3), and medium complexity and pace (both rated at 2). This would lead to the following calculation (ibid.):

Overall risk $= (0.2 \times 3 + 0.15 \times 3 + 0.5 \times 2 + 0.15 \times 2) = 2.35$

When the overall benefits and opportunities and the overall risk or difficulty for all single projects have been calculated, all the single projects (and other portfolio components) in a project portfolio can be positioned in a matrix (Figure 31.5). According to this type of risk–reward relationship, Shenhar and Dvir (ibid.) suggest that during project selection a project could be immediately approved or rejected, although some

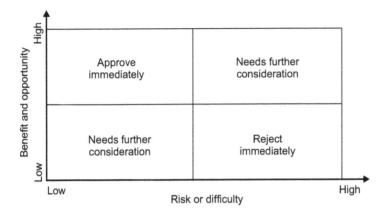

Figure 31.5 Risk and benefit matrix

projects would need more detailed analysis. The overall company strategy should be considered when making the right decisions about the appropriate reward–risk profile of the project portfolio. Further examples of risk–reward diagrams can be found in Cooper et al. (2001 – see pp. 74ff.).

Further approaches for risk management at the portfolio level

Further methods, techniques, graphic analytical methods and so on can be found in PMI's *Standard for Portfolio Management* in the section about portfolio risk management (PMI, 2013b). These include the following:

- A typical probability impact matrix for portfolio level risks;
- A portfolio risk register with a list of identified risks, the risk owners, a list of potential responses, a probability impact assessment, risk triggers and an update of the risk categories; and
- A risk component chart, showing in a table for a specific risk how many of the portfolio components (projects, programmes and other work) are influenced.

Olsson (2007) has described a methodology for risk management in a multiproject environment that requires the following three steps:

1. Analysing project issues between projects;
2. Analysing project issues with all the projects' risk data (repeat for all projects);
3. Including risk data from all projects in the analysis.

This method is a bottom-up approach, mainly based on specific, operational risks from single-project risk management. In particular, steps 2 and 3 of this method require significant information processing (Figure 31.6).

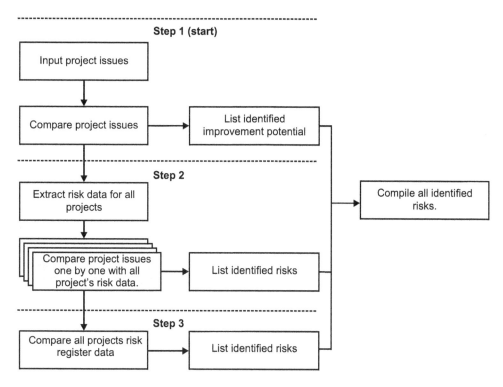

Figure 31.6 General approach for risk management in a multiproject environment

Key results of empirical studies

Empirical studies by Teller and Kock (2013) and Teller et al. (2014) have made a significant contribution to the understanding of the success implications and the contingencies of portfolio-level risk management. Their results are based on the same sample of over 175 project portfolios, which manage at least 20 projects concurrently. The principal results and implications of these two studies are summarized in this section. In addition, relevant results of the research on early warning signs and its relationship to risk management are described.

According to Teller and Kock (2013) management quality at the project portfolio level can be described by two dimensions: risk transparency and risk-coping capacity. Risk transparency includes the identification of all relevant risks, understanding their influence on the goals and the inclusion of risks in decision-making. Risk-coping capacity describes the possibility to react to risks and their sources quickly. These two dimensions have a positive influence on project portfolio success. Furthermore, this study points to the importance of an open and frank risk management culture, and to the importance of a formalized risk management process.

Teller et al. (2014) find that risk management at the single project level and the project portfolio level are highly interrelated. Risk management at the single project level increases the success of project portfolios. Furthermore, risk management at the single project level delivers necessary inputs to describe the portfolio-level risk. Therefore, risk management at the single project level should be implemented to improve the success of a portfolio. With regard to risk, successful management at the single project level is the foundation for successful portfolio-level project management. Risk management at both levels is highly beneficial.

Another result of this study is that portfolio-level risk management is not 'one size fits all'. Companies should tailor risk management to their own needs. Risk management at the single project level is more important in research and development (R&D)-dominated project portfolios. The recognition of risk information at the portfolio level is more important for dynamic project portfolios within environments with high external turbulence (Teller et al., 2014).

In addition, current research on early warning signs in projects has to be mentioned, because of its relevance for risk management at the project and the portfolio levels. Risk management is one approach to detecting early warning signs for projects and portfolios (Williams et al., 2012; Haji-Kazemi et al., 2013). The results of Williams et al. (2012) are based on 14 interviews and Haji-Kazemi et al. (2013) have reviewed the academic literature. Early warning signs can be defined as 'an observation, signal, message, or some form of communication, that is or can be seen as an expression, indication, proof, or sign of the existence of some future or incipient positive or negative issue. It is a signal, an omen, or an indication of future developments' (Williams et al., 2012, p. 38, based on Nikander, 2002).

Risk management is clearly related to early warning signs and to the approach on how to handle them. Regarding the *strengths* of a risk analysis as a source for early warning signs Haji-Kazemi et al. (2013, p. 65) state that it is: 'easy to perform the underlying analysis because it is a structured method; everyone can contribute; generally little need for collecting additional data.' With regard to the *weaknesses* of a risk analysis as a source for early warning signs Haji-Kazemi et al. (ibid., p. 65) state, that: 'Quality of the analysis outcome is dependent on the selection and insights of the participants; propensity to focus on concrete; often technical risks and overlook less tangible issue; danger of not updating the analysis to capture dynamics of risk issues.' This is important, because in complex projects informal 'gut feeling' is an important source for early warning signs (Williams et al., 2012). Therefore, it seems necessary that approaches to risk management at the portfolio level should try to include informal 'gut feeling'.

Conclusion and comments

Risk and risk management at the portfolio level are clearly established in international project management standards. Current research has provided evidence that risk management at the portfolio level can have a positive influence on project portfolio success. There are concepts, methods, tools, and so on, that are available for risk management at the portfolio level. Nevertheless, owing to the need to have tailored risk management practices at the portfolio level, the current available concepts, methods and tools for risk management do not seem to be sufficient. In addition, the difficulties in implementing risk management practices at the portfolio level are significant. More development is needed to reach a higher maturity level. To live up to its promise, risk management at the single project level and the portfolio level must deliver original, high-quality information as early warning sings, which leads to improved decision-making, including the efficient implementation of steering activities.

With regard to the future improvement of portfolio-level risk management, the difficulties with the establishment of risk management mentioned should be considered (see Figure 31.6). As project portfolio management is more strategic, the field of strategic management could be helpful for future improvement. Furthermore, my experience is that risk management is often an 'add-on' to scope, time or cost management. Maybe this is an efficient way to establish risk management in a project world in which everyone is pushed to do more with less. In addition, I would like to raise the question of whether or not it is useful to separate risk management from issue (or problem) management. It seems to be difficult for many people to distinguish between issues (current problems) and risks (potential problems). There might be also differences in perceptions. This may lead to classification discussions with questionable added value for projects and project portfolios. In the end, it is not relevant if a topic is a risk or a problem. The key point is whether or not a topic results in improved decision-making, including the efficient implementation of steering activities.

It should be mentioned that there are approaches for dealing with uncertainty other than risk management, including experienced staff and flat hierarchy (summarized by Teller et al., 2014) and 'enhanced flexibility and rapid decision-making . . . , such as reflective learning or simultaneously pursuing various candidate solutions' (ibid., p. 77).

References and further reading

Cooper, R.G. (2011), *Winning at New Products: Creating Value through Innovation*, 4th edn, New York: Basic Books.

Cooper, R.G., Scott, E.J. and Kleinschmidt, E.J. (2001), *Portfolio Management for New Products*, 2nd edn, New York: Basic Books, pp. 71ff.

Hab, G. and Wagner, R. (2017), *Projektmanagement in der Automobilindustrie*, 5th edn, Wiesbaden: Gabler.

Haberstroh, M. (2007), *Individuelle Selbstführung in Projektteams*, Wiesbaden: Deutscher Universitäts-Verlag.

Haji-Kazemi, S., Andersen, B. and Krane, H.P. (2013), 'A review of possible approaches for detecting early warning signs in projects,' *Project Management Journal*, 44(5), 55–69.

International Project Management Association (IPMA) (2015), *Individual Competence Baseline for Project, Programme and Portfolio Management*, Version 4.0 (electronic document), Amsterdam: IPMA

International Organization for Standardization or ISO (2015), ISO 21504 *Project, Programme and Portfolio Management – Guidance on portfolio management*, Geneva: ISO.

Nikander, I.O. (2002), 'Early warnings: a phenomenon in project management', doctoral dissertation, Espoo, Finland, Helsinki University of Technology.

Olsson, R. (2008), 'Risk management in a multi-project environment: an approach to manage portfolio risks', *International Journal of Quality & Reliability Management*, 25(1), 60–71.

Padalkar, M. and Gopinath, S. (2016), 'Six decades of project management research: Thematic trends and future opportunities', *International Journal of Project Management*, 34(7), 1305–1321.

Patzak, G. and Rattay, G. (2014), *Projektmanagement – Projekte, Projektportfolios, Programme und projektorientierte Unternehmen*, 6th edn, Vienna: Linde.

Project Management Institute (2013a), *A Guide to the Project Management Body of Knowledge (PMBOK Guide)*, 5th edn, Newtown Square, PA: PMI.

Project Management Institute (2013b), *The Standard for Portfolio Management*, 3rd edn, Newton Square, PA: PMI.

Raz, T., Shenhar, A. and Dvir, D. (2002), 'Risk management, project success, and technological uncertainty', *R&D Management*, 32(2), 101–109

Rohrschneider, U. and Spang, K. (2009), '1.04 Risiken und Chancen', in: Gessler, M. (ed.), *Kompetenzbasiertes Projektmanagement (PM3): Handbuch für die Projektarbeit*, Nuremberg: GPM Deutsche Gesellschaft für Projektmanagement, pp. 183–246.

Shenhar, A. and Dvir, D. (2007), *Reinventing Project Management: The diamond approach to successful growth and innovation*, Boston, MA: Harvard Business School Press.

Teller, J. and Kock, A. (2013), 'An empirical investigation on how portfolio risk management influences project portfolio success', *International Journal of Project Management*, 31(6), 817–829.

Teller, J., Kock, A. and Gemünden, H.G. (2014), 'Risk management in project portfolio is more than managing project risks: A contingency perspective on risk management', *Project Management Journal*, 45(4), 67–80.

Williams, T., Klakegg, O.J., Walker, D.H.T., Bjørn, A. and Magnussen, O.M. (2012), 'Identifying and acting on early warning signs in complex projects', *Project Management Journal*, 43(2), 37–53.

Chapter 32

Managing resources at portfolio level

Alan Summerfield

Effective deployment of an organization's resources lies at the heart of portfolio management. Clearly, without appropriate resources no organization can fulfil its initiatives for change and achieve the desired contribution to its strategic intentions. Resource management is thus a vital component in successful portfolio management.

Introduction

Although people are clearly a vital resource, we need to be clear that portfolio resources extend to other components such as cash, plant, machinery, land, support, and so on. These other resources are critical, because they are often more finite and less flexible to deploy than people.

An important part of portfolio management is about balancing changing the business with running the business. This requires judgements to balance the use of resources committed to change activities against the impact on resources used in routine operations and back office functions. Furthermore, portfolio management needs to consider resource requirements beyond the boundaries of its own organization, including the supply chain, sales agents, and so forth.

Effective resource management plays a critical role in best practice portfolio management and can bring huge rewards through more efficient resource utilization. It does so by ensuring the following:

- All parts of the organization develop their resource requirements to a consistent standard and quality as part of their business plans, and keep those requirements up to date through effective change control;
- Resources are allocated to initiatives which are aligned with the strategic objectives, and hence the strategy of the organization;
- An analysis of resource supply and demand is maintained, and actions are put in place to fill any gap between the two;
- Capabilities of the staff (and the supply chain where appropriate) are developed to optimize their potential, and close the gap between supply and demand.

By these means we ensure that resources are effectively and dynamically managed and deployed. Also, we make certain that resources are kept under constant review, redirecting them as necessary when programmes and projects do not deliver or are no longer making a sufficient strategic contribution.

In all organizations, some or all of the resources available to make change happen are limited, whether in the form of finance and cash flow, skilled people, office space, technology, facilities, support, or the capacity of the operational business to take on board and deliver benefit from a change (we ignore the latter at our peril).

Definition of portfolio resources

Portfolio resources could be defined as all those resources required to deliver the totality of change initiatives that make up the portfolio or subportfolio of the organization. Although determined organization by organization according to their needs, those resources could be seen as follows:

- People with various skills and competences;
- Technical facilities;
- Buildings and systems;
- Support services such as financial, information technology, human resources and facilities management; an
- The financial resources necessary to fund all the portfolio initiatives.

We need to define clearly the categories of portfolio resources that have to be identified, estimated and controlled in our particular organization and its environment. We must not ignore the resources required for 'business-as-usual' work, where the staff will be expected to adopt and assimilate the changes.

Definition and description of portfolio resource management

In every organization the resources available to support change projects and programmes are limited to a greater or lesser extent. Portfolio resource management has the following main components:

- Through estimates and forecasts, create an understanding of the resources required for the proposed portfolio and its component initiatives;
- Assessing the resources that are available, or that can be made available, from inside and (if necessary) outside the organization;
- At the same time understand the resources that are actually available both inside and outside the organization to fulfil the portfolio requirements;
- After the above assessments, and throughout the life of the portfolio, taking actions required to manage the gap between supply and demand, and ensure that the planned portfolio is always effectively resourced.

The objectives of portfolio resource management

Every organization will most probably face limitations and constraints on the resources that can be made available for the range of projects and programmes that make up its total portfolio. Portfolio resource management provides mechanisms that allow us to schedule initiatives more effectively, using available resources in a more efficient way. That results in fewer bottlenecks, smoothing out of peaks and troughs in resource requirements, less wasted time and fewer unachievable requirements for the scarcest of resources. This will lead to more effective and efficient delivery of projects and programmes, and therefore as a consequence more optimal realization of anticipated benefits at both portfolio and strategic levels.

Dimensions of resource usage

The use of resources has several dimensions. The assignment of each resource to portfolio tasks should reflect the portfolio priorities, focusing and prioritizing the deployment of resources on the most strategically important issues. The effect of change on resources used for day-to-day operations has to be considered carefully, because, if there is too much change taking place at the same time, people usually react badly to change overload. The reallocation of resources after changes should lead to improved utilization but may also result in surplus resources.

How effectively and holistically diverse resources are managed varies immensely from organization to organization. In some it is simply the scarcest resources that are monitored and managed. In other organizations, all required and deployed resources are understood and controlled. In other cases, little attention is paid to resource management (even across large and complex portfolios), leaving individual managers to plan and resolve resource requirements on an individual basis. This last approach can clearly be suboptimal for the organization as a whole, leading to delays and bottlenecks for individual parts of the portfolio.

Without a clear and accurate understanding of the resource requirements of all categories needed to deliver the portfolio goals and benefits successfully, it is difficult to comprehend how organizations can truly and effectively assess the relative merits of different initiatives. Indeed, how they can assess the value for money of any individual initiative if they do not understand its true cost? Resource management enables us answer these questions.

Without this clear and accurate understanding of the organization's total claim on resources, we cannot be in a position to ensure that all managers get the resources they need for successful delivery.

Effective management of resources across the portfolio will enable us to understand the resource requirements and the related availability of internal and external resources. Then we shall be better able to manage the gap between demand and supply. In addition, by having that clear and consistent overall understanding, the leadership can sign up to the portfolio strategy and enable planning, through an understanding of its content and capacity, to deliver the strategic aims and objectives of the organization. At the same time the leadership can sign up to providing the resources required to deliver the initiatives. As a consequence, those leading and managing individual projects and programmes within the portfolio should feel the benefit of being adequately resourced to meet their objectives.

If we identify and manage the business-as-usual resources required to deliver change initiatives from a portfolio, we should realize improvements in the delivery of those anticipated benefits as we assess and manage transitions and mobilizations, to ensure that the level and timing of business change is optimized for the business operational areas subjected to the change. We should see the consequences of better deployment of resources, with higher resource utilization, and with resources being allocated where they can deliver the greatest good for the organization and its strategic objectives.

We should also see an improved balance in the timing of initiatives, with planning at portfolio level taking account of resource requirements. Effective scheduling can minimize the peaks and troughs of resource requirements, and thus reduce bottlenecks and conflicting demands for resources across the portfolio.

Benefits of effective resource management at the portfolio level

Effective portfolio resource management has its own rewards. Some key benefits could be seen as:

- A reduction in costly peaks and troughs occurring for scarce and constrained resources;
- Better utilization of the available resources;
- Improved forecasting and procurement of external resources, bringing consequential savings and availability of necessary skills when required;
- More accurate planning of cash flow requirements, enabling enhanced financial management for the organization as a whole;
- Fewer risks and issues related to a lack of specific resources at key points during the portfolio lifecycle, and hence fewer delays and consequential costs.

All of the above should lead to more optimal delivery of the forecast portfolio benefits.

What needs to be done to achieve effective portfolio resource management?

We need to put mechanisms in place in order to get a clear and realistic picture of resource requirements as part of the initial stages of projects and programmes. Then we must review and update the forecast requirements on a regular basis. An effective change control system is an essential element in maintaining this watch on resources. At the same time we need to understand and check regularly on the availability of resources, looking at both internal and externally contracted resources. At the portfolio level we must then review any gap between the resources required and the resources that are available. Clearly actions must be taken to remedy any potential resource overloads. I now list 10 steps that are necessary for the effective development and deployment of resource management across the portfolio.

Step 1: as part of the portfolio framework, develop a resource management framework, including guidance on how the portfolio and its constituent initiatives will identify, monitor and manage resource requirements and deployment. This should mandate the need for resource requirements to be clearly estimated and articulated in the business case or investment proposal for any initiative.

Step 2: organize a series of briefing sessions to raise awareness of the resource management framework across the portfolio, programme and project management community (PPF), clarifying the importance of resource management, explaining what is required and what forms of assistance will be available. This education should be supported by documenting the appropriate responsibilities of the relevant roles in the PPF.

Step 3: implement consistent approaches to resource identification and estimating, giving guidance to relevant managers on what resources need to be considered, what techniques to use, what reference data and evidence they should use to contribute to their estimates, what techniques should be used to improve the integrity of those estimates, and in what templates or format the estimates should be provided to portfolio level management.

Step 4: identify the most critical resources required by initiatives and ensure that their control is given high priority.

Step 5: understand the availability of resources of all categories across the organization, together, and develop an understanding of the availability of those resources in the outside market place.

Step 6: aggregate information covering the demand for resources derived from the resource requirements identified in the business cases or investment proposals, and the information relating to both internal and external resource availability into a portfolio resource plan. This plan should be based on a timeline that reflects the portfolio delivery plan.

Step 7: undertake continuous analysis of the gap between supply and demand on a day-by-day basis, and manage the requirements through effective scheduling of in-house resources (including cash flow, people, technology or support, procurement of external resources). This rescheduling should attempt to shift the timing of tasks in the portfolio plan where necessary to level resource usage demands as far as possible (minimizing any peaks and troughs in demands for specific resources). Any such rescheduling should always be carried out with regard to task priorities, so that the strategic objectives of the portfolio are satisfied.

Step 8: implement and maintain effective change control so that unauthorized changes will not lead to unexpected demands on resources and scope creep. This should cover all areas of activity in the organization, including the portfolio, programmes, projects and business-as-usual areas that would be affected by changes.

Step 9: track and report progress against the portfolio resource plan on a regular basis through the regular portfolio reporting mechanisms.

Step 10: implement regular post-implementation resource reviews to assess and seek 'lessons learned' improvement in resource management at all organizational and work levels.

Role of an enterprise portfolio management office in resource management

Where an enterprise portfolio management office (EPMO) exists, it will often include the role of resource manager or resource specialist. Typically, such a role can support the portfolio manager and change director in the following ways:

- Through aggregation of the resource requirements defined in the business cases of each initiative, identify what resources are required across all of the organization's defined categories over the period defined in the portfolio plan;
- As part of balancing the supply and demand for resources, contribute to the development of the portfolio plan in the area of resource scheduling and, where

appropriate, take action to put forward options for reducing peaks and troughs in requirements for specific resources;

- Ensure that the portfolio's supply and demand for specific resources is maintained under change control, and that the leadership is kept aware of associated risks and issues;
- Where appropriate, support the organization in the procurement of specific resources, following corporate procurement guidelines and using framework agreements as needed;
- Develop and maintain the portfolio resource management framework including associated guidelines, process, tools and techniques for resource estimating. Support programme and project managers in their understanding and application of this, through training and facilitation;
- Undertake assurance reviews of resource management across individual programmes and projects.

Where the role of portfolio resource manager does not exist, much of the above may fall to the portfolio manager. Wherever the specific responsibilities sit, there needs to be (as with all elements of portfolio management) close collaboration and engagement on a continuing basis, with many other functions that may need to be engaged in this work. These other functions might include, for example, the following:

- Human resources management (HRM);
- Line management for people;
- Assets management for plant, buildings, machinery, and so on;
- Commercial teams connected with the supply chain;
- Financial management (particularly for cash flow);
- Sales and marketing departments or agents.

Resource scheduling

Resource scheduling at the portfolio level typically focuses on the dynamics of supply and demand, very often simply for scarce resources. Hence it encompasses what many would describe as capacity planning. At this portfolio level we should, however, also be concerned to ensure that initiatives in the form of projects and programmes within our portfolio are themselves effectively and consistently scheduling their resources, following the guidelines and using the tools, which have been defined at portfolio level.

If the portfolio management function is not provided with resource estimates and requirements that it can trust, and in a consistent manner and format, then its ability to balance the portfolio from this perspective will be severely limited. Its ability to ensure provision of resources when required, and to manage the risks and issues related to logistical dependencies will also be reduced.

There needs to be a structured approach with clarity of planning horizons. So, to what level of detail do we schedule resources against what timelines? If the horizon is too short we could fail to anticipate and make adequate resource provision for our change initiatives. Conversely, if the horizon is too long we could waste resources in planning for initiatives whose requirements will change.

Resource planning

To ensure consistency of estimated resource requirements from individual initiatives (which is essential for our ability to balance, schedule and provide resources from a portfolio perspective), we shall need to give programme and project managers clear guidance on the tools, techniques and templates to be used, and the process to be followed. All of this should be documented in the resource management framework within the portfolio framework.

In a format suited to the individual organization, using tools specified by the framework, individual initiatives will need to develop the types of skills required across the various activities and the products they need to create. All planning should be based on a work breakdown structure. Each part of the overall plan must specify the people skills (and the number of such people) needed for every task and produce the products, identifying the key responsibilities for each role. When this has been done for every task, the use of an approved scheduling tool will result in plans that can be formulated and printed.

The overall schedule should include planning the technology and tools, their specifications where appropriate, and volumes and timescales of this equipment against the timeline. Where there are significant consumables and materials to be used in the initiative, then those requirements also need to be planned against the timeline.

Individual initiatives (having created their resource plans) should each develop a strategy that explains how they intend to set about delivering to that plan, incorporating their procurement intentions, and so on.

The plan should give clarity through a detailed schedule for the anticipated use of all resources, which should include internal resources such as HRM, information technology (IT), financial management (FM), procurement, audit and any other required resource that needs to be signed off as part of the business case.

Resource balancing

Resource balancing can be truly effective only where our understanding of requirements across all resource categories is clear and consistent, and the estimates can be trusted. In addition, if it is to be more than a snapshot and a one-off balancing act, then it needs to be an understanding that is maintained on a continuing basis, and under strict change control.

For the provision of support from internal suppliers – such as procurement, technology, facilities management, finance, HR, communications, and so forth – the requirements should be explicit, and clearly articulated in business cases after agreement with supplier departments.

This applies equally to resources required as inputs from business-as-usual teams that are perhaps the subjects of the change. They might need to supply resources to activities such as the following:

- Design;
- Feasibility;
- Specification;

- Recruitment;
- Testing and training during the project or programme lifecycle.

They might need to provide resources in the form of senior users in projects, business change managers in programmes, or members of change teams or project and programme boards.

In order to provide the resources required to balance supply and demand, we do need to manage the resource requirements implied in the programme and projects in the portfolio pipeline. To do this we need to consider the capability development of our own people to give them the skills and competencies that initiatives in the pipeline indicate we will need in the planned future. This must involve understanding future requirements, gaining clarity of the current skills and competencies of our people, and supporting the development and delivery of personal development plans that meet the needs of the organization and the individuals.

We should look at the gaps in our future requirements that are best met by recruitment of new staff with new skills, or the recruitment of new staff to provide a larger volume of existing skills. We should apply this approach to other resource categories to include consideration of procurement of new internal resources (such as technology) where required to meet future needs.

We should look at the skills currently being provided by external contractors and service providers, and determine which of those could be better delivered internally, and ensure skills development and knowledge transfer that meet those needs.

Conversely, we need to consider which resources would best be provided by external sources. These could include, for example, support services such as IT, facilities management, design, construction, and so forth, or individuals with specific skills such as programme managers, project managers, analysts, planners, subject matter experts, assurance specialists, and so on. We need to understand the external market place, and ensure that the resources we shall need are actually available in the outside market – and at a cost that will allow our initiatives to remain viable and worthwhile.

In order to ensure procurement of our required resources in the most effective and compliant manner for the portfolio and its component programmes and projects, we need to ensure that the procurement frameworks in place for our organization reflect the good practice required to support procurement across the portfolio. There must be clear accountability throughout the procurement process, enabling a fair and competitive approach across all categories. The procurement framework should ensure the following:

- We meet the commercial and regulatory requirements set on the organization in a balanced manner, appropriate to the procurement requirement;
- The procurement processes are carried out as cost-effectively as possible;
- Potential suppliers are treated as even-handedly as possible, but ensuring the avoidance of corruption or collusion with suppliers or others.

Where appropriate, we should consider the development of framework agreements with suppliers (and on occasions with groups of suppliers) for resources that we anticipate needing across the portfolio over a period of time. This framework should allow for an orderly and managed draw-down of resources from suppliers, to previously tendered and negotiated price arrangements, and to previously agreed standards, roles and responsibilities, and terms of reference. All of this should remove the potential for weeks or even months of delays incurred in each initiative for the procurement of key resources, once projects and programmes start to develop.

From the outset of the development of external tendering, we should ensure that the suppliers (where appropriate) are clear on the elements of our portfolio framework with which they need to be compliant. Also, they need to be clear about how elements such as resource management (as well as monitoring and reporting, financial management, risk management, change control, organizational governance, benefits management and stakeholder management) need to be undertaken. All this is necessary if we are to retain control over our portfolio.

Conclusion

Here is a short list of key success factors for effective portfolio resource management:

- Develop a resource management framework, reflecting best practice and the needs of the specific organization, as part of the portfolio management framework;
- Ensure that the leadership sign up to the fact that, if they include initiatives in their portfolio, they are committing to the provision of the resources required to deliver the required outcomes and benefits, and at the same time accepting the impact on operations and those resource implications;
- Educate the project portfolio management community in the organizational approach to resource management, and put in place checks as part of the overall integrated assurance regime;
- Keep the balance of supply and demand for defined resources under continual review, and manage the consequential risks and issues that emerge.

Eventually we hope to see organizations in which portfolio resource management is not simply a reactive response to the resource demands of projects and programmes, but where the future deployment of resources is understood, planned and scheduled on a routine basis and under firm change control. This will contribute to the delivery of the optimal outcomes, benefits and strategic objectives of the organization.

Chapter 33

Portfolio-level change management

Michael Horlebein

This chapter deals with portfolios that consist of change components only. Portfolio management is the appropriate instrument during these critical phases, where companies have to master change programmes affecting large parts of their organizations. Fast and successful execution is very important because these activities have to run in parallel with the main business of the organization. I provide an insight into which methods of portfolio management will be successful and which aspects need special attention or focus. Typical areas of conflicts and how to deal with these are explained on the basis of a post-merger integration process.

Introduction

When companies want to implement their strategy supported by portfolio management, in most cases (when the company is not small) they will structure their complete portfolio into separate subportfolios. These subportfolios will mostly be independent from each other with regard to resources, budgets, and so on. To underline this, consider a company that is structured into a few divisions, each with its own profit and loss accounts. There will be at least one portfolio per division that is managed separately from the other divisions. But when we talk about a portfolio of *change* components, then in most cases those change components will influence all divisions at the same time. This portfolio is not independent from the other portfolios. It behaves like an umbrella that runs in parallel with all other portfolios of the different divisions and impacts them accordingly.

Before going further, I need to define some of the terms used in this chapter.

Change portfolio

ISO 21504:2015(E) (International Organization for Standardization or ISO, 2015) defines a portfolio as a collection of portfolio components grouped together to facilitate their management to meet, in whole or in part, an organization's strategic objectives. When all portfolio components are related to change, then we speak about a *change* portfolio.

Components in a change portfolio

According to ISO 21504:2015(E) (ISO, 2015) we understand portfolio component as 'project, programme, portfolio, or other related work'. In a change portfolio all components are related to make a change of organizations and their way of interaction. Although the classic project management approach focuses on the 'quality of the solution', change management focuses on the 'acceptance of the solution' within the organization (see Rothermel, 2015 and also visit www.lamarsh.com/about/successful-change-management.

To realize these components successfully we should not separate these two aspects, so both of them are part of a change portfolio. To underline this statement, what helps in a case where we have defined a new process or introduced new software but the whole organization is not using them and still works in the old mode of operation? I come back to this idea when I discuss the case of a post-merger integration and the corresponding portfolio components.

Change projects

In this chapter I define change projects as projects that aim to change organizations and their way of interaction, both within the organization and with the outside world.

Some useful methods in project portfolio management

Now I want to take a closer look at some of the methods used in portfolio management. I have chosen a selection of three from all possible portfolio management methods. These may differ from the methods we use for 'classic portfolios' (that is, portfolios without change components).

Identifying and selecting portfolio components

It is crucial to consider and select the 'right' portfolio components because, in this case, portfolio management has not only to consider the fulfilment of the strategy, but also to project those components that will be adopted rapidly in the organization and create the expected benefits. We should not forget that in change projects speed is king. The time of the transition from the current state to the desired state (see *Managed Change*[TM] – Rothermel, 2015) must be as short as possible.

Prioritization of portfolio components

Depending on the progress and success of the different portfolio components seen during their implementation, it might be necessary to change the prioritization of those components. I take a closer look later at the order and prioritization of a change portfolio in my post-merger integration use case. We must keep a very careful eye on the organization, identify the needs and the group dynamic processes, and be able to revise the prioritization whenever that is necessary and beneficial for our goals.

Resource management

Large parts of the organization will be affected by the realization of change components, even though only a smaller part is directly involved in change projects as team members. So there is always an impact on other portfolios because the change portfolio will compete for resources within the whole company. This has to be considered and managed carefully. To illustrate this I use the following example.

Consider a company that wants to introduce a new information technology (IT) system, which is to be used for customer relationship management. The directly involved team members are mainly subject matter experts from different departments who will define the new process to be supported by the IT system. But once the IT system has been configured and in place, all parts of the organization that are involved in the customer relationship management will have to adapt to this process and the new system. For all of them their way of interworking will change and they will all have to be trained on the new system. So everyone needs to be involved at an early stage to give them the opportunity to understand what is changing for them. It might be the interfaces between departments, but also their tasks and responsibilities may change radically.

This has to be considered when planning the resources in the organization. It is helpful to assign a certain percentage of all those employees who will be affected by change projects or programmes. Everyone who will be impacted by the change needs to set aside a portion of his or her time to effect the change.

Specifics of a change portfolio

When components of a change portfolio are realized, many emotions such as discomfort or fear will lead to a resistance that needs to be managed very carefully. In this case slogans such as 'Never change a running system' are not helpful and of course it takes a lot of effort to bring a change into the organization. But when the change is implemented it should pay off very soon – otherwise you should consider whether introducing this change was wise and necessary.

It is possible that the organization might have had bad experiences in the past with regard to change programmes or change projects. In this case there could well be unwillingness from the staff to begin and put effort into a new change programme in case of another flop. And isn't it easy to badmouth a new change project just to hide the internal resistance for the current activities behind historical data? We should note that, when change projects are being implemented, one can expect the following initial staff reactions:

- Roughly a quarter of the staff will be easy to convince;
- Another quarter will not want to change at all; and
- Half of the employees will be undecided.

To attain speed we need to identify the influencers and use them as multiplicators, so that they will pull the other groups in the right direction. What must not happen is to allow the quarter who would like to block the change to gain the lead and convince the undecided half to be against the change project. If we allowed this to happen it would be even more difficult to get everybody back to a change mode. So what to do?

To avoid this risk at an early stage it is essential that everyone in the organization who is affected understands why the change is necessary and what is in it for them. There can be no generic answer for all employees because they will all be impacted in different ways. To avoid confusion, motivation at the top level must of course be specific and clear. That high level of motivation needs to be shared by the different departments, groups and people within an organization. The more clearly this is formulated the easier it will be understood by the employees. For a convincing story line it is necessary to provide a detailed description of the desired state because people will move more easily when knowing how the future will look like. The better you can project a picture in everyone's minds, the easier they will adapt and move. They also need to understand how they can measure when the goals of the change project have been reached. (This motivational approach is described in detail in Fowler and Lock, 2006).

Even when people have accepted the solution, they must be given a proper chance to become trained and accept the outcome because it affects them personally. So the training part must be considered very well and the change programme managers must ensure that sufficient effort is put into the training programme.

Typical areas of conflict

During the implementation of change-related projects we have to deal with areas of conflict, and solve these in a constructive manner. Of course there is no standard solution, but I now take a closer look at some potential problems areas and discuss how to deal with them.

High information needs of the employees versus little available information from management

This is a classic conflict. On the one hand, the employees feel that they are not sufficiently informed and, on the other, the management is reluctant to give information because there is still much that is unclear and not yet decided. Best practice is to share as much information as possible as soon as possible. For decisions that have yet to be made, the employees should be told when those decisions will be taken, and when they can expect to receive the required information. Then, management must stick to the promises made.

It does no harm if you give the available information whenever there is a chance to do so, even when you think you are repeating it too often. There is a useful rule of thumb here: when you think you have shared the information so many times (say more than five times), then there is a good chance that the major parts of your organization have received the information and got the idea.

Scope of business versus internal change projects

While we work on a change project, the organization should still be focused on its real scope of business. No company can tell its customers that they will have to wait to be contacted again until the change project (for example, a reorganization) is finalized. It is essential to balance times and resources so that the fundamental tasks that need to be done during the change process from the current state to the final desired state do not interfere or block the normal business. In most cases it is beneficial to have dedicated resources (which might be external, internal or a mix of both working full time on the change activities). Of course the transition from old to new must be made by each and every involved individual, but the preparations (process definitions, training, concept for the introduction, communication concepts, and so on) should be done by a dedicated and experienced change team.

'Best of two worlds' solution versus existing solution from one of the companies

Especially in post-merger integration processes, there is a specific area of conflict. When two companies with different ways of working merge, their different processes, tools, products, and so on, will have to be aligned to reach the planned and necessary benefits.

For an alignment of the product portfolio there are different options. The two different product ranges may complement each other or one of the existing products will be discontinued. For each product developed in the future, ideas or parts from both companies may lead into this joint and new product.

When we have a closer look at processes, there are two possible options. Either one of the existing processes of one of the two companies will be used, or there will be a joint definition of a new process (the 'best of two worlds'). In terms of acceptance of a solution, the latter is the better choice because both companies will then have the opportunity to bring in their ideas and identify themselves with the new process. But, when there is a management decision to use a process from one of the 'old' companies, there will always be criticism from the employees of the company whose process was not chosen. They will complain that the non-efficient process won because the management of the other company negotiated it better.

In reality there will always be both options. The better choice is to define jointly the new way of working. This takes more time for the definition, but the speed of acceptance in the new company will be faster than a top-down decision because both parties are involved in the definition.

Atmosphere of departure versus apocalyptic sentiment

Change projects may not always influence the organizational setup of a company but will at least affect the distribution of tasks within several groups.

Some people will see big chances in the new way of working and for personal opportunities to grow, whereas other groups within the company may see no future for themselves and struggle to be receptive to something new, or dislike the possibility of handing over responsibilities or tasks to someone else. All this can be influenced by bad experiences from the past.

It is beneficial when all, or at least most, assigned individuals who are directly involved in the realization of the change project (subject matter experts and management) are positive with regard to the change because they will have to convince all other parts of the organization.

Case example of post-merger integration

This case example shows how a merger and acquisitions process can be completed successfully, joining two different companies. Both of the companies, in this case, had a large overlap in their product portfolio and distribution. But there were also other complementary areas. The products were distributed and installed worldwide. The sales contacts and fulfilments of the service contracts were mainly performed by their local companies.

Once the merger had been announced, consider what happened in the mind of the employees of both companies? All of a sudden both organizations were no longer competitors and now must share their knowledge. But the employees of both companies had become accustomed to their established processes and specific ways of working. They understood their respective product portfolios and knew how to sell, use or maintain them. To realize the expected synergies, all of this had to be aligned for the future.

Of course all employees were aware that a big change was coming (heralding, for example, organizational restructuring, change in place of work, different working methods and practices, changes in personal status, loss of management position or even redundancy). One effect was that the whole organization risked becoming paralysed because all employees immediately lost their 'sense of belonging'. When we consider the team syntax (SySt® – see Ferrari, 2013) we see that 'belonging' is the first and most important principle for teams. If this 'belonging' is unclear, it will have the biggest negative impact on teams and their performance. To give a concrete example: when during a restructuring project of a team with ten employees the decision is taken to retrench three employees, then the 'belonging' of all ten employees is lost until such time when it becomes clear who will have to leave the company. During the transition period none of the ten employees knows whether or not he or she is still part of the department. So it is very important to make the selection very fast, so as to restore the 'belonging' to this department and begin the 'healing process'.

The board of directors assigned to the merged company wanted to start the post-merger integration process as soon as possible. Therefore a portfolio manager had to be assigned at an early phase. When we talk about the decisions of the portfolio manager, we must understand that this is a simplification because these are not just the portfolio manager's decisions: they are decisions that also represent the decisions of the board of directors. Whatever personal decision power the portfolio manager might have been appointed for generally, that power is not relevant for this case.

Returning to the case study, the identification and selection of portfolio components were done in several workshops, involving the management teams of both companies. They were supported by experts of post-merger integration projects, and a change portfolio was identified. Let us assume that the assigned and experienced portfolio manager noted the components in Figure 33.1 for his change portfolio. (Note: this is only an excerpt from the real case but it shows some of the main activities to be considered.)

When we take a look at these components we can see that some elements may not be recognized as components of a change portfolio. For example, the component 'Consolidation and definition of future product and services portfolio' seems to be rather technical. But there was a big emotional impact associated with this component because many of the employees 'grew up' with their products – products that were part of the value chain before and are now in a tough benchmark against the products of the former competitor. This is why I added it here because remember that, in a change portfolio, we do not want to separate the 'quality of the solution' aspect from the 'acceptance of the solution' aspect.

Fast implementation of the above portfolio components was essential because, during the post-merger transition phase, both companies continued to work in their

Communication	Explain to the inside and outside world why the merger was done
	Develop a communication plan (internally and externally to customers)
Organizational setup	Develop an organizational blueprint
	Transfer of all employees to the new organization
	Consolidation of locations
Processes	Definition of future processes, methods and tools
	Responsibilities of departments and departmental interfaces
Products	Consolidation and definition of future products and services portfolio
Values	Definition of future company culture and values

Figure 33.1 Typical components in a post-merger integration portfolio

old manner. For the new setup of the merged company, unified and lean processes were the basis for smart interaction and success.

After selection of portfolio components, the portfolio manager started to prioritize the components in his portfolio. It was essential that the correct sequence of components be determined and maintained.

The components referred to under the communication heading already started before closing of a mergers and acquisition process, because in some instances preliminary information (whatever is possible and lawful) has to be given to customers, media and employees of both companies.

During this time, an explanation of the 'why' of the merger had to be compiled. So parts of these components were already running before the post-merger integration process began.

So now, what is the next priority in this portfolio? When we refer to the first principle in the team syntax (which was belonging), we understand that the most essential part is the setup of the new organizational structure of the new company. So this was the first priority of the change portfolio – thus, the portfolio manager had to focus on this immediately. Now all managers and employees of the two organizations had to be transferred to a new organization. So first the blueprint of the organization had to be clear and the managers had to be appointed at the first level, then the second level managers, and so on.

Note that for bigger mergers it is best practice when all employees know the timing for the appointments of the different levels of management. The employees (non-managers) will be mapped into the different departments of the blueprint. Only when all of this has been concluded will the 'belonging' become clear and the most important principle for teams will be fulfilled.

In the case example reported here, although the portfolio manager balanced, in the first phase of the post-merger integration, the portfolio between 'communication' components in his portfolio and 'organizational setup' components in the second phase, he started with the other components in his portfolio. At this point the mapping of people into the new organization had been done and so the planned responsibilities of the different departments were defined at a high level.

The next focus was to start the components related to 'process'. Only then could the portfolio manager find the right team members for the definition of the new processes and update his matrix of resources in his portfolio.

In the next stage the portfolio manager focused on the 'products' components of his portfolio. As explained above, he had to consider the two streams when implementing this component: technical and emotional streams. The decisions on the future product portfolio could have gone hand in hand with the component 'organizational setup: consolidation of locations'. However, in reporting this actual case I do not elaborate further on this portfolio component.

One specific area of conflict that we can see (especially in post-merger integration projects) is between the different cultures of the two merging companies. Each company has its own history and stands for a specific culture, behaviours and defined company values. But how should they behave now? How can we manage that they are open for a new company culture and new values?

A good practice is when representatives from both companies are interviewed separately in this context and as an outcome the results of the interviews are illustrated in two separate drawings. Each drawing represents one company. To be more comprehensible these may include some key words. These drawings will be an eye opener and can be discussed in mixed groups from the two old organizations to understand what culture and behaviours the old companies represented in the past. Providing this visibility helps everyone to understand the other company culture in a better way. This helps to bridge the time until a new culture and new values have been defined, which can be done at a later stage of operation in the new company. Best practice therefore is to build a team consisting of management and people who have an ear into the organization and appreciate what values they might be hearing. The top-down ideas from management and the bottom-up ideas can then be merged into a new set of values supported by all.

I leave this actual case at this point and trust that the portfolio manager managed all the remaining components in his list, leaving the new company to look forward into a bright future.

Conclusion

In this chapter I considered a change portfolio and elaborated on the following three processes:

1. Identification and selection of portfolio components;
2. Prioritization of components;
3. Resource management.

Components of a change portfolio show certain specific features that have to be considered wisely when implementing them. These are resistance in the organization and the fact that the explanation of the reasoning of the change is of utmost importance. Only when the organization understands what benefits the desired state offers can they move from the current state.

I took a closer look at typical areas of conflicts within a change portfolio and identified the following three as being very important:

1. The need of information versus available information;
2. Normal scope of business versus internal change projects;
3. Definition of a solution as either 'best of two worlds' or adoption of one existing solution.

All of these have to be balanced in the correct way and there is no 'one-size-fits-all' piece of advice or solution.

The case example of post-merger integration demonstrated that communication and organizational portfolio components should have the first priority, whereas decisions about the future portfolio or processes will follow. The extension on the definition of company values for the new company demonstrated that this can also be done at a later stage, when the foundation of the company has been laid down by the other portfolio components.

References and further reading

Ferrari, E. (2013), *Teamsyntax, Teamentwicklung und Teamführung nach SySt®*, Aachen: Ferrari-Media.

Fowler, A. and Lock, D. (2006), *Accelerating Business and IT Change: Transforming Project Delivery*, Aldershot: Gower.

International Organization for Standardization (2015), ISO 21504:2015(E) *Project, Programme and Portfolio Management – Guidance on portfolio management*, Geneva: ISO.

Rothermel, R. (2015), *Managed Change*™, Version 5.1, Chicago, IL: LaMarsh Global.

Chapter 34

Portfolio-level people management

John Chapman

This chapter is written from the perspective of a supplier organization that provides business solutions (financial management, document management, spend control, business intelligence and other similar systems) to external clients.

Introduction

A business solutions implementer brings to the table specialist skills in software delivery, knowledge about the different solutions and how to deliver them. These need to be aligned with the customer's team. For new project implementations such as a system replacement, the customer will not have the design skills in the product. Instead their expertise is in their own business, how it operates, what the weaknesses are and where the current systems are failing. Typically a requirements document will have been prepared stating what is needed from the new system (but not how to deliver it). Both customer and supplier want to achieve a successful project.

When each project is implemented, the customer needs to realize the return on the money, time and resources invested. In other words, post-project reviews should show that the financial and non-financial objectives were delivered successfully.

The supplier also needs to run a profitable project, from which a case history will result that can help to retain the client for future business and also win new business. But a successful, established supplier will also be running other projects for multiple customers – a portfolio of projects that seeks to maximize the use of the supplier's resources (foremost among which are the people deployed in the project teams). For the supplier this ideally means running with little or no time lost through having no bookings in the diary, while conversely avoiding unmanageable overloads.

The nature of projects

My introduction speaks of running a successful project with the client. Yet a successful supplier will run many projects. Portfolio management is the life of our business, being able to deal with competing requirements in a pool of finite resources (it is unprofitable to have individuals 'sat on the bench' and not being productive). So the first consideration is to understand the nature of the portfolio, which will then lead to definition and recognition of different project types. Once those project types have been identified, a repeatable method is developed to deliver each profitably.

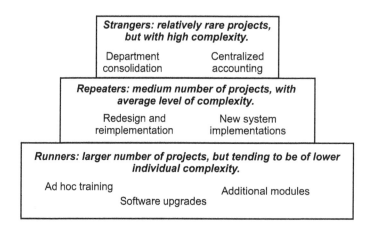

Figure 34.1 Occurrence of stranger, repeater and runner projects in a typical portfolio

It is useful to draw on the experience of the practitioners of Lean manufacturing management who use the RRS principle, where RRS is the abbreviation for runners, repeaters and strangers. When this is adopted for portfolio management (Figure 34.1) we can identify three different RRS project types as follows:

- *Runners* are projects that organizations perform frequently;
- *Stranger* projects are those that are performed infrequently;
- *Repeaters* are projects that organizations perform less frequently than runners, but more often than strangers.

Thus the number of 'runner' low-complexity projects in an organization is likely to be relatively high, whereas, at the other end of the scale, one can expect to find fewer high-complexity projects. Although there are likely to be similarities between project types (for example, the components of a 'runner' project may be the same as those of a 'repeater') there will be differences in the way that these projects are run.

Skills needed

When a model has been developed that identifies and lists the different types of projects in your own organization, each project needs to be considered from a skills perspective. For the many 'runner' projects there will probably be an unconscious or assumed competence in delivery. We know what needs to be done and how to do it. The number of project working days is likely to be small, with little planning needed. The work will probably be relatively low risk, but needing a combination of the following skills and tasks:

- Product knowledge;
- Design, on how to identify the configuration requirements;

- Configuration to ensure that the software works in a particular way; and finally
- Training the client to use the new system.

Projects higher up the rarity scale (the repeaters) will need more formal planning. Typically a team of individuals will be brought together from the supplier's side and matched with the customer's team. Project management becomes more formalized, and development of a work breakdown structure (WBS), project plan and risk register is then essential. The customer may not have its own project manager, instead looking for someone from the supplier to lead the project.

The rarer, 'stranger', infrequent projects will require the bringing together of different teams within the supplier organization. These might include a finance implementation team, business intelligence team and spend control team. Then task priorities and interdependencies will be identified, and the resource pool for each project specified and established.

The challenge is to come up with a model that defines the skill areas needed for successful implementation and then align these to the work breakdown structure. The Microsoft Sure Step Methodology (Shrankar and Bellefroid, 2011) lists nine areas that map well to this type of work as follows:

1. Project management;
2. Training;
3. Business process analysis;
4. Requirements and configuration (including solution design);
5. Custom coding;
6. Quality and testing;
7. Infrastructure;
8. Integration and interfaces;
9. Data migration.

Yet the customer's capabilities are typically in its own business and not necessarily in project delivery.

Resources and the portfolio

As a typical supplier we will have a pool of individuals who are allocated to one or more teams deployed on projects. Clearly the use of all these talented but expensive people needs to be managed as efficiently as possible. People's working time should be regarded as an expensive resource, just as much as any other more tangible resource. Any day lost through idle time cannot be recovered, adding to overhead costs and loss of money. Thus the forward visibility of task bookings is important. Typically there will be a lead time on consultant availability and this also needs to be taken into account when planning each project.

The objective of the supplier is to have a full order book, preferably with the cushion of long lead times, making possible the maximum use of resources. Woodhouse (1993) compares the objectives of the *producers* (those who generate the wealth) with the *facilitators* (those who are employed to support that function). Woodhouse makes the point that: 'Sadly one cannot achieve all these attractive goals at the same time.'

Repeatable methods

Like any business, our supplier needs to remain competitive. Estimate a project with too many days and we shall not win the order – but if we underestimate the task and quote too few days the project will not be profitable. So it's a balancing act. Stephen Covey (2004) writes about 'working on your circle of influence – not your circle of concern'. If we work on the things we can influence the size of the circle grows.

Going back to the runners, repeaters and strangers, for each of these project types we need to consider how easy it is to define a method of delivery. If we take a repeater project we need to look for any project procedures that can be developed as templates for repetitive use (such as the WBS, design workshop agendas, design documents and training agendas).

Document templates serve as knowledge repositories from previous projects of a similar type. Take the question 'What resources are required for a typical finance system implementation?'. Instead of starting with a blank page, look back to see if useful information can be gleaned from similar past projects. This can reveal project WBSs and organizational breakdown structures that can be used again, either as they stand or with a little redesign. This will tell you who needs to be involved, what their responsibilities are, the deliverables to consider, estimates of work, the quality management strategy, and so forth. These findings can help the delivery team for the new project. They will be useful to the consultants, who will have familiarity with each topic and better understand their responsibilities, the customer's responsibilities and the ultimate deliverable(s). That process can save time and greatly reduce the risks in doing business.

Estimation and team performance codes

The A-Team was a TV Series that ran from 1983 to 1987 (see https://en.wikipedia. org/wiki/The_A-Team). The term 'A-Team' means 'a group of elite soldiers or the top advisers or other staff in an organization'. Every customer wants to see their project performed by an A-Team. That means the best consultants, the most senior and capable project manager, and team members with plenty of project experience who have a high productivity rate. So how can your organization provide the A-Team? The essential skills have to be developed over time through the experience of working on multiple projects.

As a supplier we have to estimate the time that is required for us to do the work and put together a quotation that is both competitive compared with other supplier organizations and profitable for us. The estimate of work may be from a top-down perspective (which will tend to lack detail) or from a bottom-up perspective (in which case it will probably contain more detail).

The person doing the estimating must clearly have expertise in this project area. When they estimate it is important to consider team performance codes. If we assume that a typical consultant is the baseline, then the senior consultant will be (say) 100 per cent productive whereas a more junior person might be only 70 per cent productive by comparison. So estimates need to be balanced. Estimates almost always tend to be optimistic, because many difficulties and risks are not foreseen. So contingencies have to be built in, provided that the project is not so loaded with allowances that it becomes too costly and uncompetitive. Estimating is a skill that builds with time and the accumulation of experience from past projects. Estimates should ideally always be independently checked and approved.

Impossible choices

There will at times be impossible choices to make. For example, two different projects might call for the services of the same expert person on the same day. A solution might be suggested if one project is recognized as a critical project, perhaps strategically important, or possibly financially very dominant in the order book. If both projects are equally important, the time will come when a decision has to be made. Who gets the resource(s)? This is a difficult call to make. It is seemingly an impossible choice, but a choice *must* be made and prevarication is not an option.

The approach is to have a 'driver' and a 'driven' method. Take the decision as to who gets the resource(s), and what the implications will be for the other project(s). Identify who will be affected and who needs to be informed, and ensure that there is senior backing for the decision. It is better to have one happy customer and a delivered project than to try to please everyone and end up pleasing no one.

Project lifecycles and workloads in the portfolio mix

Although there are rare exceptions, typically each project has a finite start (initiation) and ending (project closure). At initiation a timeline (plan) is developed which will lead the project through its different stages. At initiation the organizational breakdown structure (OBS), WBS and responsibility assignment matrix should be prepared. All those who work with projects should be familiar with the OBS and WBS methods and the reasons for them. The WBS might be drilled down to three, or at the most four, levels.

The responsibility assignment matrix is important, but perhaps less familiar to many project practitioners. The format requires that each matrix column be assigned to one of the key roles in the project teams, whereas the rows depict the categories of tasks to be performed (not making the mistake of trying to show every actual individual task). An example, in this case for a construction project, is shown in Figure 34.2. This example is taken from Lock (2013), which also includes much on cost estimating, WBSs, planning, control and resource scheduling.

Documentation of all the above named steps is essential because all this information is likely to be referred back to during project delivery. And, of course, the documents need to be updated to reflect progress and approved scope or design changes.

The supplier will have a sales team bidding for new business. So the questions arise: 'What projects are likely to come in?' and 'Who needs to be involved in them?'. It is highly likely that each customer will have a required 'go-live' date in mind, and highly unlikely that any of these dates will coincide. So the supplier will want to plan back every project from its own 'go-live' date (preferably allowing for contingencies) to be sure of delivering on time.

At the other end of the process, there are projects closing, again with completion dates scattered over the calendar. The newly designed systems will have gone live and the teams disbanded as the projects are closed. The order book will periodically be updated with new projects, whereas successfully completed projects will be removed.

Task type:	Responsibility:	The client	Project manager	Project engineer	Purchasing mngr	Drawing office	Construction mngr	Planning engineer	Cost engineer	Project accountant	and so on
Make designs			✚		⬤						
Approve designs		⬤	◼	✚							
Purchase enquiries			◼	✚	⬤						
Purchase orders		◼	◼	✚	⬤						
Planning		◼	◼	✚	✚	✚	✚	⬤	✚		
Cost control			⬤		✚		✚		✚		
Progress reports			⬤	✚	✚	✚	✚	✚			
Cost reports			⬤		✚		✚		✚	✚	
and so on											

⬤ Principal responsibility (only one per task)

✚ Secondary responsibility

◼ Must be consulted

Figure 34.2 Example of a responsibility matrix

The workload will always be likely to fluctuate, so that insufficient orders will cause idle days for some people in the teams. The challenge is to ensure that there is always sufficient new work coming in to keep the teams gainfully occupied.

Diary availability

The facilitator objectives described above are to have the diaries booked for long periods ahead. Examining many individuals' diaries will probably reveal that they are scheduled to be busy for the coming three to four weeks; this applies in particular to senior team members. Planning must take this into account, which is a function of resource scheduling. Resource scheduling is a much-neglected subject in the literature but see Chapter 32 in this handbook. Lock (2013) deals with the subject in depth, but at project (not portfolio) level. Resource scheduling is much easier at project initiation than during project delivery, owing to changes and variations from time plans.

Scheduling where the teams include only one or two experts in a particular subject can also be tricky, and liable to upsets when tasks overrun or individuals are absent from the team for any reason. Consider the following, for example:

- A one-day workshop is planned for week 6 of a project;
- The outcome from this workshop will provide essential decisions for some imminent critical project activities;
- The workshop suddenly has to be rescheduled at short notice, owing to the unavoidable commitments of one expert person;
- The five senior people invited to the workshop have busy diaries and the next available slot when all five can attend at the same time is in week 9 (three weeks later).

So the absence of just one person for only one day in the project has introduced a three-week delay in the overall timeline.

Importance of communications and the PMO

I have mentioned several procedures above (such as creating the WBS and OBS plus planning and scheduling). It is important that such procedures are standardized as far as possible throughout the organization, so that every team handles documents and procedures in the same practical way, and the best possible project management practices and tools are understood and employed. All that presupposes the existence of at least one project management office (PMO). In a large supplier organization there might be an enterprise PMO at the top, with other PMOs handling programmes or individual projects. For more on PMOs, see Chapter 20 or Taylor and Mead (2015).

Communication is also vital to success, which means not only within the project teams but also between portfolio and project managers and other managers in the organization, such as those in finance, purchasing and (in the context of this chapter) human resources management.

Conclusion

Suppliers run portfolios of projects. One important aspect of their expertise is in the efficient allocation of resources across every portfolio. The portfolio objective is to run projects that spell success for both the supplier and the customers. Success means not only achieving the intended return on investment for all, but also building a reputation that will lead to repeatable business. A successful supplier will have projects starting, others finishing and many in progress. Deploying the essential expert resources efficiently and effectively can be a challenging balancing act. Resources in this context means people – those with the requisite skills and abilities. People working in teams at this level will typically be costly to employ, so it is important to maximize the use of their time.

References and further reading

Chapman, J. (2006), *Project and Programme Accounting for Professional Services Organisations*, Swindon: Project Manager Today.

Covey, S.R. (2004), *The 7 Habits of Highly Effective People*, 2nd edn, London: Simon & Schuster.

Lock, D. (2013), *Project Management*, 10th edn, Farnham: Gower.

Lock, D. and Scott, L. (2013), *Gower Handbook of People in Project Management*, Farnham: Gower.

Reiss, G. (1996), *Programme Management Demystified: Managing Multiple Projects Successfully*, London: Spon.

Shrankar, C. and Bellefroid, V. (2011), *Microsoft Dynamics Sure Step*, Birmingham: Packt Publishing.

Taylor, P. and Mead, R. (2015), *Delivering Successful PMOs: How to Design and Manage the Best Project Management Office for your Business*, Abingdon: Routledge.

Woodhouse, J. (1993), *Managing Industrial Risk: Getting Value for Money in your Business*, London: Cengage Learning EMEA.

Part V

Developing capabilities in portfolio management

Chapter 35

Introducing portfolio management in organizations

Reinhard Wagner

The more projects and programmes an organization is performing, the more the need for portfolio management is becoming obvious. It's the responsibility of top managers to initiate a project for introducing portfolio management. As that will be a change project, the first response of the people within that organization might be: 'Why do we need another management function?' or 'Everything is fine, why change anything?' or something similar. Therefore, the introduction of portfolio management should be based on a business case and clear benefits for the organization. Leadership and everyone involved should perform in a systematic way.

Benefits of introducing portfolio management

Why do we need another management function? It's all right, we do not need to change the system. We have no time and resources available for performing portfolio management.

Statements like the above can often be heard when considering the introduction of portfolio management in organizations. The process involves change. Thus people are hesitant to follow new processes, change their positions or report to other people about their work. Sometimes it's fear of transparency – that someone will discover that the project or programme is not running well or too much money is being spent, or things are not properly documented. One reason for objecting to the change might be that some (middle) managers fear losing power to another management function. Portfolio management is typically a rather centralized function; people in a decentralized function might fear that portfolio management will reduce their power and influence. Or people might not know about portfolio management and are hesitant to follow an approach that they do not understand. Another reason for hesitation is that the business case for introducing portfolio management has not been made clear. What are the costs and the benefits? Does it make sense to start a project and introduce project management? All these factors need to be considered thoroughly.

The benefits of introducing portfolio management are certainly very individual and depend on the organization, the leadership and the people affected by the portfolio. Discuss the benefits with all stakeholders and tailor those benefits to the stakeholders' needs in order to build a convincing and attractive case. Some key benefits are listed below and these may be applied to your own case:

- Portfolio management helps to align projects and programmes better to the organization's overall strategy by selecting and prioritizing the 'right' projects and programmes, as well as by linking the objectives of all projects and programmes to the organization's objectives;
- Through portfolio management an organization is able to better align all projects and programmes to each other, identify and exploiting synergies and avoiding duplicate work;
- Owing to the fact that portfolio management is a permanent function, it can monitor and control how the benefits of all projects and programmes are realized and help the organization to improve and achieve its strategic objectives;
- Portfolio management is instrumental for achieving transparency concerning the status of all projects and programmes. It can identify deviations and the corrective actions required. Portfolio managers can support the top management or steering committees in decision-making;
- Monitoring the risks in a portfolio can help the top management to identify and manage risk patterns or risk clusters. Portfolio management regularly evaluates the risk situation and reports to top management about necessary actions;
- Another key function of portfolio management is to identify scarce resources ('bottlenecks') from a strategic point of view in order to support the optimization of those resources in all projects and programmes;
- Lessons learned from projects and programmes can be collected by portfolio management, evaluated and disseminated for beneficial use in future projects and programmes;
- Portfolio management is a central function that should be close to the top management. It is thus a good point of contact for all project and programme managers when it becomes necessary to escalate open issues (in the process known as exception reporting);
- Portfolio managers could also support project and programme managers in applying as well as improving the practices, processes, methods and tools, structures and cultures of project and programme management.

For a business case, all available data should be collected highlighting the actual situation and the (often hidden) cost of performing projects and programmes in the organization as well as the advantages or cost savings with portfolio management. For example, an organization may take a closer look at all costs associated with the following:

- Overburden of resources owing to performing too many projects and programmes;
- Underutilization of resources through a lack of proper resource planning and allocation;
- Performing the wrong projects and programmes or not aligning them to the strategy;
- Non-conformance of projects and programmes with regard to the strategic objectives;
- Failure to take advantage of synergies between several (or even all projects) and programmes;
- Not avoiding or mitigating cluster risks affecting several projects and programmes;
- Delays caused by late (or even no) decisions taken by top management or steering committees;
- Remaining at the current level of project and programme management performance and not improving the practice (for example, not using lessons learned).

On the other hand, the business case must list all costs associated with introducing portfolio management in the organization. These costs can include (but are not necessarily limited to) the following:

- Analysing the status quo and developing the concept of portfolio management;
- Implementing portfolio management and all related processes, methods and tools;
- Performing training for all people involved in portfolio management;
- Involving external expertise and/or consultants for portfolio management;
- Selecting, customizing and implementing a portfolio management software solution;
- Performing portfolio management on a daily basis (for example, costs of staff, offices and tools).

The decision about whether or not to implement portfolio management in an organization should be based on all available information. A distinction should be made between one-off costs (resulting from the introduction of portfolio management) and the cost of performing portfolio management on a continuous basis. There can be a significant cost difference depending on whether portfolio management is being introduced by the organization's own staff or by external consultants. However, external consultants might be able to take a fresh, independent look at the situation and tailor available expertise quickly to the needs and scope of the organization.

A systematic approach to introducing portfolio management

Introducing portfolio management in organizations is an intervention into a social system, which requires a systematic approach in order to be performed successfully. Some years ago an expert team of the German Project Management Association (GPM) developed an approach for performing consultancy work for an organization, and they defined the stages and competences needed. The International Project Management Association (IPMA) adopted the concept and used it as the basis for its standard *IPMA Competence Baseline for Consultants* (ICBC, see IPMA, 2011). Their approach assumes that the change is done via a project, performed through several stages from a clarification of the assignment to a continuous improvement process (CIP). Figure 35.1 shows the respective stages and their associated milestones. The main driver is project management, focused on communication and stakeholder engagement. The following account explains how the introduction of portfolio management might work, based on a real case from the automotive industry.

Case study

The organization in this case story is a large automotive supplier with a significant growth rate over the past ten years. This growth required the owners to invest a significant amount of money and also build up the personnel.

The organization was mainly opportunity driven and the top management did not care much about systematic portfolio management. Decisions were made case by case, which led the organization into difficulties, because the investment budget was stretched too much, some resources turned out to be a bottleneck for projects, and some of the existing clients drove the organization into a certain direction, which was not always the direction the owners wanted to go.

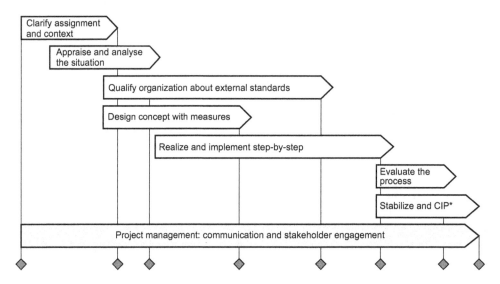

Clarify assignment and context

Appraise and analyse the situation

Qualify organization about external standards

Design concept with measures

Realize and implement step-by-step

Evaluate the process

Stabilize and CIP*

Project management: communication and stakeholder engagement

* CIP = continuous improvement process

Figure 35.1 Overview of the approach for introducing portfolio management

Source: Wagner (2015)

Step 1: clarify the assignment and context

As a result of the problems outlined above, the idea of a systematic approach to port-folio management was brought to the attention of the top management. They decided to elaborate on and implement this approach in order to deal with the challenges already mentioned.

A programme and portfolio management consultant was asked to propose a way forward, together with the manager responsible for project management and the project management office (PMO). Both developed a project brief (the project can-vas) in which they described the current situation and the forward objectives. This brief included a draft plan for implementing portfolio management, and defined the resources and project team members required.

It was also made very clear to the top management that this change project would be successful only with the full support of the organization´s leadership, and by giving this change project high priority with regard to all other activities and projects in the organization. This was already an acid test of whether the top organization's leader-ship would be able to prioritize.

Step 2: appraisal and analysis of the situation

An important step of the change activity is always to analyse the situation based on a 360° perspective. In our case, interviews were performed with some top managers, the manager of the project management department, and selected project and line managers involved in project activities (such as sales and purchasing). In addition, the organizational structure, existing processes and the actual culture were analysed. Special attention was paid to the processes for projects and programmes, the reporting lines to the PMO, the two levels of steering committees and organizational structures with relevance to project activities.

In addition, the culture was analysed with regard to actual behaviour shown in decision-making, the transparency of deviations, issues and failures, together with the response of the top management in this regard. The organization had already introduced a process for investment planning and control, which was unfortunately stand alone and not really connected to the project and programme activities.

Another issue being analysed was the resource situation and management. Many of the organization's resources were scarce, which led to significant delays in projects. The management was not really aware of the real bottlenecks and the effects that these had on projects. Furthermore, resource planning and tracking process were poor (including, for example, monitoring and controlling time spent in projects). A SWOT report highlighted the strengths, weaknesses, opportunities and threats and proposed a way forward that would build on the strengths, overcome the weaknesses, embrace the opportunities and avoid the threats.

Step 3: qualify organization about external standards

An organization should not 'reinvent the wheel' when introducing portfolio management. It is wise to build on existing, external standards and derive one's own, internal standards from them. Chapter 7 of this handbook elaborates on standards available for portfolio management.

In this case example, it was the task of the consultant to introduce available standards to the organization, highlighting advantages and disadvantages of each standard in order to reach a consensus upon which to build. The project team finally decided to apply the international standard ISO 21504 *Project, Programme and Portfolio management – Guidance on portfolio management* (International Organization for Standardization or ISO, 2015) together with a national standard for multiple project management to design their own concepts.

There are no requirements in the automotive industry with regard to portfolio management. However, in this case the organization's leadership wanted to highlight in their integrated management system (IMS) that the portfolio management is based on the best practice standards available (nationally and internationally). These standards were introduced to all stakeholders in order to familiarize them with the underlying philosophy and concepts. Also, for a change activity it is helpful to refer to international best practices because these are somehow easier to accept than their own solutions. Nevertheless, it has always been made clear that the standards were not adopted exactly, but tailored to the needs of the organization.

Step 4: design concept with measures

The concepts for portfolio management should not be designed by one person, but in a joint effort of all team members. The external consultant may facilitate this design process and provide input from time to time, based on experiences collected through other cases. This is to disallow the consultant from dominating the solution.

The people working with the solution later should be the ones designing it in order to avoid the 'not invented here' syndrome. In this case the concept paper included (but was not limited) to the following aspects:

- A process of aligning all projects to the organization's overall strategy, strategic initiatives (market position, improvement of productivity, innovation, and so on) and long-term objectives;
- A process for selecting and prioritizing the projects and programmes based on transparent criteria in a joint effort of top management, sales and the project management office;
- A process for planning, assigning, monitoring and controlling the scarce resources in order to utilize them in the best way possible;
- A process for collecting status reports, consolidating all relevant data for top management to monitor, control and decide from a strategic point of view over all projects;
- An organizational structure with roles and responsibilities (RASIC matrix) for managing the portfolio of projects (with special focus on customer projects);
- A training concept for all people involved in portfolio management (especially the members of the portfolio steering committee) on how to fill the role assigned professionally. Also how to collaborate with the other functions and roles affected by portfolio management;
- A proposal for additions to the corporate values, especially the issue of transparency and escalation of deviations (exception reporting) from project managers to the top management.

The concepts were presented for approval and detailed into documents for insertion into the organization's IMS. This was a very critical aspect. Being part of the IMS allows processes to be audited and improved on a regular basis. Finally, a detailed list of measures was developed in order to be ready for implementation. The list described the 'what', 'when', 'who' and 'how' of the implementation necessary for the next phase of the change project.

Step 5: Realize and implement step by step

Now comes the most difficult task in any change project – the implementation. Some people might be hesitant to change or adopt the proposed processes. People might do it for a while and then flip back to the 'old' ways of doing things. There might be open resistance towards the project, so that it fails in the middle of the implementation. Performing change means working with the people affected and emphasizing communication.

Thus, in our case, the top management was asked to announce the implementation, explaining the underlying reasons and pointing the way forward. Later the project team provided more detailed information through information sessions and training. The next steps were to do the following:

- Start the process of selection and prioritization with all new enquiries from customers;
- Align the project objectives to the strategy;

- Plan and assign the necessary resources; and later
- Monitor and control all projects in the new framework.

The external consultant (together with some project team members) was asked to accompany the implementation and support the steering committee and leadership of the organization in their new tasks.

Only minor adjustments to this process were necessary. Some bigger issues were detected, but these were collected for a later update of the documents. A key challenge was the discipline in the steering committee for coming to decisions. The organization was used to take the decisions, based either on 'gut feeling' or the strong interference of some leaders.

Now, there was a new process with a more collaborative and systematic approach to decision-making. This required intervention by the chief executive officer (CEO) to guide the other steering committee members into this new process. Facilitation of the steering committee meetings was also an area of improvement. The external consultant was asked to analyse the 'meetings culture' and propose corrective measures. Overall the implementation went well and reached the intended goals in the planned timeframe, with only minor adjustments of the measures.

Step 6: evaluate the process

Regular reviews of the implementation process, the results achieved and stakeholder satisfaction were necessary to adjust the process or even stop it when needed. In our case the project team made an evaluation of the progress and results achieved after six months. They checked whether the new processes were properly implemented and adopted. Interviews with key stakeholders (for example, some steering committee members, project managers, PMO personnel and sales representatives) were performed to evaluate their satisfaction with the portfolio management. Areas of improvement were collected and consolidated in a final list for consideration.

One finding was the feeling of the project managers that they were being 'policed' and did not get enough feedback from the portfolio management. Questions such as 'How are the other projects performing?', 'What are the key lessons learned from similar projects?' or 'What are strategic success factors of customer projects?' are interesting and useful for project managers. Such questions need to be addressed more by the PMO in order to benefit the project managers.

Step 7: stabilize and initiate continuous improvements

An organization could flip back to the old habits after a while, so a measurement for stabilizing and continuously improving the situation is necessary in a change project. In our case a series of training sessions was conducted to make everyone aware of the need for portfolio management and the (new) processes.

The facilitator of the regular steering committee meetings was asked to perform a feedback session after each meeting and the PMO collected the key findings. An update of the documentation was released about a year after the start of the implementation of portfolio management. The documents are updated regularly through the CIP. A quarterly meeting of all project managers is conducted in order to collect their findings on project, programme and portfolio management, and this information is used to improve relevant processes. One of the main improvements in this case was to include the head of project management and the PMO in the process for updating the strategy, and to look at implications for the portfolio activities.

Continually throughout the project: project management, communication and stakeholder engagement

As already mentioned above, the introduction of portfolio management should be managed like a change project with a strong emphasis on communication and stakeholder engagement. In our case, besides the typical project management activities the project team paid a great deal of attention to internal communication of 'why', 'what' and 'how' in order to engage the stakeholders and overcome any resistance.

Conclusion

Introducing portfolio management in organizations is a change activity that needs to be managed in a professional way. In order to avoid resistance to change, the project should highlight the benefits for the various stakeholder groups, and focus on communication and stakeholder engagement, as well as forming a project team based on key stakeholder groups. A systematic approach, starting from the clarification of the assignment to stabilization and continuous improvement activities, really helps to make the change happen and achieves high performance portfolio management.

An external consultant may be instrumental for providing know-how and experience. The consultant should not deliver the solution design, but instead needs to facilitate the team to find its own tailor-made solution and support the implementation through coaching and training. This is a more difficult role for consultants, but necessary if the solution is to be accepted.

References and further reading

International Project Management Association (2011), *ICBC Addition to the IPMA Competence Baseline for PM Consultants*, Version 1.0, Amsterdam: IPMA.
International Organization for Standardization (2015), ISO 21504 *Project, Programme and Portfolio management – Guidance on portfolio management*, Geneva: ISO.
Wagner, R., ed. (2015), *Beratung von Organisationen im Projektmanagement*, Düsseldorf: Symposion Publishing.

Chapter 36

Assessing and developing the maturity of portfolio management

Reinhard Wagner

In Germany, the share of gross domestic product (GDP) produced through projects has grown on average from 29.3 per cent to 34.7 per cent between 2009 and 2013 and is predicted to reach 41.3 per cent by the year 2019 (GPM German Association for Project Management, 2015). This does not apply to business alone. Project work is also steadily gaining importance for public services and non-profit organizations, requiring project, programme and portfolio management to be handled more professionally. Entire organizations have to change and adjust to the principles of a 'projectized' economy.

Introduction

Governance and management systems for projects, programmes and portfolios must be improved on a continuous basis. For many organizations, this results in a comprehensive change process including not only a new strategy, but also organizational structures, cultures, processes, methods, (software) tools and human resources development, among many other areas. This raises the following questions for an organization:

- What is the status quo of the organization's project, programme and portfolio management?
- To what extent do our current governance and management systems meet the requirements of external and internal stakeholders?
- What are the next development steps?
- What must be done in order to reach the next development level?

These and other similar questions must be answered by applying maturity models for project, programme and portfolio management. These maturity models are applied to analyse the status quo and to develop the organization further in accordance with requirements. Over the past twenty years, many maturity models have been developed in the domains of project, programme and portfolio management. Some of these differ significantly and require users to be familiar with their respective objectives, application conditions, benefits and disadvantages. The results of such a maturity assessment help the top management to make decisions about the steps needed for development.

Assessing the maturity of an organization's portfolio management

Maturity models result from striving for organizational perfection, improvement of efficiency (and effectiveness) and achievement of the highest possible quality level. These models were first developed as part of general quality management systems. Then they were adapted to sector-specific requirements in software development, and have increasingly gained ground in the field of project, programme and portfolio management in the last couple of years. One way of defining maturity models is as follows:

> All models for the analysis, assessment, evaluation and continuous improvement of the development status, the efficiency, the quality or maturity or the competence of organisations . . . according to defined and standardised assessment and evaluation criteria and standards.
>
> (Motzel, 2006, p. 126)

This definition emphasizes two essential functions of maturity models, which are as follows:

1.   Analysis of the current development status;
2.   Evaluation of the organization's resulting development needs.

Hence there is substantial overlap in maturity models and assessment, audit, review or excellence models in project management, which focus on the analysis and often examine only a subarea of the organization (for example, an individual project). Maturity models focus, however, on which development needs exist in relation to a defined status and the requirements needed to achieve it.

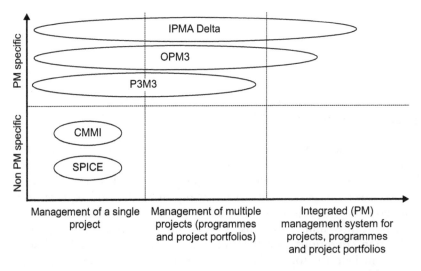

Figure 36.1 Classification of international project management maturity models

Figure 36.1 shows one possible classification of project management (PM) maturity models. A distinction between PM-specific and non-PM-specific models is made. The latter do not explicitly refer to project management, or they only partially cover project management. These include CMMI (capability maturity model integrated) and SPICE (software process improvement and capability determination) models designed for process improvements in software or systems development. Another distinctive feature is the extent to which a maturity model covers the management of individual or multiple projects (programmes and project portfolios), and whether it is designed to validate integrated (project) management systems. The following are the three internationally recognized models:

1. International Project Management Association's (IPMA's) maturity assessment model IPMA Delta;
2. Project Management Institute's (PMI's) OPM3 (*Organizational Project Management Maturity Model*); and
3. P3M3 (*Portfolio, Programme and Project Management Maturity Model*) from AXELOS (2011).

These models assess the organization's maturity in managing projects, programmes and portfolios. However, the reference models for portfolio management differ from model to model. IPMA Delta refers to IPMA OCB (IPMA, 2016) and ISO 21504 (ISO, 2015). OPM3 refers to the OPM3 Standard (PMI, 2013b) and *The Standard for Portfolio Management* (PMI, 2013a). P3M3 refers to MoP (*Management of Portfolios*, AXELOS, 2011).

These three models also differ in respect to the degree to which they take into account the organization's integrated (project) management system. IPMA Delta, for example, serves to evaluate the status quo of an organization's competence in managing projects (actual) and its development needs (Delta) in relation to a desired target state. The evaluation model distinguishes five 'competence classes', which describe PM maturity levels as follows:

- Initial;
- Defined;
- Standardized;
- Managed;
- Optimized.

Figure 36.2 shows these five levels with their characteristics. On the first level, particularly experienced project managers have positive effects on project management, but the organization does not yet have implemented standards, structures and processes for the management of individual projects, programmes and project portfolios. On the second level, initial standards, structures and processes already exist, but only some of these are applied. On the third level, standards, structures and processes have been fully implemented and are also applied. On the fourth level, the application is still monitored and corrected if required. On the uppermost level, continuous improvement is added.

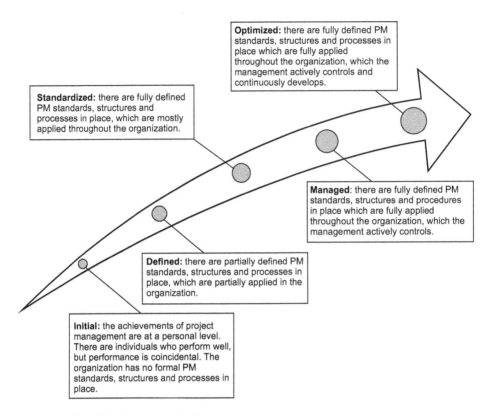

Figure 36.2 The IPMA Delta classification system

Some of the benefits that organizations can achieve through IPMA Delta are as follows:

- Obtain leading international certification of competence in managing projects;
- Identify areas of improvement and actions needed to improve project, programme and portfolio management;
- Start a continuous improvement process with measurable objectives;
- Achieve better results in projects, programmes and portfolios through more efficient and effective management;
- Raise the visibility of project, programme and portfolio management throughout the organization;
- Develop project, programme and portfolio management and learn from experienced IPMA Delta assessors;
- Determine the status quo in managing projects and benchmark this against other organizations;
- Improve your market position through the 'Delta effect'.

Such a procedure requires the active involvement of management, communicating the targets, the process and the use of the results, so that the involved stakeholders give open and honest answers to the assessors' questions.

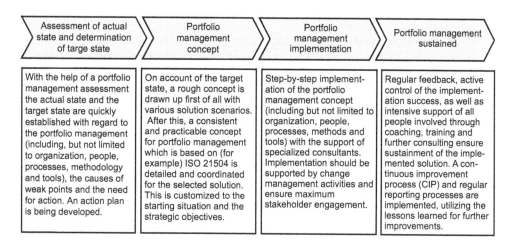

Assessment of actual state and determination of targe state	Portfolio management concept	Portfolio management implementation	Portfolio management sustained
With the help of a portfolio management assessment the actual state and the target state are quickly established with regard to the portfolio management (including, but not limited to organization, people, processes, methodology and tools), the causes of weak points and the need for action. An action plan is being developed.	On account of the target state, a rough concept is drawn up first of all with various solution scenarios. After this, a consistent and practicable concept for portfolio management which is based on (for example) ISO 21504 is detailed and coordinated for the selected solution. This is customized to the starting situation and the strategic objectives.	Step-by-step implementation of the portfolio management concept (including but not limited to organization, people, processes, methods and tools) with the support of specialized consultants. Implementation should be supported by change management activities and ensure maximum stakeholder engagement.	Regular feedback, active control of the implementation success, as well as intensive support of all people involved through coaching, training and further consulting ensure sustainment of the implemented solution. A continuous improvement process (CIP) and regular reporting processes are implemented, utilizing the lessons learned for further improvements.

Figure 36.3 Overview of the process for developing portfolio management

Developing portfolio management maturity

Based on the findings of the assessment described above, the organization's leadership needs to define a project for developing the maturity of portfolio management in a systematic way. At Tiba Managementberatung (see www.tiba.de/en) we use such an approach (Figure 36.3). This builds on the assessment of the actual state in portfolio management and a determination of the desired, future state. Based on this, one or several solutions are being developed, for example, based on ISO 21504 (ISO, 2015) or other acknowledged concepts. These concepts need to address thoroughly the gaps between the actual and the desired state of portfolio management and be aligned with the organization's overall vision, mission and strategy.

During implementation, the concepts are set into practice. This is basically a change activity. Thus it needs to be managed by engaging all stakeholders through marketing, communication and leadership. Finally, regular feedbacks, an active controlling of the portfolio management as such and its performance will help to achieve sustainability. Developing individual competences as well as conducting a continuous improvement process will support the sustainment of portfolio management.

The assessment stage

During the assessment stage, the actual state of portfolio management will be analysed by internal or external assessors using one of the aforementioned maturity models. For example, IPMA Delta uses the seven questions of the IPMA OCB (IPMA, 2016) with regard to portfolio management:

- Does the organization define the role of a portfolio and its contribution to achieve both the organization's and the project, programme and portfolio's missions, visions and strategies?

- Does the organization provide a standard for portfolio management (for example, processes, methods and tools)?
- Does the organization ensure that selection and prioritization of the projects and programmes in a portfolio is aligned with the organization's overall mission, vision and strategy?
- Does the organization ensure the balancing and prioritization of all projects and programmes in a portfolio, taking account of the available resources?
- Does the organization have a process for consolidating the progress reports of projects and programmes at the portfolio level and reviewing them on a regular basis?
- Is the portfolio management standard accessible to, understood and applied by all staff and managers?
- Do all users of the portfolio management standard provide feedback and suggestions for continuous improvement?

The assessment can be done by checking available documents (such as the *PM Handbook*, documents of the *Quality Management Manual* or templates), interviewing stakeholders involved in the portfolio management or observing the practice of portfolio management throughout several days of its operation.

The findings of the assessment could be mirrored against the maturity levels shown in Figure 10.2 and compared with the desired state or level. Any gap between the two levels will indicate the need for development. During an external assessment, the organization's leadership will get a report of the findings together with a list of recommendations, which will form the basis for an action plan.

The concept stage

The concept stage elaborates on future solution scenarios first, taking into account the findings of the assessment and the desired state of portfolio management. Based on such considerations, concepts including (but not limited to) organization, people, processes, methodologies and tools need to be developed based on the Tiba 4-Axes Approach (Figure 36.4) and perhaps by making use of internationally accepted standards such as ISO 21504 (ISO, 2015) and ISO 21505 (ISO, 2017).

We have to consider what is important during this stage. First and most important is to develop these concepts together with a group of the organization's stakeholders. Otherwise the results may not be accepted during the implementation. The development could be done in an agile way, with prototyping sessions, short sprints for achieving quick wins and also by directly involving the users during this early stage. Top management should also be involved through presentations and sounding sessions in order to obtain feedback as to whether or not the concepts fit to the overall vision, mission and strategy as well as top management's expectations. This is also why there should always be several options on hand to give choices to the management, together with economic effects and implications for achieving the organization's strategic objectives.

The implementation stage

Implementation of the concepts into an organization basically means performing change activities. People may be reluctant to adopt the new organization, people,

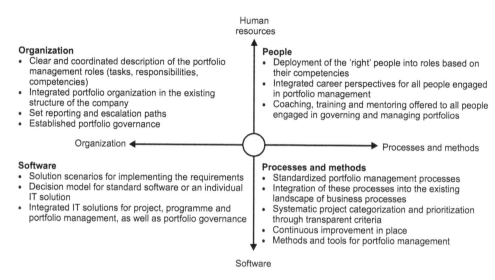

Human
resources

Organization
- Clear and coordinated description of the portfolio management roles (tasks, responsibilities, competencies)
- Integrated portfolio organization in the existing structure of the company
- Set reporting and escalation paths
- Established portfolio governance

People
- Deployment of the 'right' people into roles based on their competencies
- Integrated career perspectives for all people engaged in portfolio management
- Coaching, training and mentoring offered to all people engaged in governing and managing portfolios

Organization ◄──────────────────────────────► Processes and methods

Software
- Solution scenarios for implementing the requirements
- Decision model for standard software or an individual IT solution
- Integrated IT solutions for project, programme and portfolio management, as well as portfolio governance

Processes and methods
- Standardized portfolio management processes
- Integration of these processes into the existing landscape of business processes
- Systematic project categorization and prioritization through transparent criteria
- Continuous improvement in place
- Methods and tools for portfolio management

Software

Figure 36.4 Developing portfolio management according to the Tiba 4-Axes approach

processes, methodologies and tools. Thus, a marketing campaign should be performed by top management, explaining the case for change and the implications of the change, as well as the benefits for the individuals and the organization. Typically, the implementation is done step by step, starting with a pilot application in one area of responsibility, evaluating whether the concepts work and how people adopt the newly designed solutions. This may result in another round of development, adjusting those things that did not work well and also highlighting achievements for the next steps of implementation.

People may need to be introduced to the newly designed portfolio management. Thus introduction sessions, training and coaching may be part of the implementation process. External consultants may help during this stage to provide feedback and be open for feedback from all the people involved. In many cases, the implementation may cause additional activities for dealing with culture change, leadership behaviour, or even overcoming conflicts and crises.

The sustainment stage

Implementation of portfolio management is not the end of development activities. The end is rather the beginning of continuous improvement activities. Regular feedback loops, systematic utilization of lessons learned, internal assessments of the performance based on predefined key performance indicators (KPIs) and a continuation of training and coaching will help to achieve a sustainable solution for portfolio management. Portfolio management is mainly striving for effectiveness, which means the following:

- Realization of the intended strategic objectives and benefits;
- Utilization of the resources for projects, programmes and portfolios in the best possible way;

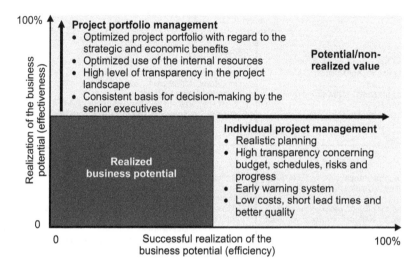

Figure 36.5 Results that an organization can achieve through professional portfolio management

- Provision of transparency with regard to the portfolio activities and the status of all projects;
- Support of the decision-making process of senior executives.

However, when portfolio management is performed well, it will also support ambitions for improving the efficiency in projects and programmes (for example, by providing transparency with regard to budget, schedule, risks and progress). Figure 36.5 provides an overview of the impact that professional portfolio management could have on the performance of an organization. This is what the activities in the sustainment stage are aiming at.

Conclusion

Assessing and developing portfolio management in an organization is typically a change activity that needs to be managed in a professional way. Internationally accepted maturity models help to gain insights into the actual stage of maturity, but they also help to define the desired state and the areas for improvement. Building on the results of such an assessment, future scenarios for a solution help to identify a feasible way of developing portfolio management. Concepts typically cover organization, processes, methodologies and tools as well as people's competences. To avoid resistance to change, during implementation the top management should highlight the benefits for various stakeholder groups, and focus on communication and stakeholder engagement, as well as implementing the concepts step by step. A systematic approach, starting from the clarification of the assignment to stabilization and continuous improvement activities, helps to realize the change and achieve really well-performing portfolio management.

References and further reading

AXELOS (2011), *Management of Portfolios*, Norwich: The Stationery Office.

German Association for Project Management (GPM) (2015), *Makroökonomische Vermessung der Projekttätigkeit in Deutschland*, Nürnberg: GPM.

International Project Management Association (2016), *IPMA Organisational Competence Baseline*, Version 1.1, Amsterdam: IPMA.

International Organization for Standardization (2015), ISO 21504 *Project, Programme and Portfolio Management – Guidance on portfolio management*, Geneva: ISO.

International Organization for Standardization (2017), ISO 21505, *Project, Programme and Portfolio Management – Guidance on governance*, Geneva: ISO.

Motzel, E. (2006), *Projektmanagement-Lexikon*, Weinheim: Wiley, p. 153.

Project Management Institute (2013a), *The Standard for Portfolio Management*, 3rd edn, Newtown Square, PA: PMI.

Project Management Institute (2013b), *Organizational Project Management Maturity Model (OPM3)*, 3rd edn, Newtown Square, PA: PMI.

Wagner, R., ed. (2015), *Beratung von Organisationen im Projektmanagement*, Dusseldorf: Symposion Publishing.

Chapter 37

Developing the individual competences of people engaged in portfolios

Reinhard Wagner

The management of a portfolio involves many people. All of them need to develop the competences needed from their particular perspective. The human resource (HR) department of the organization is typically responsible for analysing the competence requirements and actual competences available. Based on the findings, a programme for competence development can be set up in order to support people engaged in portfolios.

People engaged in portfolios

Who is involved in a portfolio and its management? Starting with the components of a portfolio, the people involved in projects and programmes and their managers are those who should be considered from a portfolio perspective. Certainly, the people directly involved in managing the portfolio (for example, the portfolio manager and the people of a project management office [PMO]) should be considered. We must also include those who have significant decision-making responsibilities, such as the senior executives of a steering board or the C-Suite. The following is a list of people who should be considered when developing competences for a portfolio. This list may not be complete and it certainly depends on the circumstances of the organization, but it's a starting point for the HR department.

- *People engaged in projects and programmes*: those concerned with components of a portfolio need to have a basic understanding of what a portfolio is, how a good interrelationship with the portfolio can be established, and how the management of projects and programmes can be aligned with portfolio management. It could be simply that knowledge about portfolios and portfolio management is what these people require. However, the alignment between the project and the portfolio require skills and abilities that are critical for success.
- *People engaged in managing portfolios* need to develop competences, knowledge, skills and abilities, in order to perform their respective tasks. The management team may include a portfolio manager and people responsible for planning and controlling. This all depends on the type, number and complexity of projects. There may be roles such as a portfolio risk manager, a change director or a benefits manager involved. Often a PMO or a specialized portfolio management office (also called a PMO) might perform the portfolio management tasks, which means that all related staff need to be competent in portfolio management.

- *People engaged in the governance, oversight or steering of a portfolio*: these people are unfortunately often forgotten when it comes to competence development. However, they need to develop the competences necessary for performing their roles, which means that they must be able to understand the purpose of a portfolio, how it aligns the portfolio and its projects with the strategic level of their organization, and what they are supposed to do. These are the people who set the framework for portfolio management. They oversee and control the execution of portfolios and take part in the decision-making. Competence development needs to address the special needs of these people and take their special status into account.
- *People responsible for resources and 'know-how'*: these people might not necessarily be involved in steering a portfolio. They will need competences that enable them to understand the requirements for deploying resources in a portfolio, balancing those resources across the line functions, projects, programmes and the portfolio. They will also need to recognize that supporting the competence development of the organization's people is key to the success of a project-orientated organization.
- *People concerned with competence development in organizations*: these people need to know the competence requirements of people engaged in portfolios, the actual state of competence available in the organization and the potential state-of-the-art approaches for developing the competences. They may include HR staff, internal and external trainers, as well as the educators at universities who deal with this specific topic. This group of people may also include the regulators, professional organizations and standards bodies that have a stake in the relevant competences.

I must stress again that the above list might not be complete, and the roles named can vary from one organization to another. However, in any organization it is necessary to perform a systematic stakeholder analysis to identify the competences needed.

Competences relevant for managing a portfolio

Most of the global standards on portfolio management are mainly focused on processes, methods and tools. For example, the third edition of *The Standard for Portfolio Management* (Project Management Institute or PMI, 2013) just mentions on two pages the following knowledge and skills:

- Portfolio strategic management and alignment;
- Portfolio management methods and techniques;
- Stakeholder engagement;
- Leadership and management skills; and
- Risk management.

ISO 21504 simply mentions that 'portfolio management requires competent individuals applying their knowledge and experience' (International Organization for Standardization or ISO, 2015), but it is silent on what comprises those competences. The same applies to the British Standard 'Management of Portfolios' (Office of

Government Commerce or OGC, 2011), which outlines portfolio management principles and practices, but fails to deliver guidance on the competences.

In 2011, the Australian Institute of Project Management (AIPM) published the second version of its AIPM *Professional Competency Standards for Project Management – Part F*, which addresses the competences necessary for people engaged in portfolios. It provides the basis for developing and assessing the so-called 'certified project portfolio executive'. It has been developed as a generic standard with the objective of applicability across a wide range of industries and enterprises. This AIPM Standard may be used by industries and organizations as it stands, or it can provide a basis from which each industry or organization can adapt the standard to suit its own circumstances (AIPM, 2011). It describes the following eight functions of project portfolio management, detailing elements of competence with the key performance criteria, range indicators, knowledge and skills, as well as the evidence guides:

- Identify, categorize and prioritize projects and programmes;
- Assess and select opportunities and balance the portfolio;
- Manage and review portfolio performance;
- Govern the portfolio;
- Manage portfolio resources;
- Manage portfolio communication and change;
- Manage portfolio risk; and
- Lead the portfolio.

The most comprehensive standard for competences is the IPMA Individual Competence Baseline (IPMA ICB). This is available for free download via IPMA's website. It defines individual competence as 'the application of knowledge, skills and abilities in order to achieve the desired results' (IPMA, 2016) and groups respective competence elements (CEs) in the following three competence areas:

1. *Perspective*: perspective CEs define the contextual competences that must be navigated within and across the broader environment;
2. *People*: people CEs define the personal and interpersonal competences required to succeed in projects, programmes and portfolios;
3. *Practice*: practice CEs define the technical aspects of managing projects, programmes and portfolios.

Within each competence area there are generic CEs that apply to the domains of project, programme and portfolio management. Each CE contains lists of the knowledge and skills required to master it. Key competence indicators (KCIs) provide the definitive indicators of successful project, programme and portfolio management for one, two or all three domains. Measures exist that describe highly detailed performance points within each KCI. The baseline is a comprehensive inventory of competences that an individual needs to have or to develop to manage portfolios successfully. The generic model is applicable in all sectors and industries. However, it does not recommend or include specific methodologies, methods or tools. Appropriate methods and tools may be defined by the organization, and individuals could choose from available methodologies, methods and tools.

Perspective competences	Practice competences
• Strategy • Governance and processes • Compliance, standards and regulations • Culture and values	• Design • Requirements, objectives and benefits • Scope • Time • Organization and information • Quality • Finance • Resources • Procurement and partnerships • Plan and control • Risk and opportunities • Stakeholders • Change and transformation • Select and balance
People competences	
• Self-reflection and self-management • Personal integrity and reliability • Personal communication • Relationships and engagement • Leadership • Teamwork • Conflict and crisis • Resourcefulness • Negotiation • Result orientation	

Figure 37.1 Three groups of competences required for managing a portfolio

The lists in Figure 37.1 give an overview of the CEs for each competence area. All competences are relevant for portfolios but the importance of single competences needed for managing a portfolio may differ between various types of portfolios (such as information and communications technology [ICT] or research and development [R&D] portfolios) or sectors (such as construction, the service industry or public administration).

Developing individual competences in the domain of portfolios

Competence development is intermingled with the activities that individuals perform through their roles and responsibilities. People engaged in portfolios acquire knowledge, skills and abilities, or, in other words, they learn. Furthermore, they interact with others and could thus share knowledge, exchange experiences and support each other in performing activities, for example, through feedback and reflection sessions. The IPMA ICB summarizes the possibilities for developing necessary competences for people engaged in portfolios and the prerequisites that should be in place before implementing the development measures. These may depend on preferences of the individual or the organization, the situation and the availability of resources, whichever of the following fits best and is chosen (IPMA, 2016):

• *Self-development*: for example, reading books, standards, case studies and articles helps to gain knowledge, reflecting on the application in practical situations and deriving learning from that. Other ways of self-development are studying, experimenting, trying things out or learning by doing. The last helps the individual to gain experience in a particular context or to develop certain skills;

- *Peer development*, such as reflecting with colleagues on how things are going, asking for feedback on one's own performance and ways for improving it. Learning partners from different disciplines could help to see a situation from a different angle and use the development for the mutual benefit of both peers (benefiting one through the questions asked and the other through the insights provided);
- *Education and training*, such as attending a seminar, lectures and training sessions, where the trainer delivers specific know-how. This could be done through a presentation, interactions between the participants and the trainer as well as using case studies, group exercises and simulation games. The development of individual competences may depend on the number of participants, the mix of methods used or the duration of the sessions;
- *Coaching and mentoring*, for example providing feedback, advice and support from a coach, leader or mentor while performing certain activities or striving to develop specific competences. Typically, a coach, leader or mentor is an experienced person who does not deliver direct answers, but challenges individuals through questions that draw each person's attention towards certain aspects and requires them to provide an adequate answer.
- *Simulation and gaming*, such as developing competences through case-based simulation games (board or computer games), reflecting on interactions and behaviours of individuals shown in such a setting. Often simulation games and other forms of game-based learning are a mix of approaches, for example enabling self-development combined with peer development and coaching in a training environment. It could also be helpful to combine these approaches based on the individual's previous experiences and stage of development;
- *Communities of practice*, which is a means for sharing experiences between people who share the same subject and technical interests but are employed in different parts of the organization, or might even be employed in different, otherwise unrelated companies. This could develop, for example, when two or more individuals meet at a seminar, discover that they share common interests and continue to cooperate and learn from each other long after the original meeting;
- *Action learning*: this is a rather extreme, but none the less effective, method for developing individual competences. It involves taking two (or even more) individuals out or their normal roles and getting them to swap their departments, with a mentor observing and guiding the process. In successful experiments, individuals were even exchanged between different, previously unconnected companies. Thus an IT specialist might be exchanged with an accountant for a few months, with both organizations and the individuals all benefitting from the experience. Reg Revans founded this idea (Revans, 2011).

Typically, the HR department is responsible for defining a strategy and the objectives for developing competences based on the organization's overall vision, mission and strategy. It sets the framework for all activities and approaches chosen for HR activities, including the competence development. HR needs to analyse the competence requirements of people engaged in portfolios and their actual state of competences. Based on this analysis, one or several of the aforementioned approaches could be chosen to develop the competences in a systematic way.

Another important actor for the development of competences is found in the professional organizations, such as the Association for Project Management (APM) in the UK or the International Project Management Association or Project Management Institute from a global perspective.

Professional organizations typically act as standard-setting bodies, accreditation centres and certification bodies. They define the standards with indicators and thresholds for individual competences, they set frameworks for assessing the competences against the standards, and they regulate processes, methods, tools and roles for trainers, coaches and assessors. Thus, the people engaged in portfolios can check with a professional organization whether they could obtain an internationally (or nationally) acknowledged certificate in order to be able to demonstrate their competence. As an example, APM provides a framework for continuing professional development (CPD), which highlights formal and informal CPD activities (APM, 2018). These activities are listed in Figure 37.2.

Conclusion

A wide range of people is engaged in portfolios. All of them need to be competent in order to act professionally in their roles and responsibilities. IPMA's Individual Competence Baseline describes the necessary competence elements, together with potential ways of developing these competences. Several professional organizations offer professional qualifications and certification for people who are engaged in portfolios. The HR department should set the framework for developing competences in an organization, based on the overall vision, mission and strategy. Approaches, methods and tools for competence development may differ, but nevertheless there is a variety of opportunities available.

Formal CPD activities	Informal CPD activities (continued)
<ul><li>Validated and accredited qualifications</li><li>Branch and special interest groups</li><li>Formal distance and open learning courses</li><li>Attending relevant courses</li><li>Attending relevant conferences and/or seminars</li><li>Attending relevant workshops</li><li>Job secondment</li><li>In-house presentations</li></ul>**Informal CPD activities**<ul><li>Learning on the job</li><li>Peer guidance and discussion</li><li>Structured reading</li><li>Work shadowing</li><li>Preparation of CPD presentations to colleagues and other professionals</li><li>Exposure to new situations at work which require action</li></ul>	<ul><li>Participating in careers conventions and seminars</li><li>Listening to podcasts, webinars and other learning for research purposes and technical information</li><li>Reading blogs, articles, e-books, journals that increase your project-related knowledge or skills</li><li>Participating in activities such as membership of committees where new ideas and initiatives are discussed</li><li>Sharing knowledge and experience with others</li><li>Acting as a coach or mentor for a fellow professional</li><li>Being coached or mentored by a fellow professional</li><li>Self-study through reading books or study pack</li><li>Volunteering</li><li>Relevant non-work activities</li></ul>

Figure 37.2 The Association for Project Management's framework of activities for continuing professional development (CPD)

References and further reading

Association for Project Management or APM (2018) *Continuing Professional Development*, available at: https://www.apm.org.uk/qualifications-and-training/continuing-professional-development-cpd (accessed 6 February 2018).

Australian Institute of Project Management (2011), *AIPM Professional Competency Standards for Project Management – Part F*, Version 2.0, Sydney: AIPM.

International Organization for Standardization (2015), ISO 21504 *Project, Programme and Portfolio Management – Guidance on portfolio management*, Geneva: ISO.

International Project Management Association (2016), *IPMA Individual Competence Baseline*, Version 4.0, Amsterdam: IPMA.

Office of Government Commerce (2011), *Management of Portfolios*, 2011 edn, Norwich: The Stationery Office (also available from AXELOS).

Project Management Institute (2013), *The Standard for Portfolio Management*, 3rd edn, Newtown Square, PA: PMI.

Revans, R. (2011), *The ABC of Action Learning*, Farnham: Gower.

Chapter 38

How people impact the adoption and practice of portfolio management

Donnie MacNicol and Adrian Dooley

In this chapter we focus on people and, in particular, their preferred ways of doing things. We examine their personal styles and how these can have a direct and often significant impact on the initiation and governance of portfolios.

Introduction

Any organization that has more than one project or programme has, by default, a portfolio. Most organizations don't even recognize their collection of projects and programmes as a portfolio, let alone apply the principles of formal portfolio management to govern and coordinate them (for reasons that we discuss).

It may seem obvious to say that to reap the benefits of a formal portfolio management approach an organization must first initiate a portfolio – by collecting and inducting their projects and programmes into the portfolio structure, and then governing it so that it runs smoothly and delivers benefits that would not otherwise be achieved. Getting the 'buy-in' to collecting and inducting is challenging for a number of reasons, including the active or passive resistance of senior managers (who might perceive all this as some form of threat, for example creating a need to relinquish power and control).

Although the need may be obvious, implementing portfolio management is not easy. It is a business change programme in its own right and, as we all know, business change involves many people and creates many opportunities for things to go wrong if we fail to appreciate the people involved, their individual motivations and their personal needs.

People are at the heart of effective portfolio management, which depends on how they perceive its value, and adopt and practise it. In this chapter we focus on how people (and, in particular, their personal styles and preferred ways of doing things) have a direct and often significant impact on the initiation and continued governance of portfolios. We provide some tools too that can help you to understand and work more effectively.

Key concepts around portfolio management to set the context

It is useful to distinguish between two types of portfolio, because both have unique people challenges. The following definitions are taken from the Praxis Framework (Praxis, 2014):

- A 'standard portfolio' comprises a set of independent projects and/or programmes. The main objective of coordinating a standard portfolio is to ensure that the component projects and programmes are managed in a consistently effective way. From a people perspective this can be a challenge because there is likely to be a very diverse group of people involved. An example would be a construction company that is performing a number of independent projects, all for different clients.
- A 'structured portfolio' comprises a set of projects and/or programmes that are united by a set of common strategic objectives. Structured portfolios will have many more interrelationships of the component projects and programmes so governance must be more rigorous – something that people may or may not welcome.

An organization may have multiple portfolios distinguished by environment, geography or operating division, creating a diverse range of people challenges unique to each portfolio. The need for a professional centralized function that is aware of and actively managing these challenges is critical.

It is helpful to consider ways of presenting the portfolio lifecycle.

The example in Figure 38.1 is taken from the Praxis Framework. It shows a closure, but in reality most portfolios evolve and change only with time, during which a large and diverse group of people will probably be directly or indirectly involved and impacted. Although the lifecycle in Figure 38.1 represents the fundamental structure of a portfolio, we need a set of processes that will manage the portfolio throughout the lifecycle and these are depicted in Figure 38.2 (again taken from the Praxis Framework).

In this chapter we focus on two elements of this process model and the impact that personal style has on:

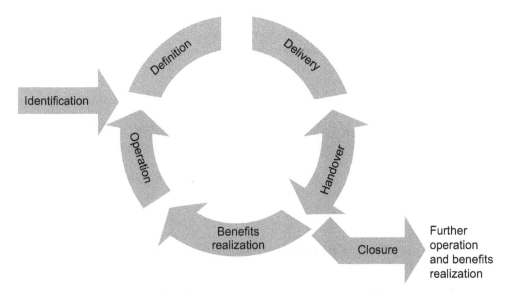

Figure 38.1 One way of presenting a portfolio lifecycle (from the Praxis Framework)

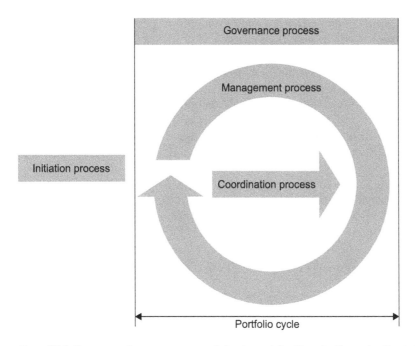

Figure 38.2 Processes that manage a portfolio through its lifecycle (from the Praxis Framework)

1. Initiation of the portfolio (and hence the initiation of formal portfolio management);
2. The management process (which most people relate to as 'being' portfolio management, although we know it requires far more than simply managing).

First, we describe a simple model for distinguishing between broad personal styles.

How to distinguish between people using personal styles

To discuss the impact that people have on portfolio management, we must first identify some way of distinguishing different styles. Distinguishing between people can be done in many different ways, using one of the hundreds of personal characteristics that go into making us individuals. Simple tools are often used to help us objectify these differences.

Some people who make use of these tools come away with the idea that they are being pigeon-holed into a particular type of behaviour, but such tools indicate a preference and ultimately are *only* an indication. The reality is that as individuals we typically have a range of responses to a situation and that we work across a spectrum, often depending on the context. Being aware of your typical approach, and being able to make it flexible as the situation and context require, is one of the key attributes of successful professionals and leaders.

We have chosen to use the iMA™ Diagnostic, because this provides a simple way of distinguishing people using four different colour styles, identifying personal engagement and communication preferences. iMA™ stands for:

- identify your own or another person's colour style;
- Modify your approach and style to suit the context;
- Adapt as necessary to the response you receive.

The iMA™ is a simple and free 10-question online diagnostic tool that identifies your colour style, as shown in Figure 38.3. Everyone is a mixture of all four of these styles but iMA aims to identify your preferred or 'high' colour styles. Each has its own typical characteristics, behaviours and preferences. You can try this free at any time at www.ima-pm.co.uk (it takes only 3 minutes to complete). Once you have done that you will have the opportunity to download information describing your own and other colour styles.

Understanding the preferred colour style of different people within a portfolio is important in terms of both what is delivered and the way in which it is achieved. As an example, if the portfolio leader is a 'high red', and a business executive who acts as a project sponsor to a number of projects is a 'high blue', the project leader should understand that their sponsor may see them as pushy and insensitive if all they focus on in their discussions is the delivery of outcomes with no regard for the impact on people.

There are multiple ways of distinguishing between people that are all worthy in helping to identify the impact and biases that people can bring to bear on portfolio management. You can consider iMA™ as a single lens but it is important to appreciate that there are many ways of doing this.

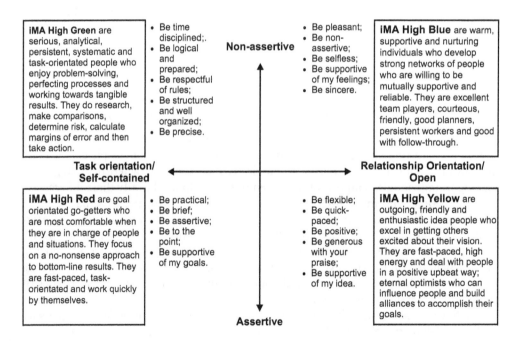

Figure 38.3 Description of iMA™ colour types

How personal styles impact the adoption of portfolio management

The one thing common to all best practice is that it assumes that we all view the content in the same way. People perceive, design, adopt, deploy on the portfolio practice, involve others, adapt, sustain its use, learn from and share knowledge differently. Surprisingly these differences are not taken into account when we define good practice and how it should be practised – something the authors are looking to rectify.

We look at the adoption of portfolio management first from a 'people perspective' by considering:

- What is adoption (to provide context as to what adoption involves);
- The evidence for the value for adoption (appealing to the *head*);
- Personal preferences and biases that leaders have in adoption (appealing to the *heart*);
- The different perceptions of portfolio management goals.

Adoption

Adoption, kicked off by initiation, is one of the most challenging aspects of the process due to the many people-related challenges that must be dealt with. Before considering these challenges it is worth considering what is required for successful adoption. A way of representing this critical stage is shown in Figure 38.4.

Just like projects and programmes, a portfolio will start with some form of mandate, which will give someone the task of initiating the portfolio. Initiation is usually a one-off process. It represents the point at which the host organization makes the decision to manage its projects and programmes as a portfolio. Often this is not a simple, single decision impacting the whole organization, but is rather the case of individual leaders deciding to implement within part of an organization. This inevitably leads to complex stakeholder engagement and adoption issues.

Broadly speaking, the decision to create a portfolio (or to consider the projects and programmes as part of a portfolio) has three purposes as identified in the Praxis Framework and repeated here:

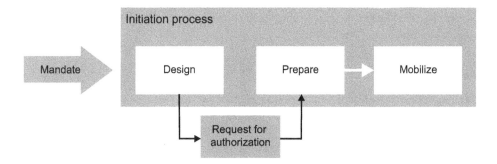

Figure 38.4 Requirements for the successful adoption of portfolio management

1. To maximize the efficient use of available resources and avoid conflicts in resource requirements wherever possible;
2. To promote a consistent approach to project and programme management that focuses on developing individual competency and organizational maturity;
3. To manage a set of projects and programmes that collectively achieves a set of strategic objectives.

Design

This 'design' person may be a board member or suitable senior manager who will become the portfolio's sponsor. The 'sponsor designate' will need to assemble a small team to investigate the way in which a portfolio should be constituted and governed to suit the needs of the host organization best. The result will be a proposal that is submitted for authorization to the issuer of the mandate. Portfolios are rarely created from scratch. It is more likely that an organization with several projects and programmes decides to collect these into a portfolio to improve management and/or focus on strategic objectives.

Prepare

If the proposal is accepted, then preparatory work is begun. Depending on the type of portfolio and its context, this could include multiple activities such as:

- Identifying and documenting managerial processes and documentation;
- Setting up a competency framework;
- Reviewing existing projects and programmes to capture good practice and baseline capability maturity.

It is highly unlikely that this preparation will start with a totally blank sheet of paper. The organization will be managing projects and (possibly) programmes, and these will already have processes, procedures and documentation standards in place. All existing methods should be assessed and the current best practice should form the basis of new portfolio-wide standards. People may be very wedded to the existing ways of working and have divergent opinions as to what is and is not best practice. There will be many personal biases. Therefore it is important to seek input, engage with all stakeholders, objectively assess as best one can, and openly communicate why decisions have been made and the impact this will have.

Mobilize

Portfolio implementation will often require significant change management activities and it is important that these are adequately resourced. If the systems and processes of portfolio management are to be embedded for long-term benefit, the existing organization and its people will have to undergo change – not just in terms of physical infrastructure but also in terms of attitude and behaviour. Mobilization may include aspects such as:

- Setting up a clear governance structure;
- Initiating training programmes and briefings that address the real needs;
- Amending recruitment and appointment processes to ensure that the people moving into the profession have the necessary skills.

Evidence for the value of adoption

With the above challenges in mind it is worth considering the evidence that exists for the adoption of portfolio management and how this evidence is interpreted by different people – most importantly by organizational leaders. In 2017 Donnie MacNicol (in his role as the Chair of the Organisational Project Management [OPM] Forum for the Project Management Institute [PMI] UK Chapter) commissioned a study to collate evidence of the value of portfolio, programme and project management. This study was conducted by Jonathan Norman (unpublished at the time of writing.

Jonathan was struck by both the extraordinary wealth of research that is publicly available through the ephemeral and haphazard nature of publications. The same organization might have research available from a number of portals, with no reference between them. Although the material is freely available and clearly designed to be referenced by the public, in many cases the location on the web is arcane and difficult to find. We have tabled some of these key references In Figure 38.5.

We take the last-listed reference from Figure 38.5 as an example, and examine it in some detail. This reveals some interesting findings which agree with some of the issues we raise in this chapter. The report highlights that many organizations still regard a collection of projects as just that; they don't see it as a fundamental and complex expression of the organization's strategy and they continue to treat the structures associated with it (such as the project management office [PMO] and disciplines like portfolio management), as an operational rather than a strategic resource.

Several interviewees for this study noted that, in the words of Steve Moysey, 'While the board and C-suite talk in terms of high-level strategy, often something gets lost in translation from the executive suite to the execution layer. Companies need to narrow that gap' (Mr Moysey is Partner and National Leader of Program and Portfolio Management, PwC in the USA).

The problem is partially one of exposition. Carrie Ferman (SVP Strategy and Business Development, Sony Pictures Television) believes that if corporate leadership 'doesn't communicate well, it makes portfolio management impossible to do because there is no clear understanding of what the company is trying to achieve'. It may also be a weakness in the strategy itself. Anthony Bramwell (Executive Director, Program Management, Ernst & Young, Germany) says companies often wonder whether, as 'strategy is done at a high level, does it provide enough detail for the portfolio or does the portfolio need to provide extra detail?'. Senior leaders need to resolve both of these underlying issues.

So the problem goes back beyond poor portfolio management. These companies don't really understand how to strategize (and certainly not how to communicate and share strategy). This presents the project director with something of a 'chicken and an egg' conundrum. How can you introduce portfolio management when the organization's current culture and capability mean that it is unable to understand what is

Title	Year	Authors	Abstract
How Project and Portfolio Management Solutions are Delivering Value to Organizations	2008	Randy Perry and Eric Hatcher, IDC	The potential for PPM as a tool for increasing project capacity and productivity, reducing cost, reducing redundant projects and failure rates
PM Pulse of the Profession: Driving Success in Challenging Times	2012	PMI	The 2012 PMI Pulse of the Profession highlighted organizational trends and behaviours in the teeth of the post 2008 recession and an environment of low economic growth
How to Prioritize your Company's Projects	2017	Antonio-Nieto Rodriguez for Harvard Business Review	C-Suite guide to the essence of portfolio management
Delivering Value	2014	Andy Jordon	Overview of the key elements required for managing a portfolio of projects successfully by focusing on a combination of financial return and alignment with strategic goals
The State of Project Portfolio Management	2013	Project Management Solutions Inc	A well-structured, short, research report on the application of portfolio management in the market place
A Business Guide to Project Portfolio Management	2016	Antonio Nieto Rodriguez for CIO Magazine	A short guide for C-suite managers to the benefits and nature of project portfolio management
Delivering Complex Change at Scale: A More Strategic Approach to Managing Portfolios of Change	Not known	Berkeley Partnership	Priority outcome and key design principles for an effective portfolio function
A T Kearney Excellence in Capital Projects: A Goal Yet to be Achieved	2017	Richard Forrest, Patrick Brown, Oliver Zeranski, Ani Chakroborty, Matthias Witzemann, Marco Vasconi for A T Kearney	The current state of play in terms of project and portfolio management in capital projects: oil and gas, chemicals, utilities, metals and mining
In Control: How Project Portfolio Management Can Improve Strategy Development	Not known	Metin Fidan, Anthony Bramwell for EY	EY article exploring the link between strategy and projects, and including a number of EY models explaining the PPM lifecycle, the corporate planning and portfolio management lifecycles and the EY PPM model for assessing the appropriateness of portfolio management for the organization
Implementing the Project Portfolio: a Vital C-Suite Focus	2015	Economist Intelligence Unit for PMI	How the C-suite can make a positive commitment to strategic portfolio management

Figure 38.5 Some documents relating to the value of portfolio management

required? This is, we suggest, a common problem at all levels of operational project management (OPM) and one that the repository is set up to challenge: project and programme teams are required to educate the business and particularly the C-Suite on the nature and value of what they do.

Personal biases that leaders have in adoption

As part of the development of *The Delivery Manifesto* (written by Donnie MacNicol for publication in 2018) some of the underlying causes why people do not adopt good practice have been identified. Some of these key reasons are as follows:

1. There is something about how portfolio management is perceived, or has previously been experienced, that is neither attractive nor seen as being of value to the person (for example, being felt as constraining or limiting of their authority and decision-making);
2. There is no motivation to take on additional perceived work that would come from adopting and implementing portfolio management;
3. Portfolio management is seen as a threat for a range of reasons. These reasons include, for example, loss of control or power (because that might effectively be owned by another organizational function) and thus there would be limited benefit from actively supporting its adoption. At a more personal level, portfolio management could expose poor performance or control by the leader, and therefore be seen actively as a threat to their career;
4. The way that it has been communicated has not engaged leaders in a way that provides them with the rationale and motivation. For example, it might be too formal, not sufficiently evidential, not linked closely enough with main business activities, seen as bureaucratic and an unnecessary additional layer that adds no value, and so on;
5. People are not exposed to it through their peer group, key influencers or professional network, that is, we must not take for granted that people have even a rudimentary understanding of what it is, the value that it adds, and so forth;
6. It is not seen as a priority or as impacting those things that are a priority at a particular point in time. For example, the focus may be on winning new business, reducing the cost base, improving regulatory compliance, and so on. As portfolio management professionals we may understand the value that can be obtained, but other people might not, or that they might not even have the interest to engage in a discussion about this.

It is therefore worth carefully considering and probing business leaders about their assumptions, biases, personal beliefs, and so on, which they might have with regard to portfolio management and how open they are to discussing and exploring alternative perspectives. This is one of the most critical elements of stakeholder engagement because, without it, no adoption will be successful.

Different perceptions of portfolio management goals

Around adoption, it is worth considering how people with different communication styles (using iMA™ introduced earlier) perceive the goals of portfolio management. These goals, taken from the Praxis Framework, are to do the following:

- Decide what type of portfolio is required;
- Design the portfolio infrastructure;
- Obtain senior level approval and commitment;
- Implement the portfolio.

When implementing these goals the different colours would focus on different areas, have different priorities, wish to see varying levels of justification, and so on.

Please keep in mind that people are rarely pure 'high green' or pure 'high yellow' and the attributes are typical only of each type. The lists of attributes are not intended to be exhaustive – they are indications of different attitudes that you need to take into account when working with others or to provide you with a fresh perspective.

High green people

A 'high green' person would typically propose or want to see the following:

- A rational explanation of what portfolio management is aiming to achieve;
- A consistent and systematic approach to identifying, delivering and realizing a portfolio;
- A long-term commitment to delivery and monitoring of the portfolio;
- Tangible and detailed financial benefits that are measureable and can be shown to be realized from the investment.

A high green person would typically be perceived as follows:

- Increasing bureaucracy and delay when insisting on evidence and facts to justify the adoption of portfolio management;
- Discounting intangible/non-financial benefits and relying solely on tangible/financial benefits for the justification.

High blue people

A high blue person would typically propose or want to see the following:

- Key individuals given the opportunity to input and influence the decision;
- Equal consideration to intangible and non-financial benefits when considering the potential value;
- A clear understanding of the impact of portfolio management on people, whether or not positive;
- Caution about how quickly portfolio management can be adopted, especially where it involves a change in people's attitudes and behaviours.

A high blue person would typically be perceived as follows:

- Being empathetic to the impact of the proposed change on people;
- A leader who wishes to ensure that there is adequate change management resource and effort;
- Focusing on the attitudes and behaviours of those impacted versus the tangible benefits of adoption;
- Focusing on the disbenefits as well as the benefits.

High red people

A high red person would typically propose or want to see the following:

- Action taken quickly to justify and implement portfolio management;
- A pragmatic view of the achievability of the perceived value;

- That they have maximum freedom to take action as they believe necessary to adopt portfolio management quickly and effectively;
- Resources being identified and committed to portfolio management in the short term.

A high red person would typically be perceived as follows:

- Focusing on short-term wins and the demonstration of value as quickly as possible;
- Focused primarily on quantifiable financial benefits of portfolio management and potentially dismissing those benefits that cannot be described in this way.

High yellow people

A high yellow person would typically propose or want to see the following:

- Clear communication on the importance of portfolio management and its role in improving team motivation (and thereby performance);
- Short-term responsibilities for portfolio management identified and clarified with people;
- Encouragement of early interaction within the team and with stakeholders as part of the adoption process;
- A broad view of the benefits of portfolio management adoption – intangible and non-financial.

A high yellow person would typically be perceived as follows:

- Over-estimating the value of particular intangible and non-financial benefits to the organization through adoption;
- Being overly optimistic about the ease with which portfolio management can be adopted.

How personal styles impact the practice of portfolio management

Effective collaboration and team working are the keys to success in portfolio, programme and project management (P3M). However, teams are made up of individuals, who have their own communication and working styles. Being aware of personal styles provides insights that improve cohesion and balance.

The P3M frameworks currently available take a 'one-size-fits-all' approach. They provide good practice in knowledge and process, but make no allowance for the different ways in which individual people perceive, understand and implement that practice. The aim is to enhance our ability to implement and benefit from the portfolio management by understanding how to adapt it – not only to the context of your portfolio but also to the people you work with.

The management process

We can now look at how the attributes described above are manifested in the functions and processes of portfolio management and (in particular) the Praxis Framework.

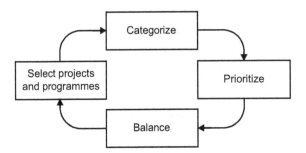

Figure 38.6 The portfolio management process according to the Praxis Framework

The management process assesses the suitability of projects and programmes for inclusion in the portfolio and maintains a beneficial and manageable mix of projects and programmes. Needless to say the inclusion (or not) and what is classed as beneficial can often end up as a subjective assessment. People therefore have a major impact. The process is shown Figure 38.6, and is similar in nature to many other approaches. The four elements of this process are described below.

Selecting projects and programmes

The main criterion for inclusion of a project or programme in a standard portfolio (described earlier) may be simply that it exists, whereas a structured portfolio would probably have a quite sophisticated system for selecting projects and programmes to achieve strategic organizational objectives that could be achieved by various means.

Categorize

Categorization is useful on particularly large portfolios and is typically defined to make it easier for senior decision-makers to understand the nature of the portfolio (for example, mandatory or discretionary; short- or long-term investments; high or low risk; significant or marginal change; and so on). This categorization will inevitably be influenced by the people who conceive and implement the categories because their personal priorities will be biased.

Prioritize

When multiple initiatives compete for finite resources, conflicts will occur and choices will have be made. The first priority of any organization is to continue to exist but, beyond this, the priorities of the leaders, often linked to their own personal priorities, will have a major impact. For example, is the purpose to innovate, secure position, benefit the employees, and so on?

Balance

Whereas categorization and prioritization can be relatively objective, finding the right balance can be more subjective. Ultimately personal preferences and priorities of individual decision-makers will have a disproportionate impact, driven by the context and values of the host organization. In a young and dynamic business it may be acceptable and feasible to have a high proportion of the portfolio generating significant change. In an entrepreneurial organization it may be desirable to have high overall levels of risk (with the associated potential for high return).

The impact on practice

When implementing or carrying out the steps in the portfolio management process described above, the different colour styles of people would typically be relevant as described below.

High green people

A 'high green' person would typically propose or want to see the following:

- The adoption and use of tools and techniques that are methodical and fact based, providing quantitative data to facilitate informed and objective decision-making;
- Propose details of the way in which valuation tools should be used (and the principles by which they should be used);
- A methodical and evidence-based approach to measuring the 'before' and end states, thus showing the value of the process objectively;
- A high proportion of information that is robust and identifiable, against which measurement can take place and performance be judged during the management process;
- A comprehensive and robust plan linking outputs to the changes needed to realize the benefits, and all steps for a successful transition.

High blue people

A high blue person would typically propose or want to see the following:

- The involvement of people (ideally through one-to-one discussions) in the selection, categorization, prioritization and balancing stages;
- Benefits and disbenefits that are people centric (often intangible and non-financial);
- Communication with people from other portfolios to benefit from lessons learned, focusing on the impact on people of the practice of portfolio management;
- The use of qualitative, as well as quantitative techniques;
- Comprehensive processes that clearly identify responsibilities (including their own);
- An approach that has been agreed by all parties, with clear responsibilities allocated fairly across the team;
- Resources being deployed to communicate with all those impacted by the decisions made through the management process;
- Focus on minimizing the negative impact on people and ongoing operations if prioritization/balancing results in major changes within the business.

High red people

A high red person would typically propose or want to see the following:

- The use of tools and techniques that can be implemented quickly and that provide short-term value;
- A focused set of data, around which logical decisions can be made;
- Lessons from previous projects taken into account, and the actions needed to implement them;
- Quantitative rather than qualitative output from the process, which allows speedy decision-making;
- Flexible approaches that are there to act as guidance for those responsible for implementing the process;
- Sufficient and verifiable information against which measurement can take place and progress can easily be monitored across the portfolio'
- Accountabilities for managing the process made clear and formally recorded;
- Timely monitoring and control to ensure that people are being held to account against their responsibilities.

High yellow people

A high yellow person would typically propose or want to see the following:

- Involvement of team members and stakeholders through discussion and workshops to ensure that a broad mix of views is considered;
- Communication with people from other portfolios, typically in a workshop setting, to obtain lessons learned;
- Less focus on disbenefits where the high yellow person does not consider them to be significant;
- Information for the process created with the minimum level of formality or resources needed for this;
- The adoption and use of qualitative techniques for valuing benefits;
- Processes that are there for guidance, allowing people to apply them flexibly;
- Effort put into marketing and communicating the process to a broad audience, to ensure their support;
- A personal role in this, potentially acting as a spokesperson for the process and helping people to understand the impact of the changes that may happen across the portfolio;
- A flexible and simple means for monitoring actions.

Conclusion

If you are a portfolio manager, there are a number of things you can do based on the insights shared earlier. If you are reading this, we can assume that you have seen the value and are interested in considering applying these ideas in your current role, or are seeking a fresh perspective and capability to improve future performance.

The following case uses risk management as an example (and in particular the identity stage) but the principle can be applied across the portfolio management process described earlier. Begin by completing the iMA™ Diagnostic and reflect on you own style, considering how adapting it could be advantageous to yourself and the portfolio.

1. Reflect on your own style and strengths

Using the different style characteristics listed above in this chapter, identify what you personally would typically propose or want to see. This will identify your own colour style (you might be a high green, for example). Then consider if your style is appropriate, given the context and how people with different colour styles would tackle the same activity. Ask which approach would add value and modify your style as appropriate.

2. Work with others (individuals or teams)

Identify your colleague's colour style and consider the implications in terms of the relationship and achieving the task. Consider how those with different colour styles would tackle the task or deal with the situation. Ask how this will impact you. Modify as appropriate. A similar approach can be taken for entire teams.

We hope that these suggestions will be of value to you, and help portfolio management professionals to improve adoption and practice.

References

MacNicol, D. (2018), *The Delivery Manifesto: How to Set Up Your Organization to Deliver Success*, Abingdon: Taylor & Francis.

Praxis (2014), Praxis Framework: An integrated guide to the management of projects, programmes and portfolios, Princes Risborough: Association for Project Management.

Chapter 39

Ten questions and answers for executives

Alicia Aitken

Executive leadership is the key to successful strategy execution. Guiding and steering a portfolio of projects and programmes are a critical capability without which strategy execution is doomed to failure.

Introduction

My organization runs nearly every kind of project: engineering, construction, information technology (IT), media, marketing, process re-engineering, product development, compliance and research and development (R&D). As we execute our strategy to shift from a world-class telecommunications company to a world-class technology company the effective management of the portfolio is critical to our success. As for most successful organizations, we have a good strategy. It is well defined, well communicated and designed to ensure that our customers, staff and shareholders thrive. The success of our organization is dependent on how well we can execute that strategy. We begin by taking the strategy, devolving it into subcomponents and creating a portfolio of portfolios. A group executive is appointed as the accountable executive for each subportfolio, and from there we create further subportfolios, programmes and projects. Many people, processes and capabilities must be aligned to execute any strategy but, as with most things, success starts from the top. Our leaders take an active role in the management of our portfolios, which is setting us up for success.

This chapter outlines the questions our executive team ask themselves to ensure that they are leading our portfolios with purpose. I have grouped these questions into the following five categories:

1. Contextual alignment;
2. Value creation;
3. Risk;
4. Capability, capacity and culture; and
5. Transition to business as usual.

For each of these questions, guidance is provided on the types of answers for which executives should be looking.

Contextual alignment

The business environment in which strategy is executed is constantly changing. Every successful organization will have an executive team that is attuned to the environment around it, with the leadership strength to change direction when needed. The questions that executives should ask to ensure this include the following:.

Question 1. Are we convinced that our plan is (still) the best way to enable the change that we need?

For my organization the answer to this question comes when our executives believe that the projects and programmes in the portfolio are aligned to our current best answer of the strategy. All organizations must make decisions on what to invest in with limited resources.

Our answer comes when we believe we have made the right choices. Sometimes we find that, although we made the best choice that we could in the past, the competitive environment, or technology, or some other factor has since moved on. So our earlier choices are no longer the right way in which to execute our strategy.

It's at this point that our executives have to make the difficult decisions on changing tack. This is when true executive leadership in portfolio management is demonstrated. The really good managers will not only act swiftly in response to changing circumstances but will also have a reserve 'plan B' prepared for an alternative route to realizing the desired benefits.

Question 2. Are there duplications, opportunities for links or 'dots to connect' – either across the portfolio or in relation to other portfolios?

Efficiency is a critical driver for any portfolio. Resources are finite, whether these are money, time or human capital. The purpose of this question for our executives is to drive efficiency into every decision. Where we have duplication we have wasted effort. Where we are not connecting up on synergies between projects or across portfolios we are missing opportunities to deliver more with less. Our executives are constantly asking the question: 'How can we deliver more value with the resources we have?'

Value creation

The purpose of business projects and programmes is to create value. It is the responsibility of the executives who lead the organization to question constantly whether the value they are driving is enough. Here are two such questions that our executives ask.

Question 3. Does the portfolio of projects and programmes selected optimize the required return on investment for the organization?

This is one of the most basic of all questions in business – and one that is surprisingly easy to forget in the face of disruptive technology and the excitement of new product ideas. But, at its core portfolio management is no different from any other part of business and the same foundation question 'Is it worth it?' should be asked. In our organization, our executives are asking the following subsidiary questions:

- Does the portfolio contain the right blend of projects that adequately address my balanced scorecard targets?
- Do we have the right operational run activities?
- Are we building capability for the future?
- Are we doing the right level of remediation activities?
- What about the balance with our people and customer-facing projects?
- Could I do better?
- What optionality and trade-offs should I make?

The other key factor to consider is opportunity cost. As with all other business decisions, the cost of different choices must be considered by executives. In this scenario our executives ask themselves the question: 'In the current knowledge of what we are doing and what we could do, is this the best set of choices we could make or should we face into a change?'

Question 4. What is the level of business sponsorship over the most critical initiatives, and are they ready to realize the benefits from the projects and programmes in the portfolio?

So much of the information presented to executives consists of lagging indicators when it comes to strategy execution and relevance to the future success of the organization. One very clear and easy-to-spot leading indicator is business sponsorship of projects and programmes within the portfolio. If you are unable to spend the time pouring over the numbers of every single project in the portfolio, the simplest questions to ask yourself are 'Who is championing this project?' and 'How hard do I think they will work to make it a success?'.

Assuming that your organization is similar to mine, where your business executives are strong, capable and clever individuals, you are most of the way to successful delivery if:

- They have backed themselves to deliver the benefits claimed by their project;
- Their project aligns to the organization's strategy; and
- They are engaged and active in their leadership.

Risk

Risk is an inherent part of change. It therefore plays a prominent role in portfolio management. For executives the key is always to maintain an 'eyes-wide-open' approach to risk. If you refuse to see risk you can have no hope of influencing it. To help face into this challenge we ask ourselves the following questions.

Question 5. Do we really understand the risks of this not creating the change we want?

One of our organizational values is *find your courage*. The risk element is particularly relevant for executives leading portfolios. It takes courage to face into the stark reality of what can and is going wrong within a portfolio, in particular looking at what is going wrong as a result of decisions you have made. A high level of self-awareness is required to lead portfolios effectively.

In my organization our executives look at risk through several lenses, including short-term versus long-term benefits, and in particular whether we are creating any short-lived sunk costs, architectural conflicts or unnecessary middle steps to a longer-term roadmap agenda

Question 6. Does the lens through which we view the success of an individual project cause an unintended consequence in another part of the profit-and-loss status or business performance?

Often the way we view the world makes us myopic to the unintended consequences of our choices. The same is true for executive leadership of portfolios. In our organization we have a particularly strong emphasis on benefits realization. For others there may be a heavy focus on delivering on time, delivery within budget, delivery or some other key metric. Whatever your viewpoint it is important to be aware of it and look for the unintended consequences. In our case we look for projects or programmes that have unintended consequences, such as revenue with unsustainable variable cost consequences or productivity that damages our customer experience.

Capability, capacity and culture

The 'three Cs' wrap around a portfolio's ability to deliver an organization's strategy successfully. The other elements discussed in this chapter can be influenced, guided or steered by the executives overseeing a portfolio. However, the three Cs are actually created by the executives involved and are a direct reflection of their leadership capability.

Question 7. Can we actually deliver the portfolio of projects?

This question goes right to the heart of 'do-ability'. There is a simple equation for answering this question, namely *capability* + *capacity* = *do-ability*. Can my organization actually achieve what we've set out to do? In so many instances projects, programmes and portfolios:

- Do not have the appropriate subject matter experts involved;
- Do not have trusted project managers;
- Have too many projects given to too few sponsors;
- Have immaturity in our technical teams or the business-as-usual teams are too busy to absorb all the change that will result from the portfolio.

The challenges with do-ability are not always solvable, even by willing and engaged executives. However, that is the leadership challenge for portfolio management.

In our organization the first challenge our executives face is to approach this question with open eyes and a willingness to understand truly the complexity of delivery. The answer is never simple. Capability to deliver is never the fault or success of one part of the organization but rather a multitude of elements working together. As an example, we are fortunate to have some of our industry's leading subject matter experts (SMEs) in nearly every part of our business. Our solution to resourcing the portfolio is to make it an official part of their role and apportion time for them to dedicate to delivery. This could be achieved by our executive team only making the decision and following through on their commitment, allowing our SMEs to work unhindered on our projects and programmes.

Question 8. Do we have the right culture of transparency?

Far too often the real information about project progress transforms as it makes its way from the project through the chain of command to the executive level. Despite many of our executives asking for the truth, they are often shielded from the harsher realities of projects and programmes than they need to know.

The root cause of this transformation from 'red' to 'green' indicators on the way up is most often fear. Where cultures of blame exist (and people experience retribution for failure or perceived failure) this fear is rational. In such cases the subsequent questions executives are asking themselves are centred on 'What have I done to perpetuate a culture of fear?' and 'Have I been active enough in creating a safe place for people to share information?'.

The more complex situation is where the fear is seemingly irrational. Where there are no obvious examples of individuals or groups being punished for sharing information in a frank and fearless way (which is the case in my organization), why then do we have information transformation occurring? The first step towards correction is to recognize that this is occurring. In many instances the fear that drives the optimistic change in information is held within a single person, or in a layer within the organization rather than as a result of a culture of blame. The solution will depend on your organization but could include deriving information in multiple forums – not through a single report that one person can control. The solution also includes looking for the data that underpin any insights being presented, and ensure that those data are comprehensive and add up to a coherent story, rather than a selected and restricted view.

Transition to business as usual

The organization's readiness to absorb the outputs of the projects and programmes into normal operations is a critical component of portfolio leadership. The following question is one that our executives ask.

Question 9. Are we as an organization ready to use the outputs of the projects from this portfolio?

Whether the projects in the portfolio are designed to change internal processes (that is, a new enterprise resource planning [ERP] system) or are to launch a new product to market, there is an impact on the business-as-usual operations. The scale of the change required and the level of support required to affect the change are important factors to consider. As projects launch out of the portfolio into operations, our executives ask a series of questions as part of their final confidence check to ensure that our organization is ready to support our internal staff, and that our frontline staff and customers make use of the outputs from the project. The questions asked include the following;

- Is the scope I expected being delivered?
- How can I be sure that the products being delivered will work?
- Do my operational teams know how to operate the new systems and products?

Question 10. How shall I know if we made the right decision?

The final question that all executives steering portfolios should be asking is about knowing whether or not they made the right decisions.

In truth there is no way of knowing whether or not all the decisions you made were the right ones or if there were better ones you could have made. However, the reason portfolios exist is to maximize the efficient use of resources to execute the organization's strategy. Executives who consider this last question as they begin the journey will set up measures for final success.

In our organization we use measures at multiple levels to give our executives indicators of success and to warn when changes in approach should be made. We use a measure at the local project level on time, cost and quality of delivery. We rigorously business case all projects and programmes coming through the portfolio and we stop to measure the actual benefits 6–12 months after project completion.

These measures and metrics are aggregated into trends across quarters and financial years to give a picture of progress to plan. Overarching all of this internal data, for us, is the external market performance of our share price. As a publicly listed company we share our strategy with the market and, if we are able to execute that strategy, our share price will respond accordingly. Coupled with this are the analyst's commentary on how effectively we met their expectations.

Conclusion

Project portfolios connect the temporary world of projects and programmes with the permanent world of operations. At times they bring together diametrically opposed management styles, cultures and ways of working. The temporary world of projects faces into the unknown, where transformational change is needed and the pace of work is constantly driven by the competing demands of time, cost and quality. The permanent world of operations offers a known base from which to plan incremental change and works towards an infinite time horizon. The management techniques that have been developed to optimize the performance in each of these contexts cover similar territory but are applied in very different ways.

The executive leadership of a portfolio requires a skill set that spans both worlds and is bound together with a depth of self-awareness and emotional intelligence. As an executive you will enter the world of portfolio management from the direction of either projects or operations and begin the journey to learn about the other side. Hopefully the questions outlined in this chapter will help you to find your path and enable you to lead your organization to the successful execution of your strategy.

Index